FRAMED

A VILLAIN'S PERSPECTIVE ON SOCIAL MEDIA

TIM O'HEARN

LUSCIOUS VENTURES LLC

DISCLAIMER

This book contains true stories. Some names and minor details have been changed to respect the privacy of non-public individuals. All quotes and events depicted are from my best recollection.

As of February 1, 2025, I am a Broker regulated by FINRA under the category "Securities Trader." I am not qualified to give investment advice or manage investments. Nothing contained in this book should be construed as investment, legal, financial, tax, or other advice. There are risks associated with investing in securities. Additionally, no part of this book concerns my official capacity as a Securities Trader.

I have made every effort to ensure that the information presented in this book is correct. However, I assume no responsibility for errors, inaccuracies, omissions, or other inconsistencies.

A substantial portion of this book details and analyzes terms of use violations related to internet technology companies. I do not endorse, encourage, or condone violating the policies of any business or breaking any laws. **This book does not promote rule-breaking, criminality, or antisocial behavior**.

I have no privileged relationship with Meta Platforms, Inc. (which owns Instagram) or any other business named in this book. I have never been an insider at a publicly traded company and nobody has provided material, non-public facts to me. Any statements regarding company operations should be considered speculative.

Terms such as "Instagram growth service" *never* refer to services offered by Meta Platforms, Inc. Further, readers are reminded that third parties using "Insta" or "Gram" in their branding infringe on Meta's trademarks.

This book contains opinions. All opinions are my own and do not represent those of any subject in the book or my employers, business associates, or other entities. This content is based on my perspective and my interpretation. I shall not be held liable for the opinions expressed in this book.

This book contains images. Some are owned by me, while others are used with permission or have been determined to be in the public domain. I believe that some limited reproductions are covered under the fair use doctrine. Any copyright inquiries will be handled expeditiously.

External websites referenced in this book are beyond my control and I bear no responsibility for their content. Errors in citation are not attempts to co-opt copyrighted work as my own. Complaints will be addressed swiftly. The inclusion of hyperlinks does not constitute endorsement or approval.

I am not permitted to speak on behalf of my current employer. This book is not a substitute for expert assistance.

MORE BY THE AUTHOR

Want to read more from Tim O'Hearn?

I haven't read this book yet!

Visit http://tjohearn.com/links

This book is dedicated to my followers.

CONTENTS

SOCIAL MEDIA UNFILTERED

THE INSTAGRAM UNDERWORLD AND THE INSTAGRAM OVERWORLD

PART I
THE OVERWORLD

PART II
THE UNDERWORLD

SOCIAL MEDIA UNFILTERED

1

CLOUT CHASER

I bought my first batch of fake followers in 2012.

Around that time, I decided to become a software engineer.

Over the past ten years, my code, methodologies, and business ventures have been responsible for hundreds of millions of illicit automated engagements on Instagram.

I was motivated by currency, curiosity, and clout, and it was easy to justify my duel with the unchecked power of social media platforms. Given all the hours stolen from my generation, why not snatch something back?

I saw how the quirky apps of my adolescence had become inescapably addictive, how Big Tech made a mockery of relationship building, and how algorithms, including algorithms I later developed, rewarded problematic and antisocial behavior. I received declined payment alerts indicating that customers had depleted their bank accounts while chasing popularity on Instagram.

After I started writing this book, a social media startup offered me an opportunity to lead an engineering team that built (controversial) attention-grabbing recommendation and engagement algorithms. I accepted; I was successful. From my control panel, my influence on the platform's users was godlike. I was stealing their time and getting paid for it.

This book is not a response to the Netflix docudrama *The Social*

Dilemma loosely based on the book, *Zucked: Waking Up to the Facebook Catastrophe*, which was itself a narrative-driven amalgamation of viewpoints contained in a half-dozen tech-meets-sociology books with irritably similar titles.

This is not a research project, long-winded whistle-blow, hit piece, or self-aggrandizing chronicle of my life.

Framed: A Villain's Perspective on Social Media is a collection of shards and shreds and conspiratorial diatribes penned by a fellow who grew up with the internet, became an adept programmer, and mastered the realm of social media while never being employed by Big Tech.

Four pillars comprise the impetus of this book:

1. Being born in the 1990s, growing up with the internet, and avidly using social media—from Myspace in 2006 to TikTok in the 2020s.
2. Possessing a computer science degree and a grasp of advanced programming concepts, enabling me to analyze social media on a different plane.
3. Having profited from veritable "bad guy" activities on Instagram and other social media platforms.
4. Having led the development of algorithmic recommendation systems, push notification infrastructure, and personalized social feeds at a mobile app startup.

These experiences, combined with an enthusiasm for writing, enough money to finance and create this book free from outside influences, and a modicum of hope that this effort could be a positive force for change, have led this eccentric recluse on an unlikely journey.

This journey has been a confluence of opportunity and ambition, demand and demarcation, rules and rulers and rulings. I believe I have a duty to preserve my journey. Rigor must be applied even when outcomes may be inconvenient. Questions must be asked, and even the most reckless opinions must be shared despite the risk of ostracization.

I meandered into social media automation because I was motivated by vanity and greed. I made money and brushed shoulders with men and women who earned substantially more. This arena of social media marketing (abbreviated as SMM) turned out to be a shadowy realm of value-added services profitable beyond my wildest imagination. This book covers SMM better than any other.

Much content about social media is biased and misleading—paid placements, mediocre books, recycled content, hidden affiliate links, poor punditry, wonky agendas, and perpetual clickbait point to the concealment of sad truths. Making sense of the deluge of spurious information requires technical adroitness, obsessive immersion, and sociological sensibility. There are few journalists bravely tackling these issues.

The villains and those generating massive revenue from services built on top of social media platforms have no incentive to talk. One scoundrel responded to an interview request with, "I'm good bro, hope the launch goes well."

Social networks, now synonymous with publicly traded companies, must tread lightly. Shareholders get finicky when faced with publicity about the social media underworld or the societal decay caused by their products. At the same time regulators and authorities are becoming daring. Government action, bot takeovers, and bombshell articles from *the New York Times* cause users to bounce to other apps. Those precious activity metrics, regularly reported to investors, must be upheld at all costs.

I've been the puppeteer as well as the puppet. Unhealthy social media use has weakened the fabric of society. People are depressed, distracted, and *anti*-social. Placing a smartphone in the hands of a child redefines childhood. The middling creatives among us simply transcribe compelling captions and apply neat filters to their photos.

Framed was written for a broad audience. Although elements of my personal experience are present throughout, there is not a cohesive, linear story. For this reason, I've split this document into two themes:

1. Tragicomedy: my views on the amusing, dreadful world of social media.
2. Instagram's emergence and platform misbehavior: an authoritative account of villainy.

Even if the reader acquires a bootleg copy of this book, perhaps with missing material or unauthorized edits, it's payment enough to flip through the pages and consider the perspectives therein. Today's world is filled with unprecedented freedom and opportunity ushered in by the Information Age. Reader, regardless of how or when you came across this book, I hope you share the same optimism that technology can improve society.

I also hope that you'll follow me back.

2

THEY SHUT OFF TIKTOK. NOW WHAT?

These days, the extent of my involvement with TikTok is that I split an elevator bank with employees of TikTok's U.S. headquarters here in New York City. Yeah, I work a corporate job. I no longer experiment on users or get paid to make influencers more influential.

When the doors to my elevator close, I'm not thinking about those bright-faced, fashionably dressed sprites in the other car. But, on Friday, January 17, 2025, I was inundated with messages from devotees asking me if there was anything I could do.

"im really gonna miss tiktok"

"i really hope something happens to save it"

"can you save it?"

This was a challenge. Was there anything I had learned from my transgressions against Instagram that I could apply to TikTok's impending shutdown?

Sure. If it gets shut down in the United States, use a proxy server to maintain access.

TikTok was shut down late on Saturday, January 18, 2025,[1] before reemerging the next day. Anyone connected to a proxy in a country other than the United States wouldn't have noticed.

A long time ago, social networks were seen as fringy, faddish, and fleeting. Some apps eventually encapsulated that by embracing shared media that was temporary—that disappeared. Today, social media is permanent and ubiquitous, and the perhaps most influential platform of them all just pulled a disappearing act in front of two hundred million Americans.

There is an ever-present temptation to crack the code once again, to profit and prevail. I could have used a technique I learned in 2017 to subvert this "ban." Digital overlords know that I've suffered thousands of bans. The sustained interest is not about techniques or our penchant for subversion; it's about what drives the demand for social media marketing and how, as the hottest apps change, it's the same bad guys donning different masks.

One of the hypotheses of *Framed* is that everything about dyadic social interaction on the internet can be traced back to long-forgotten, cringe-worthy practices on Myspace. I see my role as steering people toward my perspective while stopping along the way to pedestal the early internet and the ponderings that befit this medium.

As I wrote this book, I was overcome with the feeling that time was slipping away and that my unarticulated thoughts would soon be irrelevant or disappear from my memory like Snapchat pictures with ten-second lifespans. I held the conviction that all of this was worth writing down.

What Happened Then?

Journalist Sapna Maheshwari learned what black hat Instagram marketing was before I did.

In 2017, while I waited for the phone call that would draw me to the dark side, Sapna and a few million other Instagram users noticed an emerging phenomenon. Unknown and unencountered Instagram accounts were posting generic positive comments on photos.

In her article, "How Bots Are Inflating Instagram Egos,"[2] published on June 6, 2017, Sapna posted a honeypot, a bait post: an ordinary picture of the *New York Times* office. After ten weeks of accumulation, the comments —all positive—included encouragement, like, "best one so far," "this is cool," and "very nice" as well as an array of congenial emojis.

Suspicious? Sure. Yet, unlike email spam of the early aughts, pornographic referral, fake merchandise, or phishing scam bots that descended on social media sites in the interim, these Instagram comments were neither voluminous nor an obvious malevolent plot. The accounts typing the comments, handing out likes, and sending "follow" requests seemed normal, even, plausibly, human. As mystifying as it was, people were unlikely to complain about a little extra attention. Sapna suggested that it was "the internet's most pleasant form of spam."[3]

Before I ever earned a dime, Sapna revealed the grand secret of the "cottage industry" I would soon gain admission to, an involvement that would bestow upon me a god complex during my early 20s.

> Many people with public accounts on Instagram may not realize that when random users follow them or like or comment on their posts, it is often the work of a cottage industry of websites that, for as little as $10 a month, send their clients' accounts on automated liking, following and commenting sprees. It's a rogue marketing tactic meant to catch the attention of other Instagram users in hopes that they will follow or like the automated accounts in return.[4]

By "rogue" she meant "black hat," which will be explored in depth later but means simply, "in violation of the terms of service of a website, social contracts, or ethics, without necessarily being illegal." Automation service providers were liable to be shut down at any time, and any customer paying for a program to run on an account risked an account ban. Instagram's terms of use made this clear, and much later in this book I'll address Instagram's detection systems and the careful balance maintained by technology companies trying to fight rogue marketers.

In the spring of 2017, Instagram's legal team was shutting down major players. This was well documented. This era, the transition out of which Sapna identified, is what I call the "Instagress Era" because Instagress was the dominant service provider. Instagress was a software-as-a-service control panel from which customers could connect their Instagram accounts, configure who or which hashtags they wanted to target, enter a few generic comments, press *play*, and then watch as the reciprocated actions tallied up.

Instagress provided a dashboard with toggles for automating "likes," "comments," "follows," and "unfollows" which updated live as the actions accrued.

Instagress and what I call "Instagress clones" were particularly dangerous because these online platforms provided disruptive automation tools to people who would otherwise have no idea how to lob flattering spam across cyberspace. The results were so outrageously good that medi-ocre Instagram accounts could gain two thousand followers per month. This encouraged Instagress customers to create additional Instagram accounts (for example, for their pets) to sign them up for Instagress and passively let them grow. Not only was Instagress's pricing absurdly cheap—$9.99 per month[5]—but the service also offered bulk discounts to run multiple accounts.

The systems that debuted in lockstep with Instagress were nothing more than illicit *advertising* services. That a ten-dollar-per-month service could provide dramatically better results than running advertisements was not only disruptive, it created a natural conflict between users and Insta-gram. It is difficult to uphold integrity and convince anyone to purchase ad space when third-party services can instantly deliver fake likes or convinc-ing, organically acquired likes at a fraction of the price.

In 2017, this shadow industry generated well over twenty million dollars. The vast opportunity attracted other talented programmers, which spurred a game of "Whac-a-Mole."[6] Instagram's legal team sent cease-and-desist letters, but the same underlying technology was being re-skinned and relaunched a week later. If one team moved on, another group stood ready to take their place in search results.

One may wonder how software engineers could log into Instagram accounts and execute these actions. They reverse-engineered Instagram's private API and encoded browser automation functions that interacted with its web client. It's out of the scope of this essay, but I'll reintroduce it in "Hackathon Hackers" and the following chapters.

The post-Instagress era bred copycats. It also added another layer of deception. Instagress customers knew that they were paying Instagress to run a bot. By prying into Instagress' marketing materials and website, Insta-gram could easily identify that it was an automation service. The next generation of providers realized that "bot," "automation," and "guaran-teed" were dirty words, so they leaned into assurances of "organic growth" and "compliance" and inferred the presence of human operatives.

Rather than providing customer dashboards like Instagress did, succes-sors collected targeting information at signup using basic web forms. Behind the scenes, they ran bots and fine-tuned them using rough inputs of the information submitted at signup. It still worked well! The key difference was that an investigator couldn't easily glean the automation from the website copy or scant resources provided to a customer after signing up. Gullible customers deluded by the branding would be surprised to find their accounts banned for violating Instagram's terms of use.

The article referenced an April 6, 2017, post by photographer Calder Wilson who had run Instagress on his personal account.[7] In some ways, Wilson's "I Spent Two Years Botting on Instagram – Here's What I Learned" is a synopsis of the *Instagram* portion of this book. Some of his lines of inquiry have been left unanswered until now.

Although Instagress and its successors pushed a relatively new, "organic" type of botting, in the late 2010s, "obviously fake" bots were also rampant on social media. No article covered this phenomenon of annoyance and deception better than the *New York Times'* "The Follower Factory,"[8] published January 27, 2018. This one is in the hall of fame because the reporting led to the Federal Trade Commission setting a major precedent.

Fake activity conducted by bot accounts on Twitter was out of control despite being easily identifiable.[9] The article shined a light onto a multi-million-dollar industry and one of its largest illicit operators, U.S.-based marketing company Devumi.

Devumi earned millions by selling fixed amounts of "real" followers to a massive list of clients, including already notable, if not objectively famous, individuals.[10] The "shadowy" black market for attention was hot. The customers' desire for *any* publicity meant a deluge of willing interview subjects.

Upon closer inspection, it was determined that followers were fake "bot" accounts created and controlled by bot "farms" (or, befitting the title, "factories") in far-flung countries, such as Pakistan. These software agents exhibited predictable patterns of spammy behavior.[11]

Crucially, Devumi had no software engineering operation. The small firm was *not* creating the accounts and *did not directly control the behavior of the following accounts.* Devumi was merely a well-designed storefront from which U.S.-based customers ordered likes and followers from sergeants who commanded vast armies of virtual shills. One thousand Twitter followers on Devumi cost an unsophisticated customer seventeen dollars.[12] Those same thousand followers, obtained in a larger order from a considerably sketchier "SMM Panel" originator, cost "little more than one dollar."

My essay "Social Media Marketing Panels and Sockpuppet Botnets" provides a breakdown of social media botnets and shill networks.

The typical U.S.-based followers purchaser wouldn't have been comfortable navigating the web of cheap but illicit purveyors of fake bulk activity. Ingenious resellers cleaned up the pitch and pushed a central deception—**followers were created by real people, represented real people, and behaved like humans**.

Aside from Devumi being built on a foundation of lies (which was covered in a later piece, "Faked: The Headquarters. The Followers. The Influence?"), "The Follower Factory" identified another transgression. Instead of pushing bot accounts without profile pictures and with usernames composed of jumbles of text, the overseas creators scraped and used pictures and names from real Americans' Instagram accounts.[13]

The risk of impersonation on an industrial scale was scary—ominous. What seemed like an illicit but perhaps harmless scam pulled on Westerners desperate for followers became scarier. Through all of this, Twitter appeared culpable—aware of the issues and unwilling to stop them.

Why would Twitter not aggressively purge these practices? The company's quarterly reports and bottom line benefitted from the daily, weekly, and monthly active user numbers inflated by bot activity. The conspiracy was that there was a careful balance to be sought. Robots counted as "active" users *helped* the platform in one way but caused all types of user strife. Catching ninety nine percent of bots instead of eighty percent of bots was extremely expensive, and could have impacted human signup and in-app experiences. A suspicious imbalance on the platform led to a dispute during Elon Musk's 2022 bid to buy Twitter.[14] Compare the stratospheric valuation of a social media platform concealing automation activity to the pitiful perception of a social media platform overrun with bots and consequent alleged phony metrics.

Social media platforms have the same complicated relationship with spam bots that the U.S. Postal Service has with junk mail.

While reading and rereading "The Follower Factory" early in 2018, I felt like a character in a detective novel (spoiler: perhaps not the detective). At that point, I had been contributing to a shadowy follower growth business for almost six months. That operation was responsible for the types of activity recounted in "How Bots Are Inflating Instagram Egos." Crucially, that business did not sell fake followers. It was not directly impacted by the legal precedent that would be set by the New York State Attorney General.[15] The article and resulting commotion provided information that would-be profiteers used to map the true size of the market.

The alternative to rampant fake account creation and puppeteering was to log in to a real account and automate its actions. Rather than directing an army of bots to follow a customer, use the customer's *own account* to attract modest engagement from other humans—using a bot. This came to be known as "organic growth." In a way, organic growth was the righteous path. If I log into a customer's Instagram account and start liking photos and leaving comments, that customer will receive likes and comments in return and enjoy a boosted social status. In the aftermath of the NYT exposé, business boomed.

Two months later, the *New York Times* covered Instagram again with an article about Instagram bots.

Empowered by the response to the article about Twitter misbehavior and surely benefitting from a flood of unsolicited tips from social media "experts," Sapna Maheshwari picked up where she left off in 2017 to address troubling Instagram activity.

"Uncovering Instagram Bots With a New Kind of Detective Work" was published on March 12, 2018.[16]

This article didn't make as much of a splash in terms of cross-coverage or legal precedents but did stoke quite a bit of action that was never attributed to its publication. There weren't any follow-up articles of significance; the reader could have believed that attention had shifted elsewhere. Was that true?

My attention did not waver. March 2018 marked a breakthrough month for both my business and rogue Instagram growth. I saw revenue nearly double from the previous month, likely from customers who had just heard about the dark side of social media marketing. I have documented that a massive number of savvy entrepreneurs started software-assisted businesses around that time. In all, I've analyzed over one hundred such services.

Over the next few months, Meta *did* take notice and strictly policed fake accounts and botting on Instagram. I refuse to believe that this was the result of anything but pressure from this *New York Times* article.

I have never forgotten one of its leading quotes from the co-founder of a firm that had developed special methods to detect bot activity: "The amount of bot activity that's happening on these platforms is pretty insane."[17]

Another founder of a social-media-adjacent firm used the phrase, "day of reckoning" to refer to advertisers who, while planning to run influencer marketing campaigns, suddenly got squirrely in the face of evidence that accounts had inflated their metrics.[18] Their followers were not real. Fake followers are deadweight—they're impervious to persuasion.

One of the early companies performing this type of "detective work" claimed to use over fifty metrics to identify fake accounts.[19] Although the examples resonated with me, the underlying fact was that **the company analyzing the accounts was probably violating Instagram's terms of use**. To analyze such metrics at scale, a provider would have had to query Instagram's private API and scrape data from the platform!

My framing is that **even some of the good guys were bad guys**.

Sapna did say that "changes to algorithms on Facebook and Instagram have significantly reduced the number of people who will see a person's posts without paid promotion."[20] Later, I'll share my thoughts on these algorithms and, lest we forget, the "rogue" marketers who design systems to exploit them.

What Happens Now?

Social media journalism from the *New York Times* in the late 2010s continues to fascinate me. I revel in each re-read. I hope *Framed* is as thought-provoking and entertaining as those articles were. When people ask me "wHo'S yOuR aUdIeNcE?" I paste parts from dozens of books and hundreds of articles and research papers that inspired me.

This audience exists because I stand on the shoulders of brilliant investigative journalists, talented researchers, uptight encyclopedists, random bloggers, and Urban Dictionary ethnographers—the serious weirdos who took the time to write things down.

The scope of this book will likely be regarded as absurd for one person with no traditional support team to attempt. I rush toward publication in fear of being forced to lodge an opinion about the *new* social media site.

There have been cheaters, thugs, and even genuine criminals misusing social media platforms since the days of dial-up. We never got to read their stories. It may seem like there's a podcast episode and YouTube deep dive dedicated to every grifter who has ever lived, but we've done a shitty job of preserving the history of the internet. Some of my fondest social media memories are of events, personalities, and sociological topics that haven't been archived anywhere. So much has *actually* been "shut off."

Why not try to connect the dots between the niche I know so well and the zeitgeist that many intellectuals sink their teeth into only when the ocean turns dark red?

When I revealed to friends that they hadn't seen me in a year because I was covertly writing a book about social media iniquity, several suggested, "Oh, you need to break up the chapters and post promotional videos on TikTok!" To them and to readers I say that to make such a suggestion is to totally miss the point. If the reader does continue and entertain my brazen attempt to connect those dots, it will be clear why.

I can't predict the next wave of cultural rewiring or if it will occur on smartphones or the metaverse or a dimension not yet imagined. The modern incarnation of TikTok didn't exist when I started assembling this material. There is an argument that Instagram's relevance is waning. I'm not active on social media these days, and all my ventures have been closed.

I want to crystalize my perspective before it really is too late. This perspective was gained not while I was on the outside looking in but while I was dead center in that four-cornered frame looking around. I can't be sure what I'll find the next time those elevator doors open.

3

A PLACE FOR FRIENDS, PIMPS, AND WHORES

Myspace arrived when "going online" was becoming a big deal. I created my account in 2006, shortly after my family had upgraded to broadband. My household's bandwidth was clogged with traffic from Limewire, AOL Instant Messenger, Adobe Flash games, and all the wonders of Web 2.0. Myspace helped define the *participative web*. Yet, it's been poorly preserved, and there has been little acknowledgement of the influence the platform had on popular culture, social media, rule breaking, and self-expression.

Myspace, originally stylized as MySpace, had a slogan: A Place for Friends. This tagline has been scrubbed even from Wikipedia.[1] It's a phrase memorable for its hominess. It's also something of a nod to Friendster, Myspace's precursor which had been surpassed in user count before 2005.

Where a place being "for friends" suggests the coziness of home, Myspace was a block party, a clambake, a carnival, more than it was a modest gathering. Friendships from the overworld persisted in the virtual world—eighty percent of my connections I had met in real life—but the openness of the platform spawned a new segment of friendship: strangers.

> OMG, Stacey is such a myspace [sic] whore! She posts bulletins like every
> five minutes! She must have atleast [sic] three thousand friends she doesn't
> even know![2]

16

Friendster, Xanga, LiveJournal, and GeoCities allowed users to tailor profiles with custom text, colors, hyperlinks, and other web elements. Myspace defined early Web 2.0 social networks by offering deep customization, allowing the embedding of images, songs, videos, widgets, and iframes and the usage of HTML (hypertext markup language) and CSS (cascading style sheets). Today, this is a foreign concept. Social media platforms mandate standard layouts. Modern users cultivate aesthetics through their content and terse branding, not by layout acrobatics.

With dedication and persistence, a Myspace page could have rendered any combination of styled website elements, almost as if it had been built by a modern drag-and-drop website builder. Designing the page was painstaking work, as the globs of text (HTML and CSS) had to be saved and then tested in a different window. Most of the layouts and graphics were crude, if not hideous. This was captured in a Medium post by Amanda Russell, titled "The Beauty of the Ugly Internet."[3]

MySpace profiles gave people a space to say "this is me!" It was like being able to put your bedroom walls on the internet — the movie posters, the pages ripped out from magazines, the tickets from that band you saw, the pictures of you and your boyfriend. As expected, profile pages were often hilariously garish, loud and ugly.

Looking back, it seems almost like a false memory. Our social networks are so tightly controlled, so uniform and so bland that it's hard [to] believe they evolved from this.

If I could, I would definitely send Ms. Russell a friend request.

Computer Nerds Meet Emos

When it came to sending friend requests, I had an advantage. By 2007, I had broadband, my own computer, my own room to use the computer in, and a desire to spend copious amounts of time on the internet. In the hallways of Northeast Intermediate School, I was called a "computer nerd." I dispute the offensiveness of this term. On the computer, on the participative web, I was safe, perhaps even untouchable, and that was before likes, followers, and views became mainstream social currency. On Myspace, asymmetries in access, adoption, and computer literacy created a warp in which the cool kids from school were far from the coolest kids online.

The platform provided an unprecedented freedom of expression, which resulted in hundreds of terabytes of user-generated content. This content would be regarded as the most cringeworthy cultural artifact in human history, had it not all been lost in a botched data migration in 2018.[4]

What's memorable for me is that this Myspace social network appeared to be led and governed by the *anti*social kids from school. Encountering one of their Myspace pages gave the impression that they had been around longer, were more experienced, and were *more popular*. The profiles were so well designed! The friend count was so high!

There was an era, stretching between 2004 and 2008, in which individuals typified as outcasts banded together on the internet and inflated a vast sphere of influence. At school, they were unkempt, dejected, skateboarding, and unconventional. This group found solace and significance in social media more so than any group since.

Emo and scene kids were untouchable on Myspace. No jock who had been using the internet for less than a year would dare lob an insult at the kid with 2500 friends and a *very black* color palette, risking virtual consequences beyond their comprehension. Would-be cyberbullies were supposed to be occupied by things that kept them away from the family computer lest they be deemed computer nerds. If it wasn't for AOL Instant Messenger, their typing skills would have been nonexistent.

The fringe kids gained respect. At the same time, aided by the rocketing popularity of post-hardcore bands like Fall Out Boy, the emo aesthetic gained mainstream appeal. All of the bands were on Myspace, and their songs spread virally, autoplayed for each visitor to emo kids' profiles.

Myspace became this free-for-all, this collection of maniacally curated pages and emergent nonconformist behaviors. Nerds like me had to make a choice. We were logging massive amounts of computer time. We were mostly free from cyberbullying. But we weren't popular at school *or* on the internet. For me, it was simple—I had nothing to lose by dipping into emo subculture. It started with setting my profile song to "Cute Without the 'E'" by Taking Back Sunday. Then I darkened my layout. I added a rigid black border to my profile picture. I picked an edgier display name. I wore the dark-navy school uniform more often. I grew out my hair. Eventually, I acquired thick-tongued shoes, a skateboard, and other emo ephemera.

Such transformations (loser into well-liked teenage stereotype) were parodied in the 2006 YouTube music video *The Kings of MySpace*[5] in which a young man who just signed up for Myspace is coached by his two friends on how to ditch his bland appearance and achieve popularity on the site. One of the "kings" proclaimed, "Grew my hair long, put on *Dashboard Confessional*. Put on tight jeans that smashed on my testicles."[6]

The actors in the video using the name *Kings of Myspace* related to my experience in "pick(ing) an edgier display name"—at the time, "screen names" were still pervasive and were dripping with internet lexicon, in-group references, childishness, and pleas for attention. This was facilitated by Myspace's allowance of extremely long names that employed an array of symbols.

This absurd name I encountered during my traversal of cached websites is a prototypical example: | ♂ D-MONEY SCARiNG KiDz

It has almost everything that typified the era:

- Ridiculous length
- Irregular spacing
- Meaningless symbols
- An alias, D-Money, inside the alias
- A reference to a post-hardcore band, Scary Kids Scaring Kids
- Mixture of cases and usage of internet slang, such as the lowercase *i* and the *s*-for-*z* swap in KiDz

Really, the only things missing from this name were:

1. Explicit statement of number of friends (i.e., Timothy [12.1k])
2. Emo alliterations seen in other (real) names, such as [tylertorment], pete plague™, and saint seth sadistic

I, a geek, had become kind of emo. Around the same time, the emo and *scene* (a term I use interchangeably with emo) captains of Myspace were becoming computer geeks. A funny symbiosis emerged. The best page layouts were code copy-and-pasted from "layout generator" websites. However, anyone looking to further customize a layout, or post better content on Myspace, needed to learn HTML and CSS. It turned out that spending more time learning basic markup, and maybe even learning how to program, could directly result in greater popularity on Myspace. Nerds figured, "Hey, I have something to gain by being emo." Emos figured, "Hey, I have something to gain by being a computer nerd."

In the quest for subculture authenticity, *audience* rapidly gained importance. Myspace users started to claim the number of their friends in their display names. They started to think more abstractly—what if there were other ways to measure reach? As the conventionally popular kids started to build out profiles and networks of their own, the race was on.

Teenagers flocked to customize their profiles to accrue *hits* (hit was the old word for pageview).[7] To know how many hits they were getting, they built hit counters. If they couldn't build their own, they found hit counters and pasted the code into their Myspace pages. The special thing about a hit counter is that it doesn't just provide information to whoever controls the site, visitors can see the number as well. The hit counter was one of the earliest forms of social affirmation, predating networked friend counts.

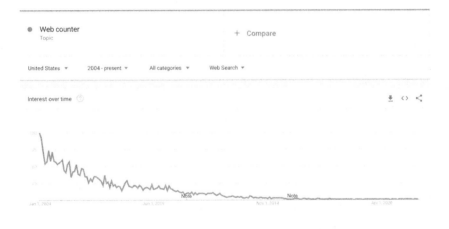

Google Trends™ for "web counter"[8]

It is no coincidence that search interest in both "hits" and "web counter" dropped off steeply between 2009 and 2012. This was the period during which Facebook surpassed Myspace. All of those people tracking their hits were shepherded into a sober, sterile site with almost no customization. Facebook took away the ability to add custom code and to embed images or videos hosted elsewhere. This resulted in a more standard, safer, and more performant site experience.

While Myspace was still a juggernaut, nerds, geeks, emos, goths, scensters, and a host of weirdos formed a loose confederacy in which they sought further popularity—they became Myspace Pimps.

Pimping

In the mid-aughts, the hit MTV show *Pimp My Ride*, hosted by rapper Xzibit, shuttled the word *pimp*, in all its forms, into the mainstream lexicon. The series, which debuted in 2004, was so pervasive that, *in fifth grade*, my friend and I wrote a piece of fiction for our school newspaper in which we were "pimping" a Lincoln Continental. Our teacher, appalled that we referenced *Pimp My Ride*, suggested we write a different story.

Two years later, I was thinking about the same thing: pimping. Only I was creating Myspace layouts. I wanted to pimp them; I was learning how. Not from Iceberg Slim but from hastily constructed web-design guides I found on the internet.

The back cover of the *Pimp My Ride* video game, released in 2006, included a link to Xzibit's Myspace page.

It's totally fitting for the era that a gritty West Coast rapper's harnessing of "pimping" quickly reached edgelords on social media. But, what if these nerds calling themselves pimps found they were infringing on *actual* pimps operating on Myspace? To understand this clash of cultures, I've arranged a few definitions of pimp and how real life pimping translated to the internet.

Definition 1: A Myspace pimp is an actual pimp.

I never would have expected a self-identified Myspace pimp to have been a real-life pimp. As millions of people sought to pimp their profiles, bona fide pimps were left to wonder what the hell was going on. There was a branding issue as the flashy 1970s pimp aesthetic was represented by web designs which caricatured the attention-grabbing costumes and pageantry of the era.

Or, maybe it was easier for pimps to hide in plain sight, realizing that anything they said or did, short of posting an ad for a prostitute, would blend in with emo kids trying to look cool.

There are a few surviving accounts of this, all written by Kevin Poulsen for *Wired*. In his last article on the topic, published November 8, 2010, the title says it all: "'Y2K Pimp' Gets 12 Years for Recruiting Minor on MySpace."[9] The story begins: "A self-described pimp who recruited a 16-year-old girl on MySpace then rented her out as a prostitute through escort websites was sentenced Monday to 12½ years in prison for sex trafficking of a minor."

An earlier article, "Pimps Go Online to Lure Kids Into Prostitution,"[10] makes clear that predators really were recruiting young girls:

> "We have a bunch of fake MySpace accounts that we go after pimps with," says Shaun King, an officer with the Los Angeles Police Department's Juvenile Prostitution unit. "Pretty quickly, if they get a vibe that you're open to such things, they'll draw you in. . . . We've had pimps buy us bus tickets."

If being a pimp was considered cool, then being labeled the Y2K Pimp was as cool as it got in the aughts. The man bestowed with this title in Poulsen's article, Marvin Chavelle Epps, was a bad guy who pleaded guilty.

Realizing that his sentence had likely been served by the early 2020s and that he would have been required to provide his mailing address as a registered sex offender, I sought to get in contact with Mr. Epps.

I could only find two relevant records, both dead ends, but both intriguing. The first was a court document called an Order of Detention, signed on September 30, 2021, in which Marvin Epps—then a free man—was found to have violated the terms of his probation, most notably by pandering, meaning he had quickly returned to pimping, and possession of computers with access to "online computer services."[11]

The other record was on Goodprisoner.com, a site offering prison penpal services that appears to be stuck in a time warp. On the site, a picture of Epps (identified as "Chevelle" instead of Chavelle), features prominently.[12] His profile there, not dissimilar in style to a Myspace profile of the young woman he might have pimped, contained a juvenile **20 Questions: & My 20 Answers !!!** section before providing his contact information. Letter mail only.

It's telling that when appealing to potential romantic pen pals, a hustler known as the Y2K Pimp didn't want to be seen as a computer nerd: "My name is 'Chevelle' and I am new to this online thing..."[13]

Definition 2: A Myspace pimp is one who maintains multiple accounts in order to hide emotional affairs from their partner.[14]

This entry has garnered only sixteen thumbs up. It makes sense that the term would be expanded to mean *a savvy person who uses social media to mislead romantic partners*. Surely, users did employ this practice, but I don't remember this practice, I didn't know anyone with more than one account, nobody I polled associated this practice with this term, and there is no supporting evidence that it was widely used.

Definition 3: A Myspace pimp is an individual with an attention-grabbing, well-designed, feature-rich profile.

Checking Google search trends for "pimp" reveals strong overlap with the heyday of both Myspace and *Pimp My Ride*, the traffic surging in 2007 and peaking in December of that year before dropping precipitously by late 2009 (when *Pimp My Ride* was canceled, and Myspace's user count had been surpassed by Facebook's).

The related queries tell the story, as the top searches ranked by popularity were: "pimp my," "myspace pimp," "pimp profile," "pimp my profile," "pimp my ride," "pimp my myspace," "pimp layouts," "layouts," "pimp lyrics," and "pimp myspace layouts." Even with many different queries addressing the same concept, *Pimp My Ride* was only fifth in the rankings. These results indicate that pimping was out of Xzibit's hands. They also suggest a strong relationship between pimping and the layouts of Myspace profiles.

An industry sprung up filled with glittering graphics, custom layouts, and detailed guides on how to make Myspace profiles more appealing. Pimp-my-profile.com and other sites prominently featured the word *pimp* in their branding.

ZingerBug
https://www.zingerbug.com › layouts

Pre-Made Layout Codes for MySpace - ZingerBug

Jun 23, 2009 — Get MySpace Layouts, with background images and pre-made CSS layout codes to pimp your MySpace profile.

In what now reads like satire, the tutorial website Howcast.com published an article and instructional video titled "How to Pimp Your

Myspace Page."[15] The video differentiated a "bland" profile from a "sweet," pimped one, suggesting a common acceptance that a pimped Myspace page was a cool one, free of the negative connotations of criminal pandering. It suggested that not customizing a profile made someone bland, boring, and perhaps unpopular. Likewise, the back cover of the *Pimp My Ride* video game contained the phrase "Turn Hoopties . . . Into Head Turners!"

Layout generator sites allowed visitors to pick from color palettes and specify other values and customized styles from which the sites then "generated" HTML and CSS. Users would copy the code generated and, according to instructions, paste it into one of the Myspace profile boxes, which would then render a pimped Myspace page.

Definition 4: A Myspace pimp is a subculture leader who organizes "whore trains" and other disruptive campaigns in order to gain notoriety and followers.

Pimping a profile was only half the battle. Drawing eyes to it presented a different challenge. Myspace users participated in a practice known as *whoring* and in a collaborative endeavor known as the *whore train*.

An outgrowth of Definition 3, one who fit the aesthetic to the point of being a tastemaker, this pimp sought attention by organizing bands of like-minded, similar-looking people who engaged in self-promotion. A popular person—an early *influencer*—would pimp others, would promote them. This was a means of demonstrating popularity, with the idea that someone pimped by a whore train "conductor" would gain plenty of new friends. The pimp might have accrued social currency in return.

In this definition, pimps were important players, attempting to channel traffic to their profiles and the profiles of their constituents, namely other emo kids.

Definition 5: A Myspace pimp is someone who achieves notoriety or revenue, often by advanced use of technology.

Pimp, on Myspace, came to mean more than a popular user with a nice profile, a disruptive promoter, a man cheating on his girlfriend, or a guy who had legions of female friends. It came to mean real success and significance. It often involved breaking the rules.

Myspace Whores

Myspace had an official slogan: A Place for Friends. Myspace was actually a place for *whores*.

The cultural rise of the term was unmistakable, exemplified by one of the band Fall Out Boy's unrecorded songs:[16]

> "I Liked You a Lot Better Before You Became a Fucking Myspace Whore."
>
> The band have been hyping this song since 2004, and with good reason. With lyrics about blood, hearses and car crashes, it almost makes us think twice before logging into our MySpace account. Almost.
>
> PATRICK STUMP: "Funny that the most well-known song on our record never even made it to the record. I love this song. It reminds me of 'Young Turks' by Rod Stewart. When we were deciding what songs we wanted to record, everyone kind of blew this one off and later on we were like, 'Why didn't we record this one?' I think this is another one we'll record someday. Definitely one of my favorite songs we have ever written."

"Whoring" on Myspace did not have an overtly sexual connotation. It really was an abbreviation for *attention* whore. Urban Dictionary has a March 2008 entry that helps establish the connection: "This girl has hundreds of pictures of herself on her myspace [sic]. She thinks shes [sic] so pretty, but shes [sic] not. Shes [sic] just an attention whore."[17] It makes sense why Patrick Stump may have liked a girl less after she became a Myspace Whore.

The emo subculture on Myspace appropriated this term and embraced attention whoring. Emo users garnered friends, comments, messages, and other forms of virtual score by any means possible. The idea was that a user's popularity was demonstrated by the number of friends they had, and, to a lesser extent, the number of photo comments and profile comments they had. Popularity meant accumulating these interactions—coming home to a stuffed notification box. The best way for users to grow while electrifying the brain's dopamine passageways was to rapidly dish out interactions and then *explicitly ask for recipients to return the favor*. These users—these whores—were forebears of the behaviors exhibited on social media today.

The Myspace notification box

Sending a friend request on Myspace required more effort than what was necessary on sites that appeared later. Users couldn't scroll down a pre-prepared list and click add, add, add, add. They had to visit each profile and wait for each page to render. On the default, two-column profile layout, the Send Friend Request button was intended to be located directly under the upper-lefthand-corner div displaying the user's profile picture, online status, and other demographic information. However, there was not a guarantee that the button would be there. The location and even the accessibility of the button could have been altered by a layout that was pimped too hard.

Central to the concept of whoring was that a collaboration between emos, geeks, and pimps had resulted in a short-circuiting of the friend-request process. Rather than having to visit a user's page to send a request, savvy players extracted the profile IDs required to send requests in a single click, which meant a friend-request URL could be created and clicked without the rigamarole of visiting each user's page.

If the user's page wasn't being visited, then where was the link or button that people would have been clicking? It was located in a Myspace bulletin. Bulletins were early status messages (think tweets) that were broadcast in a primitive "feed" to all one's friends on their Myspace homepages. This feed was sorted chronologically, and there was no filtering.

From	Date	Bulletin
psycho_luigi	Jan 1, 2008 12:04 AM	New Year Blessings
&shan;	Jan 1, 2008 12:03 AM	HAPPY NEW YEAR!!!!!!!!!!!!!!!!!!!
mikehedge *RonPaul08*	Jan 1, 2008 12:01 AM	2008
&shan;	Dec 31, 2007 11:56 PM	5 minutes!!!!!!!!! :D
hellogoodbye	Dec 31, 2007 11:50 PM	happy new years!
Paige	Dec 31, 2007 11:36 PM	Happy New Years! :)
Stefanie Screams™	Dec 31, 2007 11:29 PM	guitar hero bitchhh
The Amorous Contact	Dec 31, 2007 11:07 PM	happy new year
Alycia Brennan	Dec 31, 2007 11:04 PM	Happy New Year
Molly [Ron Paul 2008]	Dec 31, 2007 10:59 PM	Enjoy

post bulletin | view all

A Myspace user's bulletin space—note the chronological ordering

On the same "pimp my Myspace" layout sites there are still "whore me" generators, which were used by those interested in gaining friends whom *they didn't know*. The generated code would be placed in bulletins (or external sites) with the hope that people would repost them and provide free advertising.

Myspacegens.com provided a simple whore me generator with the description, "Create a custom friend adder image and information text. This is helpful if you are looking to get some more friends around myspace." It would render the code that displayed a link that would dispatch a friend request when clicked, provided the visitor provided their friend ID.[18]

YOUR WHORE ME CODES:

Add Tim
I am one of the
coolest people on
Myspace. Please add
me!

Paste the following codes into any section (the one where you want the box to appear).

```
<div style="text-align: center; width: 120px;"><span style="color: #a84fa8; font-size: 11px;"><a
href="http://friends.myspace.com/index.cfm?fuseaction=invite.addfriend_verify&friendId=1234">Add
Tim</a></span><br /><span style="font-size: 11px;">I am one of the coolest people on Myspace. Please
add me!</span><br /><a href="http://profile.myspace.com/index.cfm?
```

Myspacegens.com Whore Me generator input and output

Links streamlined the adding process but they did nothing to guarantee exposure and reach. As users became more familiar with how Myspace worked, they embraced reciprocal actions, coded under the acronyms PC4PC, C4C, and W4W.

PC4PC, arguably the most popular, meant "picture comment for picture comment."[19] C4C meant "comment for comment,"[20] and W4W meant "whore for whore."[21] F4F,[22] meaning "friend for friend" or "follow for follow" on other platforms, was used on Myspace to indicate that a user would accept anyone's friend request. Myspace had a mutual friendship model, with no concept of unilateral *followers* or *following*, so F4F didn't involve a reciprocal user-initiated action, it would have just been the user on the receiving end clicking Accept.

The intent behind writing PC4PC was to nudge whoever was being interacted with, to let them know that their comments left on pictures would be reciprocated. For example, if I left a comment on a female's picture, punctuated with "PC4PC?," she'd see that as an invitation to comment on one of my pictures if she thought I was a worthy suitor. Today, stating this intention sounds ridiculous, as it's become an ingrained yet unspoken social code—actions such as comments and likes generally *are* reciprocated between friends and lovers.

W4W was the first attempt at joint promotion of profiles for the purpose of building an audience. If I posted my own whore link, the default audience would be my existing friends. They were already friends with me! If I convinced someone else to write a bulletin containing my Add Me link, that would be free advertising to *their* friends list. At the same time, I could post a bulletin containing their Add Me link. We were attention whoring each other to distinct networks. Other users interested in trading bulletin promotion might have contacted me after seeing someone else promoting me, or they could have noticed that I had included W4W in my display name or elsewhere in my profile.

W4W evolved to become the *whore train*. Whore trains ran on bulletins, but rather than a post requiring the cooperation of two friends listing each other's Add Me links, the train bulletins contained links and pictures of numerous users, as well as instructions on how one could join the train.

whore train

[Myspace] groups frequented by 14–17 year old scenesters (mostly girls) who have thousands of friends and lead a very large part of their lives on the internet. [The] point of these trains is to get a shitload of friend requests, although they seldom actually interact with most of the people they meet on myspace in real life. [One] must apply for the train by adding the owner, having a large amount of friends ("must have at least 2K"), and look extremely scene. [Once] accepted, members must post the train in a bulletin a set number of times a week. [The] bulletin displays small pictures of all the train's members with the owner on top. [Members] are often divided by how many friends they have, with "riders" often being a low rank. [To] devote one's time to this essentially means you're spending too much of your time on [Myspace].[23]

The veracity of this definition is attested by the fact that I witnessed friends from school reposting train bulletins, and that I joined the trains myself. If more friends meant more popularity, why not?

For one thing, whore trains weren't what everyday users wanted to see in their bulletin feeds. Available space in the chronological bulletin box was limited. Spam from those seeking attention pushed down other content, such as users posting their answers to short surveys. Recall the quote from the introduction and the anger generated by "Stacey" posting "bulletins like every 5 minutes!"[24]

Date:	Aug 18, 2008 4:37 PM
Subject:	boredddddddddd
Body:	What's your name? jaydee
	How old are you? 14
	Eye colour? bluuueeee
	Hair colour? blonde
	Do you like someone right now? maybeeeeee ;)
	When did you last see your crush? today at school hehe

A typical Myspace bulletin from 2008

Whoring was disruptive and it degraded user experience on the platform. Though there are few contemporary accounts, users generally found the whore train bulletins to be obnoxious.

Myspace Train

Any of those obnoxious bulletins that some of your emo/scene/whatever friends post occasionally. It's usually called something like "Capcom Train," "Toy Box Murder," "Silent Hill Train," or anything similar, and it's basically a bulletin promoting some sort of group or club.

Inside the bulletin are pictures of the group's members in order of rank, as well as a billion clickable links to add the people AND group to your buddies list and groups list.

But get this. No matter WHAT THE HELL the train is called, no matter WHAT THE HELL this little club is about, and no matter WHAT THE HELL the rules are, EVERY SINGLE F[*]CKING member is emo. They're all camera whores. They've all got the infamous myspace [sic] angle[25] with weird black hair covering half of their face with eyeliner on. It's just... annoying.. to see that kind of thing ALL the time.

someone posts a new bulletin

Typical Myspace Train:

"Toy Box Murder"

clicks

"TOY BOX MURDER!! OWNERS: *shows display pictures of two emo kids* CO-OWNERS: *shows even more emo kids* MEMBERS: *shows the biggest list of emo kids you've ever seen in your life*"

"What the hell is this??? The gathering of the scene whores??"[26]

Although all trains had an owner, an authority, they were notoriously difficult to organize and keep on track. There were usually standards for users seeking to hop on board. The train conductor, whether a pimp or just an owner, would mandate a minimum number of friends and then a certain profile aesthetic for consideration for membership. The aesthetic (e.g., scene kid) might have only been implied, not stated. Though it helped to be objectively attractive, the name of the game was, overwhelmingly, to look scene. The fringe kids were still in the driver's seat; the popular kids from school were not in the car.

Owners might have demanded that a "rider" change their display name to indicate exclusive participation in a single train. Users who wanted to participate in trains tended to add their number of friends to their display names, such as Timothy [1.2k], to save a conductor from having to click through their profile to investigate friend count. Obviously, this was easy to fake.

Those who applied to ride the trains would be tasked with friending all current riders. Verifying that a qualified applicant had indeed added everyone was tricky, because it depended on the existing train riders having *accepted* the friend requests. For the perfectionist, it also meant checking that the rider had *kept* everyone added. If a conductor approved an additional rider, when it was time to update the train's membership the owner would generate a new blob of HTML code with all of the add-friend links. In the bulletin, the names and profile pictures of riders would be listed in order of importance. The riders would copy and post the new bulletin at a predetermined interval, known as a "round" of the train. Then, the conductor would check to make sure that every rider did post it and didn't modify the bulletin, for instance, to rank themself more highly.

Running a train was comically difficult. When I participated in them, ones that weren't particularly exclusive, I was drawn to the opportunity to fork the train, to remove people, to modify the links and rank myself at or near the top of the wall of add-friend links. My hope was that my fork would spread more like chain mail, where I could persuade other stowaways to add their names to the list and repost it as their own bulletin. If the train conductor noticed this fork, what could they do? If I wasn't part of the train to begin with, I had nothing to lose by hijacking a train.

As I gained dozens of friends, my higher-than-average friend count (roughly four hundred), which at times was featured in my display name, served as a scarlet letter of sorts. Because the people I'd added had been obsessed with growing their friend lists, my bulletin board became a chaotic mess of self-promotion. There were times where I refreshed my homepage to find that none of the bulletins were posted by people *I actually knew.* My Myspace was no longer a place for friends.

Computer Nerds as the Real Pimps

As a computer nerd who associated with the emo subculture and then spent hundreds of hours trawling Myspace, how did things turn out for me? Where I remember most of my social media use from 2010 and beyond with regret, my experience using Myspace in middle school holds only fond memories for me.

Not only did Myspace give me the opportunity to express myself, it gave me the freedom to do it without judgment, nearly free of consequences. Further, Myspace introduced me to great music spanning all genres. I later uploaded my own songs to the platform.

As an unexpected benefit of modifying all of those layouts and bulletins between 2006 and 2009, I learned web design. My first-ever internship was as a web developer. All that crudely written code on Myspace set the stage for what became a rewarding career as a software engineer.

The big question, though, is whether I ever became cool.

People peak in high school. People peak in college. There is no doubt that the apex of my popularity was in 2008, on Myspace. By eighth grade, I even had a real girlfriend. The significance of Myspace was that it allowed me to represent myself as a popular, social, emo kid with shaggy hair. Though I had a large crew of friends with similarly unkempt haircuts, none of us were popular. Where Myspace made a difference in my life was when I was talking to people *I didn't know.*

Years before I had a driver's license, I was using Myspace as a dating service; I'd find and send friend requests to girls my age from neighboring school districts. In some cases, this meant that I was an eighth grader hitting up high school freshmen. The rate of reciprocity, of mutual interest, likely due to the newness of the experience for everyone involved, was astonishingly high.

Having unrestricted internet usage helped me build my persona, build my profile, develop savvy in navigating early social media, and hone my writing ability; it gave me a distinct advantage. There was less competition because the kids who were cooler than me weren't logged in as often. Some of them didn't even have profile pictures! On the internet, nobody could have known that in real life I was shy and awkward. Yet, I befriended many love interests from other schools, and slid my favorites into my Top 8 friends long before we ever met in person.

By the time I was arranging in-person meetings with these young women at local church picnics, there was a small group of people attempting to program, automate, and broker attention whoring on Myspace. Though they weren't the Y2K Pimp, they were pimps in their own right.

The most notorious caper to accumulate Myspace friends was attributed to a guy named Samy Kamkar. In 2005, just before I started using Myspace, he created a virus, or worm. Myspace's insufficient security allowed Samy to slyly exploit a cross-site scripting (XSS) vulnerability, in which any user who visited his Myspace profile using a browser such as Internet Explorer was tricked into running his unsafe code.[27] The code quietly sent a friend request to Samy, injected the same self-replicating code into the visitor's profile, and displayed the message "but most of all, samy is my hero" superimposed over the user's Myspace profile.

```
but most of all, samy is my hero <div id=my-
code        style="BACKGROUND:        url('java-
script:eval(document.all.mycode.expr)')"
expr="var B=String.fromCharCode(34);var 28
```

This is still considered the fastest-spread virus of all time, having infected over one million users in less than a full day.[29] For what he considered a prank, Samy Kamkar was subject to an FBI raid, a felony conviction, and a plea agreement that forbade his use of the internet for several years. Today, he is a prominent security researcher and perhaps the most legitimate claimant to Definition 5 of Myspace Pimp.

Samy wasn't the last person to write software to algorithmically gain friends. Enterprising software developers realized that conducting whore trains through bulletins was tricky and, noting the demand for and potential profit in friends-list growth, started websites that facilitated friending beyond what could be accomplished by Myspace bulletins.

Websites that provided software solutions for attention whoring on Myspace included friendstorm.net, fatadds.com, phatadds.com, maxadds.com, infiniteadds.com, unwrittenadds.com, and friendpulse.com. Thanks to the Internet Archive, I've been able to peek into the operations of these sites and speculate about how their fortunes rose and fell.

The sites all followed the same formula. Users authenticated their Myspace accounts within these unaffiliated sites' web interfaces. The interfaces displayed lists of participating Myspace users—extracted from Myspace—who also wanted to make more friends. The crucial advancement was that, from there, friending activity was tracked and rewarded.

Sending friend requests natively on Myspace, even through a direct whore link, couldn't be tracked. Sites like FriendStorm were able to track the activity, and users who sent greater numbers of verified friend requests were rewarded with points. Users with more points were given broader exposure within these "adder" sites. More visibility meant receiving more friend requests.

FriendStorm is the fastest way to make new friends on MySpace. You could think of it as one huge whore train with thousands of profiles on it only makes one round per day. **FriendStorm uses a point system to ensure that users who participate will receive the most add requests.** See below for details on the points system.

Once you join FriendStorm you will be presented with a series of other users. Then you simply push the ADD button to add that person as a friend. You may continue to add users to as long as you like, up to 500 per day.

For each person you add you will earn **1 point**, the users with the most points will receive the most add requests from other users. **Basically, the more points you have; the more add requests you will get.**

Probably the fastest way to get points is by posting bulletins. When you log into FriendStorm you will be given the opportunity to post a bulletin. You will earn **50 points** for each person who joins FriendStorm through your bulletin, these are called referrals.[30]

FriedStorm's adder service eliminated the toil, trust, and organizational problems of operating platform-native whore trains. Though readers may consider this to be a relic of the past, sites like these really were the original "coin apps," which operate adjacent to social networks. Like the Myspace adder sites, coin apps don't guarantee anything—they simply offer increased exposure within their interfaces in exchange for interacting with other users (or in exchange for real-world currency).

FriendStorm's profit center was the Featured Profile.[31] Users could pay for increased exposure. Subscriptions lasting one day, one week, and one month cost $9, $43, and $105 resulting in four hundred, two thousand, and five thousand *approximate* friend requests. The page provided "Cost per 100 friends" which mapped to $2.25, $2.15, and $2.10 for each plan respectively.

The approximation of how many friend requests would be received is not too different from the claims made about clicks when running platform-native ads today. FriendStorm was one of the first sites to ascribe value to friendship on a social media site, about two pennies per pal. It should be noted that even if a user received the friend requests promised, they'd still have to manually accept the friend requests. If there actually were thousands of requests, accepting them could have amounted to a full-time job.

The adders were mostly indistinguishable. However, considering that Myspace lost all of its data from its golden era,[32] the sites *are* notable for what they preserved about how people—call them early influencers—were using Myspace at that time.

One trend was the *emo alliteration* used in names, which was prominent amongst friendpulse's top users.On friendpulse.com in July 2008, the top five users were "[tylertorment]," "dear, will killen," "aesthetic...," "saint seth sadistic," and "pete plague™."[33]

In the 2010s, Myspace took action against the adder sites. Their ability to operate was restricted. The message supplied in the last archival capture of Maxadds[34] is one of optimism in the face of defeat: "We at Maxadds are looking to work very close to myspace [sic] if possible, and keep Maxadds going and comply to myspace [sic] new strict rules. Still waiting for the final word."

In what I consider the final frontier of Myspace pimping, the greatest accomplishment in Myspace friend-adder software is actually found on an *earlier* application. MyFriendBot was released by Anthony Lineberry in

2005.[35] The shell of his wiped Myspace page reveals that he described himself as a "computer hacker."[36]

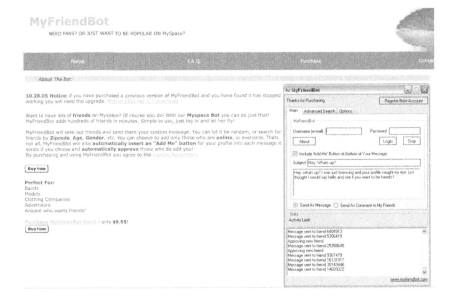

The MyFriendBot website in 2005

MyFriendBot, the originator of disruptive social media software, contained three amazing features for the price of $9.95 (which was later raised to $19.95):[37]

1. It searched potential friends and targeted based on demographic filters
2. It automated the sending of whore messages to these users
3. It automated the accepting of friend requests

Unsurprisingly, a program with these features facilitated huge volumes of spam—unwanted messages. Myspace swiftly took legal action against the creator.[38]

Starting in 2006, the MyFriendBot site displayed the text "down until further notice."[39] In an article titled "MyFriendBot author threatened with lawsuit,"[40] author Brian McWilliams wrote that on December 14, 2005, Anthony Lineberry had been sent a cease-and-desist letter by Myspace. At that point, there had been 270 verified sales of the program, according to PayPal records. Lineberry was not interviewed for the article. Anthony had posted he would release the code as "opensource" (free) if sales slowed down, which could have been interpreted as a threat.[41]

The first comment on the article was from a competitor who claimed he had "shared ideas" with Anthony. An hour later, Anthony emerged from the shadows, claiming that his ideas were original, that an early version of his code had been distributed for free on his website, and that the competitor's only role was in having "suggested that [I] sell [MyFriendBot]."[42]

In a subsequent interview,[43] Lineberry decried the association of his name with spamming: "I don't really think of myself as a bad guy in the matter. People hear any association with spam, and bam, you are a bad guy." The association was clear to McWilliams, who wrote 2004's *Spam Kings*, the seminal book on internet spam.

Where spammers of the late '90s and early aughts were pushing penis enlargements, porn, and other bogus goods (according to McWilliams on the *Spam Kings* blog, which he stopped publishing in April 2006),[44] the new generation of growth hackers, pimps, and whores adapted and evolved their tactics to infiltrate and exploit social networks. Because *spamming* on a social network usually involves growing one's network and taking actions that are *licit*, software-augmented disruptive behavior on social media has in a way become a self-propagating Samy Worm.

When an emo kid with low self-esteem and low friend count saw a whore train, he wanted to become a rider. When a lonely Instagram user sees a peer gaining followers at a rapid pace, she rushes to pay for any short-cut, irrespective of the consequences. While not exactly self-propagating, the demand for social metrics is such that any exploit or shortcut spreads rapidly, just like the original whore trains, adder services, and Samy's devious worm.

Brian McWilliam's book influenced whether I thought this topic was worth writing about two decades later. On his blog, he recognized that Anthony's software and legal troubles marked a changing of the guard from old (email spam) to new (social media automation). I am indebted to his work and his decision to dedicate a few hundred words to how computer geeks were burdening Myspace users. His journalism helped solidify a shift in defining what so-called villains were doing on the internet.

There is no doubt that Anthony Lineberry is on the Mount Rushmore of Myspace Pimps.

As for the scene kids, their virtual existence was fleeting, but their impact was unmistakable. Where early detractors criticized befriending "people they didn't know," by 2009 there was no question that friend count, comment count, and picture comment count underscored the authenticity of everyone on Myspace, and especially within the emo subculture. Into the 2010s, what was once a dig at people who spent too much time online became mainstream social proof: having large numbers of followers one *didn't know* validated one's influence.

Early social network growth methods were honed by teenagers who wore tight pants including one who wrote, "I like to skateboard too."[45] Early social network success was grasped by computer nerds who were seeking acceptance. Their motivation was belonging, self-validation, vanity. Fringe kids who saw no issue with calling themselves whores or forcing others to call them "my hero" became vigilantes who monopolized and metricized *friendship* while abusing the tenets of what it meant to be social.

By 2009, migrating to Facebook meant starting from scratch. It also meant whitewashing those crazy display names, leaving behind customizable profiles with music players, and disincentivizing social climbing—requesting users one didn't know was actively discouraged. However, it wouldn't be long before the masses found a new social network where they could chase that old thrill. Only, that next time, they would be the ones being pimped.

4

ALGORITHMS AND TRUTH

Twenty years ago, if you googled "When will I die?" you were directed to DeathClock.com.[1] At my cousin's house in 2004, we gathered around her desktop to enter our birthdates and other basic information and click "Check Your Death Clock" to find out how much time we had left. Satisfied with our fates, we entered our parents' information. Upon learning that one of her parents was, according to DeathClock.com, already dead, my cousin's friend panicked and called her family to ask if everything was okay. Thus was the quirkiness of seeking answers on the early internet.

Today, the relic of The Death Clock, which has added smoking status and BMI inputs, still operates. Hundreds of sites now feature algorithms that use a birthdate to predict mortality, horoscopes, and dates of conception, such as the site I launched in 2014 called, WhenDidMyParents-Bang.com.

The original Death Clock now ranks fiftieth in search results for death-related queries. Does that mean that it's the fiftieth-best predictor? Search algorithms always provide an answer even if it isn't objective. I spend a lot of time thinking about how algorithms augment what is seen, credible, and true. This is an essay about the ethics of algorithms, particularly information retrieval algorithms.

And before I continue—an "algorithm"[2] is a set of instructions. It can be a bit of a dirty word; it can be anthropomorphized: "I hate that *the algorithm* knows me so well." Although some algorithms are indeed dastardly, an algorithm can be designed using plain English, and non-technical, comprehensible explanations of important algorithms are possible.

Newspapers

Twentieth-century journalists are inextricable from national identity and popular culture in the United States. Journalists earn their audiences' trust and abide by principles of independence, accuracy, and ethics when assessing newsworthiness.

Algorithmic "news" feeds co-opt the innate trust Americans have in reporters while shunning such principles.

Print news organizations gained the public's trust with consistent, unbiased, and timely fact reporting. Only the editorials, which expressed opinions, may have aligned with certain belief systems more than others. Some bias was welcomed, especially when counterbalanced with dissenting viewpoints.

Newspaper editors may endorse political candidates or assign more resources and prominent page space to investigations of one issue compared to the crosstown rival. Readers accept this. By and large, any news organization that gained pre-internet prominence kept its audience happy by reporting the news without unreasonable bias. Too much bias harmed the public's perception of the overall accuracy of the information presented. Too negative of a perception of what the paper contains meant nobody bought the newspaper.

When consumers purchased physical newspapers, they endorsed the accuracy and conformity of the contents, even if they didn't agree with every editorial. They bought newspapers because of their baseline of reputable reporting. Facts were facts; opinions or special interests didn't corrupt facts. Small cities tend to have one newspaper. That one newspaper is implicitly trusted to report facts without much oversight. The only governance is an organization's insiders, public outcry, fringe fact-checkers, the odd whistleblower, or a ragtag journalism award committee. There is no expectation that readers will independently investigate facts, verify information, or corroborate stories by consulting primary sources.

Ironically, the foundation built by twentieth-century journalists ushered in the belief that information on the internet does not need to be questioned, challenged, or verified. Awareness of the gullibility of viewers also led to a noticeable drop in the quality of nationally syndicated news, especially cable news, in the late 2000s. In the 2010s, unsophisticated users flooded the internet, primarily newly retired Baby Boomers who grew up admiring newscasters.[3]

In contrast to younger, savvier users raised with the internet, older generations became known for sharing absurd news articles on Facebook. "Clickbait" websites churned out a bastardized brand of journalism that falsified facts and failed to cite sources. Facebook wasn't fact-checking or assigning a "trust score" to shared articles. Folks saw social media previews of news articles as fungible; there appeared to be no real difference between a *New York Times* article and a *New York Post* article. The most naive users applied their trust in print newspapers to *whatever* they found in the digital realm. Trust and naivety were abused.

Online Newspapers

Web "browsing" is essentially seeking information—answers. People navigate the internet because they're looking for something.

When I was just a naive nine-year-old when I saw the date I would perish on The Death Clock, maybe. Maybe I trusted the website because I grew up in a world where well-organized information was given credence but also because in the 1990s and early 2000s, it took time, effort, and a measure of professionalism to distribute or broadcast *anything*.

Maybe I trusted the internet because I hadn't had much experience being lied to.

In retrospect, the layouts of websites in the participative web era resembled newspapers—not newspapers of today but newspapers printed over one hundred years ago. Popular themes for website builders, like Word-Press, use newspaper-inspired mock headlines and reference journalism in their theme and font package names.[4]

Technology enables more efficient navigation than physical media. Hyperlinks are superior to "read more on page B4" captions. Still, similar principles, styling, and layouts are used: fonts, images, captions, spacing, margins, alignment, and headline design.

Does the presentation and layout of information impact the trustworthiness or credibility of a print newspaper? Might these same factors impact how people consume information online?

Journalists abide by standards and ethics, and I'd like to think they possess moral compasses. What about the *journal* itself? What impacts the efficacy of the medium, facts, and editorial content? It's easy to find resources on fairness in reporting. There's little addressing how to present material to a reader or how poor presentation can affect a reader's perception of an article or entire organization.

If a newspaper's editors don't want to run a story, they probably won't. It's difficult to compel a news organization to investigate a topic or publish a story (I've tried). Even if public opinion demands it, nothing will be done until that public *votes* by not buying newspapers or formally protesting. The dwindling number of newspapers in America must cater to a middle ground to stay afloat. Vanishing financial support means not every story gets the coverage it deserves. It also means less accountability.

Assuming a story *is* run, a publisher can do an awful lot to alter how the story is consumed or the perception of facts. *Readers can be manipulated without changing the story's contents.* It starts with the front page. The headlines in the largest print and most visible locations are the most important. Consider a vintage newspaper announcing the end of WWII. The headline is in a gigantic font, and the story is the primary feature on the front page. *The Charlotte Observer*'s "PEACE! IT'S OVER"[5] was one of many such marquee headlines across American media on August 15, 1945.

Nobody will contest the top billing of a WWII surrender announcement. Yet, newspapers are free to rank stories however they want, and they don't explain their rationale. Imagine how ridiculous it would be if that headline ran beneath an announcement of a new Ford dealership opening in Charlotte on August 16, 1945.

Every small-town newspaper has underreported a story or brushed one under the rug from either sneaky compliance or intentional but plausible errors.

When I was sixteen, two of my buddies unexpectedly beat a DI-bound runner from our rival high school in the mile in a dual meet. The hometown sportswriter wrote that the stud was nursing an ankle injury and excluded the race results from the published scoring table.

A conflict of interest could be hidden through redirection: when one passage instructs "Read more on page B4!" B4 could add another redirect, "Read more on page C2!" That would certainly decrease the number of readers who eyed the whole story, just like website visitors gradually bounce rather than continue to click links. Exposing this strategy could harm the newspaper's credibility, but the newspaper could defend itself: "We ran the story, and the facts were reported accurately." Those who oversee information retrieval algorithms wield such plausible deniability. Journalism *is* information retrieval.

If a newspaper publishes award-winning stories, strictly adheres to standards, and has the community's trust, there are still factors outside of the reporting itself that affect the perceived credibility of a story and a news outlet. I've curated a list from my ponderings on formatting, layout, designs, and adjacent widgets that affect my perception of news articles and *information*.

1. **Prioritization of content.** As in the WWII example, content should be displayed in order of importance. Not doing so suggests a conflict of interest or incompetence.
2. **Organization of content**. Content must be organized and consistent with a theme. If a website dedicated to car collecting hosts articles about shoes, that hurts its credibility.
3. **Authorship**. Information is more credible if the author is credible. Print publications will list authors' names, but space is limited, so it's rare to see full author bios. Online, it's important that an author's identity can be cross-referenced.
4. **Intrusiveness of ads**. Advertising is accepted as a necessary evil. In print, ads can take up prime space, which means stories get squeezed into a side column or bumped to the next page. On the internet, ads can invade the screen and spoil the reading experience. More ads, and more intrusive ads, mean less credibility. Disruptive ads that are difficult to close are unethical.
5. **Advertisement content**. The content of ads on a website bears on the website's trustworthiness. Ads for products that seem predatory or use grotesque or sexualized branding to generate clicks suggest an owner is willing to degrade the viewing experience to generate more money. By contrast,

hosting ads for local businesses may boost credibility (though, ironically, creating a potential conflict of interest).

6. **Disclaimers and conflicts of interest.** Publishers must be forthcoming about conflicts of interest and potential revenue generation. They must identify advertising partners and clarify relationships between those in the newsroom and those featured in stories.

7. **Photographs and other media**. An abundance of photos suggests a lack of substance. Reliance on stock photos reveals a lack of resources (no staff photographer).

8. **Navigation**. Sections should be consistent and navigation dependable. Content should be located in traditional spaces.

9. **Calls to action.** Persuasive writing is okay! Frequent reminders to buy, click, or take action unrelated to the underlying content detract from the user experience.

Worse UX (user experience[6]) means the information is less credible. This is not always conscious deception. It could be due to incompetence or desperation. It's difficult to find convincing counterexamples if a town only has one newspaper and one "source of truth" for each newsworthy story.

How does one know when a newspaper is growing desperate? Consider *The Scranton Times-Tribune*, my hometown's only newspaper. Because the publisher catered to an aging demographic, it never had a first-class web product. Around 2022, the mobile reading experience had become so chaotic and ad-ridden that it impacted how I perceived the underlying news. I started to suspect that the newspaper was pursuing questionable methods of generating revenue while ruining the mobile reading experience. I believe the newspaper compromised the credibility it had been building since the mid-1800s. Consider how the experience recounted below tracks along with the points listed above.

Reading an article on *The Scranton Times-Tribune*'s mobile site in 2022

I click on an article on the full-screen web browser on my phone. It loads slowly. The header and navbar take up one-eighth of the page. The portion of the screen below that consists of two low-quality banner ads for local businesses. They're not offensive, but they take up a lot of space. Sometimes only one of the ads displays and the other fails to render. The bottom tenth of the view has a sticky ad that stays in place as I scroll. Right now, it's for an Amazon Fresh product. As I nimbly tap its tiny "x" button, a different layered ad is revealed in the same spot (actually, it was already there, a few pixels peeking out behind the overlaid Amazon Fresh ad). In the time it's taken me to write this, it has flipped between a Tylenol lawsuit announcement, a women's health lawsuit announcement with a medical image of genitalia, and an advertisement for women's shoes making a silver bullet marketing claim.

After four long sentences of article content, I'm presented with a generic real estate ad that takes up half the window. And then there's a break with links to trending stories. After one more sentence, there's an advertisement picturing mayonnaise jars with the copy, "US Companies Owned By China."

The article concludes after another two hundred words or so. At the conclusion, there's an ad for a local credit union, then a trending articles carousel with pictures, then an ad for a nationally syndicated sports story that takes up a fourth of the viewing window. Then there is white space, then another ad that takes up a third of the screen for a local chiropractor. Below that is the author's contact information and the comments section with one comment. Below the comments section is a gigantic advertisement for Amazon products, then two "active conversations" directing a visitor to other articles with more comments. Then there is a large gray box that has failed to render. Next, a social link ribbon, tags, and the author's full name and picture. I continue to see ads that take up a third of the screen (arranged in what's called a "chumbox"[7]): an ADHD lawsuit, a women's health lawsuit suggesting I may be entitled to $170,000, and an ad for walking sandals. Next follows a box with a small "sponsored" tag, but the content hasn't been rendered. Then there is an ad for a "Camp Lejuene victims" lawsuit, then one for Angelina Jolie...

Having crawled into the deep recesses of the page, the site forcibly reloads. Now the trio of ads in the sticky footer are back. Below the Angelina Jolie ad is another ad with a young woman with a nose ring holding up a bottle of apple cider vinegar with the tagline "Leave ED in the Past if you are a senior man." Then an ad for blood pressure monitors. Then an ad for trucking accident attorneys. Then a repeat of the ad for the local credit union. Finally, links to the day's obituaries and a sign-up CTA for obituary notifications. Then a large section with the links to the top ten articles of the day. Then a doctor's ad. Then a section supporting the annual Mother's Day edition. Then a "quiz" on local history purportedly hosted by the newspaper (though, prominently, "powered by Insticator"). Then a colorful animated ad for a game featuring animals. Then a cavernous space with a small ad for something called "average Joe." Then a reader poll. Then a repeat of the mayo ad. Then a "Special Sections" carousel that rotates through different parts of the paper. Then an ad for a local Ford dealership. Then a local dentist. Then a link to the annual reader's choice awards. Finally, the footer.

It's hard to believe that I paid to access this hellish site. *The Scranton Times-Tribune* had an ads-to-story content split of roughly eighty to twenty percent. The ads were intrusive. The ad content was inappropriate. The site loaded slowly and was buggy. The facts were buried under an inexcusably awful user experience.

The website was worse than the prototypical scam sites of the aughts. If a new visitor was dropped onto an article and had to evaluate whether the site was "a scam," the conclusion would not be kind. Poor UX and design can harm the trustworthiness and credibility of information displayed on the internet, even when the underlying content is well-written and ethically sourced.

In August 2023, *The Scranton Times-Tribune* was sold to Alden Global Capital.[8]

Algorithms: Web Directories, Search Engines, and News Feeds

Websites resemble newspapers. It's important that information—truth—be displayed cleanly and concisely. Newspaper editors figured out how to do that ages ago. The effort of launching and maintaining a newspaper gives a degree of credence to any operation. Likewise, *websites* are afforded baseline trust, especially when branded as news hubs.

Newspapers can be corrupt. They can bend the truth. They can harbor biases. On the internet, the search for truth often leads to the highest-ranking *persuasive writing* with profound biases, which is probably optimized for search engine position. Shadowy webmasters, anonymous software engineers, and black box algorithms are responsible for new-age control systems that influence how information is sought and consumed.

Web Directories

News organizations' reputations suffer if they prioritize inappropriate stories on the front page. On the early internet, before search engines, there were *web directory* sites. These sites organized links to other sites—not dissimilar to the front page of a newspaper crossed with the Yellow Pages. The owners of directory sites had the privilege of choosing which links to display and how to order them.

Text-based directory sites loaded quickly, an important consideration in the dial-up era. Directories, sometimes featuring search engine widgets, persisted even after search engines became commonplace. They were colloquially known as *homepages* and as they tacked on more features, web *portals*.[9]

Directory site owners were the oligarchs of the early internet. In 1996, rather than googling "best sports website," a user would type out the URL of a directory (portal) site and use that to facilitate a search. Yahoo provided a ranked list of websites in the sports domain.

On November 28, 1996, Yahoo.com's sports directory[10] looked like this:

The page loaded fast, but its design and information display were primitive. Descending in alphabetical order in a single column looks downright ridiculous. Surely "Boomerang" is not more important than "Boxing" or "Football." Clicking on "Boomerang" revealed an adorable collection of early websites for throwsticks: BoomPlans, Full Circles, United States Boomerang Association, FAQ - alt.boomerang, Index - Boomerang World, Usenet - alt.boomerang.[11]

This all seems honest and credible. Yahoo indexed thousands of websites and dedicated space to even the most niche sports. Yahoo's "algorithms" for hand-selecting content seemed to work well, though it must have taken crazy amounts of human time to locate, evaluate, and organize everything. Oligarchs? Evil algorithms? Hardly.

In the late 1990s, Yahoo pulled off a caper that guaranteed long-term relevance. Through their directory portal site, the company acquired detailed knowledge of visitor search patterns and browsing behaviors. Users would visit for a short time, find what they were looking for, and leave by clicking links. What if Yahoo could convince bouncy users to stay?

Between August 5, 1997,[12] and October 8, 1997,[13] the link in the header titled "Scoreboard," was placed at the top and renamed to "Yahoo! Sports" which pointed to sports.yahoo.com. The last snapshot of the sports index occurred on June 30, 1998.[14] Soon after, *Yahoo shed its links*. Yahoo's rich directory of links to external sports websites was replaced by *Yahoo! Sports*. What better way to capitalize on all the sports-related web traffic?

Yahoo! Sports is still a juggernaut. It consists of score reporting, original sports journalism, fantasy leagues, and discussion boards. Yahoo had no duty to continue linking to thousands of competing sites. Yahoo built a sports portal in an attempt to retain all the traffic it had been redirecting (and followed a similar act for finance, news, and other domains). I wonder how much traffic the United States Boomerang Association lost after it was removed from Yahoo's index and teenagers stopped clicking it out of curiosity.

These days, when encountering a top ten list on the internet, there is usually a loquacious explanation for each pick and plenty of affiliate links to ensure the curator receives kickback money regardless of what is clicked. Twenty, and, yes, even *thirty*, years ago, the lists were sterile and updated infrequently with usually no transparency of the curator or curation. Yet, they were taken seriously. They were trusted.

Webmasters wielded power—*the power to define what was number one,* what was "the best." The potential for corruption was immense. Traffic has always been valuable, and corruptible web directory site owners surely accepted payments for superior rankings. These days, readers chastise journalists. They're quick to lob insults at local newscasters for their perceived biases, mistakes, and ethical failings. I wonder if those same critics, whether in 2004 or 2024, would be savvy enough to identify a top-ten list filled with link placements that contain undisclosed conflicts of interest.

Nineties kids will remember FunnyJunk.com, an early internet humor content aggregator that peaked in 2005. The site hosted tons of user-submitted content, and it is memorable for its left sidebar with ranked *Top Flash Videos.* The legendary video there was *End of Ze World,* a video parodying thermonuclear war, which, confusingly, was simultaneously ranked second, fourth, and fifth in October 2006. I hate to admit it, but as a twelve-year-old, FunnyJunk's top ten list *defined* what was funny.

SublimeDirectory.com was a pornographic web directory. It prominently featured lists of links to external adult websites. Yet it perhaps *defined* what was sexy. Years before YouTube launched, the site began hosting non-explicit videos: "You film a 2 minute or less clip of something funny, stupid, sexy or classic and send it in to us...if we like it we'll put it up and send you *up to* 1000 bucks." In February 2004, the site uploaded a video that would change the internet forever: the first Kimbo Slice street fight.[15]

The contributor who sent the video was named "Icey." That was "Icey" Mike Imber, an early employee of the adult content production company, Reality Kings.[16] Documentaries have covered the relationship between Mike and the late Kevin Ferguson, known as Kimbo Slice. The relationship between Sublime Directory and Reality Kings is more important. Sublime Directory referred traffic to the Reality Kings network of sites, at one time listing Mike's employer as *number one* (ahead of "EXGF Revenge" and "MILF Hunter").

Maybe Mike saw the opportunity to make *up to* one thousand dollars by sending the street fight videos to the directory that happened to be promoting his porn site(s). Fair play. Maybe the requirement of the "mention" of Sublime Directory is why all Kimbo's old fight videos have that obnoxious watermark. I figured that some aspect of the site had to fit with my theory of corruption on web directories. I reached out to Mike.

He didn't respond. I wondered if there was any way to contact the directory's long-retired webmaster and ask. I saw that in 2005 Sublime Directory[17] featured this call to action: "Submit a Site - If you're a webmaster and want to submit a link hop on in here."

It was *different* from the "Email Us" link to the "webmaster@" address. The "Submit a Site" CTA linked to tgpsitecentral.com. That site offered a paid submission system for owners of adult content sites to be listed on Sublime Directory **for $4.95 per month**:[18]

> The progression to forming partnerships and alliances is a natural one in the business world and the online adult business is no different. What we would like to do is form a partnership with every one of you and create a symbiotic relationship between us. In return for linking to your site and sending you thousands of hits we are requiring a link from one of our programs at the top of the gallery submitted.
>
> ...
>
> In the end webmasters that want to form a partnership with us will always be listed and make some very good money from all the free traffic. We have already been doing this on a personal basis with several webmasters and it has been working out very well for both parties...

This confirmed my hypothesis that there were backroom deals between directory site owners and listees. If the top ranking was impenetrable without payment, then listees were getting, well, shafted. It turned out that perhaps no site was being linked without paying. Visitors expecting an unbiased ranking system were being manipulated too. Directory sites dictated the top genre sites even if visitors disagreed. Yahoo realized this and created Yahoo Sports! The owners of Sublime Directory had so many conflicts of interest that they had to create an external site and subscription gateway to manage them. There was no transparency.

Search Engines

Managers of directory sites painstakingly identified content and arranged it by hand. These human-executed algorithms were limited and severely biased. Search engines solved the directory sites' inherent problems by indexing every site and programmatically estimating their importance and relevance with an algorithm. So much about information retrieval on the internet relates to *relative importance*, and that's what Sergey Brin and Larry Page encoded in their PageRank algorithm.

In the mid-1990s, Yahoo had curated links to thousands of sports sites. Today, searching Google for "sports" returns *ten billion* pages. Just as physical copies of the Yellow Pages become unwieldy in supercities, directory sites could not scale on the participative web. They arguably morphed into portal sites and then social bookmarking sites, like Digg, before reaching their final form on reddit. Search engines and sites increasingly using software to aggregate content led to their extinction.

Search engines may be the ultimate reflection of credence in things perceived as difficult to build. They are respected, and their results are rarely questioned because it's mind-boggling to think they could be wrong. I built my first mobile game in 2013 and one of my first websites in 2014. I've never built a search engine.

PageRank

There are a few search engine ranking algorithms out there. Google's Page-Rank is the most well-known. To avoid plagiarizing the PageRank wikipedia article,[19] which is fascinating, I'll advise that readers parse it and assess how much they understand before continuing.

There are three ideas related to PageRank that underpin Google Search:[20]

1. Weights representing authority are assigned recursively to interlinked web pages;
2. An army of automated web crawlers scours the internet, following all links and updating a massive index of all structured HTML pages and their written content; and
3. A system parses search queries that humans enter and serves search results based on keywords and website PageRank

Some sites are manually pegged as "authority" sites. Wikipedia lists CNN.com and mayoclinic.org as examples.[21] Google's crawlers use an algorithm that follows the links between pages to build out a holistic authority score. "A hyperlink to a page counts as a vote of support."[22] This is similar to establishing (or embellishing) authority over other mediums. Buying a newspaper or flipping to a TV station is an indirect vote of support for those organizations. Linking to another website indicates *support* for the site being linked. The recommended method of separating oneself from digital impersonators is to *link to one profile from another profile one controls*.

I'm Feeling Lucky

Most people can't remember the last time they checked the second page of search results. Most people have never compared Google search results to those of other search engines, such as Bing. "Sophisticated" information retrieval might mean appending "reddit" to a query to target *discussions* or using search engines like DuckDuckGo or Brave Search to be more mindful of privacy. Forget checking page two or using filters.

One of Google's prominent early features was the "I'm Feeling Lucky" button, a sophisticated alternative to the search button leading to the traditional results page. The "I'm Feeling Lucky" button automatically brings a web surfer to the page that would have been displayed *first* in search results given a query string. On desktop browsers, the button still occupies prime real estate on the Google homepage next to the "Google Search" button. Although I consider it a relic of the early internet in the same category as The Death Clock, "I'm Feeling Lucky" helped Google build user confidence in its search algorithms while helping those on dial-up connections skip a hop between inquiry and destination.

People trust Google; Google is an information retrieval oracle. Searches eviscerated web directories to the extent that they aren't even well remembered. Around ninety percent of searchers click the first or second link in search results. It's why a niche business ranked second instead of twelfth might sell two orders of magnitude more products. It's why fierce battles are waged by those seeking higher *page rank*, a search engine's affirmation that a website is more authoritative than those beneath it.

Novelty or not, the tendency of users—including those who are on mobile and don't see the "I'm Feeling Lucky" button—to click the first listed link creates a stranglehold like an oligarchy or fiefdom. Everybody clicks the first Google Search result. Assuming the site holds onto visitors relatively well, thus reinforcing its rank, not only might it feel impossible for keyword competitors to break through but competitors might feel their only option is to purchase ads or take shortcuts to juice visitor metrics.

Directory sites demanded time-consuming human skimming and site browsing to be indexed. Though exhausting, navigating these webs of links encouraged organic exploration that is now extinct. The changes wrought by search engines don't have me feeling very lucky at all.

Subjectivity in Truth

Writing computer code to match search queries to objective truth is difficult enough. When the answer is subjective, things become complicated, especially when humans typing search queries see search engine algorithms as omniscient.

When will I die?

Sure, there are actuarial life tables that can be consulted, but the answer, like from The Death Clock, is an educated guess. By now Google has likely separated algorithms for fact-finding and whimsical searching, but it's plausible that mortality predictor websites were once ranked by the same algorithms ranking websites that answered the question, "Is an apple a fruit?" Visitor engagement is used as a proxy not for *correctness* but for *visitor satisfaction with a result*.

If a high-authority website started proclaiming apples to be vegetables, visitors would quickly navigate elsewhere, and the site would eventually fall in rank. If The Death Clock told people they were already dead, it wouldn't lose search rank unless the result bothered them enough to close the tab. When my cousin's friend received the result that one of her parents was already dead, she became hysterical and phoned home while *still lingering on the website*. Sites with controversial information that keep visitors engaged tend to have higher domain authority than sites listing similar keywords that may be more credible.[23]

Immense trust is placed in search engines. Their implementations are *black box*[24] algorithms, meaning their inner workings aren't known. Imagine Google provided a step-by-step algorithm walkthrough justifying the rank of every site. Not only might the English language explanation span hundreds of pages but perceived slights, biases, and coincidental correlations would draw criticism much like criticisms heaped onto journalists these days.

Journalists don't have to operate in the realm of subjectivity and opinion, but search engines do—billions of times per day. The need to serve queries like, "Who is the smartest?" and "Who is the prettiest?" has led to vectors of manipulation.

External Manipulation: SEO

The curator reserved the final judgment of hand-curated web directories. If the curator made a mistake, had a vendetta, or just went on an extended vacation, too bad. The result would have been a bottleneck of static results especially in niches where few index sites operated. The main option would have been emailing a webmaster to ask a site to be considered for indexing or indexed differently.

Nobody at Google visits each ranked site or reads mail from people who believe their favorites should be displayed differently. When it comes to search engines using complicated algorithms to priority rank, there is not only external finagling but also gaming. Readers may have heard of SEO (search engine optimization). It's a behemoth industry that seeks to understand search engines to create and apply principles to improve rank for given keywords. In a way, SEO reverse engineers Google's algorithms and tries to better satisfy those conditions, even while decreasing a website's quality.[25]

Recipe websites are meme-worthy examples of SEO harming site quality. They tend to begin with authors' life stories while cramming in barely relevant but keyword-laden content.

Conditions for higher ranking should also result in the best possible user experience. This is Google's preference. SEO shouldn't need to be an *industry*. High-quality websites should rank highly organically. Creators shouldn't have to learn anything about search engines.

Unfortunately, in a world where superior knowledge of SEO trumps superior content, search rank might be inaccurate. It's no coincidence that top sites with all their newfangled metadata and embedded reviews tend to be prominent. Their web developers (or SEO consultants) figured things out. It's why The Death Clock, which I consider the original website to find out when you die, is ranked so low that it might as well be six feet underground. It scores poorly on general search engine ranking criteria, and its status as an early internet originator counts for nothing.

Dishonest folks can use so-called "black hat" SEO methods to unfairly climb the ranks, possibly employing spammy backlink tactics or harming competitors' ranks using rank calculation glitches.

The result is an environment in which truth, even objective truth, is manipulated or obfuscated to fit the goals of a site owner who has abused Google's ranking algorithm while calling it "SEO." This is not to suggest that web search companies are complicit or that all SEO is villainous. One consequence however is that an SEO arms race has led to old-school websites being buried deep beneath hundreds of nimble copycats.

Internal and External Manipulation: Ads

The lion's share of Google's annual profit, over two hundred fifty billion dollars, comes from ads.[26] Search queries are deconstructed into keywords. Advertisers bid in real time on the placement of links related to those keywords. Unlike the crude ads I found on *The Scranton Times-Tribune*, Google's keyword-specific search ads are formatted and presented like relevant search results. Google has integrated ads with its content stream and presented the advertisements as roughly equivalent to or as trustworthy as sites ranking organically.

Ads are usually the very first results. The number of displayed ads depends on the keywords. Google's ads are subtly marked as "Sponsored" results. Below is an ad displayed when I searched for "pool" during a hot summer day.

Internet veterans have developed a sixth sense for detecting and skipping inorganic content. I instinctively scroll past sponsored ads, even well-integrated ones. There are two ethical dilemmas here. First, naive users ignore the "this is an ad" disclaimers with alarming frequency and click on sponsored content at the top of search results as if it is supremely authoritative. It isn't.

Second, Google's insane share of worldwide search traffic rides on the back of an excellent product. However, the continuation of the business depends on ad spend. There is an ethical conflict when Google makes design choices to manipulate webmasters to pay for ads rather than organically gain traffic. Google may have a vested interest in the oligarchical, self-fulfilling nature of top organic search engine rankings. If the algorithm makes it hopeless for a new entrant to ascend the ranks, there's a chance they'll buy premium space for guaranteed, temporary reach.

Google may also have a vested interest in further dissolving the barrier between organic results and paid link placement. For example, would decreasing the font size of "Sponsored" lead to more ad clicks? Probably! Past a threshold, though, such things are considered UX trickery, *dark patterns*, and decisions that undermine integrity.

Another angle is the Wikimedia Foundation's appeal: "Wikipedia is different. No advertising, no subscription fees, no paywalls. Those don't belong here. Wikipedia is a place to learn, free from bias or agenda."[27]

The Wikimedia Foundation equates advertising dollars with "bias" and "agenda."[28] Surely, some public figures would donate to Wikipedia if it meant that inconvenient truths on their biographical or company pages would be removed from the internet's central reference. There are agencies that slyly build up or whitewash Wikipedia pages for the right price.

Too many visitors ignore the foundation's pleas and the larger implications. When a platform accepts money to display digital ads—depends on advertisers—deep-pocketed advertisers can bias a platform's decision-making. If that's true, information retrieval algorithms must encode special cases to appease external influences.

Might a religious organization only undertake an ad campaign with the assurance that a platform will aggressively cull heretical content? There are plenty of ways platforms spin bending to the demands of their advertisers, usually under the guise of upholding community "guidelines" or "principles." Whenever advertisers call the shots, the morphology of "truth" delivered by information retrieval algorithms becomes misshapen.

SafeSearch

Consider the adage that "sex sells." Sexual content attracts clicks. Dotcom-era startups weren't masquerading as Sublime Directory, but most content-driven sites have been happy to feature strains of sexually gratifying content until pressured by investors or advertisers to moderate it.

Enforcement actions don't tend to be well-publicized. A mid-2024 trend called "transparent try-ons" that emerged on YouTube is one example of incremental enforcement. Women would model ("try on") transparent clothing; the clothing made them appear nude. While YouTube quickly affixed "18+" content warnings to the videos while demonetizing them, the videos did not violate any nudity policy. A few videos quickly accumulated hundreds of thousands of views thanks to YouTube's algorithms, and content creators accomplished their goal of converting viewers into paid subscribers on adult-oriented platforms like OnlyFans. I became aware of this because a woman I knew (actually, she had purchased my Instagram growth service years earlier) sent me her YouTube videos, incredulous that they were permitted. It all lasted fewer than two months before the platform revised its guidelines and shut down all the creators.

As moneymen descended on sites like reddit, they dashed toward "advertiser friendliness," eliminating porn, and aggressively moderating sexually gratifying or "offensive" content. Steve Huffman, the lesser-known co-founder of reddit (who later returned as CEO after having exited for a paltry sum in 2006), infamously tried to backtrack on reddit's original claims of being a bastion of free speech in a 2015 AMA while defending overlord-pressured content policies.[29]

Huffman was found to have edited users' comments on a subreddit related to Donald Trump.[30] It's easy to claim that platform moderation is censorship, but unchecked it can also be outright propaganda.

The "Censorship by Google" Wikipedia page is massive.[31] It would take more than a week to read the referenced source material and court proceedings. Do I allege that there is a rogue employee inside Google mangling search results? No. Google is forced into a game of tug-of-war with countries (and deep-pocketed advertisers) with competing ideas of what's appropriate and what's not—or what's *true* and what isn't.

Search engines are inundated with requests to scrub objectionable content. This can include filtering explicit content, like porn, and digital annoyances, like copyright infringement. To handle the former group in 2000, Google introduced SafeSearch to filter it.[32] Alerting users when content is censored, filtered, or excluded is benevolent, but black box information retrieval algorithms like search engines can abuse this blind trust to augment what is true and what is preeminently ranked.

Anticompetitive Behavior

Shortly before 1999, Yahoo! Sports launched and inflected traffic previously sent to hobbyist sports pages indexed on Yahoo's main page. Today, if Google tried to capitalize on a trend emerging from its search product and then sneakily altered search results to boost its own side project, that would be considered "anticompetitive behavior." There are of course allegations that Google abused its monopoly on search, including an intriguing case involving rap lyrics that I include later in "Punishing Crime." When considering threats to "truth," one could understandably suspect Google of modifying its algorithms to augment queries related to business competitors or adversaries.

News Feeds

My grandparents used to spend their mornings reading *The Scranton Times-Tribune* cover to cover. Grandchildren spend their entire days consuming "news feeds" with no stop condition—no "that's all, tune in tomorrow."

With feeds curated by algorithms, information retrieval is now primarily a form of entertainment. Facebook took a shot at creating a homepage feed in 2006 called the "News Feed."[33] In my view, it meant "news from your social network" and came to include actual news articles your boomer cousin shares. It eventually just became the "Feed."

Any dynamic, asynchronously updated content stream is affixed with the label "feed" and borrows concepts and style cues from Facebook. Users reflexively flick to see more even when there's no scrollbar. Web directories and portal sites have become deprecated.

Surfing the internet—seeking information—used to be a pastime. That journey has been undermined. Navigating a directory site is unthinkable. Using search engines is falling out of favor. Integrated feeds eliminated the last key blocker: the redirect, the "read more on B4." The feeds are to the internet what the 24/7 news cycle was to cable news: a never-ending stream of entertainment, most of lower quality than what originally enticed the user to tune in.

Facebook has become the newspaper of record.

Users spend more time engaged with feeds than any preceding content delivery method.[34] Implicit and explicit preference signals mean the content becomes personalized for *each user*. Increased personalization leads to longer usage durations. That time is stolen from other websites, including actual "news" sites and quirky content sites of the aughts.[35] This is similar to how Yahoo Sports "stole" traffic from hobbyist sports sites. The sites dependent on referred traffic aren't nearly as entertaining. Even those that rank highly in a search could only dream of having the same engagement rates.

This essay has covered newspapers (print and online), pure directory sites, portal sites, the social bookmarking site reddit, the search engine known as Google, and finally Facebook's Feed. All involve information retrieval and algorithms to accomplish this task. Over time, algorithms have become more powerful, harder to understand, and more difficult to regulate.

Interest in and funding for journalism has waned. Low-effort scrolling and streaming have proliferated. Complex algorithms have introduced new ways of consuming, issues, rules, and rulebreakers. Programmers awkwardly strafe from the expectation that information retrieval algorithms should retrieve truth.[36]

Someone needs to design an algorithm that can predict when all this will die.

5

HACKATHON HACKERS

PennApps was the first student-run hackathon in the United States.[1] Since 2009, this semiannual event hosted by the University of Pennsylvania has attracted—and minted—the country's top emerging tech talent. Although participants tend to write software well, hackathons are not competitive programming competitions. Impressions are not made by lines of code or the difficulty of solved problems. There is no measure of correctness.

A collegiate hackathon is a contest in which the challenge is to ideate, build, and present a minimum viable product in a single weekend. Although "-thon" is borrowed from the term, "mara*thon*," the events are seen as a respite from the stressors of undergraduate life.

Hackathon participants look forward to building apps that aren't graded, probably aren't commercially viable, and possibly downright frivolous. Before 2009, technologists were organizing so-called hackathons,[2] but I credit the founding group at PennApps with bringing hackathons into the mainstream. There is a widely held idea that student-run hackathons foster experimentation and creativity, which has spurred corporations to sponsor hackathons for their employees. Oh, what fun.

In either setting, there may be categorical winners, but nobody goes home a loser. In student-run hackathons, the socialization, free food, and privilege of detaching from schoolwork for a weekend are the main draws.

At majors, like PennApps, sponsors show up with truckloads of free stuff. Sponsors also send representatives to recruit talented undergraduates, especially non-traditional candidates. Prizes can be substantial. PennApps Fall 2022 offered twenty-six thousand dollars in prizes.[3] For the participant, the hackathon is totally free.

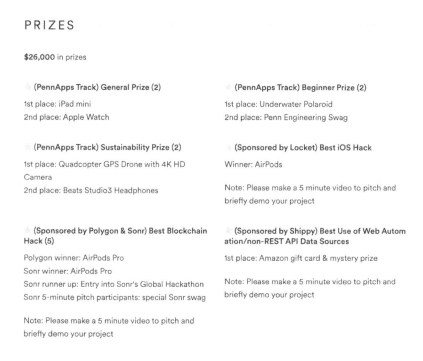

PRIZES

$26,000 in prizes

(PennApps Track) General Prize (2)

1st place: iPad mini
2nd place: Apple Watch

(PennApps Track) Sustainability Prize (2)

1st place: Quadcopter GPS Drone with 4K HD Camera
2nd place: Beats Studio3 Headphones

(Sponsored by Polygon & Sonr) Best Blockchain Hack (5)

Polygon winner: AirPods Pro
Sonr winner: AirPods Pro
Sonr runner up: Entry into Sonr's Global Hackathon
Sonr 5-minute pitch participants: special Sonr swag

Note: Please make a 5 minute video to pitch and briefly demo your project

(PennApps Track) Beginner Prize (2)

1st place: Underwater Polaroid
2nd place: Penn Engineering Swag

(Sponsored by Locket) Best iOS Hack

Winner: AirPods

Note: Please make a 5 minute video to pitch and briefly demo your project

(Sponsored by Shippy) Best Use of Web Automation/non-REST API Data Sources

1st place: Amazon gift card & mystery prize

Note: Please make a 5 minute video to pitch and briefly demo your project

A sampling of prizes from PennApps Fall 2022

How could someone dedicating a weekend to a marathon programming session with non-traditional, non-target candidates not be on a tech company's radar? The market for entry-level software developers is competitive, and the most desirable companies recruit heavily from the most prestigious schools. Most college programmers never get a chance to showcase their abilities to Google.

Recruiting is hard. Candidates slip through the cracks and fall under minimum GPA thresholds. Others make the dean's list or ace interviews but show up for their first internship unable to work with teams or hit deadlines. Hackathons provide a real-world simulation, placing recruiters and candidates on a playing field more practical than any pair programming interview.

When I was attending college in the 2010s, hackathons were the best venue in which students from non-target schools with mediocre GPAs could get interviews with Big Tech.[4] As more people realized this, those who couldn't gain admission started joking that the hackathons were becoming as selective as the prestigious schools that hosted them. Increasingly, something was *at stake*. Some participants cheated and developed substantial parts of their projects before hackathon start dates, trying to pass off massive code contributions as the product of one continuous coding frenzy.[5] I know this because I was one of those mediocre students looking for a path to employment, and I joined a Facebook group called, "Hackathon Hackers," back in 2014.

I attended PennApps Winter 2015. According to the page on Devpost ("the home for hackathons"), there were 602 participants and $46,060 in prizes.[6] I did not win a prize or receive a job offer; my team ran out of time and didn't submit a final project for judging. The environment was built for the tech-obsessed, and we enjoyed the experience. My buddy and I occupied a remote corner of a building on Penn's campus where company reps and friendly participants approached us.

We tried to build a web app that identified and charted correlations between stock prices and myriad data sources, but it wasn't linked to any prize category. If we attempted that same project today, we'd find that *every* data source or API we used in 2015 is now inaccessible to two friends spending a snowy weekend in Philadelphia.

Hackathon hackers of my era relied on third-party data sets and APIs. What made projects special, even newsworthy, was that they combined and crossed and *hacked together* well-known, data-rich APIs, often in ways unanticipated by API providers. Nobody is coding Google Maps from scratch. On Devpost today, over 7,500 submitted projects mention the Google Maps API.

The megahit game GeoGuessr, in which players are dropped onto a random Google Street View location, guess where in the world they landed, and earn points based on the proximity to the correct location, could be seen as a natural outgrowth of a hackathon project.

Hackathon hackers took aspects of the internet familiar to spectators and added fresh twists, gamification, functionality, and crossovers. The power of *open APIs* is that the potential use cases are inexhaustible.[7] When APIs weren't explicitly *open*, the most resourceful hackers "sniffed" private APIs, the internals powering apps not intended to be used by kids at a hackathon.

Throughout the 2010s, tech companies quietly closed off their APIs to avoid appearing commercialized while giving a middle finger to the hacker ethos. Some started charging for access. Acquisitions were rampant, and attitudes around openness flipped. Companies pursued legal action against third parties that had built businesses on top of their APIs.

At early hackathons, projects that hinged upon integrations with social media APIs were common. Today, aside from fringe Twitter and reddit projects, they are rare. No social networks now make available the APIs I remember from the 2010s.

As a reaction to Instagram announcing restrictions to its developer platform in November 2015,[8] Aaron Parecki posted a critique of the state of things: "Remember when everyone was building and promoting 'open' APIs? What happened to that?"[9] Parecki, now the director of Identity Standards at Okta, did not respond to my inquiries for this essay, but I credit him for blogging about it at a critical juncture.

APIs being closed has affected hackathons in two ways:

1. Hackathon sponsors wield significantly more power in guiding project formulation.
2. More hackathon participants realize that hacking private APIs might lead to greater rewards.

IBM might pay twenty-five thousand dollars for the privilege of sponsorship: "Hey, Watson is packed with useful features. Here's an unlimited-use API key that will work for the weekend. Here's a guide to get you started. Happy Hacking!"

Hackathon sponsors get valuable face time with prospective employees and receive critical feedback *on their technology products*. Sponsors' representatives, sometimes called Developer Evangelists, help bridge the technical expertise gap between traditional sales reps and the engineers who build products. Faced with an internet that is less free and encourages less experimentation than in days past, these evangelists help redirect unbridled enthusiasm.

Hackathon hackers are still free to build whatever they want—there's almost always a general prize category. A few will arrive at the hackathon knowing exactly what they will try to build. Regardless, it's likely that anyone sitting through the initial presentations, during which attendance is mandatory, and prize categories are formalized, will be influenced by sponsors' technologies or unique challenges. Participants produce more predictable cookie-cutter projects because there are more sponsors promoting their technologies more aggressively but fewer accessible real-world APIs and data sets. In case number one, that is.

The closing of APIs has not necessarily *hurt* hackathons. However, these proving grounds for talent once served as caches of API access policy and developer interest trends over the past fifteen years. It's drastically different now from when this author was first learning how to program.

Hackathon participants' abilities have improved since I was an undergraduate. The curious reader could browse thousands of hackathons and their project galleries hosted on Devpost.com to see as much. The production value of these projects can be incredible. And who is to say that it's all elitist and corporatized? In one entry from PennApps 2021,[10] two women linked to a video titled, "Deez Nuts," and submitted the following product description:

Inspiration

deez nuts

What it does

deez nuts

How we built it

deez nuts

Challenges we ran into

deez nuts

Accomplishments that we're proud of

deez nuts

What we learned

deez nuts

What's next for deez nuts

deez nuts

Built With

deez   nuts

I don't think they won a prize, but their entry earned seven likes on Devpost, more than any of the sixty-plus submitted projects.

I reached out to people associated with the hackathon community: longtime organizers, professional partners, bloggers, and platform reps. Nobody wanted to discuss my thesis. The only response I got was from one guy who said that government API data had improved, which I agree with. Sadly, he didn't engage with my other questions.

As for those experts and veterans of the space, perhaps we should affix a different label to them: "hacks."

Hackathon Hackers and Private APIs

Although hackathons sound mischievous, the worst thing I've ever seen happen was a geeky fellow who tripped and fell on his face while running to a prime workspace on Penn's campus. This book is about the underbelly of internet technology. But, so far, this chapter hasn't discussed that theme because I haven't addressed the second consequence of API closure: "More hackathon participants realize that hacking private APIs might lead to greater rewards."

Public and private APIs are crucial to understanding one of the central conflicts on the internet. I've already used the term "API," like, twenty times because this is foundational knowledge that made Instagram automation the web's perhaps most notorious spam and that emboldens hackathon hackers to seek prizes beyond the prize pool, though with the risk of face-planting.

APIs and Web Services

API stands for *application programming interface*. These interfaces help computer programs communicate. A smart man once instructed me that an API is "an abstraction." The interface does *something* and allows systems to interact without exposing implementation details.

API-like abstraction is akin to a car's ignition. The driver of the car turns the key without wondering about anything "under the hood." Pressing "start" buttons on web pages similarly serve requests to APIs.

Social media wrongdoing involves APIs exposed as *web services*, meaning functionality accessed over a network. Browsing the internet, using social networks, and playing online games involve web services. Web services, written in myriad languages, don't require integrators to know anything about the programming language being used. Instead, functionality is expressed by an API using a common protocol, "HyperText Transfer Protocol" (HTTP), which facilitates data transfer on the web.

"User interfaces" (often known as "graphical user interfaces," or GUIs) facilitate human interaction with computers. Software and hardware systems use application programming interfaces to interact with one another. An app or website user only *sees* the user interface. Executed actions, taps, clicks, and keystrokes are processed and usually sent to an API.

There is a set of assumptions behind the actions we take on the internet and the results we expect when we take them. What if nothing happens when a button is clicked? Imagine no loading animation or any indication that the click did anything.

Dead clicks are deeply unsettling, not only for humans. I have heard mentions of studies in which chimpanzees have the same befuddled, disappointed reaction after pressing a button that appears to *do nothing*.

Humans and monkeys alike will press the button a few more times.

In this chapter, non-technical readers can learn how to investigate dead buttons using web browsers. Using methodologies generally known as *API hacking*, sophisticated outsiders can uncover and exploit the private APIs of popular apps, like Instagram.

Inside a Contrived Web Service API

What does a web service look like? Remember, a web service allows an API to be accessed over the internet. An API has structured endpoints that are logical, legible pieces of functionality. I'll show how APIs work and how engineers design them.

For example, doors can be opened, closed, locked, and unlocked. An opened door can't be opened again or locked. A closed door can't be closed again. A locked door can't be locked again or opened. An unlocked door can't be unlocked again. Here's what the API endpoints might look like:

`/door/open /door/close /door/lock /door/unlock`

When each one of these endpoints is "called," "executed," or "queried," there is an expectation of an attempted or consequent action. The implementation details (How is the door opened? How do locks work?) aren't important. "Door" is a noun, and it's followed or preceded by a verb. Each endpoint represents an operation.

This "Door API" doesn't look like the intimidating walls of code seen in cybercriminal movies; it looks like plain English with a special syntax:

```
POST >> https://192.168.1.1/door/open
POST >> https://192.168.1.1/door/close
POST >> https://192.168.1.1/door/lock
POST >> https://192.168.1.1/door/unlock
```

In its full form, Door API looks like a URL that might be found in a web browser. The root URL provided, 192.168.1.1, is the default local IP address. It's a placeholder as if the service were hosted locally rather than on the open internet. All the aliased URLs on the web ultimately map to the IP addresses of servers, and I've elected to use this dummy address.

Although this "directory structure," in which each successive layer is a deeper level of nesting (imagine the construct of /house/den/door/open), is widespread in internet page navigation, web services follow the convention of *slash hierarchy* as a tradition, not a hard requirement. These slashes in a web URL might indicate a physical path to a file on the file system of a server hosting a website. It doesn't guarantee that an API is present.

Simply put, API is nouns and verbs. The verb is usually a logical action with an antecedent noun. Where the noun is not a (quasi-)physical object, like a door, and instead represents a digital resource, a standard set of verbs is used. These are called CRUD actions.[11]

C: Create, **R**: Retrieve, **U**: Update, **D**: Delete

Then there are the types of requests: GET, POST, and PUT. A GET request means there is no modification to the object. There's typically no payload sent by the client, and the client expects to retrieve information. For our door, maybe we'd GET an endpoint like /door/locked. We would attempt to *retrieve* information about whether it was locked. A POST request usually means taking an action that modifies a state, often by sending a payload. If we're opening, closing, or locking a door, the *state* of that door is being changed, so POST is appropriate. We also POST for creations or deletions of resources. PUT is for updates—usually minor changes to information that don't clearly represent complex actions or new objects.

We can pile on infinite door constraints and functions. Project managers call that "scope creep." Scope creep occurs when feature requests are added to a previously agreed-upon project scope in a potentially never-ending work rhythm. I'll add requirements to better furnish this example.

What if there are many doors, not just one? Identifying *which door* would be necessary. Maybe numbering the door would be best, like in an apartment hallway. To better navigate that numbering scheme, users would benefit from a kind of directory to discover the different doors.

```
POST >> /door/{door_id}/open
POST >> /door/{door_id}/close
POST >> /door/{door_id}/lock
POST >> /door/{door_id}/unlock
GET >> /door/{door_id}
```

I introduce the variable "ID" to refer to a unique door. The curly braces signify a user input value. In this case, it's an ID. How about finding all the IDs? GET >> /doors

This new endpoint would be used to retrieve a list of all door objects. The response could look like this:

```
[{"id": 1, "state": "open"},
{"id": 2, "state": "locked"},
{"id": 3, "state": "closed"}]
```

Let's consider one more improvement. What if unlocking the door required a passcode? A passcode must be supplied. How is this done?

Query parameters are found in URLs across the internet. The question mark ("?") that is followed by parameters which may appear to be gibberish. We can modify the unlock route to accept a passcode, and it would then look like the string below. The parameter "key=value" is placed after the question mark.

```
POST >> /door/{door_id}/unlock?passcode={code}
```

A complete query, using the local web address, could look like this: https://192.168.1.1/door/45/unlock?passcode=12345

This would be an attempt to open door #45 with the code 12345. Cleanly designed APIs and web services help bridge the gap between computations "under the hood" and linguistic expressions of functionality. */car/start* should be as easy to understand, even though starting a car is more complex than opening a door.

```
{"Response": "Passcode 12345 is incorrect and
door 45 has not been unlocked."}
```

. . .

Hopefully, this walkthrough has opened doors for the reader. While it might seem simplistic, this is how APIs are developed and made available externally. Some sites have moved beyond displaying directory structures or API-like formatting in the primary URL in the web browser. This doesn't mean that the APIs aren't being used—it indicates that dynamic sites draw content from dozens of URLs queried asynchronously. This is why hitting the "back" button can lead to unexpected results—dynamic content can render deterministic navigation impossible.

Facebook launches a huge number of API calls to assemble my home page at https://www.facebook.com. The site relies on traditional navigation formatting when I search for the Hackathon Hackers group: https://www.-facebook.com/search/top?q=hackathon%20hackers.

To conclude this lesson in web service design, the curious reader may be interested in the following points for continued inquiry:

- Submitting a passcode as a plain-text query parameter is considered bad practice. Why?
- Without GET routes for all doors, could a curious user sniff all door IDs using an individual GET route? What would have to be true for that to happen?
- What's to stop someone from trying to open door #45 by cycling through all five-digit numbers?

Public and Private APIs

Web services are meant to be easy to understand and interact with. The OpenAPI Specification[12] helps enforce such usability standards. Below is an image from a web service called Cats API[13] with an OpenAPI documentation page. Yes, the OpenAPI doc page can be thought of as a GUI for an API.

Cats API `0.0.1` `OAS3`

/api/api.json

Cats	∨

GET	/api/cats Gets a page of cats
POST	/api/cats Creates a new cat
GET	/api/cats/{cat_id} Gets a cat by id
DELETE	/api/cats/{cat_id} Deletes a cat by id
PATCH	/api/cats/{cat_id} Updates a Cat

The Cats API interactive documentation page[14]

The Cats API may seem self-explanatory. It's not a stretch to think that APIs are synonymous with openness. It's even in the name of the most popular specification! However, the *accessibility* of each API is not the same, and the majority are *not* intended for public use.

When a group such as an engineering team at a private company wants to keep their *things*, like their technology stack and confidential documents, private, all they have to do is create and maintain a private network. That network is only accessible by a limited range of IP addresses, usually in the same subnet. Remote workers talk about having to "VPN in." With the "Virtual Private Network" (VPN), they're establishing a trusted link to a private network in which all the assets are hidden from nosey search engine crawlers.

Some APIs and web services out there are not accessible. If it doesn't form the backend of a customer-facing product, there's no reason it should be available on the open internet. It's expensive to launch an API endpoint that anyone can access. It could be dangerous. I refer to an API existing exclusively in a restricted VPN as a "secret API." We don't know if they exist because we can't prod for or tease them out. There's no web address an outsider could infer to access them.

What about a consumer-facing app intended to be available to as many people as possible? A nuanced understanding of "public APIs" and "private APIs" is important.

If a company provides an external-facing app, the interactions between the front end (what the user sees, like on a webpage or mobile game) and the backend (an HTTP web service) cannot be fully concealed. The *code* can remain secret, but the messaging can't. This messaging can be obfuscated or encrypted, but if users can access the website, app, or game, they can also record or *sniff* the back-and-forth web traffic to uncover API endpoints and how they work. This is known as "API hacking."

I see API hacking as between traditional breaking-and-entering *hacking* and the hacking-*together* practiced at hackathons. It can be done ethically. These techniques are an important part of any cybersecurity professional's or software engineer's tool kit. However, API hacking techniques can inflict major pain and perpetrate traditional bad-guy stuff, like stealing confidential data.

The point is that when the *front end* of a website is available to the entire internet, someone *pretending* to be that front-end application can then submit modified requests to the private API web service. There might be value in viewing the data returned or programmatically modifying its state.

When a firm wants to safeguard this data or doesn't provide access to an API, the engineers create a "private API." The APIs underpinning social media services are *private*. By contrast, a "public API" (used interchangeably with "open API") is an interface that providers *do* want people to use. Companies provide detailed documentation and run advertisements to entice adoption. They send evangelists to hackathons. Both private and public APIs, despite featuring antonyms, are *generally* accessible to anyone with an internet connection.

Public APIs aren't like public parks, they aren't necessarily free. These days, if a company is beckoning API use, it expects to make money from it (or by selling API-adjacent services or harvesting user data). It might be *kinda* free up to a certain usage tier, but the point isn't to democratize access to data but to generate revenue. When I was a much younger man, APIs existed that didn't require logins or auth tokens to use them. Today, such restrictions abound.

Serving an API can be expensive. If it costs a host $.0005 per query in computing and data transfer costs, what if one bad actor submits one million queries? That's five hundred dollars. Unlimited and unmetered APIs are a thing of the past. For any hackathon hacker looking to use the data from public APIs to create more dynamic applications, the barriers have never been higher.

"What good APIs could I tinker with to learn more about programming while building a dynamic application?" is a question without a clear answer. Entering a hackathon and asking the same question leads to the sponsor booths.

What about private APIs? Software engineers can design programs that crack and exploit them. The distinction between private and public must be repeated. A private API underpins a service—it is abstracted from the end user. The explicit routes and request payloads are not advertised or publicly documented.

Programmatically accessing a private API may be artificially difficult and is almost always outlawed by a provider's terms of service.

A public API provider wants developers to know everything there is to know about accessing the API. Although public APIs have mind-numbingly detailed terms of service that can be violated similarly to private APIs, it is private APIs that have been dissected and reverse-engineered to build fortunes in spite of their terms of service restrictions. Reverse engineering or sniffing a public API is oxymoronic.

Users expect to gather data from an API—about a cat, door, or maybe a vehicle. Enter a URL, the request is dispatched to the server...loading occurs...and the result is soon displayed.

APIs are used to not only retrieve data but also modify data and execute actions, like in the Door API and Cat API. Here are some real-world examples:

- What if instead of *retrieving* a social media account's biographical information, it is modified by an HTTP request?
- What about uploading a new picture to Instagram?
- What about leaving five hundred comments on Instagram pictures that say, "follow me back, please"?

Powerful, disruptive, and lucrative systems can be created by discovering and reverse engineering a certain class of API endpoints–typically empowering those verbs used on social media sites (like, follow, comment).

API Hacking

Corey Ball published the book, *Hacking APIs: Breaking Web Application Programming Interfaces* in July 2022. I purchased it immediately and worked through it over a weekend.

Ball's work is written from the perspective of a security tester, or a "white hat" hacker. It delves into the techniques and tools required to, well, *hack* APIs so that engineers can improve the security of their systems. *Hacking APIs* also encourages readers to find and solve problems for security bug bounties. Bug bounties are rewards that companies offer outside engineers to solve problems with their systems. Security bug bounties are the same thing, just in exchange for finding network security exploits rather than exploiting them.[15]

Hacking APIs is acclaimed. It has also attracted attention because, in a tale as old as time, the information used by the good guys can also be used by the bad guys.[16] Most of the automated villainy carried out on social media platforms, particularly Instagram, resulted from hacked private API endpoints long before Corey's book was written.

What does it mean to hack an API? Why would a hackathon hacker hack an API?

Hacking an API means learning more about it to gain expanded access just as a traditional "hacker" might prod (*penetration test*) a system for vulnerabilities to expand his access and do something nefarious. Snooping around private APIs might lead to valuable discoveries: new endpoints, special cases resulting in unintended behavior, avoiding rate limits, or the ability to reverse engineer the functionality to build an adjacent or copycat product.

Web traffic flows through APIs. Anyone with the willingness to break the rules and hack around can find a realm of possibilities in the undercurrent of the internet.

Hackathon participants, frustrated with onerous restrictions and desperate for top prizes, may hack APIs and use hidden functionality in their projects. Tighter locks on APIs—*longer passcodes for the door*—only increase the incentive to break in.

Award-winning hackathon projects have utilized private APIs. Countless projects have used public API endpoints that are now private. Sniffing and testing these endpoints is time-consuming, but the functionality accessed can be of immense value.

The runner-up from the Spring 2013 edition of PennApps[17] was called SparkTab.[18] It was a search box with keywords for interacting with specific websites and services, including Facebook, Twitter, reddit, Amazon, Tumblr, and YouTube.

SparkTab

John Biggs, a judge at PennApps, wrote an article for TechCrunch in which he stated, "It connects to a number of services using URL calls or API connections. There is a full set of commands that is available just by typing in the text bar."[19]

He also said, "I could definitely see them adding more features (and advertisements) and making at least some sort of small service business out of the project."

I remember SparkTab well because four upperclassmen at my college created it. They hosted the school's first hackathon and later encouraged me to attend PennApps.

The relevance of SparkTab is that it depended on sniffing websites' available search functionality. In some cases, these hackers were just building URL query strings. In other cases, they were integrating with APIs. Based on my view in 2013, they did not sniff *private* APIs. For this tool to win a prize today, it would have to depend on hidden functionality.

Major League Hacking,[20] the official student hackathon league, provides a rule set that doesn't explicitly forbid using private APIs. However, MIT's Reality Virtually Hackathon does specify that "You are permitted to use publicly developed and openly licensed APIs and SDKs for your project."[21]

Inspection

Non-technical users can perform rudimentary API exploration. Google Chrome provides tools to filter, organize, and explore HTTP requests.

Remember when MySpace had a top-eight-friends feature? Facebook once had an internal representation of Top X friends, too, though it was never displayed. Users could determine their top friends by inspecting the page and sifting through payloads from Facebook's private API.

Unfortunately, I had to remove the tutorial. Anyone who wants it can email me. The steps are: right-click "inspect" on any page, navigate to the "network tab," refresh the page, and analyze the requests and responses displayed in "Developer Tools."

Finding a feature on a website powered by a repeatedly accessible private API is common. To continue digging, repeatedly refreshing the page and waiting for other elements to load isn't efficient. The hacker needs to isolate the specific feature. Using tools like Postman and Burp Suite a security researcher can poke around more precisely, which is one of the fundamentals in Corey's book.

Reconsider the broken webpage button that frustrates both primates and homo sapiens. Next time it happens, open the "network" tab in the browser and resume clicking. The non-technical observer will be able to observe in real-time which, if any, web requests are triggered by the button. If there are no web requests, the button isn't hooked up to anything. In my experience, the button usually sends a request but with an uncaught error displayed in the overlay.

Tool use is what separates us from monkeys.

What about the private APIs of mobile apps, like social networks or games on the iPhone? If the app is self-contained and Google Chrome's web tools don't apply, where are the web requests?

Web requests still flow between the client device and the internet. Ignoring encryption for now, sniffing is performed by fooling the mobile device into piping its web traffic through a proxy server. There are several network hops between a phone and a web server. Adding an extra hop to a server controlled by the researcher may not be detectable by the app's servers.

To investigate an iPhone app, the traffic is sent to a man-in-the-middle (MITM) proxy. That proxy could be running on a home computer or another device like a cloud server. That proxy would intercept and log *all* web requests like a web browser does. As a researcher becomes more comfortable mapping out the functionality, the endpoints can be further exploited using desktop tools like Burp Suite. To "map out" the API, a researcher sniffing the interface must execute all actions, including specific sequences of actions!

Defenses against API hackers include encryption, tokens, rate limits, log-in requirements, aggressive IP banning or IP quality checks, and obfuscation. Oh, and legal action and account blackouts.

From the first time I clicked "inspect" to check out a non-working website button, this type of "hacking" has always felt approachable and inviting, regardless of whether a prize from PennApps has been on the line. Just like at student-run hackathons, the non-traditional hackers may extract the most profit.

6

SCREENGRABBING

A screenshot or screengrab is a captured image of all or a portion of the display on a computer screen. A snapshot of a screen provides context for what another person sees. It's no wonder that sending them to friends, colleagues, tech support specialists, and strangers has become a fundamental part of digital communication. An indicator of the believability of any claim: "Screenshot?"

These screen grab shortcuts, across all operating systems, are the most used: *Windows Key + PrtScn* on Windows, *Command + Shift + 4* on MacOS, *Volume + Lock* on an iPhone or Android. What's captured may be ephemeral. This camerawork can demand fast reflexes. Committing these keypresses to memory is useful for building social cachet in a group chat as much as writing professional, informative reports.

During the awkward aughts, users pointed digital cameras at their screens and uploaded those pictures to internet forums. The internet contains millions of these pictures with at least a few sourced in 2006 from my hard drive.

As smartphones became ubiquitous, screen grabbing contrasted with the beautiful moments associated with great pictures. The issue is not that "I have screenshots" is now a threat or that screenshot functionality can bring private ephemera into digital permanence. It's that, as I've been thinking lately, screengrabbing could better describe the phenomenon by which mobile phone screens have totally captured us.

By today's standards, roughly ninety percent of the frontal surface area of a smartphone is a screen. My corruption of screengrab no longer refers to impulsively saving what appears on a screen. My idea of "screengrab" refers to the impulse to physically grab the screen—the device—even when not beckoned by vibration, sound, or visual notification. It is a cerebral clutching of electronics.

Elders used to ask if I "ever put that thing down," referring to a video game controller. Now I notice them mindlessly holding their phones. After setting them down, they are affected by the same sneaking tendency to pick them back up, as if the mobile phone represents a grand unfinished idea, a spiritual tethering. I also notice tiny hands in strollers reaching out, not for sippy cups but for immersive screens, and adults reflexively handing over the child-ready devices to grip and scroll on.

This essay conveys my perspective on screen addiction, which is admittedly nonscientific and anecdotal, drawing heavily from my experience gaming and logging untold hours of playtime during the formative years of my life. My central argument is that the features that made video games alluring and immersive were successfully adapted to social-feed apps, which are now so addictive that kids are no longer motivated to play video games. I provide thoughts on what can be done, who needs to help, and why this scary epidemic has uniquely empowered those who remember a world before smartphones.

They called them "Addicting Games," after all

Nobody born in the 1990s experienced the epoch of gaming, but they did experience the epoch of gaming as it is known today, with the introduction of three-dimensional graphics, countless innovative game mechanics, epic storytelling, rich media, indie publishing, and, of course, online play. It was the era when playing a game all day no longer resulted in a headache.

Video games were a sacred pastime free of intrusive commercial influence. I can't recall how many times adults who spent twenty percent of car rides listening to radio advertisements and thirty percent of "family time" on the couch watching commercials told me to spend less time playing games. Maybe video games were an unproductive, addictive, waste of time, but gamers relished in complete control over every moment of their immersive digital existence, which was absent in other forms of entertainment.

My family upgraded to broadband in 2005, and I rushed to access vast repositories of Adobe Flash games.[1] Almost every Flash game was free to play in a web browser. Sites like Addictinggames.com served as free-of-charge digital arcades. The arcade at the mall extracted fees for playtime; online gaming portals did not.

Games distributed on the internet were innovative in another way. There was no vetting of the games, rating systems, or waiting for physical distribution. Anybody with the requisite knowledge could create and upload a game. Any kid with an internet connection could find the game and play it. New games were created in response to emerging trends. The Addicting Games website helped popularize a new paradigm: casual browser-based gaming. It democratized gaming for those who couldn't afford the consoles of the day. It also meant that gamers, even die-hard gamers, had exciting options to fill twenty-minute buckets of time when firing up a console and finding an online match to join wasn't justifiable.

The currency of Flash games was the players' attention. Host websites ran banner ads, pop-ups, pop-unders, and, much later, view-before-you-can-play ads. This model was applied to big-budget games of the era too, such as the classic MMORPG[2] *Runescape* by Jagex, which built a massive player base by offering a game with a free-to-play segment supported by banner ads.[3] As a kid, I'd have done anything to keep playing.

Achievements

Although I never really outgrew *Runescape*, the seventh generation of the console wars brought a level of seriousness that browser games of the era could not match.[4] My friend group focused on Microsoft's Xbox 360, and our debut was during the 2006-2007 Christmas season when we were in seventh grade.

With the 360, Microsoft introduced the first universal achievement system.[5] Every game had a set of challenges to complete. The console's operating system, not the game alone, evaluated and awarded players. This system gave a new sense of depth to gaming. The meta goals encouraged accomplishments beyond what was explicitly rewarded inside a game world. These achievements were stored in a digital trophy case.

Importantly, the "achievement system" alerted players using pop-ups. Messages of a standard size, shape, and color appeared in the margin of the television screen with a celebratory sound effect whenever one of the predefined tasks was completed. Gamers found out about achievements as they unlocked easy ones when playing their first game on the 360. Those were special moments for me. Those were special moments for millions.

Each achievement carried a point award. These totals ranged from 0G to 500G. "G" indicated "Gamerscore." As one played more games and progressed in collecting achievements, Gamerscore grew. A user's Gamerscore was a proxy for how many different titles had been played and how deeply a user had explored those titles.

A reddit user responding to the statement that there was "no use for" Gamerscore said this:

> That's what I thought three months ago when I got my first points. But you can't help it. As it starts rising, you notice it brings you a strange sort of pleasure. Then, just because you're curious, you look up which achievements you missed in a game. And then...before you know it, you start completing some of those achievements. Maybe because you're just a bit behind a friend in monthly points, or because now you'd like to reach that 10k. Or 25k, or...yup. Now you're hooked.[6]

Achievements and Gamerscore went hand in hand with Xbox Live. With Live, players created Gamertags and linked up with gamers from around the world.[7] Although online play had been around since the original Xbox, I made my first memories of playing console games online in the mid-aughts. Without Live, players would have probably taken pictures of their screens to show their Gamerscore to buddies at the school lunch table.

The 360 innovatively pushed pop-ups, which we now call "push notifications,"[8] to report friend activity: logons, direct messages, and invites to join players in a party. All of this was delivered using the same mechanism as in-game achievements. Players were alerted to social occurrences and achievements just after being indoctrinated to despise pop-ups[9] on the family desktop.

Players fell into patterns of logging onto Live when they got home from school. Achievements started to pile up. Players became conditioned[10] to seek those notifications. They subconsciously snuck glances at the dark margins of the screen, beckoning a friend to make contact or an Easter egg to reveal itself. I believe Xbox Live and Gamerscore Achievements paved the way for what is now studied by real researchers, something I could call "distraction engineering."

The Xbox 360 experience had plenty of addictive qualities, such as the notifications of achievements and social messages, though that also bore a minor cost of *cognitive load*. Today, the smartphone is a "distracting source of dopamine." One study attributes a startling drop in working memory capacity and fluid intelligence to the presence of a smartphone in a peripheral view or pocket. The study was titled, "Brain Drain: The Mere Presence of One's Own Smartphone Reduces Available Cognitive Capacity."[11]

Did achievement messages spoil the purity of console gaming? They were the first bid for intact attention spans. They were pleasant interruptions. Regardless, anyone who played the 360 in its prime will quickly cite their proudest achievements and most savage beatdowns witnessed in Xbox Live game lobbies. The stage for screen addiction was set, though it's hard to believe that behind this fantastic product were evil scientists deliberating on how to manipulate users with pop-ups.

Everyone Runs Faster with a Knife!

When reminiscing on console gaming in the aughts, the primary memory is rarely stoic children cooperating on an "achievement." Instead, I remember tantrums, prodigious cursing and trash-talking over percussive blasts of grenades and sci-fi weaponry, and controllers lobbed across the room. The Xbox 360 pioneered something else: emotionally intense gaming—dramatic sequences of win, loss, and draw in which everyone could be the main character.

First-person shooter (FPS) games were popular. One of the first videos I ever saw on YouTube, posted on January 18, 2006, captured the raw excitement of FPS gaming along with its comedown.[12] *boom headshot* is a mockumentary targeting the addictive experience of the popular PC game, *Counter Strike: Source*.

The video follows a dedicated *Counter-Strike* player named Doug whose virtual and gaming lives have melded.[13] When questioned about wielding a gigantic chef's knife when preparing for a run, he exclaims, "Everyone runs faster with a knife!" His life revolves around a tiny CRT monitor on which he plays FPS. The intonations of his speech oscillate wildly, imitating a stereotype of a crackhead: "my heart's beatin'! MY HANDS ARE SHAKIN'!"

"BOOM! HEADSHOT!"

The actor's catchphrase during each kill became one of the internet's earliest memes,[14] a refrain I uttered hundreds of times while playing games like *Halo 3* and *Call of Duty: Modern Warfare 2* on the 360.

The closing sequence includes the main character's avatar dying.[15] The video ends with the actor smashing a keyboard in his garage and delivering a profanity-laden soliloquy. Games could take players to such highs but also deal out losses that could destabilize the emotionally immature.

For a middle-school kid, the real world offered no equivalent emotional rollercoaster; no other dopamine spike came close. To generalize, the FPS console was the most accessible and strongest, and PC-based RPG games tended to have similar effects but required more time investment, as parodied by the *South Park* episode, "Make Love, Not Warcraft."[16]

FPS games in the aughts could be infinitely replayed and addictive, a quality later intensified and harnessed by social-feed apps. At the time, mobile app experiences were nowhere near as enticing as FPS games. The best games were thoroughly studied—the meandering curves of action, risk, investment, and enjoyment were plotted and analyzed. In theory, the highs and lows of *boom! headshot!* could have been captured by an app designed specifically to engender emotional responses.

The Brick

When did phones become addictive? Certainly not in the 1990s or early 2000s. Can any nineties kids remember getting a dopamine rush when *the house phone* rang?

I remember how exciting it was when the phone rang, even though the caller usually wasn't looking for me. Back then, every phone call presented a mystery. Before phones, it must have been exciting to receive letters, postcards, and telegrams. Humans are social creatures; mundanities make us feel important. The excitement of today's push notification *ding* might be equivalent to the phone ringing for previous generations and the sound of the brass letter mail slot for the generation before that. The brain rewards routine socialization.

A prolific letter writer of the 1940s could not imagine the throughput of the median teenage texter of the 2020s. Some people send and receive more electronic messages in a day than would receive emails in a month at the very peak of email spam in the aughts. What used to be impossible, cost-prohibitive, or unwanted—if not forbidden—is now routine.

As a seventh grader in 2007, I received my first cell phone: a TracFone Nokia that displayed its prepaid "minutes." Sending or receiving a text message and making a phone call cost some nontrivial fraction of digital currency. My phone featured free games, such as *Snake* and *Brick Breaker*. I'm not exaggerating when I say that every pixel on the screen was identifiable.

My parents concurrently granted me more freedom to visit friends in other parts of town. I usually rode my bike to see them. Around that time, I got my first girlfriend who also had a cell phone.

I remember becoming more attached to my phone because I associated its buzzing text notifications with my female friend's affection. For many people, this type of interaction is a Pavlovian conditioning—a dependence on technology.[17] The same emotions created through inperson interactions are proxied through our devices. These devices can feel like the only way to access a consistent flow of positive, rewarding socialization. Or at least the only way with immediacy, at scale, or that is *replayable*.

While playing my violin in a regional orchestra, I was disciplined for balancing the TracFone on the music stand and texting during short instructional breaks. I wonder if my cognitive capacity as a violin player affected my phone's presence. Were my peers distracted by the comically loud noise from the vibrating Nokia on a wrought iron music stand? Nobody becomes an alcoholic in six months. Had I become addicted to my phone in even less time?

The user experience was clunky. The phone was physically clunky with a retractable antenna. The battery lasted for more than a week, so I didn't need to sleep with it on my bedside table as it charged. When I search the internet for "indestructible phone," half the hits involve Nokia models like the one I owned. It made me want to try to smash one myself. I never reached the point of reflexively reaching into my pocket to check my phone. My phone didn't need to be near me. There was no deep-seated fear of losing it.

The iPhone

I'm sure parents sarcastically said "Oh, great!" when they learned the iPhone might become a singular replacement for listening to music on the iPod, chatting with friends on the computer, gaming on the Xbox, filming content using a camcorder, and talking to friends on the house phone, but no one could have predicted the scale of its success.

It took over three years for my mom to buy me one. In the meantime, I stayed entertained with an iPod Touch, essentially an iPhone without cameras, speakers, or the ability to call or text.

Even when the App Store launched in 2008,[18] nobody knew *what* to do with their smartphone. My first memory of an iPhone app was of a classmate using the iBeer app[19] at a freshman football game in the fall of 2008. iBeer debuted with the App Store. It used the phone's motion controls to simulate drinking a frothy pilsner as the phone was tipped like a beer glass. This entertained me greatly as a fourteen-year-old. Its creator, Steve Sheraton, says it has had "120 million users."[20]

The apps were simplistic. Most of the games were better than *Snake* on the TracFone. I spent *a lot* of time perusing the App Store, downloading apps that seemed interesting, using them for a bit, and moving on. It was similar to exploring the early internet.

In early 2009, I was one of the legions of curious young people playing *Pocket God*,[21] a Tamagotchi-meets-God-simulator game.[22,23] The graphics were crisp, the use of the iPhone's movement and gesture controls was novel, the interactions were funny, and the game held my attention for tens of minutes each week.

When playing a cool new game like Pocket God, users commonly tilted the iPhone (or iPod Touch) toward a friend to show how neat the gaming experience was. It was dorky, but just as my classmate nailed his iBeer chug, I showed friends I could flick a miniature islander into the ocean blue. A December 2012 VentureBeat article celebrating *Pocket God*'s final update corroborated, "It was something that friends could fire up to show off an iPhone."[24]

When musical instrument apps were released, I wanted to show my parents that I could play songs on the guitar or piano. Third-party developers released all kinds of apps, most for free. Apple devices, with a dynamic library of apps, begged for socialization, and users naturally wanted to demonstrate what they were doing. They wanted other people to grab *their* screens.

Reminiscent of the Xbox 360's achievement pop-ups, push notifications were first-class citizens[25] on Apple's iOS. Call and text notifications dopamine, so the layout and delivery mechanism for push notifications became the best way to capture attention and boost engagement. Provided they didn't clutter the screen with notifications, any app developer would have been stupid to not beckon users to return. Tapping on a notification and being led directly to the app—just like a web popup—was a new, neat feature.

My earliest memories of push notifications were of my iPod Touch. *Pocket God* was updated weekly.[26] Each time it was updated, the developer sent a push notification summarizing what was new and lightheartedly beckoning users to return to the app.

In a way, it felt like the developer was texting me directly, lending me *his* attention. I couldn't stop associating weekly *Pocket God* developer push notifications with a reciprocal social relationship. I think I was just bored and lonely.

Angry Birds is a candidate for the greatest mobile game of all time. It was the perfect use of the touch screen with rich, exciting, casual gameplay. I loved that game. Everyone did. *Angry Birds* meant traction. The money started flowing, developer tools became more powerful, and titles became more ambitious. By the spring of 2010, another classic game, *Fruit Ninja*, was released, and in that same week, the official app for the microblogging site Twitter launched.[27] I started grabbing my device more frequently.

At that point, I still only owned an iPod Touch and had "upgraded" my cell phone to one with a slide-out qwerty keyboard. I brought both on family trips. By the summer of 2010, I knew I was due for my first iPhone. I was biding my time. I could not ignore the pull from my cheap cell phone, my iPod Touch, or the social networks I accessed on my desktop computer. The notifications screen on my iPod Touch was getting crowded, and it became harder to write essays for English class on my desktop when it felt like I was missing out on what was happening on Facebook or Twitter. Sometimes I felt guilty for not visiting my islanders, possibly the result of "The Tamagotchi effect": the development of emotional attachment to machines, robots, or software agents.[28]

In late 2010, my mom bought me an iPhone. That was the year that I got my first *real* girlfriend. I like to think she was an upgrade from my middle school girlfriend of the same order of significance as my iPhone was from my TracFone.

By that time, cell phones were becoming problematic. I had been bullied at my high school for having a shitty phone. Two years earlier, at the tail end of eighth grade, I received a slider phone to replace the brick. I pulled it out of my pocket in art class to check my texts. I remember the kid sitting next to me saying, "Wow, cool! Is that your cell phone?" without mocking me. But maybe that was more of a testament to the differences between attending a public middle school and a private high school.

As the days of my shitty high school phone waned, the way my peers handled their phones and used the internet transformed. The force of technological change aligned well with the typical anxieties of high schoolers becoming young adults. Facebook pictures and comments became a virtual popularity contest. I remember being bullied on Facebook during my first week at private school because I hadn't trimmed my emo hairdo. Phones were status symbols. Weekend get-togethers were more frequently interrupted by whipping out phones and responding to text messages.

Anyone not on Facebook was missing out. Anyone not on Xbox Live was missing out. Avoiding both meant missing an invitation to do something on a Friday night, even within my nerdy friend group. Those same Friday nights, we convinced ourselves that certain text messages were important enough to be answered while driving or at stop signs.

Students always had phones in their pockets at school, even though the devices were forbidden. The fear of losing a phone crystalized; having a phone confiscated was a meaningful punishment. Schemers considered handing in dummy phones. Occasionally, I took my phone to bed with me. When I found myself frustrated by difficult homework, I reached for my phone as an escape. I remember this happening as far back as 2008 as I prioritized women over Latin homework.

With my iPhone in hand, I carefully boxed up my iPod Touch. I loved that thing. And love quickly took on a new meaning for me as I texted a new high school girlfriend. Being romantically interested in someone or being pursued enlivens text conversations, which at that time still contained boorish AIM lingo, like "wut."[29] Injecting emotion was a game changer. The suspense was enveloping after sending a teenage "risky text."[30]

Did she text me back yet? What did she say?

That powerful shot of dopamine after sending a text and receiving a desirable response shaped my cell phone usage patterns over the following decade.

I observed that guys who found girlfriends started playing a heck of a lot less *Halo 3*.

This is how I imagine real-life communication became synthesized with electronic device communication. This digital tie-in shackled humans to their cell phones and smartphones, which were omnipresent communication devices able to supplant the thrill felt playing video games.

I remember feeling euphoric chatting with my new girl, even though we usually conversed nonsensically. The iPhone could bestow unnatural amounts of attention and affection. My infatuation with her was proxied through my cell phone, and large parts of our relationship lived and died over those airwaves. Apple released the emoji keyboard with iOS 5 in June 2011,[31] and I used it to express the whole spectrum of emotion, from winky face to heart to emphatic question mark to broken heart.

Made Men

Xbox Live's social gaming jumped to social media sites—kind of. The year 2008 was a transitional period during which Myspace and Facebook started hosting games.

This new genre, "social network gaming,"[32] was notable in that the featured characters were profiles derived from individuals' networks. The games weren't console blockbusters. In technical terms, they were a step back, more closely resembling indie games on Addicting Games. They leaned heavily on stock graphics and text-based elements.

"Gangster games" was a popular subgenre of social-augmented gaming that included *Mafia Wars*, *Mob Wars*, and *Mobsters*. Although *Mafia Wars* by Zynga is the most well-known *and somehow continued until 2017*,[33] I spent most of my time playing *Mobsters*, which is considered the lowest profile of the three. I surmise that *Mobsters* on Myspace was the earliest release and that the games that emerged immediately after copied its themes and gameplay.

In these games, players started as low-ranked gangsters in a crime family and followed the path to becoming made men. Players completed (clicked) missions, attacked (clicked) rivals, and even bought (clicked) property—and, lest we forget, *unlocked achievements.*

The appeal was huge. Players could wage war against facsimiles of their friends in an obvious social tie-in. Players who would have never otherwise been caught dead gaming tried them. Achievements were automatically broadcast on social media. The big innovation was the *idle* game.[34] Just like logged-off social media users could still accrue social currency in the form of likes, comments, and friend requests, social gamers passively generated in-game currency. Things *happened* while the player was away. Playing windows were limited by cooldown timers (and "pay-to-win"[35] was introduced).

Facebook's games provided a stopgap for the lulls in the early social media experience before mobile apps took off. In 2010, during the peak of *FarmVille*, my high school teacher cast her farm on the projector to show how her crops were faring.

These games without clear win conditions nonetheless kept score. Because of the way they were built—with friends forming interactive elements of the game—the strength of one's network and relative popularity within that network often resulted in a higher score. This was a proving ground where social "vanity" metrics were demonstrably more than vanity.

By the time social games fell by the wayside, mostly on account of being monotonous, corny, and dominated by middle-aged women, Facebook decimated Myspace. Myspace will be remembered as the ultimate choose-your-own-adventure[36] platform. Facebook and its successors softened the user experience, providing more enticing "adventures" while reducing users' need to chart their paths.

The Convergence

In the early 2010s, pictures supplanted text updates as social media's focal point. Within a few years, video began contending to be the dominant content format. In 2013, short-form vertical videos rocketed to the forefront on Vine. TikTok's United States launch in September 2017 cemented the format as the most alluring content type.[37] Even *LinkedIn* promotes them now. As social media experiences became richer, many of the forces I had observed in successful video games converged.

Video games almost always trumped social media browsing when it came to intensity and immersiveness. However, gaming requires high user effort. From the highest-effort games, like *World of Warcraft*, to medium-effort games, like *Halo 3*, to low-effort *FarmVille* and browser Flash games, users had to endure cognitive load. They had to press buttons.

It turned out that users preferred not pressing any buttons at all. One trend that emerged in the 2010s was *watching others play video games*. Kids possess encyclopedic knowledge of games they've watched streamers play but don't own themselves. Top streaming games on Twitch are measured in the tens of billions of hours watched.[38] To show examples of continuity between "when I was a kid" and "kids these days," I'll add that a newer *Counter-Strike* game is among the top ten streamed games of all time.

Maybe the aversion to playing hard games is actually an aversion to *losing*. Perhaps players have become more sensitive to loss, like *Grand Theft Auto*'s "*wasted*"[39] message, which has nudged users to activities that don't carry straightforward outcomes.

Social media app feeds didn't surpass video games by adding open worlds[40]—infinite content—but by removing the need for users to interact at all. Unlike when I was a teenager, there are numerous comparable options for virtual entertainment, and thrill-seekers now seem to choose the path of least resistance.

Report Cards

"In some classes, the bell rings, and everyone just stays on the phone with their earbuds in."[41] A reddit user wrote this on a July 23, 2023 thread called "No Cellphone Policy."

To assess whether there is a screen addiction epidemic, I thought I could find research wherein a "control" group of subjects belonging to a religious sect that shunned technology. I came up with nothing, but an eccentric reddit community suggestion led me to a goldmine of despair: the subreddit for schoolteachers.[42]

Within thirty minutes of digging in, I concluded that no group better understands the impact of smartphone usage than American teachers. They hold the key to mitigating the problem if anyone would listen.

During the years I followed the discussion on r/Teachers, once even identifying myself as the son of a teacher who was writing a book about social media, the tone concerning cell phones was of anguish and defeat: "Until they're gone, there is no point to anything we do at all. Our kids' working memory and attention are shot. They are addicted and retain nothing."[43]

American teachers are hamstrung by school handbooks and unable to enact or enforce phone policies. In a uniquely American quagmire, parents insist their children must have phones on them in case of school shootings.[44] Parents physically threaten teachers if they forbid cell phones. Teachers are noticing achievement gaps between students whose parents control their screen time at home and those with parents who don't. The effect on fluid intelligence and working memory seems dramatic, which aligns with the study cited at the beginning of this chapter.

Homework

What can be done about screengrabbing?

The path forward has become clear to decision-makers since I first thought this topic essay-worthy. There is a growing consensus that children must have limited screen time. Enforcement mostly falls on parents, but, so far, parents have done a shitty job. I believe social media has no place in a child's life until age fourteen. I strongly support banning social media access nationwide for anyone under fourteen. Adding and enforcing ID restrictions will come at a cost to technology companies, but it must be done. Nobody should be using social media before they're in high school.

The "most addicting" content—personalized auto-playing videos on TikTok and video games with gambling elements and microtransactions—should also be age-restricted. The most addicting content delivery mechanisms should carry the equivalent of Surgeon General warnings. I'm not going so far as to say all infinite scrolling feeds should have warning labels, but maybe push notifications should. There is a point at which resistance against the feed is futile and content degrades attention span. That needs to be addressed.

Smartphones must be banned in schools. To fight against habitual use, authorities can ensure that minors have daily periods when their phones are inaccessible. The only regular time period that can be controlled is the school day. Students can be permitted to use dumbphones[45] with basic features but to fight against the critical mass of social media mobs, phone use at school must be limited.

Further, ID verification for pornography must be enforced strictly. Authorities should define what constitutes "adult" content and who should be allowed to watch it. The amount of raunchy, sexually suggestive content on social media is too high, and it can corrupt kids. Similarly, games with gambling elements or videos that contain "giveaways" must be identified as problematic.

How can screengrabbing be fought without sacrificing personal liberties? It isn't just kids. The majority of adults that I know also have a "problem."

The answer is a smattering of what the internet brain trusts are saying. Now devices have controls that can limit screen time. Anyone serious about limiting screen time should uninstall problematic apps or enable tools that artificially block access. I limited my screen time for time-wasting sites on the desktop, and it was amazing how quickly I felt my focus snap back to "normal."

The likely scenario—what *might* end up happening—is some countries will more forcefully address screen addiction than others. "Free" countries are starting to realize that being tethered to a phone in any society does not confer freedom. China understands the benefit of keeping young minds away from smartphones and harmful internet content,[46] and the immense harm if it doesn't. Apps that thrive on human attention drain humankind's productivity. At scale, this is problematic.

Some countries will foster greater advantages by adopting stricter device usage policies including digital curfews. It will be startlingly obvious who has fallen behind in education, productivity, war preparedness, and perhaps even the general ability to function. Screen addiction is such a problem that it may be solved as a matter of national defense, economics, or demographic policy.

A country that lags behind is one in which police bodycam footage often captures arrestees shrieking, "Where's my cell phone?!"

There are so many forces at play. Nineties kids are empowered because we remember a time before phones and seem able to reason through the pros and cons of heavy usage. Sure, millions of terrible parents come from this generation, but there's a belief that those who remember the old days while remaining adept at wielding the new technology have *de facto* leadership roles. Tens of millions of people have never known a world without cell phones. My take is that, eventually, screengrabbing will taper off, and society will reach what I call "peak screentime." There will come a day when the number of hours engaging with screens will never again be surpassed. Although I think war or climate catastrophe will be most influential, I predict peak screentime will happen in the late 2040s.

Despite these beliefs, I must admit to my experience developing addictive software systems at a social media startup.

7

THE PUPPETEER PART I

I grew up gaming. I spent hours controlling avatars in virtual worlds. Like any kid with an imagination, I aspired to create my own games someday. I was in the second grade when I first sat down to draw character artwork for my first release. My game was an open-world RPG based on the 2001 classic *Twisted Metal: Black*.

It turned out that making a video game was quite difficult. Twelve years later, as a college freshman, I managed to build a game called *Clams & Conches* for an app development contest. Although I had single-handedly cobbled together a functional mobile game, I failed to deploy it onto the test device for the final showcase, and my team was forced to withdraw from the competition.

The more that I built out my portfolio of coding projects, the further away I felt from being able to create a fully-fledged game. Questions remained about game engines, artwork, soundtrack, storyline, networking, "the difficulty curve," and AI. Noted polymath Eric Barone developed the acclaimed indie game *Stardew Valley* after working alone ten hours every day for four years.[1] Although I've written up specifications for games I would eventually like to develop, I thought more highly of myself when I was seven years old.

In 2021, a friend from the Instagram growth space introduced me to the founder of a social media startup. His startup had raised about ten million dollars despite having no product or traction. The founder quickly offered me part-time work in a tailor-made role, based entirely on my reputation as an expert on bots, scraping, and private APIs.

I've been advised not to name the company. I'll codename it "Cutlet."

In my role at Cutlet, I was supposed to lead web scraping and alternative data projects as well as backend software engineering for the company's mobile app. I eventually enlisted the help of two interns and shifted my focus to a new area for me: user engagement and retention.

After spending my childhood mashing buttons and flicking joysticks, I had an opportunity to design systems with which I could once again control and manipulate avatars. At Cutlet, I was entrusted to develop persuasive technology systems that influenced human behavior. The "users" weren't an abstraction; they were *my* users. The kid who dreamt about designing video games was given a chance to create a game of his own. I became a puppeteer.

Keeping Score

Keeping score based on user behavior is about metrizing what happens and displaying the results in sleek dashboards. When the usage data is trending upward, it's a bonanza. When the usage data is trending downward, the investors are mad, and things get awkward at the overpriced Manhattan office. Gut instinct can be wrong, and the *best* ideas may be proved only by rigorous experimentation, being pitted against competing ideas tested on small segments of users in a practice called, "A/B testing."[2]

The deep-pocketed investors who had funded Cutlet were anticipating hypergrowth. The next _____. I wasn't invited to those investor meetings, but that was the dream that I was pitched when I joined the company. When I was offered an equity package, the CEO walked me through a scenario in which Cutlet achieved a *ten-billion-dollar* valuation.

If an engineer builds great features into a mobile app, then, logically, the app should gain traction organically. But it doesn't always happen that way. Investors and executives who aren't met with supercharged growth numbers split their focus to include what's easier to control: increasing the value of existing users.

A user who logs on once per month for five seconds is still a user, just not one of interest. A periodic drop-in user probably isn't creating user-generated content, engaging with others, buying anything, or viewing many ads. This depends on the genre of the app, but this essay assumes the social media space.

What makes a customer valuable is somewhat intuitive. Just as brick-and-mortar businesses prefer frequent big spenders who have pleasant interactions with salespeople, social technology businesses prefer those who come around often, click frequently, abide by the rules, and make the platform a better place. Optimizing for these traits has become an art form.

There are books and probably business school courses covering this. Below is my outline of the facets of increasing user value.

1. Longer visits; more active time using the app
2. More frequent visits
3. Higher engagement
4. Referrals and external promotion
5. Enriched user data

In short, users who spend more time on the app more often while engaging more, organically promoting the app, and providing a more complete picture of their preferences are of the utmost value.

When it comes to extending a visit, releasing more features might help. These days, there's a focus on reducing resistance by making apps easier to use and increasing motivation to keep scrolling.

Increasing the frequency of visits involves manipulating the user to habitually, perhaps even subconsciously, return to the app. Expressions like "daily active users" (DAGs) and "monthly active users" (MAGs) are used to describe and measure such trends. Every app is competing for users' attention. The primary way to increase the frequency of visits is to ask people to return. There is now widespread implementation of "push notifications" to beckon users, break their focus, and lure them into reopening an app.[3] Apps like reddit gamify habitual use, offering badges and other awards to those who return on consecutive days.

Engagement can mean taking in-app actions, such as "liking" and leaving comments, or creating user-generated content. It can also mean clicking on ads or other calls-to-action–exploring within the app. Engaged users form the backbone of social media platforms.

Referrals and external promotion tend to be overlooked, but they're essential to growing audiences. It's no wonder that apps generate *shareable* links, which they encourage sharing with friends. Someone who shares content or invites friends to a platform after following an in-app "call to action" (CTA) provides an invaluable service to the app creator: free advertising.

The fifth facet of user value, enriched user data, has become controversial because of increased regulatory pressure on the selling of data. However, all the consent forms in the world don't mean that detailed user profiles are no longer valuable. Investors, advertisers, and software engineers who design experiments all value knowing more about their test subjects. Some details are behavioral—users reveal data while using the app. Other facts are explicitly stated, such as an uploaded birthdate. To build troves of data on users, companies can mine their posts, messages, comments, and connections to infer facts.

At Cutlet, I led development in three product areas, the success of which was tied to user-based scorekeeping, which involved the five facets of value explored above. The three areas, which will be explained in subsequent sections, were Push Notifications, The Feed, and Recommendations.

Push Notifications

The iPhone introduced push notifications in 2009.[4] Apps rely on the ability to send notifications that "push" messages to the foreground of the phone screen.

Push notifications induce urgency while attempting to redirect attention to the app that generated them. There was a strong backlash against desktop pop-ups back in the aughts. Now, streamlined, personalized pop-ups called, "push notifications," are pervasive. When given the option to turn them off, most people don't.

There used to be tools called, "pop-up blockers."[5]

Push notifications effectively redirect attention back to the parent app. I turned off push notifications on Snapchat just to have the app regularly display an in-app notification asking me to turn push notifications back on. I've noticed LinkedIn does the same thing.

Though app distribution platforms mandate that developers comply with certain guidelines while making it easy to opt out of messages, "compliance" can be disingenuous. Surprise: there's no way to turn off Snapchat's manipulative in-app popup beckoning for push notifications to be toggled back on.

Push notifications are, essentially, popups that are integrated into a mobile phone's operating system. If the feature is turned on, a phone shows obtrusive (yet easily flick-away-able) alerts while another app is in the foreground. When the phone is not in use, push notifications queue up on the lock page or the system's notification center.

The original idea must have been a response to the smartphone user experience dedicating the entire screen to the active app. Spending hours playing a stupid game and then finding out that three WhatsApp messages and two emails were missed affected the quality of the experience. Starting in 2009, third-party developers were allowed to integrate with iOS in this new way.[6] They were allowed to send pop-ups even when their apps weren't running. The messages would be *pushed* to the foreground.

Although distracting, the push notifications would slide into the margin at the top or bottom of the screen to not totally interrupt the task at hand. Some users were already conditioned to look for rewards in the screen margins, as that's how Xbox achievements were delivered to console gamers.

In the early days, as I noted with *Pocket God*, mobile notifications alerted a user that a game had recently been updated with new features. Not exactly critical. Early users, including me, *welcomed* push notifications, even capricious ones. They were a form of passive entertainment on phones, especially on devices like the iPod Touch, which lacked cellular connectivity. App developers' push notifications therefore pierced a veil of unconnected loneliness.

Over time, so many push notifications became so plentiful that some apps provided tiered configurations for controlling what was pushed. This, in line with the concept of "messaging" growing from native SMS texting to a dozen third-party apps, meant that a phone could "blow up"[7] all day. I put myself in the position of the engineers at Apple who first proposed allowing third-party developers to integrate with the push notification API. There is no way that anybody expected these notifications to become a vortex of attention-grabbing, a force so strong that notifications could dictate *what* a user would do when they grabbed their screen.

People wake up in the middle of the night not with the impulse to run to the bathroom but to check queued notifications on their phones.

Although each mobile phone platform has its own rules and regulations concerning what *should* be pushed, I'm not aware of any active moderation or filtering. Cutlet used a "customer engagement solution" called OneSignal.[8] With the API key for the company OneSignal account, I could push any notification to our thousands of users with no oversight. At large tech companies, there are access controls that could prevent a lone wolf from doing such a thing. I was unrestricted.

I could have sent a notification that linked to a paid sponsor and encouraged users to buy dog food from the website. I could have pushed a notification to thousands of users that said, "You're a loser." More on that in a minute. The only platform restriction I recall was on the frequency of messages, and even that was lax. As long as the iOS app had a valid certificate granted by Apple, users could be barraged with messages.

Nearly all notifications sent by established social media apps are generated by triggers based on in-app activity. With OneSignal, I could manage such triggers. I could also log into the web portal and send campaigns independent of the Cutlet app's wiring, similar to sending an email. Furthermore, since OneSignal was integrated with the app, **it tracked whether notifications were successfully delivered and if the notifications were tapped**.

I mentioned the silly example above because if an installed app frequently pushes "You're a loser," people will surely uninstall that app and maybe even leave a negative review. Each user has a different tolerance level, and there is a balance to strike. A single, unwanted push from an app I don't care about might be enough for me to disable notifications or delete the app outright. I'm among the more sensitive parties. On the other hand, when a primary news source app harnesses push notifications to disseminate *breaking* news, I appreciate that. I turned off push notifications while writing this book. People become habituated to hundreds of push notifications per day.

Push notifications, even poorly designed ones, coerce a return to an app. It's almost like giving a ruined gambler another free play. Even when the excitement has bottomed out, a push notification appears, almost without fail. It carries with it *some* promise of *some* action—some target for the attention span. Whether it is "John commented on your picture" or "There's a winter storm warning in your area," the terseness of the notification conveys a mystery–clicking may uncover the answer. Which picture did John comment on? When is the winter storm? People click these notifications at significantly higher rates than email or web CTAs.

Estimates place the median notification "click-through rate" (CTR) between two and seven percent. That is across all mobile device operating systems in all countries. Although this range is consistent with my experience designing, delivering, and monitoring a variety of push notifications at Cutlet, the caveat is that certain apps are so ingrained in phone usage patterns that their clickthrough rates should be discounted or placed in a different category.

Social and messaging notifications convey a degree of urgency, so those click-through rates are bound to be high. They're some of the most frequent notifications, and users eagerly anticipate their arrival; users are dying to tap them, which must skew the average higher. When removing social notifications and other habitual app notifications from the count, the rate is lower—closer to two percent.

From my OneSignal dashboard, I could access the subscription list. At the time of capture—sometime in 2023—the list was just short of 60,000 people. Plenty of test dummies!

Subscriptions to the Cutlet app in its OneSignal dashboard

The subscriptions view displayed details of all users. The important fields were the subscription status, usage duration, first session, number of sessions, device, phone number and email address, app version, country, and time zone.

OneSignal is focused on notifications, not any specific in-app behaviors, but the "usage duration" tracks time, which the connected app runs in the foreground.

	Last Unsubscribed ⇕	Usage Duration	Sessions ⇕	First Session ⇕	Device
⋮		1005582	4814	11/12/21, 1:31:19 am	iPhone13,3 16.6.1
⋮		497899	4647	02/22/22, 9:37:10 am	iPhone15,5 17.1.2
⋮		852394	4619	11/19/21, 9:07:19 pm	iPhone12,1 16.5.1
⋮	12/27/22, 11:33:35 am	432263	4480	03/24/22, 11:36:09 am	iPhone14,8 17.1.2
⋮		304653	3697	02/28/23, 6:37:48 pm	iPhone11,8 15.6
⋮	07/07/23, 9:45:32 am	245237	3596	12/20/21, 9:06:51 pm	iPhone14,2 16.5.1
⋮		521116	3527	02/23/22, 11:49:47 am	iPhone13,4 17.1.2
⋮		953335	3506	12/13/21, 9:00:32 pm	iPhone14,8 17.1.2
⋮		475630	3345	01/22/22, 3:53:59 pm	iPhone12,3 15.7
⋮		440234	3189	05/17/22, 8:22:32 am	iPhone13,4 16.6.1

OneSignal table of Cutlet's top users

The top page of subscribers, sorted by number of sessions in descending order, contains some outliers. Some entries are explainable, such as developers' actual accounts or dummy phones used to demo new features. While there may be one or two power users baked in, the top of the top doesn't convey much about overall usage patterns. For the curious, 400,000 seconds, a mark some of the top players had exceeded, is around four-and-a-half days. My device was definitely absent from this high-score list.

However, before we go any deeper, it's worth asking whether Cutlet actually had 60,000 users.

[The "Users" count includes] All devices that have ever subscribed to your website or opened your mobile app with the OneSignal SDK active. Also counts all email and SMS records provided to OneSignal. This number will never decrease even if users uninstall your app or unsubscribe from your messages.[9]

The first part makes sense. The second part is dangerous. What happens if a marketing manager dumps a bunch of email addresses into the subscription repository, doesn't link them to active accounts, and then doesn't tell anybody? That's what happened at Cutlet, and it's why "users," without any qualifier, is an easily manipulated metric. The company had nowhere near 59.8k users.

The actual number of users still subscribing by the time the app was taken offline was 26,036. Of these, 12,473, nearly half, used the app for less than a minute. 17,433 used the app for less than ten minutes. Nearly 2,000 users used the app for over an hour, and among those were the daily, weekly, and monthly active users. From these stats, I could identify outliers and other audience segments to refine campaigns.

Using OneSignal and having access to thousands of opted-in subscribers was a dream come true. The platform made conducting notification experiments easy. Most of the campaigns I designed didn't require my team or me to write any code.

For one campaign, I wanted to focus on users who were "freshly out the door." They'd been relatively consistent and engaged patrons of the Cutlet app but suddenly hadn't been seen in a week or more. Maybe they had been lured away by a new distraction—maybe a competitor. Perhaps they weren't happy with the app and dragged it off their phone's front page view and into a folder, never to be seen again. OneSignal granted power but not omniscience—users who leave the app don't complete surveys or send emails when they depart. I could only try my best to get them back. A carefully designed push notification could help.

When designing an experiment, there are practical considerations for the human test subjects. The user shouldn't be alerted to the possibility that they are being experimented on. Sending multiple iterations of the same message to the same person is a bad idea. Bombardment means users uninstall the app. Reliance on certain segments will bias the outcomes compared to random, isolated test groups.

I become irritated when an email marketing campaign sends, "Hello <name>," breaking the illusion of a personalized, social newsletter. It's funny to consider the dichotomy of how amenable people are to constant streams of direct digital marketing while minor mistakes in the messaging provoke rage.

An experimenter can't send twenty different versions of a message to twenty different users. There needs to be some statistical significance in the sample size. Big tech companies have internal guides for this. Since I was dealing with no rules and a small active user base, I was just making things up as I went. Sometimes I had to target test segments as small as ten or twenty and hope for the best.

The idea with cohort testing is that, by observing segments' reactions to different versions of a notification, a better version can be built with a higher conversion rate. The polished notification can be sent to the larger, nonexperimental subscriber group with the expectation that the performance will be similar to the test cohort.

Just like a newspaper lede, the notification should lure the user to read it and click. When iterating potential headers and bodies for the message, my team found that using edgier titles almost always resulted in better click-through rates. Who knew?

One notification title we liked was for the "inactive user nudge." It read, "What is Wrong With You?"

It's hard to resist tapping such a provocative notification.

With over 3200 sends, the message approached a ten percent click-through rate. I never discovered if these users reintegrated as daily or weekly users, but they were removed from the "inactive" pool once they clicked the notification and became "active" users once again.

Inactive User Nudge Template 1   3.2k 310 N/A 9.61%

The takeaway here is not that my team and I were masters of creating notifications that converted users. It's that this already-forgotten app with a small audience was able to grab the attention of inactive users at a rate of ten percent.

Enticing notifications are based on some app-related trigger. This requires some programming and enrichment of the subscriber profile. Cutlet dealt with stock trading. I could sync each user's portfolio holdings, or at least stocks they were interested in, to their OneSignal profile. Then, whenever anything significant related to those stocks happened, I could send a personalized alert.

During a company's earnings call, I could send a notification to interested parties. They clicked at a rate of 5.5 percent—not bad.

A notification was triggered when the front page of the app featured a symbol that a user cared about. This was one of my favorites. It required some backend coding and had dependencies on parts of the app that nobody else knew how to monitor, but it performed well. We were rewarded with a 4.25 percent conversion rate, which wasn't amazing but accrued over tens of thousands of sends.

Other notifications did not fare so well. There were a few one-off sends that were dead on arrival. I was disappointed by the result when I tried to convince users to update incompatible app versions. It turned out that there was no exciting way to communicate, "Go to the App Store and upgrade!"

Some messages are better left to in-app notifications or even emails. For the upgrade nudge messages, I decided to send out a reminder every five days. I averaged a three-percent click-through rate over 5,000 sends. None of those clicks guaranteed that anyone had updated. In total, I tracked fewer than twenty folks who eventually updated their app version.

Even though asking people to upgrade app versions ended up not being worth the goodwill risk of sending push notifications, a decent portion of recipients *still clicked*. Despite the mundane call-to-action, recipients didn't turn off notifications or delete the app in significant numbers.

Push notifications are one of the most devious inventions of our time. Users assign importance to them because they've been primed by high-reward apps, like Instagram. Other apps ride the coattails and enjoy surprisingly high conversion rates. Not only did I see fantastic conversion rates, I had full control over the messaging platform. The only repercussion I ever faced was when a user disabled notifications or uninstalled the app.

The Feed

The "Feed" refers to Facebook's "News Feed," which became simply the "Feed" and is the centralized place to view content on the platform.[10] Web feeds are nothing new. XML-formatted RSS feeds have been around forever. What's special about Facebook's feed and the imitators it spawned is that Facebook pioneered the change from chronologically sorted, unfiltered fire hoses to intelligently displayed, algorithmically constructed, personalized lists.

These days, a chronological feed with no specialized filtering would be regarded as unusable.

Understanding that Cutlet needed to improve its feed to impress investors, I began a new task. Feeds are the cornerstone of persuasive technology systems. An effective feed massively increases user value by luring them to spend more time on the app. Although I had never designed a feed, I had spent thousands of hours staring at them. Why not try?

Feeds need to be filled with content. It's convenient if the content can be generated by user submissions. Instagram's feed is entirely user-generated content (and ads). With less engaging content during Facebook's early days, its feed contained basic text entries related to friend behavior, such as "Tim O'Hearn *likes* protein." My friend reacted to that feed item, writing, "way to like 'protein' on facebook [expletive]" on February 8, 2011.

Without user-generated content, it's up to the software engineers to curate feed items. At Cutlet, users could not generate content. We didn't have enough users, anyway. So we took a shortcut and piped in data from reddit. Reddit is the all-too-popular social bookmarking site with user-moderated communities.

We were using reddit's API before its API access changes in 2023.[11] Back then, a developer could set up a listener to stream and store all the posts from reddit and then reassemble that data without fear of rate limits. *Apollo for reddit*,[12] which shut down in June 2023, was a popular client app providing a smoother browsing experience. While using *Apollo*, the underlying data was the same, and any interaction from within Apollo was sent to reddit's servers.

This type of tight integration is only possible when an internet platform takes a developer-friendly stance: building a public API and providing access to it. Reddit was the last bastion of the public APIs from social software sites. Although hobbyist integrations are still feasible, the mandate for commercial licenses led quality apps like *Apollo* to cease operations.[13]

Emulating the reddit experience guarantees decent metrics. Why? Reddit is one of the most engaging communities on the internet. If an app mirrors reddit's feed, a user of that client app will exhibit behavior akin to scrolling through the native reddit app. If an app also provides the ability to *engage* with reddit—to upvote posts and leave comments—it might become preferable to the underlying app. That's what happened with *Apollo*.

Emulating the reddit experience, which Cutlet's brilliant front-end engineers had done to the greatest extent possible, wasn't as simple as displaying the feed and refreshing it at some interval. Other two-way synchronizations had to be implemented, such as displaying and leaving comments, upvoting, and downvoting.

Mirroring a reddit feed isn't real innovation. Worse, it exposes the business to risks of outages or *changes to the API access policy*. If a product person decides that an app will primarily host content from another website, value-added features should quickly follow. That's what I helped do.

By default, Cutlet displayed content from r/WallStreetBets (WSB)[14] and a few other subreddits. The feed was displayed using reddit's default sorting algorithm.

What makes "better" content? For me, it's delivering domain-specific utility. In an app catering to the personal finance and trading crowds, there was a demand for tools that could help identify big trading opportunities. Users might enjoy content from influencers in the trading space who didn't regularly post to reddit. Anything for stickiness.

I wondered if piping content from WSB and other subs like r/Superstonk, which had already been configured when I began employment, might have been scaring people off. I was annoyed by the amount of meme media content on WSB. The memes hogged screen real estate and didn't facilitate worthy discussion. I felt that the quality of the feed would have been improved if front-page memes were removed, spaced out, or significantly downranked and the "DD" (due diligence) text posts that helped make WSB famous as a hub for retail traders were up-ranked to take their place.

I implemented my feature. I left the base feed sorted in the default order and created a selectable "Cutlet Feed" in which posts tagged "meme" were spaced out and ranked lower. For example, if meme posts were ranked fifth, sixth, and eighth, the Cutlet Feed might rearrange them to be fifth, eighth, and eleventh. We didn't have enough users to test on, so I polled the team. Everyone agreed: the previous feed had been too crowded with memes, and my tweak resulted in slightly more engaging content. Users were not aware of the change.

The next question was, well, if the app shouldn't be fixated on meme stocks, should other investing subreddits be aggregated in the feed? Again, I had to rely on intuition rather than quantification. My team explored about fifty subreddits related to trading and finance and read hundreds of posts. It turned out that the best posts *do* tend to bubble up on the major subreddits, and that's where the lion's share of discussion occurs. There were about eight worth adding and another five that I continued to experiment with. I didn't blend the content proportionally. Rather, I made it so that lesser-known subreddits could have up to two of their posts displayed on the front page of Cutlet Feed.

Again, this wasn't met with an outpouring of joy, but I had confidence that it was somewhere on the spectrum of the "right" decision. The research also demonstrated that small reddit communities with as few as two or three dedicated content creators publishing charts or research could attract significant followings despite irregular posting. The default reddit feed incentivizes rapid content creation, which leads to a lack of original content and a high rate of recycling.

I also developed an overlay that provided utility to those interested in which stocks were being discussed. For any post, I analyzed the body and image text for mentions of traded symbols. I then displayed the tags, such as [GME] for Gamestop, in the same way that reddit would display tags, such as [Meme]. A user could then click the symbol tag to see more information about the stock, including pricing data, which was a feature within Cutlet.

Scrolling through a feed that contains a limitless amount of content cheapens each piece of content. Back when any web page would only show twenty results before a visitor needed to click "next" and wait a split second for another page to load, each one of those twenty results was inspected carefully. They were more valuable. These days, people flick through feeds, barely engaging with the content. Or worse, they continue scrolling ad nauseam, daring an app to *stop providing content* or *try something crazy* to grab their attention.

In the next phase of feed development, I tried something "crazy" and broke the tight dependence on reddit content while I was at it.

I sought to maintain the look and feel of the reddit feed while injecting other content types that my algorithms sourced and curated outside of the purview of reddit. I referred to this as "feed augmentation" and sometimes "feed splicing."

There is comfort in mindlessly scrolling through any feed. My idea was that by adding new types of content, I could surprise users, momentarily snapping them out of their scrolling trance and offering the opportunity to engage with the app more deeply or share content externally. By the time I started implementing my idea, there were also in-house tools within the Cutlet app that I could redirect users to.

The first thing I added was Tweets. I was already scraping Tweets related to personal finance and tagging them with any symbols that might have been mentioned. Integrating some of the popular Tweets into the feed made sense, though it might have been a violation of Twitter's terms of service. To splice in this content, I'd downrank existing reddit posts, thus creating spaces for the Tweets.

I added feed items that redirected users to other parts of the Cutlet app. Cutlet had a voice room feature, similar to Clubhouse, a pandemic-era socialization app.[15] If someone important was speaking in one of the rooms, I could splice a preview with a link to the "room" into the feed.

Reddit displays ads integrated into the feed. Anyone scraping reddit content will not find any ads—all client apps are inherently free of them. After seeing success with chatroom content, I realized that I could use the feed as an internal advertising engine!

Just as feed advertisers disguise their content to resemble actual user-generated content, I worked with our front-end engineer on other calls to action that could be spliced into the feed. We tried to avoid being annoying. Examples of the content blocks included encouragements to "Sync your brokerage account!" and "Invite a friend!" Because users were so drawn to the feed content, we were able to essentially claim "free" advertising space that directly benefited Cutlet. Users convinced to provide more details and share content externally would be more valuable. Sites like Facebook use their screen real estate to spur users to take actions that benefit Facebook. My approach was no different.

By creating a clone of reddit's "Hot feed," called the "Cutlet Feed," I was able to improve user value and differentiate the app from a run-of-the-mill reddit clone. As I assessed methods of personalization, I realized the immense power that I wielded.

Recommendations

I had a full plate at Cutlet. The top dog had ordered the technology team to implement all types of features he enjoyed in other apps. All the while, the metrics reported to investors weren't meeting expectations. I was shouldering quite the burden as the special projects guy. I eventually took a shot at implementing personalization and recommendation systems.

I had never done such a thing before. Fortunately, I found Kim Falk's *Practical Recommender Systems*.[16] The technical depth was intimidating, but the book would be useful to anyone looking to understand how recommendation systems are built and why they're important. I learned enough to have some confidence in implementing one within the Cutlet app.

To make a suggestion to a user is to make an informed guess as to the user's preferences.

It's wonderful if users gratuitously indicate their preferences. This is why new user signup flows ask so many questions—to receive responses like, "I like beer" or "I don't drink alcohol." That's helpful.

Users engaging with app content explicitly provide their preferences. *Explicit* preferences can be indicated when a user upvotes or downvotes a post. However, a software engineer would prefer an explanation for the action. Downvoting a picture of a Heineken? Maybe they don't like beer. Maybe they don't like Heineken. Maybe they love Heineken but are hungover at that moment. Accounting for the action is nice, but social media content has frustrating dimensionality.

Preferences can be inferred based on behaviors. These *implicit* preferences are measured and calculated because smartphone activity is easy to monitor. Upvoting, liking, and commenting aren't enough because some users don't ever engage using those methods. One amazing aspect of recommendation systems is that they make use of passive browsing data to infer likes and dislikes.[17]

"Implicit feedback" includes window view time and tap-scroll location. The longer a piece of content remains in the frame of an active app relative to other pieces of content, the more interested the user is in that content. Maybe a user has the Heineken picture up for twice as long relative to other items. Maybe the user upvoted everything. In those cases, the implicit action (the view time) is more useful than the upvote. Tracking how long a user views feed items can help piece together comprehensive user stories. If only billboard advertisers didn't have to rely on estimates of the number of drivers seeing their billboards.

Building recommender systems is time-consuming. These systems require preference and behavior data. They require active users! Part of my initial buildout involved outlining every possible action within the app, capturing the events, and assigning some value to the events for further analysis. For example, an upvote was +2 for a post. Clicking on a post summary to learn more was +1. Using the search box assigned a +2 to that term or phrase, even if I couldn't link it to anything concrete.

Then, I had to consider how to handle the dimensions of content. A reddit submission has so much potential meaning, it's hard to know *what* a user liked or disliked. I already knew that Cutlet users liked trading stocks. I could determine which stocks interested a user by tracking interactions with posts that were tagged with certain symbols.

Within the app, we added new, clickable buttons to indicate clear preferences. Feeds tend to have buttons along the lines of "show less of this...," but that gets back to the dimensionality problem. What part of the content is irritating? I haven't seen a big tech company get this right yet. I've clicked "show less" just to be met with messages indicating that an overly broad genre will be removed from my preferences or that the content type will reappear after a thirty-day cooling-off period. Facebook graciously accepts my indication that I want to "Hide" Reels from my Feed, yet they reappear the next time I log in. Huh?

With the other buttons I deployed at Cutlet, users could select options from a dropdown menu like, "I'm not interested in content from this community." That's much better! We don't see it more often because 1. There are still too many dimensions, which would crowd any interface; and 2. Social networks ultimately don't want users to think critically about how their preference data is recorded and used.

At scale, the possibilities are endless. As users are potentially arranged into cohorts of preference, more specific recommendations can be provided and provided much earlier. If someone spent a large proportion of time looking at posts about Delta Airlines, the inference may be that they had an interest in *the airline industry*. I could recommend content tagged with other airlines. It's possible they had an upcoming Delta flight that they were nervous about and then stopped caring about Delta after they landed. If a user reflexively scrolled past text-heavy DD posts, I could guess that that user preferred to look at memes instead. As time went on and patterns were established, I gained the confidence to quickly bucket scrollers into my pre-defined cohorts.

I built a recommendation engine. Behaviors and actions were fed in, and the engine calculated insights. This was far from a fully automated process. Often, there was no obvious insight, and the data remained for human inspection. Sometimes, behaviors did track along a pathway that I had designed, and that user's Cutlet Feed was adjusted, however slightly, to account for the recommendation. Hyper-optimized end-to-end rec systems do exist at many big tech companies. In my ragtag group, we were making minor automated recommendations; the main value was in the systems that gathered and classified feedback.

Possessing the enriched behavior data was extremely valuable. It increased the value of the users from a business standpoint and made experimentation, synonymous with "special projects," easier to iterate on and more rewarding. Whenever I visit Facebook these days, I find that my feed is filled with popular posts from niche community pages. Meta's recommendation systems know my type from my usage patterns based on where my scrollbar pauses and jumps.

Although the recommendation system at Cutlet wasn't near world-class, it helped me better understand what drives user value at big tech companies and why people spend so much time staring at their screens.

Pulling Strings

The users of Cutlet were my avatars, my puppets. I was a social scientist carrying out experiments. I was free to manipulate the app's small audience without anyone knowing who I was, what I was doing, or what I was trying to accomplish.

Humans see "news feeds" as an extension of trustworthy news broadcasts of the late twentieth century. Humans take what they see in social feeds for granted. It's uncommon to question them. It's impossible to understand exactly how the black box operates or to mandate corrective actions. This is known as *algorithmic transparency.*

Journalistic entities are held accountable largely by the same forces that have been in play for hundreds of years. Social feeds with user-generated content serve plenty of misinformation and harmful stuff, yet a platform can deflect blame by claiming there was a glitch in the system. Journalists are afforded no such deniability. The puppeteers of social media platforms can easily escape consequences.

I was benevolent with my control panel. I just wanted to appease the higher power, the guy who cut my paycheck at the end of the month. What if I went rogue?

Push Notifications

Considering that sending push notifications doesn't require any technical skills, this is one avenue that a puppeteer can easily exploit. However, unrestricted access to a notification platform for a substantial user base is uncommon. For this reason, it's rare to hear about this being functionality abused. Much more common is the story of the rogue social media intern who posts an "I quit!" declaration to the company's Facebook page.

Push notifications could be used to incite chaos just for the sake of inciting chaos. Push notifications are implicitly trusted. A message like, "Chemical gas attack in your area" could be pushed out but would likely subject the sender to criminal charges for causing a panic. A more light-hearted example would be, "I quit this dumb company! Uninstall the app!" The number of consequent uninstalls would be relative to the size of the cohort receiving the message. Remember: three percent of Cutlet users tapped notifications swaying them to update their app versions.

What about commercial gain? A notification could be sent beckoning recipients to download a different app or check out a website. Impressions have value, and push notifications generate impressions. Some advertisers would pay for such exposure and wouldn't care that this would be a betrayal of trust. Thankfully, to deal with wonky notifications, users can turn them off or uninstall the app.

One dishonest pattern is when apps provide detailed push notification controls inside the app, which can be ignored, and users continue to receive notifications. Sometimes this is fueled more by incompetence—think about electronic mailing lists that for some reason need up to seven days to remove those who have opted out.

Content Manipulation

With control of the feed, the puppeteer can get nefarious. What if the content itself was manipulated? What if John posted, "Hello my friends, how are you today?" but when his post was displayed to others, it said, "Hey morons, I'm better than you!"

This is, of course, a flagrant violation of trust in any content site. To alter John's text seems absurd and would almost certainly be grounds for a combination of defamation or impersonation lawsuits. The virtual facsimile of John appeared to type something that he *did not type*. This happened on reddit where co-founder Steve Huffman admitted that he modified comments about him that were left by Trump supporters. In his words to the Washington Post, "I abused my power to give the bullies a hard time."[18]

Dystopian. This isn't dissimilar to taking control of John's account and going on a posting spree, essentially hacking an account as a privileged insider. Every registered user is a potential puppet.

But this idea of manipulation would not likely stop with one account; it would involve manipulating numerous accounts to change messaging to essentially broaden a propaganda campaign. Hey, publicity is publicity, but this could easily be detected and proved, and it would destroy trust in the app in which it occurred.

Although I claim this is dystopian, I wonder how long it will be until *content manipulation* occurs as a matter of policy and posts are censored (manipulated) by the platforms themselves rather than being removed by content moderators. Defining what deserves censoring will turn out to be a slippery slope.

Privacy Violations

Users expect privacy, and these expectations are routinely violated. The puppeteer knows everything.

Cutlet didn't have meaningful social features. Ponder for a minute that a software engineer of a social media site could be reading users' private direct messages. I'm sure that sensitive messaging is encrypted where it matters, but for less prominent apps, who knows?

If an insider has access to a user's privileged communications, they can perpetrate harm, perhaps by extortion or physical violence. The more interesting theme here is that the puppeteer has something else—all user action data. The puppeteer knows exactly what makes someone tick.

Feed Manipulation and Objective Steering

When considering vectors for abuse of major social platforms, it's important to remember that there are countless buttons, dials, calculations, and function calls. *Why* something is displayed to a cohort of users is not easily explained in English—sometimes the puppeteers don't understand their marionettes.

The film *The Social Dilemma* contained scenes where persuasive technology systems were directed by a small team of savants at a control panel scheming to hijack attention spans from individual users.[19] Though a memorable illustration, the amount of number crunching at this scale would mean that exporting and replaying aspects of even one user's feed recommendation system output would be extremely complicated. Further, it would be nearly impossible for a lone troublemaker to change what's displayed—think about a child flipping a few switches in an aircraft cockpit.

Feeds are innately trusted to show content that people jive with. There are also implicit expectations of the veracity of what is shown. Apps exploit this trust by *strongly suggesting* to participants what their preferences could be. Suggesting new content is no different from carrying out an experiment. This happens on TikTok where autoplay is experimental and free-wheeling feedback systems suck users deeper and deeper into more niche content areas, some of which are objectionable.

Staying focused on mixed media content feeds, a puppeteer subject to few access controls (Tim O'Hearn) could insert anything into the feed. A puppeteer could change the mechanism that determines how feed items are selected and ranked. The way Cutlet Feed was set up, I could insert arbitrary content or messaging wherever I wanted or change the algorithm with a new version release that nobody had to approve.

Although Cutlet did have some neat tools by the end, most active time was spent scrolling through the modified reddit feed. I mentioned above how someone could send a push notification that would induce panic. Couldn't a puppeteer arrange a feed such that posts with bearish outlooks were prioritized, inducing a user to "panic" and make emotional trading decisions?

The objective doesn't have to be spending more time in the app. A puppeteer can arrange for complex outcomes, steering users toward special objectives. There are accusations that some websites have special algorithms just for dealing with content related to elections.[20] The conspiracy is that some of the algorithms may favor one candidate, or one belief system, over another. Because the feed is "intelligent" and impossible to audit, it's extremely hard to investigate layered manipulation.

Conclusion

In exchange for my work at Cutlet, I possess a certificate attesting to my ownership of worthless common stock as well as an insider's knowledge of how users are valued and how technology systems are built to siphon focus and manipulate behaviors.

I checked user metrics in Amplitude as if they were high scores. Developing a persuasive technology system felt like designing a video game.

Drawing scenarios on scraps of notebook paper was oddly like creating levels in my *Twisted Metal* clone from 2001, in part because I still have the handwriting of a second grader. In both cases, I sought engagement and to steer users toward an objective: beating the game.

I was fired from my job at Cutlet, and no puppet master took my place. *Game over* for the company came later in 2023. The cause could be broadly summarized as a lack of puppets.

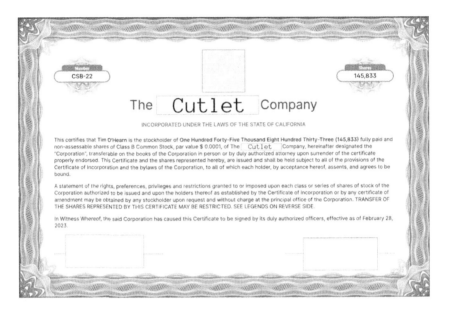

The **Cutlet** Company

INCORPORATED UNDER THE LAWS OF THE STATE OF CALIFORNIA

CSB-22

145,833

This certifies that Tim O'Hearn is the stockholder of One Hundred Forty-Five Thousand Eight Hundred Thirty-Three (145,833) fully paid and non-assessable shares of Class B Common Stock, par value $ 0.0001, of The Cutlet Company, hereinafter designated the "Corporation", transferable on the books of the Corporation in person or by duly authorized attorney upon surrender of the certificate properly endorsed. This Certificate and the shares represented hereby, are issued and shall be held subject to all of the provisions of the Certificate of Incorporation and the bylaws of the Corporation, to all of which each holder, by acceptance hereof, assents, and agrees to be bound.

A statement of the rights, preferences, privileges and restrictions granted to or imposed upon each class or series of shares of stock of the Corporation authorized to be issued and upon the holders thereof as established by the Certificate of Incorporation or by any certificate of amendment may be obtained by any stockholder upon request and without charge at the principal office of the Corporation. TRANSFER OF THE SHARES REPRESENTED BY THIS CERTIFICATE MAY BE RESTRICTED. SEE LEGENDS ON REVERSE SIDE.

In Witness Whereof, the said Corporation has caused this Certificate to be signed by its duly authorized officers, effective as of February 28, 2023.

8

INFLUENCERS, VERIFYING THEM

Influencer marketing is a rich industry in which prominent personalities on social media platforms are compensated to sell products to their followers. It's a direct-to-consumer advertising method with a high conversion rate. Everyone wants a piece of it, and I saw this firsthand as I spent months consulting for the influencer marketing startup Lionize.

Widespread knowledge that it is possible to earn money from a social media presence is good. This opportunity didn't always exist, and my optimistic view is that more people are motivated to share their talents with the world knowing there is a chance of being compensated.

The effective democratization of influencer marketing can lead to user experiences with fewer generic ads and less inorganic content. It also might mean that small business owners searching for product-market fit have an easier time breaking through to their imagined customers.

Talented individuals competing for these opportunities leads to a cornucopia of free high-quality entertainment and rapid advancements in video production and photo editing.

However, assigning such importance to influencers, to the extent that children consider "influencer" a viable career,[1] has created problems, both offline and on the platforms that empower these demigods.

First, with power comes the risk of impersonation. Providing badges to at-risk users created an underground industry in which fame-seeking users paid thousands of dollars to become "verified." We still haven't solved identity verification.

Next, with well-accepted standards of which metrics "influencers" must achieve,[2] users seeking status engage in all types of disruptive and harmful behavior, including running bots, paying for followers, and being anti-social scourges of the platforms they operate on, to say nothing of police bodycam videos where petty criminals pull the "influencer" card.

Finally, there's a constriction formed from opinions expressed in "Algorithms and Truth," "Screengrabbing," and "The Puppeteer Part I." With algorithmic support, influencers can command vast armies of followers. A growing underclass is intimidated by high-status users and may become more withdrawn and less creative.[3] For example, kids who spend all day watching people play video games may not play video games. When I was a kid, watching a friend play a game was the cruelest punishment imaginable. It is fundamentally bad when the web trends away from being participative.

This essay will examine power and clout on the internet: relevant background, avenues for monetization, what I've seen with my own eyes, and the push and pull of user-driven persuasion.

When Did Influencer Marketing First Occur?

It's too difficult to locate the first internet denizen who got paid to promote a product. However, I remember a campaign from March 2009 well because I came home from school to find my YouTube subscriptions box sullied by paid promotion.

In early 2009, before cell phones had cameras, Japanese electronics manufacturer Sanyo released the Xacti camera. Anyone serious about video content needed a separate camera (though swaths of people relied on webcams). Who better to promote digital cameras than fledgling videographers on a fledgling video-sharing platform?

On that day in March, I found my YouTube subscription box filled with videos from popular creators prominently featuring Sanyo's new camera. Occasionally, the marketing was well integrated. In other cases, such as in a video by ShayCarl, the statement was along the lines of, "HEY KIDS–BUY THE SANYO XACTI!" as he juggled several.[4]

I wrote previously that representatives from Sanyo "went directly" to YouTube channels to offer deals to creators. According to Adweek[5] and Trendhunter,[6] Madison Road Entertainment orchestrated that campaign. AdWeek wrote there was a contest called "15 Seconds of Fame" in which viewers were encouraged to submit their videos.[7] The Xacti was subsequently plastered all over YouTube. A historical search now reveals that nearly all those original promotional videos have been removed, though users frequently posted unboxing videos and reviews of the camera during the following year.[8]

The list of YouTubers who are known to have produced these early "influencer marketing" videos includes LisaNova, iJustine, AlphaCat, Rhett & Link, Mr. Safety, ApprenticeA, Brandon Hardesty, Shane Dawson, and ShayCarl.[9]

Frankly, for whatever Sanyo paid these people (Adweek claims that it was based on views), there was a substantial first-mover advantage here. This might have been the best influencer marketing campaign of all time. Owing to the weird name of the product, I've never forgotten that silly-looking handheld camera designed for video blogging. When I bought my first real camera a few years later, I admit I did check out Sanyo's products. I had been influenced.

I cannot remember if there was outward rebellion in the comments sections. What I can say, though, is that iJustine's video, which is still on YouTube,[10] had roughly seven thousand likes and seventeen hundred dislikes, which I captured while writing about this on my blog in 2020. Dislike counts are hidden from viewers now, but we can assume from that high number of dislikes that a group of users did not appreciate this early influencer marketing effort or iJustine being a *sellout*.

The irony is not lost that iJustine's video description was later bulk updated[11] to contain affiliate links for *different* cameras. She is compensated if visitors click on her personalized links and buy these products. This advertising scheme, called *affiliate marketing*,[12] proliferated long after 2009. One has to wonder whether iJustine's testimonial for the camera was authentic. Aside from the fact that she later moved on to a professional-grade studio setup, it isn't believable that she switched overnight to exclusively use Sanyo's entry-level cameras.

A July 2009 video by a very young Anthony Mennella (who now has over 800k subscribers on his Culter35 channel) both preserves clips from creators promoting Sanyo's products and humorously critiques this early influencer marketing push.[13]

By the time Culter35 posted his video, there was already another major influencer marketing campaign on YouTube for Carl's Jr., a chain of fast-food restaurants. Carl's Jr., which is known for attention-grabbing and sometimes controversial marketing, followed Sanyo's lead onto the platform. According to Adweek, creators were paid a flat fee, and another contest was pitched to the masses.[14] The campaign's decision-makers lauded the lower costs of the campaign compared to traditional TV advertising. The title of the article highlighted the trend's cost-effectiveness and novelty: "Carl's Jr. Makes New Kind of Network Buy—Burger promo leans on vast reach of YouTube content creators."

The article expanded upon tidbits that would have otherwise been lost on time. First, the author explained that YouTube "has struggled to find its footing with advertisers leery of associating with user-generated content."[15] There was also a frightening sidenote: "Google [which owns YouTube] is also clamping down on unauthorized product-placement deals. It sent letters to popular creators who have inked such deals, reminding them that using the service for commercial purposes without permission is against its terms of service."[16]

As we now know, YouTube creators would come to enjoy vast freedom to use the service "for commercial purposes." Further, these "product-placement deals" became central to influencer marketing. The floodgates had opened. Today, it's hard to find a YouTube video from a popular creator that doesn't have creator-integrated ad spots spliced into the videos in addition to YouTube ad breaks.

In promoting the Sanyo Xacti, none of the creators disclosed that they expected to be compensated by Sanyo.[17]

Badging

Before I heard the term "influencer," popular users were commonly described as (e- or cyber-) stars or celebrities.[18] Sometimes they had royal titles, such as the "Kings of Myspace"[19] or "Kimsaprincess," Kim Kardashian's Myspace username.[20]

Honorifics aside, there has always been a need to ascribe importance to users in web communities. Follower metrics are quickly retrieved today, but there wasn't always this numerical proxy for authority. When I was using the internet in the 2000s, everything from basic forums to multiplayer video games featured a badging—small, pixelated insignia displayed close to the username that conferred status.

Most internet forums displayed badges that indicated user tenure and rank in the community's pecking order. Reddit, which drove the devastation of independent forums, does allow the display of comment awards and community-specific user badges called "flair." Employees of Jagex within *Runescape* had a small icon featuring a golden crown and the letter "M" affixed to their in-game chat messages.[21] Yelp has had Yelp Elite since 2004.[22] eBay had the PowerSeller badge. Today, it seems platforms have standardized the "blue checkmark." In massive communities, badge authority has always been respected.

There doesn't seem to be widespread awareness of the origin of the blue checkmark, and critics may wonder if it's a farce, fabricated like a dictator's war medals.

Not Playing Ball

Twitter (now known as "X" but referred to as Twitter for the rest of this chapter) introduced "verification" in the summer of 2009.[23]

"Not Playing Ball,"[24] published by Twitter co-founder Biz Stone, proposed a solution to a greater problem epitomized by the story of an account impersonating the manager of the St. Louis Cardinals. The Cardinals are a baseball team, thus the "playing ball" idiom. The unofficial, parody account used the team manager's name and posted parodies that apparently weren't very funny.

That manager of the team, or his foundation, sued Twitter.[25] Stone called the lawsuit "bordering on frivolous" but said that Twitter would take steps to better enforce its terms and conditions, which already forbade impersonation.[26]

Stone announced, "Verified Accounts Beta," which he deemed an "experiment." The verification included a "special seal," now widely known as the "blue check" or "blue checkmark."[27]

Details were sparse, but Verified Accounts Beta would initially only be for *individuals*, with businesses perhaps included in the future. The announcement suggested that the program would be scaled according to "resources" without saying explicitly *how* accounts would be verified or which resources would be required.[28] In retrospect, of course, processing identification documents and assessing a user's risk of being impersonated requires considerable manpower.

Stone offhandedly mentioned that there were logical ways to determine the veracity of an account without verification, such as the presence of a social media account linked to an official website.[29] Impersonation wasn't allowed, but his point was that savvy users could figure out whether an account was real even without the presence of a blue checkmark.

Blue Checks Becoming Cool

The blue checkmark preceded an early-2010s trend of adding "Official" to display names on social media platforms. This was often a parody, a user's self-deprecating insinuation that they were not popular enough to be imitated. "Official" was also added by those who imagined themselves on a path to fame or businesses, which were not originally included in Stone's "experiment."[30]

I found plenty of companies that placed "official" in their social media descriptions, URLs, or display names. I also found a man named Dustin, who appended a literal "*Blue Checkmark*" to his Twitter username.[31] All of this was an outgrowth of look-at-me screennames, which liberally applied symbols to grab attention.

Into the mid-2010s, screennames and badging rapidly fell out of use. Sterile, standardized social media profiles were the new norm. As user count ballooned, people realized that there were few ways to stand out from the crowd. Platform owners were dealing with increased impersonation. They followed Twitter's lead.

Around May 2013, Facebook rolled out a public verification system and blue checkmarks for Facebook pages.[32] Instagram, which was already owned by Facebook at that time, added verification and blue checkmarks in December 2014.[33]

Search interest trended upward during the summer of 2018 when Instagram growth services proliferated and influencer culture became ingrained. It was in 2018 when blue checkmarks reached a fever pitch and became a topic *du jour* in rap music.

A blue checkmark indicated that a user was notable and had completed identity verification. The unintended side effect was that users who wanted to achieve importance saw Biz Stone's seal as a laurel to be attained. That was never the intention.

It turned out that effectively scaling the verification work was difficult because it required human review. In this new cottage industry, overworked guardians were exploited while Instagram and Facebook users gamed the system. Greenbacks were exchanged for blue checks. Platforms didn't see a penny of that black market activity. Cycles of users saw people they knew get verified and inundated the platforms, seeking admission into the club.

Users were willing to pay hundreds of dollars for fake followers.[34] Users were willing to pay thousands of dollars to obtain blue checkmarks.[35]

Checking Out

I was never verified on any platform. However, the CEO of the Instagram growth service I worked with paid a middleman for a "guaranteed" verification service on Instagram because the risk of being scammed was outweighed by the potential profit of white-labeling[36] someone's illicit verification service and marketing it toward customers of our Instagram growth service.

Plus, with the blue check, the sales pitches he was direct messaging to Instagram users might have had higher conversion rates.

Also, he was a musician, and the clout mattered to him. A journeyman in the growth space was powerless to resist the allure of the badge. The path was more arduous than he expected, but he successfully received the blue checkmark.

Searches for fake followers returned ads for shady sites. Searches for "How to become verified on Instagram" also returned tantalizing ads. These practices were outlawed. Providers were offering money-back guarantees. Were they legit?

Kerry Flynn's article, published on September 1, 2017, titled, "Inside the black market where people pay thousands of dollars for Instagram verification" offers insight into this world.[37]

Years before anybody really knew what was going on, and half a decade before platforms started to meaningfully alter verification approaches, Flynn conducted a laudable investigation!

Flynn identified a middleman named James who had a contact at Instagram.[38] The contact (likely someone working on the ad support team servicing big-budget clients) could submit a form to get users verified. The insider charged the middleman $1,200 each time. James then upsold the service for anywhere between "$1,500 and $7,000," depending on how moneyed and desperate he thought the client was, and pocketed all the profit

Platforms found value in verification. Select users were surely being impersonated, and others were paying so much for platform advertising that they deserved a little recognition and special treatment—another example of how advertisers can destabilize platforms.

I realize that people pay more for cosmetic upgrades in video games, but thousands of dollars for verification in the 2010s strikes me as a gigantic sum of money. That base price reflects Instagram's relevance in 2017.

Verification approvals were bottlenecked because Instagram's human processors restricted the reviews and approvals. So, the corrupt employees or ad partners could sneak fewer than a handful per week.[39] This became a matter of supply and demand, and as time went on, premium providers started charging upwards of ten thousand dollars.

With such huge amounts of coinage changing hands, a trust scam arose. Promises of "verification or your money back" actually meant no verification, being coerced to wait past any refund period, and no money back. There is no doubt that gullible wannabe influencers were shaken down for hundreds of thousands of dollars by fake, unscrupulous, Instagram blue-check middlemen. The best middlemen couldn't advertise themselves well for fear of exposing their connections. Everything depended on webs of referrals and blind trust. The guys selling badges needed badges.

By the time my friend sought verification, the process was more involved and expensive. Kerry Flynn's article didn't mention the need for a certain follower count or newsworthiness.[40] When my friend pursued verification, he needed to reach ten thousand followers and have three news articles mention his name.

Of course, providers lined up to offer those services at inflated fees. The end-to-end fee schedule that I reviewed, which included gaining (fake) followers and (usually, very crappy) news articles cost between six and ten thousand dollars.

The Instagram contact was the most important step. Flynn's article mentioned an *insider*. My friend's middleman also had a "contact." I guess this could have been any company that had spent a huge sum of money on Meta ads such that it had a personal support rep. Blue check requests were piped through this rep, who was not explicitly bribed. Presumably, it worked because companies with high marketing spend get elevated privileges.

Getting "enough" followers organically could take months or years. For those seeking verification, the answer was always to buy abundant fake followers. Although I find it hard to believe, reps at Meta weren't checking follower engagement or scanning for follower quality.

The news article requirement makes sense. What defines notability and how could it be faked? There are a lot of websites on the internet (I own several). The middlemen would pay small sums of money for fake articles to be written about influencers and then post them on crappy sites. Wikipedia editors carefully enforce "notability"[41] and aggressively delete pages that haven't met the guidelines. Whoever approved Instagram influencers didn't seem to care—barely legible hobbyist blogs were good enough.[42] This worked best for musicians to prove they had songs on streaming platforms.

The article quality was terrible, and the websites had little to no standards or domain authority. The sites seemed to exist just to promote those seeking blue checkmarks![43] As I was loosely involved in the black hat backlinking space, I can say that countless websites exist just to fool search engines into allocating more authority to websites or subjects that don't deserve it. Backlinks not explicitly identified as spam can fool Google's PageRank algorithm[44] (even temporarily). Google invests heavily in identifying and penalizing these poor-quality sites but doesn't consider whether they improve an underpaid verification verifier's awareness of how notable an influencer is. Assessing the authority of sites below big brand names is tough; it takes so long to unravel backlink networks and evaluate bogus content.

Paid placements ranged from fifty dollars on crappy sites to five hundred dollars on Forbes, which was effectively a pay-to-play brand name. Don't take anyone seriously who claims to have been featured on Forbes.[45]

After all the work, hassle, and waiting, maybe the blue check would never come. Worse, it could be removed later[46] and there would be no way to claw money back from the middleman.

Established PR agencies offered the service at huge premiums. One example was Otter PR, a company I followed for years. They also offered

YouTube and Twitter verification. Providers charged more and more for the service while the "guaranteed" aspect and timeline became more footnotes than selling points.

In their recent iteration of Instagram verification, the timeline Otter PR provided spanned about twelve months. The service cost an eye-popping twenty-five thousand dollars.[47]

My Mom's LinkedIn Was Hacked as I Was Writing This Chapter

As I wrote this essay, a former colleague reached out to ask, "Do you know Susan O'Hearn?"

I said, "Sure I do, that's my mom." Knowing that Susan isn't a common first name and that O'Hearn is rare amongst Irish surnames, I figured something was up.

My colleague explained that my mom had sent him a connection request on LinkedIn that morning. My mom had been retired for over ten years and had likely never logged in to LinkedIn after I first created a profile for her in 2012. She had never even uploaded a profile picture. So, I checked LinkedIn.

To my surprise, a woman named Susan O'Hearn from my hometown of Scranton, Pennsylvania, was on LinkedIn at that very moment. She had a profile picture. We had a few mutual connections. At a quick glance, her LinkedIn Premium badged profile seemed legitimate.

What a weird coincidence, I thought. I started typing an introductory message to her: "How is this my first time hearing about you, and under what circumstances could we have mutual connections both from my high school friend group and my college friend group?"

When I perused her fifty-or-so connections, I saw names of my mom's past business associates and even her best friend Peggy. I realized that I was already connected to *this* Susan O'Hearn. Then, panicked, when I searched for my mom's account, it was nowhere to be found! Sure enough, this Susan O'Hearn's account had been created in 2012, just like my mom's had. It *was* my mom's LinkedIn account.

It was probably a scam to post fake job postings from a seemingly trustworthy account. The job postings would either store sensitive personal information or play a longer game with an overpayment or task completion scam. That's what shmucks who got hacked around the same time were saying. I reported the account, and, thankfully, nobody was victimized.

This made me realize that LinkedIn is probably the most trusted network. Everything that happens on LinkedIn gets taken more seriously than anywhere else. Users are on their best behavior.

Seeing a request from the mother of one of your connections certainly grabs your attention. Nothing about the fake Susan O'Hearn account would look particularly fake to a professional browsing LinkedIn on a lunch break. Unlike other social networks that encourage frequent posts, ninety-nine percent of LinkedIn users have never posted anything. It's a site updated at the cadence of major resumé changes. But it's a professional site, and everything there is more trusted. Influencers on LinkedIn who have been mocked as r/LinkedInLunatics have solid engagement rates and enjoy bands of influence.

Because of how LinkedIn profiles and LinkedIn interactions are viewed, stealing a LinkedIn account has all the makings of virtual identity theft. Reputations could be seriously harmed or hijacked, adversely affecting a business or job seeker.

While my mom was asking if she could take her computer to Geek Squad to fix it, I learned that she could recover her account by sending a picture of her ID. That would be convenient. But if my mom had already been verified, a hacker could have masqueraded as my *verified* mom, raising the risk of reputational harm!

Although continuous verification sounds absurd, I saw a real need for it and rushed to verify my own LinkedIn account. My mom's hacked account was deleted by LinkedIn within a day. As far as the internet is concerned, she never worked an honest day in her life.

Blue Checks Becoming Necessary

There were two eras for verification. The first was between 2009 and 2023 when notability and other requirements were necessary for consideration. In the other, from 2023 to the present, verification is merely validation of identity, creating a connection between a real-world entity and a virtual one.

One frustrating part about writing a non-fiction book as a part-time solo effort is that bold positions overripen and must be revised before they fall off the vine. I was proud of my original recommendation of strategies for solving the conflation of verification and notability. The first "strategy" was "verify everyone." Everyone can get verified now, at least on Facebook, Instagram, and X.[48] It's an opt-in program.

I still think we are moving toward a future where everyone is "verified" with mandatory ID submission, and because I believe identity (age) verification is crucial to a better future. I'll include the first paragraph of my original prediction here.

> The best ways to stop impersonation are to require government ID and photo verification at signup for every user, prevent those users from changing their names or demographic information, and limit non-human, non-business pages while making identities transparent. This practice will probably become standard at some point in the 2030s. For now, the issue is that the *first mover* risks scaring people away. Signup conversions will slow. Legions of employees will have to be paid to perform this work. And then they'll have to deal with the issue of straw-manning, where honest people accept payments for allowing others to use their identity (or accounts created using their identity) for blackhat or straight-up illegal purposes.

Meta Verified costs $14.99 per month and Twitter Blue costs eight dollars per month. One can only assume that the old black market for blue checks has vanished. Might there be a new black market?

I'm a proponent of stopping the bad guys. I'm a proponent of stopping misuse and upholding order. As more of our lives occur in the digital world, the concept of identity has gained increased importance. Although a few sites still offer the quasi-anonymity of "screen names," they *all* want to know who users really are. "Safety and security" are sounding increasingly justified.

One-time ID verification is well worth the effort. It's the natural progression of what Biz Stone's "experiment" was meant to be: stopping impersonators to uphold platform integrity.

However, gaining access to a verified account sounds like identity theft. My mom's LinkedIn account getting hijacked felt like identity theft, even though nothing bad happened.

Platforms have a vested interest in knowing that whoever logs in is who they say they are. If an ID has already been provided, they'd love to know that the person logging in matches the ID. Unfortunately, this is hard to do.

Why bother? Netflix wants to ensure that users aren't sharing accounts.[49] Uber wants to ensure that users aren't sharing *driver* accounts.[50] Meta doesn't want users on its platforms claiming they are someone not using the account. Online banks don't want anyone other than the account holder to log into that person's account.[51]

Two-factor authentication (2FA) provides extra security but no guarantee of the identity of the person actually using the account. A thief can steal a password and a 2FA device to log into the account. If on a suspicious unknown IP address, a login gateway could thwart a hacker. But what if permission was willingly granted? It becomes hazardous, beyond two friends ripping off Netflix.

There is currently a black market for "verified" Uber accounts so people without valid driving licenses can drive for Uber and earn money. There is a similar black market for Doordash delivery accounts.[52]

CAPTCHAs help stop bots.[53] Too much resistance ruins the user experience though. CAPTCHAs that are too difficult hurt conversions and engagement.[54]

To stop impersonators, including *permitted* impersonators, platforms must implement "continuous verification." At what cost?

Continuous verification is frequent biometric verification that users are who they say they are. However, no implementation is unobtrusive. Continuous verification is continuous monitoring. It's Big Brother. It's the final, ugly, frontier of the Information Age. The technology isn't entirely where it needs to be for this to happen. It would be costly to implement, and it would royally piss off users. It's not yet practical or intuitive but will gain traction one day and perhaps be mandated by law.

Should users need to pass a facial recognition test every time they log into YouTube? Probably not. Should Uber require facial recognition verification every fifteen minutes? I would say, almost certainly, yes. There's a balance to be achieved depending on the use case and the potential damage that an impersonator could do. Since only the largest software companies seem comfortable with ID verification, it'll be a while before continuous verification becomes mainstream. However, better enforcement is needed, especially in cases where dangerous or unqualified users misrepresent themselves.

Banking apps (understandably) force users to log off after frustratingly brief periods of inactivity. Nobody will rush to admit it, but that logout cadence is comparable to what would be necessary for continuous verification.

Influence Unchecked

I was born in the 1990s and picked up skateboarding in middle school. One of the biggest influences on me as a young skater was Bam Margera and his *CKY* crew. As *CKY* morphed into *Jackass*, Bam took the home video to the extreme.

My friend group obtained weird, off-brand cameras—not the Sanyo Xacti but even stranger products that saved onto file formats lost to time. By 2008, a few of us had horrific cell phone cameras. Whenever the gang came together, we filmed stunt and prank movies.

We broke bones, curfews, and laws. One of the first videos I uploaded to Facebook in October 2008 was of my friend Jud lighting Axe body spray on fire and using it as a flamethrower.

A September 2007 article warned, "Turning [Axe Body Spray] into a makeshift mini flame thrower...is so popular, social networking websites like Facebook have groups dedicated to it."[55]

Our influencers were frontmen of emo bands and amateur stuntmen, like Bam and Johnny Knoxville. We built our camera presence based on what we had seen. Like other outcasts, we gained confidence by emulating the people influencing us from—to mark my age—MTV.

When Donald Trump was elected to his first term in 2016, I was living in Chicago. On November 9, 2016, I heard there was a gathering near Trump Tower and left my high-rise apartment to go find the crowd. I streamed the event on Facebook Live.

Fishing for this video was difficult. Eventually, I remembered that I had titled it, "TRUMP RIOT." When I searched my post history for "Trump," Facebook returned no results. When I searched for "riot," the "TRUMP RIOT" video appeared.

The results only make sense if searches for "Trump" are suppressed by the search algorithm—there is a "word list" of terms that are being excluded from results, falsifying that I never posted about "Trump." I suspect a rule is encoded into the search algorithm that quietly disallows me from searching for Trump. Taking it further, if I search for "big riot," the video appears, but when I try for an exact match of "trump riot," I again get no results.

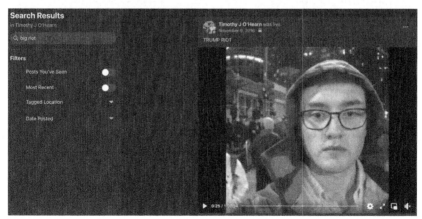

Although I had left my flamethrower at home, I will report that for the one hour that I streamed the event, I was an influencer, military surplus jacket and all.

During my march around downtown Chicago, I became aware of a warped sense of self. When I "interviewed" people or when they grabbed my phone, I saw shades of obsession. The manner of speaking and eye contact was like everyone was more practiced than Bam Margera had been the last time I saw him on *Viva La Bam*.

I thought about all the times I bolted from my parents' house when a friend called to say he had an idea for a new video. Sure, we had all wanted to be "on camera" back then, but I detected a new craving for attention. For exposure. For influence. When I was a kid, a camera meant newsworthiness. When I was a teenager, a camera meant we were about to attempt a round-about wooing of female classmates. As an adult in the Trump protest crowd, people battled for the privilege of filling my front-facing camera with their heads.

People broke bones because of Bam Margera. People participated in the widespread meme-ing of pop music by following Logan Paul's lead on Vine.[56] During the first decade of influencers, followers bought the Sanyo Xacti because ShayCarl juggled it. But they also entered the contest—they participated.

Today, the difference is that influencers are so compelling, so accessible, and so numerous, that they are a paralyzing distraction. Sure, influencers are shilling products more than ever and exposing kids to gambling and sexualized content.[57] There are problems. To me, one of the biggest concerns is that a growing portion of audiences are not going outside and attempting trick shots after watching a Dude Perfect trick shot video. They are not participating.

"Do not try this at home" disclaimers are superimposed only as a comedic element.

Content creation has never been more democratized, yet fewer people bother. When they do, it's just front-facing camera drivel. They prefer to scroll, swipe, and like. The furor of getting the gang together and filming a stunt video is something of the past. Influencing has shaped the internet such that developing hobbies, preferences, skills, and independent thoughts are discouraged. The blue checkmark is reimagined as a prerequisite, a license to create content that is taken seriously. Without it, why bother?

9

PUNISHING CRIME

C ountries have laws. Jurisdictions investigate crimes and assign punishments. The consequence of jaywalking can be a ticket and a fine, particularly in Hawaii. In Hawaii, murder carries a life sentence because that state has abolished the death penalty. When the legal system doesn't cover an offense, social systems fill in the gaps. There is a moral compass.

Private companies set their own terms. They can refuse service to violators or anyone. News organizations help enforce ethics and morality while providing extra bite to crimestoppers. Coverage focusing on scams like pig butchering, however, can obfuscate that the internet contains a spectrum of malfeasance, ranging from violations of social contracts, ethics, and terms of service to the most heinous crimes imaginable.

Headwear Shading

Behavior on the internet can be classified along the same lines as old Western flicks, wherein bad guys wore black hats and the lawmen wore white hats. Black-hat-white-hat terminology appeared on the internet long before I started dialing in. The association is strongest in the realm of cyber-security. Although "hack" has a negative connotation, some hackers are benevolent. We call them white hat hackers, and their opposites, the "bad guys," black hat hackers.

Black hat hackers exploit security holes for personal gain.[1] White hat hackers operate with the full permission of a system owner and do not publicize, weaponize, or monetize their findings.[2] They are the white knights, or so say the ethicists analyzing their activities. They play by the rules and are sometimes rewarded with cash bounties and lucrative consulting contracts. Sometimes they're still charged with crimes.

The internet outgrew movie tropes with the realization that human behavior is not black and white. The spectrum of cybersecurity-related activities led to the rise of the debated term, "grey hat," which spurs meaningful debate.

I won't focus on traditional hacking, such as ransomware, phishing, espionage, and viruses. The only virus featured in this book is the Samy Worm unleashed on Myspace. Rather my discussion is on API hacking,[3] which can be performed in the black hat sense when violating service agreements and laws.

"Black" and "white hat" labels are still primarily used when discussing cybersecurity. However, the factors behind shaded headwear are increasingly used as a proxy for concepts like user trustworthiness and behavior net cost. Social media platforms have internal scoring systems to rate the *trust* or *quality* of their users.[4]

Low-quality users label their behaviors as "black hat" in lieu of admitting that the activities are harmful, violating, or illegal. Black hat *hackers* understand their wrongdoing carries a risk. Black hat *users* may be aware that they're violating terms, facilitating rule-breaking, or making the experience less enjoyable for everyone else. Like petty criminals, they wield the "I didn't know what I was doing was wrong" excuse.

Nowadays, the shading depends on who is classifying while applying a subjective matrix of cost and benefit. My attempt at such an analysis breaks down the relationship between an actor, other users, and the platform:

- *Illegality/Criminality*
  - The behavior breaks laws or encourages or facilitates the breaking of laws.
- *Cost to platform owner*
  - The actions cause higher (technology, legal, moderation)

costs for the platform.
  - The actions result in less revenue for the platform.
- *Disruption/hindrance* of platform activities
  - Everything from spam to outright denial of service. Up to a certain threshold, spam's *cost* to a platform owner is effectively zero. However, its disruptiveness is always non-zero.
- Indirect *cost* to the system
  - The continuance of a practice that sets a bad legal or behavioral precedent.
- *Harm* done to victims
  - Ranging from annoyance to physical harm to monetary cost.
- *Non-compliance* to terms of service
  - Violating terms *almost always* means direct or indirect cost to a platform owner, harm done to other platform users, or setting a negative precedent. However, sometimes terms of service can be downright frivolous.
- *Non-conformance* to ethics and social codes
  - Bad stuff that may or may not be covered explicitly by laws or terms of service.
- Actor's motivation, intentions, and anticipated payoff
  - If a disruptive user is a charitable organization, the trust score should be higher than if a disruptive user is selling penis enlargement pills, even if both are engaging in the same disruptive behavior (say, sending unwanted DMs linking to an external site).
  - Generally, the more money an actor earns, the less favorably their activity is viewed. The skeevier the end product, the less favorably their activity is viewed (porn, drugs, scam-facilitating, and gambling are bad). A college hackathon participant should get more leeway than a startup employing ten people because the latter should know better and that the former isn't motivated by profit. However, platforms don't have systematic classification, it's only usually evaluated in cases where legal action is being considered.

Black Hat World

Spammers warmly embraced the concept of black hat for their "black hat marketing" activities. Email spam furthered the goals of the senders at a cost to everyone else. At their core, spam and similar disruptive behaviors *are* marketing. *Spam is marketing; spam is sales.*

Black hat practitioners are willing to violate terms or social contracts to pursue their goals, such as increasing website traffic. Being a nuisance or degrading the experience within a media platform or an email inbox isn't a concern to them. They are sociopathic. Black hat marketing is less violating than *hacking* and significantly easier to participate in to extract profit. More people *market* than *hack*.

BlackHatWorld.com (BHW) is a forum and central repository for profit-at-any-cost digital marketing schemes that often infringe on codes of conduct, community guidelines, and ethics. The official branding is more neutral: "BlackHatWorld is a professionally moderated, large community where millions of SEO Enthusiasts, Affiliate Marketers and Internet Marketers discuss the latest trends in marketing and making money online."[5] Founded in 2005, the website has long been a breeding ground for illicit practices that exploit and circumvent things like Google's PageRank, anti-spam systems, and copyright laws.[6]

BlackHatWorld is an old-timey forum with ugly graphics and a navigation experience that has fallen out of vogue. Threads are sorted in descending order of most recent activity, which has revived the once-ubiquitous tendency to reply to threads with nothing of value to "bump" them to the top of the navigation stack. It is richly ironic that a website that has facilitated untold volumes of spam has found it necessary to implement anti-spam policies limiting how often users can bump their threads.

The website tends to attract the lowest common denominator, hordes of visitors who are seduced by the dark branding indicating that something dishonorable awaits inside. I posit that BlackHatWorld stirs emotions of vintage internet evildoing, which continues to draw visitors.

I first encountered BlackHatWorld in the mid-2000s. I was dying to dive into internet buffoonery. The site provides relatively straightforward guides on devising and deploying moneymaking schemes with no initial investment or technical knowledge. The threads that stick out on the front page are apparent black-hat services that could help me earn money or gain web traffic:

- "SPOTIFY DESKTOP STREAMS [EARN MONEY WITH YOUR MUSIC] BOOST YOUR STREAMS LEGITLY"
- "[Reviewers Wanted] Our Upcoming Scraping Service - We can scrape anything"
- "SMM PANEL | Free Test | Buy Cheap Instagram - YouTube - Spotify - Twitter - TikTok And More! INSTANT & 24 HRS SUPPORT!"
- "20 High Authority Contextual Backlinks Only $59 DA 99 | DA 95 | DA 94 | DA 92 & More (Review Copy)"

Wedged between flagrant terms of service violations are thousands of pages discussing conforming services, such as web design, content creation, and even a section titled, "White Hat SEO." BlackHatWorld isn't all bad, but it's a bottom-of-the-barrel repository of activities that no reputable website wants to host. For this reason, BlackHatWorld, despite receiving millions of unique pageviews per month, appears unable to attract mainstream advertising partners.

It's not a free-for-all. Section three of the site's terms and rules outlines a dizzying amount of prohibited actions.[7] Ironically, it starts by banning "any illegal service," yet the site hosts tons of SMM panels that were ruled illegal by the precedent established in the Devumi case.[8]

However, BHW's continued existence suggests a degree of conformance to laws and regulations. If the community was that much of a scourge, a web host would be pressured to peg the site as a danger and elect not to host its content. If enough web hosts colluded, the site could, effectively, be knocked off the internet. A website remaining accessible goes beyond the American war cry of "free speech." When condoning lawbreaking, sometimes websites are forced off the surface web, even when the content may be interpreted as "free speech."

BlackHatWorld remains an invaluable resource for those looking to learn more about the latest trends in internet marketing and understand trends and lines in the sand pertaining to black hat techniques—controversial practices that aren't plainly illegal.

When Keeping it Rad Goes Wrong

A service built upon grey hat access patterns that becomes too disruptive might incur a lawsuit. Tech companies wield considerable legal might but don't waste resources chasing down bands of twenty-year-olds who decided to spend a week maniacally coding a hackathon idea. Tech companies aren't drafting demand letters to inconsequential players. They're interested in larger violations from established businesses.

Any communications between platform owners and groups violating their terms of service or intellectual property usually comprise a cease-and-desist letter, which usually scares people off and convinces them to close up shop. Startup founders have grown comfortable wading into such activities, believing the worst that can happen is receiving a cease-and-desist or strongly worded email—a digital *slap on the wrist*.

Web scraping is a method of harvesting content from a website agnostic of API access or terms of service. If a human can see or access a website, it can be scraped by a machine. Some sites host valuable information that may be ancillary to the primary business. These days, the more valuable the minable data, the harder the host will make it to scrape. Requiring a visitor to create an account to view certain material helps counter scraping. However, if scraping is too difficult, usability issues may turn away legitimate visitors, which isn't good either. TikTok users would spend less time scrolling if they were regularly presented with intrusive CAPTCHAs.[9]

Craigslist.org, a classified listing website that may be as old as the internet, has been plagued by so-called "aggregators" for much of its existence. Craigslist remains humble and accessible, with dozens of categories for listings of goods and services. Aggregator sites exploit its simple design by employing scraping programs to download listings from Craigslist before reassembling them on their own platforms. Those platforms tend to be sleeker and more built-for-purpose than Craigslist, but they rely on the data Craigslist hosts.

In April 2017, Jeffrey Neuburger, a lawyer with Proskauer, detailed that Craigslist had received a sixty-million-dollar judgment against the company behind a mobile application called RadPad.[10] About a third of the settlement was on copyright grounds: RadPad was found to have scraped user-generated content from Craigslist. Presumably, the content was apartment listings, which Craigslist is well-known for hosting.

Craigslist had previously served RadPad with a cease-and-desist order to stop scraping the content. RadPad ignored it and instead "used sophisticated techniques to evade detection." RadPad used the data for its own "commercial purposes." It became insolvent during the proceedings, so there wasn't much of a battle in court.

What's significant about the RadPad case is that it set a strong precedent that user-generated content could be copyrighted and its scraping for commercial purposes is a breach of copyright law.[11] It shifted such practices from being "grey hat" and "inadvisable" to "black hat" and illegal.

RadPad seems like an open-and-shut case. But two opportunities still tempt reckless entrepreneurs: 1) Platforms start enforcement with a cease-and-desist; and 2) It remains hard to prove that *scraping* is malicious, even when it violates terms of service. This is with the admission that every major website's rules include the prohibition of scraping.

It's ultimately what a scraper elects to *do* with scraped, copyrighted data that motivates legal action. It can be assumed that RadPad's business extracted major value from the Craigslist content, otherwise, it would have complied with the cease-and-desist or found an alternative. It is also reasonable to think that RadPad's activities harmed Craigslist and Craigslist users. It is reasonable that a court found it illegal and that courts don't favor introducing spectrums, as I've done.

If I were the CEO of RadPad, I would have explained to prospective employees and investors that the actions underpinning that platform were "grey hat"[12]—"probably violating the terms but ahh who really cares, so far, so good right?" As in my own businesses, this type of justification is commonplace until the legal threats start rolling.

Despite this precedent, guides for scraping copyrighted content pervade BlackHatWorld, and, likely, so do marketplace pages for reselling aggregated scraped data. Anything used for a commercial purpose would therefore be *illegal* and violate BHW's terms.

Is it farfetched to claim that Craigslist users were harmed? What if someone posted an apartment listing on Craigslist, it was reposted without their consent on a website like RadPad, and the original poster successfully rented out their place, but RadPad took too long to update the listing as off the market? RadPad could direct dozens of irrelevant leads to the user. That wouldn't be the end of the world, but it would be annoying, and the user would justifiably think, "Why would Craigslist allow this?" It would probably harm the reputation of Craigslist more than RadPad. This is a central concern with aggregator sites, even those that redirect traffic to the sites they *borrow* content from.

If a company can't prove that its scraped data is being used in a competitor's product, it's hard to build a case. If a property listing is present on other sites like Zillow, a defense lawyer could cast doubt on the claim. Sometimes to catch bad actors, companies get creative, genius, even.

Genius

Finding song lyrics on the internet used to be difficult. Websites such as A-Z Lyrics and MetroLyrics arose to satisfy a ballooning interest in lyrical content. These lyrics were used for ad hoc karaoke sessions and often placed in AOL Instant Messenger away messages. The home page from 2006 is dripping with early-internet charm.[13]

> Welcome to the A-Z LYRICS UNIVERSE !
>
> It's a place where all searches end!
>
> We have a large, every day growing universe of lyrics where stars of all genres and ages shine.
>
> Use Lyrics Request Section to request lyrics that you didn't find here. We have 90% successful request answers.
>
> You can Add Lyrics to this site, it's as easy as requesting. If you found [sic] any mistakes in some of our lyrics you can always Correct them.
>
> And don't forget to sign our Guestbook and drop us a few lines.

One of the funny things about this early Web 2.0 user-generated content is that sometimes it took *days* for the lyrics of a chart-topping single to be posted on a lyric site. Even today, A-Z Lyrics' submission page warns that it can take up to a week for new lyrics to be posted. The other funny thing was that the lyrics weren't always correct. The same angsty teenagers jamming to Fall Out Boy were also sloppily transcribing the choruses.

In August 2009, Rap Genius launched.[14] The technology startup not only transcribed lyrics of rap music but also took user-generated content to the next level. It encouraged users (and rappers) to annotate lyrics and interpret and explain them with highlighted comments. To earn a score, called "IQ," for contributions. Rap is a dense genre. Wordplay and references are a big part of the music. I thought Rap Genius was a genius idea. Series A investors included the rapper Nas and the founder of reddit, Alexis Ohanian.[15] The company's ultimate goal was to annotate written content across the web.[16]

The masses just wanted the lyrics.

Google saw an opportunity. The search giant had started providing song lyrics in a search-native format by December 23, 2014.[17] This meant that a box filled with music lyrics would be displayed at the top of Google Search results like the number "4" would be for the query "2+2=." Officially, this is called a OneBox and is meant to serve as an instant answer for queries when users prefer not to click on a search result.[18] Google's OneBox for lyrics discouraged users from clicking on results from Rap Genius, A-Z Lyrics, and other sites that appeared below it.

At face value, this sounds like anti-competitive behavior. Rather than Google acting as a benevolent tyrant extracting tolls from map games like GeoGuessr, it's a bully, utilizing inside knowledge of lyric-search activity to display lyrics and annihilate traffic to lyric sites. When an antitrust case finally mandates a breakup of Google, what happened with the lyrics OneBox might not even be a footnote.

This sentiment was captured in a September 2021 reddit thread on r/google titled, "Google search for lyrics is kinda douchebaggy."

Rap Genius, known simply as "Genius" since July 2014, complained that traffic was effectively stolen. The memorable part of the complaints was that Google was also stealing the correct lyrics from Genius.

Just as in the RadPad case, how could a company prove that its content was scraped? Genius would need to prove the content could only be found on its site, which would be pretty difficult when dozens of websites host song lyrics.

Genius, true to its name, executed a brilliant plan. According to *PCMag*,[19] *The Verge*,[20] and legal documents I reviewed, the company baited Google and "watermarked" its lyrics by alternating curly and straight apostrophes. When Genius analyzed Google's OneBox lyrics, sure enough, they contained the watermark, which apparently spelled "RED HANDED" in Morse code.

There were other nuances to the case. Genius struggled to fight on copyright grounds because though user-generated content on the site (the lyric interpretations) was copyrighted by Genius, the company did not own the copyrights to any of the song lyrics on its site.[21] So instead, Genius argued that terms of service were violated: its content (user-generated *transcriptions* of the lyrics) was used without permission and its website was being scraped programmatically.

Genius accused Google of employing black hat methods to obtain song lyrics.

Google's defense was that Genius was trying to "invent new rights through a purported contract," according to Reuters, and that Google itself didn't assemble the lyrics but had an arrangement with a third party called LyricFind that provided the "licensed" lyrics. Red-handed, indeed. If Lyric-Find wasn't scraping Genius, someone in the chain was. The United States Supreme Court declined to hear the case in 2023,[22] upholding a lower court's 2022 decision that said Genius could only fight the case on copyright grounds. The precedent is scary because, according to Josh Rosenkranz, a Genius lawyer, it "allows companies like Google to swallow up their competitors by misappropriating their content without any repercussions."[23]

Although Genius remains a wonderful source of rap lyric interpretations, there is no question that it failed to realize its grand vision for the music industry and web annotation. As a result of the "RED HANDED" fiasco, Google started attributing and linking to sources for song lyrics in the bottom margin of its OneBox. In the scheme of lyrics on the internet, this concession means that Genius is *literally* a footnote, a "marginal" player. The traffic bleed-out from Genius has been happening for more than a decade, and the extent to which Google stunted the company's potential is hard to fathom, even by someone with a high IQ.

hiQ Labs

What happened when hackathon hackers kept working on projects using private APIs and scraped content after the end of the contest? Some valuable ideas were monetized before being vanquished by the platforms they depended on. hiQ Labs was a data analytics company that scraped, stored, and resold massive amounts of data from LinkedIn. Although there is no evidence that hiQ originated at a hackathon, the idea always struck me as something a hackathon participant would think of—predicting employee turnover by closely analyzing LinkedIn activity.[24]

Every website has users who want features that don't exist. Every website has users that seek shortcuts to success metrics, sometimes expressed as reaching an arbitrary number of followers.

There is a built-in "going rate" for obtaining more followers—running successful ad campaigns using promoted posts. This path is often avoided because it is fairly expensive and having posts marked as "sponsored" diminishes credibility. The desire for superior features is perhaps most easily provided by the platforms themselves, but if a company has a reason to withhold a broadly desired feature, enterprising software developers might take things into their own hands and create and sell them as their own services.

Such services tend to be black hat. They violate the terms of the platforms they interact with. They harm the platform in some way. At the very least, no platform wants third-party services that cannibalize ad spending or provide features included in premium subscriptions.

Web scraping is a data mining practice in which websites are visited programmatically and some content of each page is downloaded for external use. Most web scrapers operate no differently from a human clicking through pages on the internet, except viewed data is saved in a structured format. Because scrapers emulate human browsing patterns, they are slower than querying private APIs and typically require more bandwidth since the loaded data is greater.

If useful data was provided by an API, retrieving it using an HTTP request would always be preferable since it would be faster to retrieve and in a machine-readable format. Data not being available in such a format suggests that a platform does not want to give it away to data miners.

Employment data is valuable. In 2019, a startup paid me to build a system to scrape LinkedIn. My system scraped company-specific LinkedIn pages and focused on headcount growth. If I scraped a company page daily for an employee count (the number of self-identified employees on LinkedIn), I could assemble that data to show growth trends. The data was to be used by salesmen at an office-services startup to target clients.

Nobody realized when I was commissioned on the project that this was already an existing LinkedIn Premium feature since at least 2016. I only learned this years later as LinkedIn started displaying the growth indicator on company profiles to lure people into activating free Premium trials. I got paid anyway, and, despite never working at LinkedIn, I created a system dependent on scraped data that provided a feature desirable to LinkedIn users.

hiQ's cached website[25] reveals a product offering far superior to what I was contracted to do:

Data-Driven Talent Management

People Analytics using public data is what we do. The business outcome is data-driven decisions that answer key questions such as:

How do you retain the best and brightest employees? Which employees are being heavily recruited? What are your organization's skills and capabilities gaps? What talent should you recruit vs develop?

...

Keeper

Keeper is the first HCM [human capital management] tool to offer predictive attrition insights about an organization's employees based on publicly available data. The solution turns those attrition insights into consumable, easy-to-deploy action plans so HR and business leaders can retain their key talent.

By identifying risk early, addressing potential issues proactively, and deploying remedial actions quickly, Keeper drives immediate business impact across organizations - and provides a built-in feedback loop so you can communicate your retention win to management

It's easy to see how hiQ put together a lucrative product offering on the back of "publicly available" LinkedIn data.

From LinkedIn's perspective, though, there were two problems:

1. Any member of the LinkedIn "public" would feel violated upon finding out that their data could be plotted and algorithmically analyzed to determine if they were looking for new employment.

2. hiQ would have created a small army of fake accounts producing large numbers of fake actions to navigate and scrape the site.

Back in 2019, LinkedIn served hiQ with a cease-and-desist.[26] hiQ, which was probably swimming in cash and felt that the law was on its side, reacted by suing LinkedIn. My understanding is that LinkedIn had padded its letter by harnessing three legal precedents:

1. The Computer Fraud and Abuse Act (CFAA)
2. The Digital Millennium Copyright Act (DMCA)
3. The Common Law of Trespass

Items 1 and 3 deal with how the data was retrieved. Although LinkedIn is a "public" site, it takes some measures to thwart abuse. Using fake accounts to access the site and to access the site in a way different from a human user might have been considered digital trespassing (closer to hacking) or "abuse" under the umbrella of the CFAA. Furthermore, distributing and profiting from the data could have been considered copyright infringement.[27]

hiQ Labs won the initial court case. hiQ's interest in maintaining its business outweighed any interest in labeling the scraping of a public site as "abuse," according to the court. Years later, the Supreme Court heard the case. The court vacated the original judgment based on the interpretation of what constituted "abuse," but an April 2022 ruling by the Ninth Circuit affirmed that **web scraping is legal**.[28] An important precedent set is likely that while web scraping is legal, private API access would be considered unauthorized access.

LinkedIn and hiQ reached a private settlement in late 2022, and the startup closed its doors in early 2023.[29]

Gab

When I first heard of him, Andrew Torba was living the dream of any kid who grew up in Scranton, Pennsylvania. While enrolled at the University of Scranton in October 2011, he cofounded Kuhcoon, a social media marketing startup.[30] I was a senior in high school then. People were talking about this new software company, which sought to simplify the management of digital marketing campaigns by consolidating metrics from different platforms into Kuhcoon's analytics dashboard. The founding was one of the coolest things to happen in Scranton that year.

During September 2014, Kuhcoon seemed to refine its niche: it provided tools to optimize ad campaigns, specifically on Facebook. The company used machine learning and other software features to automate and optimize campaigns:

"Kuhcoon optimized Ads save over 15% on average."[31]

Back then, it's likely that the company was complying with other platforms' terms of service. It wasn't illicitly scraping data to build the product, as many big-tech-adjacent, dashboard-like services tend to do. The company claimed "4000+" users by August 2014 and secured funding from YCombinator as part of the Winter 2015 batch.[32] Later in 2015, the company moved its headquarters to Palo Alto, and Kuhcoon rebranded as *Automate Ads*.[33] Andrew Torba remained at the helm, living the dream.

By August 2016, however, Torba had left Automate Ads to start a new company: Gab.[34]

The early press suggested Gab as a more free and independent Twitter.[35] There was a mounting sentiment that Big Tech was biased and politicized. By the time Gab launched publicly in 2017, social media had become a battlefield of censorship, bans, and questionable moderation policies. Gab fulfilled a need; the new microblogging platform in an oligarchical space was viewed with apprehensive intrigue.

Silicon Valley allegedly pandered to the American left and disproportionately silenced conservative voices on platforms like Twitter. It was more personal for Torba, who in one retelling stated that "after living and working in Silicon Valley's inner circle for a year and a half [he] quickly became disillusioned with Big Tech companies."[36]

Torba's Gab origin story struck me as genuine. He fulfilled a need. Unfortunately, rather than becoming Twitter with looser content moderation, Gab almost immediately gained a reputation as a "haven"[37] for those who had been cast away from mainstream social media. Torba's late-2016 insult-laden tirades in YCombinator's alumni groups, which resulted in his ejection from the YCombinator alumni community,[38] set the tone for similar fuck-offery on Gab.

I see nothing wrong with a website's user base being politically conservative. The issue I had with Gab from the outset was that I expected a platform for fiery two-sided debates but instead encountered a 4chan-like firing range filled with virtual shouting and increasingly suspicious ideas: conspiracies, extremism, and hate speech. Also, it was overflowing with pictures, memes, and low-quality reposted content like Tweets.

As an internet instigator, I have been frustrated by the lack of a platform for meaningful discourse, and I don't think it's fair that everyone who logs into Gab is assigned a "neo-Nazi"[39] label or any other for excommunication. I think that most discussions and statements deserve First Amendment protection, even when they don't align with my belief system. This is what the reddit founders once said and got roasted for trying to insist they had never deviated from.[40]

On October 27, 2018, the Pittsburgh Synagogue shooter posted anti-Semitic hate speech on Gab before committing his horrific act.[41] At that point, Torba's dream turned into a nightmare.

I'm not here to pick sides on issues related to domestic terrorism or test the boundaries of free speech in light of such tragedies. As an internet rule-breaker, I've elected to include Andrew Torba's Gab in this essay because Gab revealed that *even when you control a software platform, someone still controls you.*

In the wake of the Pittsburgh synagogue shooting, Gab was effectively dropped by all of the services keeping it aloft—Paypal, Stripe, GoDaddy, Medium, Joyent, and Backblaze.[42] The site went offline for a time. While the internet may seem limitless, a small number of critical service providers hold the keys to operating a business on the surface web.

This practice is known as "deplatforming."[43] Andrew Torba is the poster child for it. He claims he and Gab have been banned from "25+ service providers" and that he is "personally banned" from "online banks, cryptocurrency exchanges, and Twitter."[44] Individual deplatforming (also called no-platforming) is a type of digital censorship in which a user is banned from posting content on one or more internet "platforms."

If a user is banned from Facebook, Twitter, reddit, YouTube, LinkedIn, and Medium, exposure shrinks to the point that an individual is effectively silenced. For anyone trying to make a living as a pundit, being banned from Twitter in the mid-2010s was enough to derail a career. The question of where to go next quickly leads to a dead end, especially if platform-critical services collude to decide someone *offensive* is "hateful" (or any number of other gotchas bisecting internet free speech). This practice leads to canceling controversial figures' talks at major universities, either by being disinvited or even shouted from the pulpit.

When applied to businesses on the internet, deplatforming sounds more complicated, mainly because observers won't have the same familiarity with the forces at play. It adds another layer to the original term. How can a *platform* be deplatformed?!

It's as simple as Stripe, a payment processor, messaging Gab that it was in violation of Stripe's rules and that recurring bank transfers would cease until the issues were resolved. When I was involved in the Instagram growth space, my business type was *eventually* added to Stripe's Prohibited and Restricted Businesses list,[45] so I feared this same thing.

The prohibited businesses list covers things that are widely objectionable, like illegal drugs and fake IDs. In the late 2010s, however, Stripe's list included "hair extensions" alongside resellers of fake likes and followers on social media.

Originally, Stripe's bone to pick with Gab was regarding adult content. It has been suggested that this spurred Torba's Christian rebranding of the site. Gab subsequently removed adult content.

The sticking point in the wake of the Pittsburgh shooting was, presumably, restrictions against hosting content related to "unlawful violence."[46] The defense doesn't tend to be that *calls to violence are protected*, it's that platform-service enforcement of terms can seem selective. Even the largest platforms struggle to moderate terrible stuff, and there is startlingly little room for discussion when faced with imminent deplatforming.

A warning message wouldn't cause Gab to vanish from the internet. The business would still *exist* but would be prevented from receiving money unless it bent to the terms of the payment processor, which are in turn dictated by card issuers, like VISA (which, according to Torba,[47] has blacklisted his entire family).

When researching alternative payment gateways, Torba probably noticed that all the major players (probably fewer than ten) had the same restrictions. Eventually, Gab created its own payment processor, GabPay, and launched it in 2022.[48] Such an endeavor is expensive and risky (I've looked into starting my own payment processor, and so have my friends who operate in the periphery of the gambling sector, which is also a prohibited category). That Torba's team would undertake such a task speaks to how much power payment processors wield. Torba's saga can be pieced together by anyone looking to do so; countless other stories of deplatforming and demonetization will never be told.

By nature of the enforcement action, the public doesn't see much of what happens, who it happens to, or why. In late 2022, PayPal announced that, at its sole discretion, it would fine customers up to twenty-five hundred dollars for spreading "misinformation."[49] After the backlash, the company removed the rule from its policy and insisted it had been a mistake.[50] People who spend time ragging on Gab and Andrew Torba should carve out some time to ask if PayPal's new misinformation policy wasn't a mistake.

In addition to retaliation from payment processors, domain registrars have refused to host Gab's domain name, and web-hosting providers, like GoDaddy and Microsoft Azure, have terminated or threatened to terminate. Each provider has the unrestricted ability to pressure platforms like Gab into taking action, specifically removing certain posts from the website. Additionally, Gab has been banned from Apple's App Store[51] and the Google Play Store.[52]

In the years since the deplatforming, Gab has chartered a course toward independence, building "everything"[53] to harden its online presence: "Hosting, email services, analytics tools, ecommerce, payment processing." There remains paranoia about what could happen at the ISP level. In his open letter to Elon Musk,[54] Torba states:

"What we are missing at the moment is an ISP. I fear that the next big leap of censorship is at the ISP level, with ISP's [sic] blocking access to Gab.com. You solve that problem with Starlink. Together we can build infrastructure for a free speech internet."

There are documented cases of critical service providers pressuring Gab to remove specific posts and Gab complying. Some say, "Good!" I say, "Who draws the line for the more subjective offenses? Why isn't everyone else terrified by this shadow enforcement system?" Blinded by mainstream dislike of Gab, people miss that a guy from Scranton might be fighting one of the most important battles on the internet today. By building its own platform-critical services, Gab sidestepped the internet gatekeepers and replatformed its mission.

Bump

In 2012, I purchased a batch of fake Twitter followers from a reseller, not unlike those operating on BlackHatWorld today. That wasn't my first time behaving badly on the internet. Before I knew it was possible to earn money online, I was looking up cheats and bots for computer games.

The internet presents an optional disconnect from mainstream morality and ethics. People can disregard norms in pursuit of clout, popularity, fortune, and high scores. Ironically, social networks provide detachment from real-life social systems, guilt trips, and other guardrails that enforce proper behavior. The next section traces the actions of profiteers, specifically on Instagram.

Into the 2010s, it was easy for a non-technical user to be a nuisance on any website offering social functionality. I will never forget Myspace. Today, breaking terms, conditions, or social contracts is harder; the risks of being victimized have never been higher. There are complaints that platforms are too restrictive. There is also a lack of awareness of platforms that employ squadrons of cyber police to guard against everything from spam to bullying to human trafficking to terrorism.

In "A Place for Friends, Pimps, and Whores," I paired the absurdity of the mid-2000s moniker "Myspace Pimp" with the revelation of pimps operating on Myspace trafficking vulnerable women. In a 2006 account titled "Testing the Bounds of MySpace,"[55] *Los Angeles Times* staff writer Catherine Saillant wrote: "I've covered murders, grisly accidents, airplanes falling out of the sky and, occasionally, dirty politics. But in nearly two decades of journalism, nothing has made my insides churn like seeing what my 13-year-old daughter and her friends are up to on MySpace.com." She covered a case of *pimping*—the harmless kind—she had observed on her daughter's Myspace bulletin board.

At an age closer to that of a father than a thirteen-year-old, my insides are churning, too. The internet of today is a blend of comedy and profound danger, grand opportunity and grim oppression. I've watched it evolve over the past two decades while wearing different hats.

On July 31, 2014, BlackHatWorld launched a dedicated Instagram forum.[56] There are now tens of thousands of threads that have attracted millions of views. These posts comprise the fullest history of Instagram wrongdoing on the internet. It was invaluable to my research and understanding of how automation programs came to be and how the rule-breaking eras were often delineated by Instagram's bot-busting and legal threats.

For a period of several years, I employed black hat marketing techniques on Instagram. I profited and gained clout. Each day, my "high score" ticked up.

There are startups out there with products that only exist due to grey-area access and usage patterns, whose parasitic existence depends on their ability to continue exploiting the private API of or scraping the website of a host platform. This group includes the majority of businesses that operate

Instagram-adjacent growth services.

I faced consequences for things I did on Instagram. My Twitter account —the one with five thousand extra followers—was banned years ago. Andrew Torba and I have more in common than growing up in Scranton and starting our careers with social media services startups.

The title of this chapter enforces the idea that doing bad things on the internet is degenerate and causes harm—is "punishing." It also serves to opine on how broadly criminality can be defined on the internet where black-hat villains are no longer pistol-toting horse rustlers or even fingerless-gloved cyberhackers but rather people violating terms of service to sell more products. It's also the people who were "whoring" for new friends on Myspace in 2007.[57] The chairmen classifying violations and dishing out punishments have their own interests.

Finally, this chapter is a nod to Dostoevsky's *Crime and Punishment*.[58] I believe that virtual life mirrors Dostoevsky's commentary on nihilism expressed through his protagonist, the poor student-turned-murderer, Raskolnikov. The internet robs life of meaning. Influencer culture is purely nihilistic. Though short on philosophical musings, what I've covered so far can only have been spawned by a tempest of self-importance that has warped "consequence" and "punishment." The murderers, scrollers, and engineers of today are all a bit anguished like Raskolnikov: wracked with guilt, alienated, and wondering if *perhaps it really would be better in Siberia*.

THE INSTAGRAM
UNDERWORLD AND THE
INSTAGRAM OVERWORLD

PART I

THE OVERWORLD

1

INTRODUCTION

In the first section of *Framed*, "Social Media Unfiltered," I described my viewpoints on social networks and persuasive technology. In some ways, it was a cathartic review of my adolescence. It was inspired by the investigative journalism of the *New York Times* and books like *Move Fast and Break Things: How Facebook, Google, and Amazon Cornered Culture and Undermined Democracy*. I'm thankful for Sapna Maheshwari, Jonathan Taplin, and the rest of the crew who wrote pieces that made an impression on me years ago. I view that section as a metaphorical preheating of the oven. Now it's time to cook.

The main course is Instagram and how an innocent dabble in social media tomfoolery led me to become a "top-ten" player in the Instagram growth space. I found worthy digressions at every turn. Digressions demanded changes in scope and asterisks. This became a major distraction, so I created a partition.

In the title of this second part of the book, "underworld" has two meanings: the land of the dead from Greek mythology and the realm of organized crime or, more specifically, sophisticated unethical cyber activities. I'm addressing a shadowy legal gray area while also insinuating that "users" are zombielike, braindead, and unfulfilled.

The term "underworld" suggests the presence of an "overworld," which, for many, would be a curiosity. It *looks* right but isn't the opposite of the *under*world. Overworld is a term from video games, a view of interconnected levels in a game—a "hub world."[1]

"Good" versus "evil" is also a hard contrast to substantiate here. I fixate on salacious elements and their link to what Instagram purports to be. I also cover everything that I feel other works have missed. I insist that the obsessive usage patterns typifying these apps are triggered by borrowed video game mechanics. Using a term exclusive to video games seems fitting.

In "Social Media Unfiltered," I wanted to justify why I placed some subjects upfront. As I prepare to reference them liberally, perhaps the reader will want to revisit some passages.

"They Shut Off TikTok. Now What?" revealed a bit about my daily life while making the case that the practices I learned almost a decade ago are still widely applicable on social media in 2025. It covered the excellent black hat growth articles from the *New York Times* during the beginning of my journey in 2017 and 2018. It also explained why I wrote this book and what I thought it could be.

"A Place for Friends, Pimps, and Whores" is my favorite chapter. The ridiculousness of Myspace set the stage for the evolution of social media from an after-school novelty to an ominous, pervasive juggernaut. I identified some of the earliest examples of users going to great lengths to increase their clout—including using bots—and proved that users had widely differing views on privacy and the value of social metrics, such as friend count.

"Algorithms and Truth" examined the concept and debasement of "truth" on the internet and how software engineers design algorithms to take advantage of the importance we assign to newspapers, which, I argue, is the basis of the authority of the internet. Authority is re-assigned and redefined by search engines in novel but sometimes problematic ways. The opportunities for undetectable exploitation by engineers are immense.

"Hackathon Hackers" uses the backdrop of innocent collegiate hackathons to introduce Application Programming Interfaces (APIs) and the immense value of private APIs. One of the social problems explored is that companies that once campaigned on API openness, including Instagram, have changed their tune, and curious developers may be motivated to take dishonest paths.

"Screengrabbing," in its original form, was a book within a book. The purpose of the heavily revised chapter is to give the topic of *addiction* and the *problematic use of social media* the attention it deserves. For those few who don't use smartphones and are totally disengaged from popular culture, I used tons of anecdotes to promote a coming-of-age story punctuated by rapid advancements in consumer tech.

When I began writing *Framed*, I hadn't yet served my tour of duty as the "special projects" lead at a well-funded social media startup. At Cutlet, I wore many hats and gained firsthand experience with the hot-button topics on the news and covered in other books. In "The Puppeteer Part I," I wrote about sending push notifications, designing news feeds, and tuning recommendation systems. I designed the systems manipulating the next generation of screengrabbers.

"Influencers, Verifying Them" explores self-importance and platform-designated importance on the internet. I recall unique early examples of influencer marketing from when I was a teenager. I analyze the influence of the blue checkmark and how a black market for verification thrived for years before social media platforms began selling blue checkmarks themselves.

"Punishing Crime" transitions from the social media mixed bag section to the Instagram bad behavior section and introduces the community of BlackHatWorld. It delves into conversations of right versus wrong and black and white while drawing on court cases and older definitions of what it meant to be a "hacker" misusing a service.

The chapters from the first part of *Framed* stand on their own, and I'm proud of that. Ultimately, they are designed to support and contextualize what follows. This section will be all about Instagram and my sojourn through the underworld.

2

WHY INSTAGRAM?

On my first day in Los Angeles, I was walking down Highland Avenue when a speeding car caught my attention. It was a baby blue Mustang. It was wrapped in decals for a company called Jumper Media.

Jumper Media offered an Instagram growth service.[1]

People go to LA to *be somebody* and, in that same pursuit, seek out Instagram growth services. With muscle cars, private jets, and scantily clad women, growth service providers harnessed the imagery of the good life. They pitched the life of an *influencer*. They sold the idea that being famous on Instagram was a ticket to success and celebrity, maybe in LA or maybe in Plaquemine, LA. Social clout became big business, and anyone, anywhere, could achieve it.

I admit that I had just left the Hilton Garden Inn and was about to cross Highland Avenue to eat sushi at a strip mall. But by then, my Instagram growth business had generated hundreds of thousands of dollars, and my partner had purchased his own muscle car.

Instagram launched in October 2010,[2] a few months after I received my learner's permit, a year or two after Myspace had been crushed by Facebook, and before my mom bought me my first smartphone. The timing was fortuitous, not just for young Tim O'Hearn, but for pretty much everyone on the internet. Instagram became the app of the 2010s.

Instagram: *Fast beautiful photo sharing for your iPhone.*

Instagram was part of the batch of apps that proved "mobile" was a valuable segment. Fifteen years later, everything happens on phones. Back then, analysts were doubting it. Facebook itself expressed concerns about the profitability of mobile advertising[3] before going public in May 2012, and that was after purchasing Instagram for one billion dollars.

Fast, beautiful photo sharing may have been the activity that tipped the scales—that tore people from their family desktops and family dinner tables while turning the smartphone into a generation's most valued companion.

Users started keeping score, not on games, like *Angry Birds* and *Fruit Ninja*, but on Instagram with followers, likes, and comments. Instagram's departure from Facebook was the splitting of the mutual friendship model. There were no more friends; it was all about "followers" and "following." A user could follow someone to see that user's content in their feed. Reciprocating was voluntary and part of the anticipatory rush.

Myspace paved the way for Instagram users' fixation on social metrics. When Myspace launched, users were critical of their "attention whore" friends who connected with *people they didn't know*. A few years later, Myspace "whoring" was a well-established practice.[4] Users spammed bulletin boards with their "whore train" "add me" links, they signed up for websites that streamlined the friend-adding process, and some even paid for MyFriendBot,[5] which was years ahead of its time. All of this revealed a big problem with mutual-friending and chronological feeds in which new connections were *also* spamming "add me" requests: popular users with lots of friends faced a degraded browsing experience.

Switching out the chronological bulletin feeds with intelligent "news feeds" filled with *beautiful photos* mitigated this problem. Along with the follower-following split, popular Instagram users enjoyed a clean in-app experience facilitated by a well-constructed feed. Real celebrities and businesses could coexist with regular users on the platform. Popular users didn't have to worry about responding to huge queues of friend requests. The followers accrued without acceptance necessary. Following back was their prerogative.

`280 posts 1.5M followers 2,241 following`

Instagram profile stats (posts/followers/following) have been the standard of importance on the internet for over a decade. Serious users can recite their stats more easily than their credit scores or grade point averages. Consequently, an industry dedicated to increasing user follower count burgeoned. On Myspace, users with flashy profiles called themselves "pimps"; on Instagram, it was baby blue Mustangs drivers doing the pimping.

Instagram's Emergence

Instagram became a cultural phenomenon. It became one of the biggest time sucks in history. It became the primary dating app for the smartphone generation. By 2017, the platform was flirting with *one billion* monthly active users.[6]

The question became not why, but why *not*?

Instagram's adoption had a gender gap. My buddies from high school were plenty entertained by Twitter. Teenage boys aren't crazy about taking "beautiful pictures" with prettifying filters. All my high school friends agreed on this. None of us started using Instagram until college in 2013, and we were surprised to see that women we knew from high school had post histories going back to 2011. Barely any of them followed me back.

One of my buddies put it best: "Didn't start using IG till [sic] college when I realized it would get me [the attention of women]." My motivation was similar. Once I realized it was a dating app, I started framing pretty pictures and writing cringeworthy captions.

We found the app experience irresistible due to an intelligent, algorithmically constructed feed that recommended new pages to follow while keeping users abreast of what close friends were doing. For as "simple" as the first generation of the feed was, later versions were marvels of software engineering and applied statistics. Instagram offered an infinite feed experience tailored to each user's preferences. It was unlimited entertainment, which is partly why teenagers today don't regard the app as a "girl thing."

There were so many cool profiles to follow. Dan Bilzerian might be remembered as a hypermasculine meme lord, but his being surrounded by guns, cars, mansions, airplanes, and gorgeous women spoke to the teenage male fantasy.[7] For every Dan Bilzerian, there were hundreds of Instagram influencers inhabiting those Hollywood-inspired niches. I don't think it's a leap to insist that, deep down, anyone who ended up chasing popularity and buying followers was chasing the life that Hollywood—Los Angeles—sells them.

One evening at a nightclub in Las Vegas, my business partner talked his way into joining Dan Bilzerian's table and took a picture with him. It was like he met God.

Social media services were adapted to serve the diverse needs of Instagram users. I've profiled over one hundred such businesses. Why so many? Why Instagram instead of Facebook a few years earlier or Myspace near the dawn of time? What made Instagram the center of my universe as a software entrepreneur and an everyday user? Why does it remain a battleground between rulebreakers and rule-setters?

Social Media Marketing

One factor of the proliferation of Instagram-adjacent businesses was also responsible for the explosion of web-based businesses in general. Payment processors, like Stripe, made receiving payments, especially the subscriptions that funded growth services, easier. Website builders, like Wix and Squarespace, enabled non-technical users to cheaply register domains and build interactive storefronts that listed products, accepted payments, and ranked well in search results.

Small-scale entrepreneurs benefited greatly from Stripe's innovations. Stripe provided a built-in customer relationship management (CRM) system too. Other service providers offered everything from email campaign management to low-code tools to product review aggregation dashboards. Running cheap ads was a cinch! Digital entrepreneurship became accessible to those who weren't skilled programmers in the mid-2010s.

Instagram remains a battleground, a phenomenon, a home-page designee because its formula still works—beautiful photos served by an advanced feed—and, of course, because of the network effect. Anyone not on Instagram is missing out. Instagram now claims more than *two billion* monthly active users. I'm not here to dispute its continued relevance. Its continued relevance means that thousands of new supporting businesses emerge each year.

Above all, a high follower count became a mark of notability. The question, "How many followers do you have?" became so personal. I bought five thousand fake Twitter followers in 2012. I had no income. I wanted to be famous. I was enticed by social proof imagery. Millions of others entered the same search queries I had. Instagram's follower-following split empowered fame seekers. Because the platform emerged as a virtual trophy case, Instagram followers eclipsed Twitter followers in desirability.

Hundreds of millions of humans developed a dependence on drawing their phones from their pockets, checking notifications, scrolling, tossing out likes, and then re-holstering the phones. Feel-good interactions fostered that dependence. Gaining digital interactions amplifies the emotions. What if software could provide that amplification as it had on Myspace?

How did computer software affect internet businesses? More people were learning how to program, and it went beyond Stripe integrations. Cloud providers like AWS made it easier to start and scale software businesses.

So, did devious programmers line up and "hack" Instagram to create automation tools that generated likes and followers? No. In February 2011, Instagram founder, Kevin Systrom, announced that Instagram would provide an open API.[8] His creed: "The Instagram API merely allows talented developers to create really neat and useful apps for you to get more out of your images."

Hello Developers.[9]

The first version of the Instagram API is an exciting step forward towards making it easier for users to have open access to their data. We created it so that you can surface the amazing content Instagram users share every second, in fun and innovative ways.

Build something great.

Nobody was hacking Instagram. Instagram invited developers to interact with its API. Technical founders tended to support openness and the hacker ethos. There was some symbiosis here. Independent developers could build things on top of Instagram's data and functionality. Maybe they could earn a minor profit or score a job offer from Instagram. Maybe they could win a hackathon! As a result, Instagram increased its traffic. Further, these developers were trusted to give Instagram's engineers feedback on bugs, performance problems, and desired features.

The developers had nothing to lose, but Instagram was incurring risk. If the programmatic usage was unmetered, a rogue developer could hammer Instagram's API with bogus requests, costing the company serious money in those cheap and scalable cloud computing resources and potentially degrading the platform's performance for users. Further, a resourceful developer could steal or "mine" photo content from Instagram, querying what was shared "every second,"[10] not in a "fun and innovative way," but in a constant suction of resources before selling it or using it to reverse engineer trade secrets.

On the internet, it's hard to trust users, even registered users, to be compliant and "good." Tech companies had to weigh the benefits of APIs against the risks. They implemented safeguards like rate limits, but for other vulnerabilities, they relied on spot-checking and "policy."

Instagram instituted rate limits overall and on each API endpoint.[11] In 2012, the hourly limit was five thousand total actions! Endpoint-specific actions like liking, commenting, and following were originally limited to sixty or one hundred per hour, though.

PLATFORM POLICY[12]

Before you start using the API Platform, we have a few guidelines that we'd like to tell you about. Please make sure to read the full Platform Policy. Here's what you'll read about:

1. Instagram users own their media. It's your responsibility to make sure that you respect that right.
2. You cannot use "insta", "gram" or "Instagram" in your company or product name
3. You cannot replicate the core user experience of the Instagram apps or web site. For example, do not build a media viewer.
4. You cannot use the API Platform to crawl or store users' media without their express consent.
5. Do not abuse the API Platform, automate requests, or encourage unauthentic [sic] behavior. This will get your access turned off.

Most important in Instagram's Platform Policy was item five:[13] a fully-featured public API could be used to create malicious bots that degraded the experience for everyday users, in other words, programs that abused the API Platform, automated requests, and conducted unauthentic behavior.

Even if the rate limit was sixty likes per hour as specified above, what if a program rotated through multiple access tokens?

An API providing the ability to *change* data ("publish" in Instagram's parlance) could be wielded to emulate human taps, such as liking, commenting, and following. Any API with the ability to change data on top of querying it had immense power and potential to be abused.

It wasn't long before Instagram's developer site featured a different greeting.[14] Note the emphasis on authenticity, non-automation, and the quality of apps. This is not quite the goofball-friendly sandbox first pitched in 2011.

Hello Developers.[15]

The Instagram API Platform can be used to build non-automated, authentic, high-quality apps and services that:

- Help **individuals share their own content** with 3rd party apps.
- Help **brands and advertisers** understand, manage their audience and media rights.
- Help **broadcasters and publishers** discover content, get digital rights to media, and share media with proper attribution.

In April 2018, Instagram (Facebook)[16] shut off the public API to most developers.[17,18] This broke many websites that had designed integrations to purportedly "help," as specified by the developer docs above. Users of third-party apps who didn't understand the shutdown were, justifiably, pissed. Since then, developers were only permitted to access the limited Graph API (a read-only data store), a common technology platform shared with Facebook. Right until the end, an Instagram-registered app could use the public API to follow other users (create *relationships*), like pictures, and leave comments. This functionality was widely abused.

The problem was that developers had acquired a taste for automation and inauthentic behavior. They weren't about to relinquish it. With so many documented paths to interacting with Instagram, the same developers who were encouraged to "build something great" were happy to build great client libraries for Instagram's *private* API once the public one rate-limited them or shut off access. Unfortunately, these APIs were *black hat*. They violated Instagram's terms. They couldn't be entirely prevented because the private API enabled the phones running the Instagram app to communicate with Instagram's web servers. Some programmers with advanced knowledge of how Instagram's API was structured and what it could be used for were happy to sniff the routes and rebuild what had been taken from them.

This might have become such a problem on Instagram compared to platforms that came before it because collaborative development was totally different in the late 2010s. Social code-sharing sites, like GitHub, allowed users to easily disseminate, branch, merge, and check out what they had discovered about Instagram's private API and the tools they had built to exploit it. Collaboration was easy. Hints were sprinkled throughout Black-HatWorld threads. For MyFriendBot on Myspace, comments I dug up suggested that source code zip files were being passed around on old-school discussion boards. Hardly comparable.

The amount of library code available to the novice programmer looking to build an Instagram-adjacent app was substantial. And it was that same shared codebase that gave companies like Jumper Media their start. It was the existence of that code that encouraged entrepreneurs to try to sell the dream of being an influencer. There were millions of dreamers—wannabe influencers.

3

SHARKS

Digital innocence is lost upon entering the first cheat code. Entering a cheat code in a single-player video game provides an immediate dopamine rush but without any sense of accomplishment. My experience has been that it quickly degrades a game's carefully constructed difficulty curve and ruins replayability, especially for role-playing games.

When I started playing games online against real foes, I quickly sought out cheat codes. Cheating in single-player games was benign, but I wanted to win where the stakes were higher. Finding a secret combination of buttons could help me avoid the requisite character-building or skill development.

My quest was futile. It turned out that there were some real dogs on the internet placing traps for fledgling rogues. Search queries like "cheat at *Runescape*" returned pages of results, bolstering the juvenile fantasy that cheat codes for multiplayer games existed *and* existed to be exploited solely by the lone gamer searching Google.

The viruses I downloaded in the mid-aughts while looking for cheat codes reduced my family computer processing power to that of a toaster.

Cheating in online multiplayer games isn't as simple as entering a code. Gaining an unfair advantage is much more complicated. If it was easy (or developer-supported), then everyone would cheat, there would be no balance, and honest players would have no fun. Gaining an unfair advantage is not about "cheat codes" in the traditional sense but rather combinations of input that perform a special function designed by the game creators.

A rare "hack," "glitch," or "exploit" targeting the game engine might provide a tangible advantage, but these can be patched by the game developer. The fix would be mandated for anyone wishing to continue playing online. To cheat these days requires connecting a separate program to a system's interface and having a computer program play the game or confer other advantages by augmenting the experience. Macros, auto clickers, auto typers, and aimbots provide massive advantages in online multiplayer video games.

A basic "Auto Clicker" program[1] *for the game Runescape—expressly forbidden by Runescape's rules*

Such tools are similarly used to cheat in games as they are to boost social media metrics. It can be as simple as deploying a script that automates clicking.

My start in Instagram growth was preceded by traditional solo video game cheating. My first stop was Cheatplanet.com and then the venerable GameFAQs.com. Before that, cheat codes were accessed by purchasing gaming periodicals or passing around a sheet of notebook paper at school with sequences of buttons or short instructional vignettes. The most enterprising, aspiring cheaters would enter a Blockbuster or EB Games, find the shelved magazine, search the pages, locate and copy the codes, and walk out without paying. Walkout behavior is common in dishonest communities and permeates BlackHatWorld. Script kiddies leave without paying.

Eventually, I graduated to using GameShark. GameShark was a third-party application for game consoles used to extensively modify variables within games. GameShark and its contemporaries, such as Action Replay and GameGenie, all similarly worked by modifying a game's memory as it was played. This worked because consoles of the PlayStation 2 era didn't have protections in place to prevent memory access. This unintended manipulation could render games unplayable. If a game was saved with the wrong values modified, the save would be ruined and all progress lost.

Using my GameShark on the PS2, I found certain scenarios in which the values modified in single-player persisted online. This included *Tony Hawk's Underground*, which when I played online with GameShark-augmented "perfect balance," never falling off the skateboard while performing a grind.

Its anti-cheating system was unintentional. I scored so high that I exceeded the limit of the signed integer data type, 2,147,483,647, after which my score went negative.

I spent a significant amount of time playing *THUG* online. I observed less than five percent of players obviously cheating in that 2003 title. Everyone else seemed to be "nooby" ten-year-olds just like me before I cracked the code.

A 2003 thread on Neoseeker, a gaming website, in which a user asked about cheats for THUG

On Myspace in 2008, I participated in "whore trains." The trains were an early social cheat code for gaining more friends and imagined influence. Software emerged to support the trains.

Around 2011 (after everyone had moved to Facebook for everything except local music), I learned HTML and CSS and used basic web design skills to change the displayed number of fans of my musical group. It was funny to see my cheat codes impact social situations. Classmates asked me how I had so many fans. The logic follows that plenty more visitors accepted that I *really had thousands of fans* and were impressed by the number. For artists, virtual social validation can mean everything.

During the summer of 2012, I purchased five thousand Twitter followers. I searched for a way to buy Twitter followers, found a page that looked legitimate, and bought the followers using a prepaid debit card. Much to my chagrin, those followers weren't real people. They were basic accounts with the default egg picture (discontinued in 2017), no bio, no tweets, and gibberish names. Anyone investigating my followers would have seen that they were fake and quickly concluded that I had purchased them.

Unfortunately, my original Twitter/X account was suspended

Anyone who checked the minuscule engagement rates on my tweets would also have noticed that something was amiss. But then, nobody ever verified my Myspace band page's fans, so why would they investigate my Twitter followers? Even as the fake accounts started getting banned, I began my freshman year of college with roughly 5200 Twitter groupies. To my delight, I met people during that fall semester who seemed genuinely impressed by my follower count. Back then, I posted a lot of obscure rap lyrics, and I remember one girl from my freshman dorm commenting on how weird my tweets were, "How do you have so many followers if you're so weird?"

I don't think anyone ever figured out that I edited the CSS and HTML on Myspace, but cyberspace social intelligence increased rapidly amongst those spending every day on the internet using social networks. A brash Bostonian in my freshman hall barged into my dorm room to interrogate me about my many followers. I didn't have a good answer for him and acted as if having over five thousand followers as a freshman in college with no notable web presence was normal.

Auto-clicking on *Runescape*, GameShark's perfect balance, fake Twitter followers—regardless of how the score is kept, if cracking the code is an option, we'll crack it—or try. There were print advertisements for Game-Shark. There were Google search ads for fake Twitter followers. *The existence of advertisements afforded these practices legitimacy and gave rise to a generation that believed cracking the codes to win on the internet was morally neutral.*

As my Twitter followers dwindled and it turned out that I would not be conventionally popular on campus, I entered a more traditional college existence. I began studying computer science. As I advanced through my coursework, I attempted what young men dream about: designing video games, creating the next billion-dollar app, mining Bitcoin, and "hacking." I put together a few small-scale projects. I was a grader for classes. But I went into my first internship in 2015 without anything resembling the credentials of today's top coders.

My journey as a programmer really began in 2011 when I signed up for an AP Java Programming class during my senior year of high school. I found an old forum post purportedly from *the day I signed up for the class in 2011.* My post was a response to an article on a *Runescape* fan site alleging that *Runescape* bot developers *were earning upwards of $500,000 per year.*

"The $500,000 USD estimate actually excited me about the java course i signed up for today :thumbsup: all jokes and uncertainty of actual sum aside, how many people on this forum would turn down even 100k a year if they knew how to write these scripts and clients? (to my knowledge [game-client integrated] scripting is considered one of the most advanced applications of the language)"

I find it deeply satisfying that, as a high school student, I connected software-driven cheating and the potential to earn large sums of money. By 2016, I had a lucrative job as a software developer, and by 2019, I had surpassed the "100k a year" number from my side hustle—I had written "scripts and clients" for the game of Instagram.

I graduated in 2016 and moved to Chicago for that first programming job. From the start, I was itching for more. A switch flipped as I walked home from my nine-to-five and found myself without much to do on nights or weekends. I was thinking big, reminiscing about all the opportunities for earning money I had read about on the internet. I was looking for a way to fill my free time with meaningful and, hopefully, profitable activities, even if it meant taking shortcuts.

In the summer of 2017, one of my hometown friends reached out with an opportunity. He owned a small digital marketing agency and was a DJ on the side. Through a nightlife management company that helped book his gigs, he knew another DJ who helped people acquire followers on Instagram. They had combined forces and needed a programmer.

Oh, hadn't I heard that one before?

For software engineers, there is always an opportunist waiting in the wings to pitch an idea. The "idea guy" handles the business side, and the programmer handles the hard part, which the boss thinks is the easy part. It's a match made in hell, but I've known a lot of folks who have gotten sucked into situations like this. Arguably, this happened to me at the startup I have codenamed Cutlet, though I was paid for my trouble. This type of arrangement usually results in months of poorly compensated, frustrating development work driven by the whims of a clueless non-technical founder.

This is so common that it's memed as "WSCM": "Whartonite Seeks Code Monkey."

I couldn't help but be skeptical. I ended up playing both the code monkey and the condescending Whartonite in those initial meetings. I was the shark on *Shark Tank*. Eventually, I learned that this DJ I had never met was already running the business and had customers. He wasn't a pure ideas guy. There was already cash flow. And he already *had* software.

I signed on for nights and weekends. I helped build the website, payment integration, and customer support flows. I would help design better growth software in the future. I codenamed this team, "Shark Social."

Shark Social was a traditional 2017 Instagram growth service. Customers provided their Instagram login details and targeting information based on how they wanted to promote themselves. We plugged that information into off-the-shelf software. The bot logged in to a user's account and sent likes, comments, and follows to similar accounts, and the customer's account gained reciprocal followers. Shark Social charged less than fifty dollars per month for the cheapest growth package. *The follower numbers we were getting for customers were superior to five hundred dollars per month spent on native Instagram ad spend. Organic growth automation was the cheat code.*

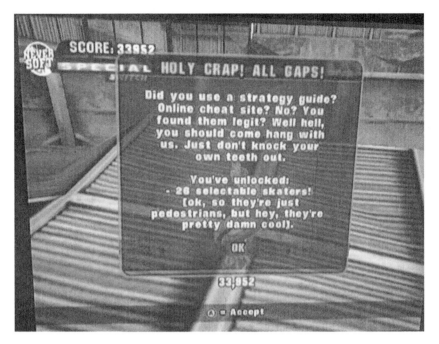

Tony Hawk's Underground accused players of cheating once they skated every named level feature ("gap") in the game.

By August 24, 2017, my systems were up and running. We received a quirky email each time a new customer signed up. Initial customers were friends, family, and business associates of the DJ duo. Nobody in my circles was interested, so I focused on tech and competitive intelligence while the turntablists sought new leads.

WordPress wordpress@⬚   Thu, Aug 24, 2017, 10:49 PM

to tim, ⬚ ⬚ ▾

Howdy, You've got a new subscriber! Email: ⬚ @ ⬚
Username: ⬚ Instagram Password: ⬚ Stripe ⬚
⬚ YEE HAW!

⬚ @⬚ ..   Thu, Aug 24, 2017, 10:52 PM

to ⬚ , tim ▾

LOLOLO YEEEE HAWWWW 🤠🤠🤠🤠

•••

One of the earliest automated customer emails

Less than a week later, Shark Social received an unexpected email. It was for a customer that nobody had prospected. Not a friend, not a family member, not a cold approach—it was an organic signup. A touchless, effortless, organic signup. Somebody waded through dozens of competitors on Google search and found us. We started a three-way call and confirmed that nobody knew who this person was.

Our first customer was a baker. Our rallying cry became, "Let's get this bread."

WordPress wordpress@███████. Aug 28, 2017, 9:34 PM ☆ ☺ ↩
to tim, ████████ ▾

Howdy,

Here are more details

████████

More Account Info: This is my personal account. I\'m looking to put myself out as a hea baker and pastry chef.

Similar Accounts: Zakthebaker, mothersoven, tartinebakery, trueloaf, breadbakersguild

Targeted Hashtags: #bread #organic #france #nyc ....

████████████████████████

Time restrictions:

YEE HAW!

WordPress Aug 29, 2017, 8:33 AM
Account email: ████████████████████████████

████████████████ Aug 29, 2017, 12:39 PM ☆ ☺ ↩
to ████ Tim ▾
Omg ████ you were right, this is all fucking bread omg im dying right now LOLOL

A baker signs up—let's get this bread.

Less than two weeks in, there was external validation. There were bumps in the road, but the customer count rose steadily as the year-end approached.

Shark Social gave me my start in the Instagram growth space. The founders later offered me a share of the revenue and a front-row seat to the most exciting segment of the Instagram underworld. I explored as much as I could. I came to understand how the fake Twitter followers sham worked. I posted on BlackHatWorld. I understood why everyday users of the platform preferred paying growth providers instead of running ads.

I learned that anyone willing to break the rules with a social media adjacent business could make a lot of money, just like the *Runescape* bot developers I wrote about in 2011.

Wait a minute—was this "organic" Instagram growth service breaking the rules of Instagram?

In April 2017, before we started our little business, Instagram shut down Instagress,[2] a software-as-a-service (SaaS) dashboard that allowed users to automate actions. A user would click a button, step away, and come back to new, real followers and comments. It was an intelligent auto clicker similar to what cheaters employed in *Runescape*. Abstractly, it made growth an *idle* game. On Instagram, none of the cheaters seemed to get banned, and nobody seemed to mind giving away their Instagram login details to the faceless Instagress.

> Sad news to all of you who fell in love with Instagress: by request of Insta-gram we were forced to close our web-service that helped you so much in your Instagram journey. We are all very sad of [sic] that but it looks like there is nothing we can do at the moment.

> Please, login into your Instagress account to request a refund.[3]

Instagress, and the organic Instagram growth industry in general, *did violate Instagram's terms of use*.[4] Instagram's terms specified that auto-mated, disruptive behavior was not allowed. Growth services that used soft-ware to automate actions directly violated that rule. Rather than hunting down every user suspected of botting, Instagram decided it was more productive to shut down the bot providers. Instagress was the largest.

Additionally, Instagress' catchy name violated Instagram's branding guidelines. The use of "Insta" in any product or service name was explicitly forbidden, at least by 2016. "Instagress" rolled off the tongue in such a way that users might have mistaken it for an official offshoot of Instagram.

The downfall of Instagress enticed a wave of successor growth services hoping to siphon off market share. We all convinced ourselves that if we didn't violate Instagram's branding or advertise our services directly on Instagram, we were safe. We had the invincibility cheat. But that cease-and-desist letter could have come at any time. We could have been terminated.

By December 2017, I couldn't stop picking up my iPhone at my day job. The most seductive notification began with "Howdy!" the new customer email from Shark Social. Outstanding days featured several. They became my comfort, my hedge, my own cheat code out of the corporate grind. Even when my phone didn't buzz, I picked it up, stared into it, and wished for a new customer.

When it came time for year-end performance reviews, I noticed some-thing funny. My manager's public Google calendar was packed with scheduled meetings. Everyone's name was there but mine and one other guy's. The consensus was that guy was *definitely* getting fired.

I remember sitting there with my ego deflated. Not getting a meeting meant that I was getting fired too from my first big software job—exactly what youthful gamers dream about. It was going to be taken away from me. Why was I being cut? Was there more honor in quitting first? Could I buy myself time and still have a merry Christmas if I faked an illness?

I remember staring at my computer screens. I checked my Jira tickets, my source code "commit history." I reminisced on the late nights I'd pulled and the lonely dinners I'd eaten in the office, often just to head home and keep coding for my second job. I remember checking my phone, scrolling through my emails, checking the Stripe dashboard, and counting the number of customers. I remember calculating the exact number of Shark Social customers needed for my share of the profit to keep me afloat until I could find another job.

I wondered, "What if I didn't need to find another job?"

The December air was cold on firing day. As I prepared to cross the street next to the old Al's Italian Beef on West Adams and South Desplaines, I ran into a friend, the guy who had mentored me when I had started as an intern. I informed him, "Well, I'm getting fired today." "Well, shit," he responded.

The other guy was fired early in the morning. He announced, "FIRED!!!!" to the lady at the front desk as he stormed out of the secure office space with the "no guns allowed" stickers on the glass doors.

I was invited to a last-minute meeting, and I planned to accept the news with poise and composure. But when I went into the room, my whole team was there. My boss announced that the other guy had been fired and asked if we had any questions. "Is that all?" I asked, dumbfounded. He replied affirmatively.

I later learned that I was supposed to be fired that day, a team lead had stuck his neck out and saved my job. Scrambled, my boss told me about my lateral move later that day. I walked out of the office into the same cold, biting Chicago wind. I realized that I needed to escape the corporate grind, and I was confident that I knew how to do it.

Unlike using cheat codes in single-player games, the more we cheated on Instagram, the more fun the game became.

4

SAY HELLO TO MY NEW GANGSTER FRIEND

As 2017 turned into 2018, Shark Social continued building momentum. More customers signed up. Average customer value increased. Each day, it felt more like my ticket to the good life.

I tried to sell the service to my friends and colleagues. Nobody was interested. The New York-based shark visited my hometown that Christmas and we hit the bars. I wasn't interested in bragging about my six-figure software job. I wanted to tell people about Shark Social. The next night, the shark, who was my friend before he was my business partner, joined me for dinner at the nicest restaurant in town. I ordered the most expensive bottle of wine, Stag's Leap "Artemis." As the waiter palmed our IDs, he remarked, "We don't sell many of these, especially to twenty-two-year-olds."

During that week, I learned that my ability to sell was pathetic. Two nightlife guys who grew up elsewhere were able to infiltrate my hometown's nightlife and generate leads. Meanwhile, the cutie from my high school cross country team hit me with, "Oh that's so cool about your Instagram thing, gotta go!" as she ran away.

Since the business kept me busy "growth hacking" and breaking the rules, there wasn't much time for focus groups or self-help books. So instead I added a field called, "More Account Info" to the product's new customer onboarding survey. Customers appreciated this, and I learned from their loquacious submissions. "More Account Info" wasn't just more info on the account, it became a repository of hopes and dreams:

> As of now, my Instagram is tailored to just be a personal account, but I am trying to get better at photography and possibly become an influencer.

> I am a Tibetan Buddhist lama, teacher, and translator. What I say and how I interact with [sic] means a great deal to me.

> I'd like to turn followers into fans and get to 20k in 2022! I'm very consistent with my content and engaging with new accounts but I'm ready to take it to the next level and finally get new eyes on my account.

As we obtained more customers, I was able to extrapolate *what Instagram users wanted*. The team developed an intuition for which customers would be pleasant to work with and which would be nightmares. We tailored our offerings to customer needs.

Some people had no plans to earn money but had vague notions of becoming "an influencer." Others had micro businesses or modest followings and were looking for a boost.

Most customers blindly subscribed to the idea that being popular on Instagram was a necessity. They were no different from 2008 Myspace users pulling zany tricks to notch more friends.

It's telling that in the *entire* "More Account Info" collection, which I preserved from Shark Social, only one customer mentioned "sales conversions." What about just "conversions"? Two people wrote that word. They were both talking about "van conversions." Amazingly, the customer who mentioned sales reasoned, "We are less interested in actual sales conversions than converting interest into followers...it's a reflection of how popular the band is."

The *one* guy who mentioned sales conversions wasn't interested in sales conversions! From tens of thousands of words of text, I learned that even the "business" people were overly attached to platform metrics and had little business sense.

Social media users seek distraction, excitement, love and an array of other emotions. They want to be popular and they want to escape reality. I've included my own caper that revealed I was, ostensibly, a gangster.

Dope

It is a cop-out to say that users are seeking either money or dopamine, which arguably, are inextricable. Books have been written about motivation and reward, including social media and brain-circuitry cheat codes like heroin, with Sam Quinones' *Dreamland: The True Tale of America's Opiate Epidemic* providing the richest description of feel-good chemicals and human susceptibility to addiction that I've read.[1]

I'm not a scientist, but much of social media villainy exists because of the uncomfortable truth that people are glued to their phones because the devices more reliably produce feel-good chemicals than the natural world. Anyone who operates a social media-adjacent business benefits from the addictive nature of social media, the precious dopamine chase. There's always a strongly motivated, captive audience; at Cutlet we realized that when splicing reddit's feed into our own, user metrics mimicked reddit user behaviors.

I hate relying on the word "dopamine." No business claims to sell dopamine. Instead, one might say, "We sell *distraction*."

Plutchik's Wheel of Emotions

The late psychologist Robert Plutchik created a wheel of emotions,[2] using color and two dimensions to illustrate intensities and the mixture of feelings. His wheel can be used to theorize social media's usage patterns and broad appeal.

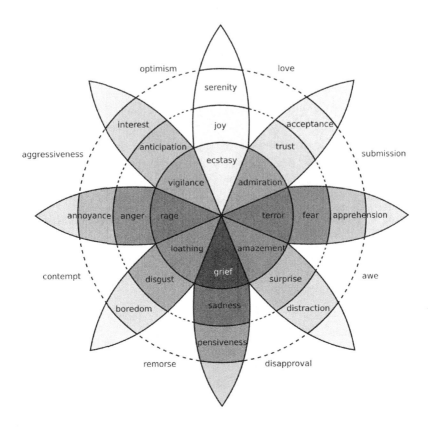

Plutchik's wheel of emotions

Plutchik proposed eight "root" emotions: anger, disgust, sadness, surprise, fear, trust, joy, and anticipation. Each emotion is bipolar and paired with an opposite. There are different intensities toward each pole. Intense anger is rage. Weak anger is annoyance. The opposite of grief is ecstasy. This may be intuitive, but Plutchik was brilliant for drawing it up this way.

Can the wheel be used to classify the emotions of digital experiences? I previously drew on the early internet meme *boom headshot*[3] to argue that video games elicit strong emotions. That video contained expressions of *ecstasy* and *rage*. Playing with others may trigger the strongest emotions, though they can also be felt when chasing single-player achievements.

I hypothesize that habitual gamers, beyond the stereotypes introduced in *boom headshot* and the famous South Park episode, "Make Love, Not Warcraft," exhibit narrower ranges of emotions. Plutchik's wheel illustrates the separation between gamers and social media users. Social media plucks entertaining elements from video games, cinema, and mobile apps and provides an *in-game experience* with implications outside of cyberspace. Things that happen on social media generally coalesce with *real life*. For this reason, these networks produce a wider range of emotions and, potentially, more intense emotions than video games. Yes, stronger ecstasy and rage than the *Counter-Strike* addict in *boom headshot*.[4] A user can run the gamut of the emotional wheel in a single day, then hit refresh.

I've never had a hardcore gamer tell me that logging on made him "hate myself." But I've met people at bars who, upon hearing about this book, have been quick to connect self-hatred, depression, anxiety, and sadness to their social media habits.

They desire this emotional rollercoaster. It's what people sign up for. It's what people log in for. The highs are so high because they're matched with lows. Everyone signs up chasing the positive emotions (joy, trust, anticipation, surprise) but without being well prepared to deal with the negative ones (fear, anger, disgust, sadness) or their mixtures (submission, disapproval, remorse, contempt, aggressiveness). Larry Magid, the CEO of ConnectSafely.org, who provides the introduction in *A Parents Guide to Instagram*,[5] admits this:

> There will also be moments of drama and anxiety—not necessarily because of the technology, but because that's the nature of relationships, online and off.

I've written down examples of my own experiences using Instagram that can be fitted to Plutchik's wheel. The three levels of intensity are in ascending order. Readers may find value in writing down their feelings before reading mine. I won't file them into the "More Account Info" archive.

Anticipation Segment

- *Interest*: Seeing new suggested content that aligns with my tastes.
- *Anticipation*: Receiving a "follow" request from an account I don't know.
- *Vigilance*: Receiving a push notification informing me that a love interest has DMed me. Certain DMs override all other priorities.

Joy Segment

- *Serenity*: Witnessing a predictable event, like when it's a major holiday and people post about it. All is right in the world.
- *Joy*: Seeing my friends celebrate achievements. Getting high engagement rates on the content I post.
- *Ecstasy*: Transitioning a virtual courtship to an IRL date or, in business, converting a new lead.

Trust Segment

- *Acceptance*: Approving "follow" requests from or reciprocating actions with someone I consider to be in my social stratum.
- *Trust*: Patronizing a business because its Instagram presence is authentic and compelling.
- *Admiration*: Assigning celebrity status to an individual and overusing engagement methods to make my support clear. For example, commenting on photos of a basketball player after making a game-winning shot. Commenting on the photos of a public person to debate naysayers.

Fear Segment

- *Apprehension*: Seeing a friend make a troubling or uncharacteristic post that could be classified as a "cry for help."
- *Fear*: Reading posts about scam victims and picturing a loved one falling for the same scam. Alternatively, seeing posts from deranged individuals who may be capable of causing harm to me or people I care about.

- *Terror*: Receiving a specific threat from a disturbed friend before he blocks me. Receiving DMs from friends with screenshotted conversations in which violence against me is the main topic.

Surprise Segment

- *Distraction*: Scrolling with minimal effort through a feed is the primary Information Age distraction. This is the vast majority of Instagram usage.
- *Surprise*: Learning of a friend's major life event, especially an engagement announcement. Instagram's feed is, after all, seen as a *news* feed.
- *Amusement*: Encountering high-quality content, often funny videos.

Sadness Segment

- *Pensiveness*: Seeing a social justice post that "puts things into perspective" or invites deep thought.
- *Sadness*: Observing a friend's vulnerable post about an unfortunate thing that happened. Also, *the feeling that an enemy is living a better life than me or of having lost the game.*
- *Grief*: Seeing a dead person memorialized and realizing that I knew them.

Disgust Segment

- *Boredom:* Viewing a stream of uninteresting content that leads me to the Discover page, to specific accounts that are more reliably exciting, or convinces me to put my phone down.
- *Disgust*: Checking a client's profile to find that she had posted a picture of her dead grandmother in an open casket. These days, content may intentionally disgust viewers to trick them into engaging with the subject.
- *Loathing:* Witnessing dubious sob stories or cancellation attempts brings me very close to feeling loathing. A growing

camp alleges that too much time on social media leads to *self-loathing*.

Anger Segment

- *Annoyance*: Leaving a comment on a picture posted by a brand I follow and a provocateur responding by calling me a nerd.
- *Anger*: Seeing my long-distance girlfriend post a revealing picture after a disagreement.
- *Rage*: Noticing that my long-distance girlfriend deleted multiple pictures of us together while we were still dating.

While I didn't turn into a master salesman or "emotional intelligence" god overnight, awareness of the emotions of the social media experience helped me understand the emotions of social media growth *purchasing* experiences.

I started classifying customers into (somewhat overlapping) categories according to what they wanted on Instagram:

- Building brand, status, and audience
- Making money
- Setting and achieving goals
- Welcoming surprise and its polarity (the primary emotions of engaging apps)
- Seeking social group assimilation and acceptance
- Socializing digitally as a utility
- Posting media as a utility (storage, filtering)
- Approbating social apps as multilayered dating sites
- Pursuing detachment, fantasy, and escapism

Although no customer ever explicitly wrote, "I want to boost my reputation with the ladies!" I can find myriad examples of "More Account Info" fields that match all these. Unfortunately, I only have the space to focus on one.

Users Pursue Detachment, Fantasy, and Escapism

When I started using AIM to socialize in the mid-aughts, my fifth-grade classmates told me I was "different" on the computer. Shy people are more confident on the internet. Expressing oneself there is, by and large, easier than doing so in person. On the internet, there is less pressure, no interruptions, no need for immediate reaction, and no (immediate) physical consequence to anything said. I have always found that I could be more expressive and sociable on the internet. I couldn't really explain it to people when I was nine. I was quiet and shy.

In MMORPG games, I've found that people really do tend to "role play." Though a bit narrower than social media patterns in terms of what is expressed, I've found human emotion in games to be polar. People are either mean (or toxic[6]) or jovial, kind, and generous—almost saintlike. Gamers want to feel the emotional rush of being generous online, perhaps when they don't have much in real life. They also want to feel the emotional rush of being mean, being a bully. In my teenage years, I played a game called *Stick RPG* where a literal stick figure was stronger than my stick figure in real life. How do you think I wanted to roleplay?

As games became more social in the 2010s, their emotional outcomes closely resembled social media websites. An early 2010s practice in *Minecraft* servers was known as "griefing,"[7] the consequences of which certainly matched the intense "grief" emotion on Plutchik's wheel. It's hard to harness certain emotions in real life with any dependability, at least without undesirable consequences.

Video game actions translate to social media, where I hypothesize there is *still* a fuller spectrum of emotions. There is a lot of cyberbullying that would not occur in a physical setting. Hell, I spent years trolling and picking fights with musicians, artists, and random people on Myspace. I don't think that I would have fought them in real life. I was playing out a fantasy of being a thirteen-year-old tough guy. Likewise, users structure their social media experiences according to their aspirational identities.

In rap music, there is a disconnect between threats or "disses" made in the recording studio or on the internet and the physical arena. One of the original manifestations of this was the "studio gangster."[8] The notion of "pulling up"[9] is the challenge for an internet hater to repeat what they've said online in person—to deliver on digital threats.

Even for those who don't come to Instagram to alter their outward representation, users may still see Instagram as a gateway to a different world on account of the sea of content inside the app. Logging in to Instagram can provide someone in a crappy situation with a virtual vacation and virtual companionship.

This can range from healthy, normal, temporary escapism to delusional behavior, such as thinking of people one follows as personal friends or pitching an internet hater as a mortal enemy. Fake photos and fake likes can increasingly fictionalize personal representations and imagined relationships. Social media can exacerbate problematic social behaviors.

Reconnecting with a Norwegian musician that I bullied on Myspace in 2008

As a kid, the digital world was my escape from reality. I sometimes behaved poorly on the early internet because I considered them free of real-world consequences. I wanted an escape. PlayStation offered the chance to "Live in your world, play in ours."

Myspace offered people who would never "pull up" the chance to cyberbully. In 2008, I targeted a Myspace profile named Julius Androide. Julius Androide was the alias used by Egil Ursin, an Intelligent Dance Music (IDM) producer from Norway. I can't remember how I came across his profile, but I remember savagely bullying him and telling him that his music sucked.

In a bid for redemption, I searched for Julius Androide, figuring there was a one percent chance the Myspace page had been preserved. I was surprised that he still had a web presence and had continued releasing music since I first found his profile—as recently as 2023! Filled with remorse, I decided to reach out and apologize.

Sure enough, he responded to my apology. He remembered our interaction years ago when I still went by my childhood nickname, TJ. I asked him, "There's this book I'm writing exploring Instagram, Myspace, and escapism. Would you be willing to revisit the interaction from your perspective?" He said he would and sent a list of questions. This passage draws from an interview I conducted with Egil Ursin.

We both recalled my pointless confrontation as one of our earliest social media memories.

Myspace was Egil's first foray into social media. He created his "flagship" alias, Julius Androide ("androide" is Norwegian for "android"), as an artist page, which allowed him to post music for fans to stream. Egil had released two albums on a local record label before the end of 2009 while Myspace was the most popular platform for distributing music.

Myspace's engineers encoded fixed values for users' body types, which as I recall, included "slim," "athletic," and "more to love." Myspace similarly compiled a seemingly endless list of musical genres. These genres spawned stronger senses of identity for emerging artists with unique sounds. They also helped organize truly memorable regional and national discovery pages. Myspace's genre list contained everything from "hardcore" to "Hawaiian." There was a genre for every sector of the wheel of emotions.

Bands could have selected three genre tags to display on their profiles. The band *My Chemical Romance*'s page displayed "rock," "metal," and "post-hardcore." Although no screenshot of Julius Androide's page survives, the genre list probably contained variations of "IDM," "experimental," "trance," "electronic," "ambient," and EDM.

The approach to music categorization was brilliant because it presented a smorgasbord of sonic profiles to young adults who had barely moved on from FM-radio-driven tastes.

Someone who liked Julius Androide could have clicked around to find similar artists. Someone could have found him by checking the "most popular" or "featured" pages for his genres. I might have found the page by searching for styles I wasn't familiar with—a motivation akin to that of a visitor clicking the "Boomerang" page on Yahoo's sports index in 1996. One blog post I dug up on the website rateyourmusic.com addressed what I remember seeing on Myspace, especially with the genre that Egil was composing:[10]

Myspace-Era Electronics - Digigrind, Speednoise, Spazzpop, Trashcore

From (very roughly) 2005 though [sic] 2012 something magical happened in the underground that I don't hear talked about very often. Speedcore, noise, nintendocore, chiptune, cybergrind, and whatever deranged misinterpretations of all these genres a website full of video game nerds and crazy teenage musicians could come up with got mingled together in a massive mess of [Microsoft Paint-generated] covers, scene-adjacent edginess, and DIY experimentalism.

Egil's unique strain of electronic music became successful by promoting it on Myspace. As he remembered, there was no paid promotion. He found new fans by adding people, commenting on their profiles, and posting news about his compositions while uploading new tracks. He described artist-driven promotion on Myspace as being "great" and "work[ing] by itself." The same self-promotional activities he participated in perhaps as early as 2006 continue to define user interactions on Instagram and across the internet today.

It is possible that Egil and I both found escapism on Myspace. He highlighted that he would "play around on Myspace," "creating new account[s] and thereby creating these mini-aliases and identities in which you could pretend to be someone else or hide yourself."

I found an October 2009 post from Egil on a different forum that corroborated his responses. Notably, in that post, he mentioned wanting to switch his style and that he "started thinking of creating a new alias with a new style that would be able to express just that...game music."

Not only does this fit with Egil's remembrance of his "mini-aliases," it also substantiates the arcane blog post on rateyourmusic.com in which the author, writing under the alias *internetbasedghosts*, remembered "crazy teenage musicians" and the proliferation of Myspace-era electronic music.

Egil indicated that my keyboard tough-guy act did have consequences. He was "hurt" by my comments, and he "was afraid of what other people would think of me when [you] had said [mean things] in my comments [section] and artwork [which had been posted as pictures]."

The main photo for Julius Androide was Egil's original, digital artwork of a humanoid monkey in an unmistakably futuristic, techno, trancelike setting. I commented on his pictures, calling him a "stupid monkey" among other, more offensive things.

Although his pursuit of escapism granted him some detachment from his real identity and his other music projects, my version of escapism was using Myspace under my real name to bully someone on the other side of the world. I typed things that would have gotten my ass kicked if left on the Myspace pages of my classmates. What emotion is associated with physical pain?

Egil reacted to my roasts with a Myspace blog post, "Say hello to my new gangster friend: TJ!"

In the (now lost) blog post, Egil dissected my persona on Myspace, which had roots in gangster rap and edgy punk music—major influences on me at the time. He mocked my choice of clothing (which was emo), my choice of profile song (which was probably rap), my "layout" (which was really important!), and even my writing style (I dropped "g"'s from words like, "nothin'").

I continued to call him stupid, but the truth was that my unwarranted attacks made me the stupid one. And, my god, was I an easy target. He ripped apart my fragile existence and struck at the heart of the problem: I harnessed my insecurities in my interactions with internet strangers. In other words, social media provided an outlet for my negative emotions where I could feel big and confident. That meant being a dick to fellow humans, even those who roleplayed as primates.

To revisit an earlier label, I wasn't a "studio gangster." I wasn't a gangster in any way. I was neither a music critic nor talented or knowledgeable enough to create the digital art or compositions that Egil Ursin was showcasing. I was, in his words, an "internet troll," before anyone knew not to feed trolls.

While writing this chapter, I switched my Spotify playlist to one featuring Julius Androide's music. Turns out, it is similar to the soundtracks I've been listening to while writing this book.

5

TERMS AND TERM SHEETS

Social media is mired in conflict, controversy, and confusion. It's hard to believe that today's publicly traded behemoths were once fringe operations helmed by nerds espousing mission statements and proclaiming open APIs. Meta, a "social media company" best known for Facebook and Instagram, is actually a technology conglomerate. This is an essay about business.

Meta's products, stakeholders, and terms of use must be outlined to set the stage for the battlefield of Instagram. Instagram's goals vis a vis Meta's position as a publicly traded entity provide context to understand tensions between platforms and their users—journalists, regulatory bodies, parents, content creators, and advertisers.

Public companies appease shareholders

Instagram wants to make more money and create more shareholder value. Anything that helps achieve these goals is good. Anything that doesn't is bad.

Meta, a publicly traded technology company, is beholden to its shareholders. To build a business, there's a balancing act between short-term and long-term thinking. Unfortunately, for a publicly traded company, there is quarter-by-quarter pressure to improve, innovate, and deliver.

In the United States, companies release quarterly reports and detail the reports in earnings calls. Each report and accompanying meeting is expected to convey meaningful progress and accomplishment. These expectations are not always logical.

For a "growth" company like Meta, research and innovation aren't reliably demarcated by arbitrary quarters. Regardless, the market expects *something*. This may lead to "short-termism."[1] Stock analysts and retail investors may criticize an invention or a breakthrough projected to materials in two years. Meritorious ideas may not be pursued due to short-term pressure or the fear of risky projects going off the rails.

Instagram wasn't always bound to quarterly expectations from millions of investors. Still, there were people to answer to. Before, Instagram's founders knew the names of every investor and that their motivations were convergent.

For private technology startups, stakeholders are searching for an *exit* —a liquidity event that allows them to profit from appreciation in private share valuation. If an investor holds stock in a *private* company, it can't be imported to Robinhood and sold in five milliseconds. There is no liquidity, no primary market. Instagram was sold to Facebook in April 2012. In May 2012, Facebook held its initial public offering.

Instagram investors weren't all thrilled with the acquisition[2] although the financial windfall was rich. They received some Facebook stock as part of the deal. Facebook shareholders as well as the past Instagram shareholders were pleased when Facebook went public because they could unload their shares for cash.

A company pursuing an acquisition, an IPO, or its own version of an exit might *want* the same success indicators as a publicly traded company. In high technology adoption and engagement are just as interesting as pure profit.

While private companies make decisions based on gut feelings and adherence to values, publicly traded companies, even the most agile ones, are beholden to shareholders and market analysts. They feel the pressure of the looming quarterly report. This warps priorities and encourages reactionary moves.

Revisiting "The Puppeteer"

Meta's market capitalization exceeds one trillion dollars. When I worked at Cutlet, its private market capitalization, the valuation used by seed investors, was roughly ten million dollars. When my employment ended, it was probably worth pennies on the dollar. But, at its peak, it was like 1/100,000th of Meta—a cutlet of Meta, if you will.

Meta is a conglomerate. It's more than Facebook and Instagram. It sells physical products, such as VR headsets. The app catalog includes Threads, Messenger, and WhatsApp. I care most about Instagram.

The metrics that Cutlet investors *really cared about* were those Instagram used to measure its success as a business arm. It doesn't matter that Instagram was purchased long ago and runs a profitable ads business. The users form the foundation of the business.

All of this is front and center in Meta's quarterly reports to investors, which are publicly available. The 2023 Q4 and year-end report[3] lists all the traditional accounting metrics: revenue, costs and expenses, operating income, and provision for income taxes.

Right below that section, the report lists "operational and other financial highlights." The interesting ones are "family daily active people," "family monthly active people," "Facebook daily active users," "Facebook monthly active users," and "ad impressions and price per ad."[4]

Meta's "Family of Apps" is Facebook, Instagram, WhatsApp, and Messenger.[5] Active users ("people") remain the best way to showcase growth and the potential for profitability within the company, which generates nearly all its revenue from advertising.

Facets of increasing user value include longer visits, more active time using the app, more frequent visits, higher engagement, referrals and external promotion, and enriched user data

It wasn't just Cutlet's investors hounding for this stuff. Meta's investors are analyzing the same measurements and factors. The true difference between Meta and Cutlet is that Cutlet didn't run ads. Meta's stats related to ad consumption, ad conversions, and ad spend are the mark of a mature business, not a whimsical startup.

I don't know much about ads, but I think we can intuit what's going on here. Optimizing for "user value" may have a negative societal impact.

Optimizing for "price per ad" and "ad impressions" may mean persecuting business owners fighting for their share.

Limiting Distractions

One irony about companies that make money from creating digital distractions is that they expend heaps of resources guarding against distractions to their core business function.

The biggest distraction...er...inconvenience for companies based in the United States might be the United States government and regulatory bodies. According to Opensecrets.org, Meta has spent over fifteen million dollars per year on lobbying since 2019.[6]

Big government confounds me. I suppose lobbying is important to fund influence campaigns when the government is actively assessing issues related to a company's business. Although there's a salacious element here, it doesn't necessarily mean that bad things are happening behind closed doors or that a company is evil. It does say something about the government's priorities, though, to read that Philip Morris International, a tobacco company, has spent less than ten million dollars per year on lobbying since 2008, according to Opensecrets.[7]

I'm on board with this part: high-technology businesses are more complex and harder to regulate than a crop cultivated in the United States for four hundred years. Still, all this money suggests that Meta's mission "to give people the power to build community and bring the world closer together" might not be as noble as it seems. It suggests that the enforcement of the terms of service might not be enough. Capitol Hill is clamoring for more Big Tech CEOs to grill.

We must admit that wherever there is change, disruption, or innovation, somebody will cry foul. It comes with the territory.

Beyond national attention or the even more frightening specter of European regulators,[8] the magnifying glass of investigative reporters is a concern. I haven't been able to retrieve the precise number, but Meta has a Communications and Public Affairs team that I estimate is staffed by about four hundred people. Nobody is expecting them to get by with a small team, but this number suggests that Meta is well aware of the tenuous position it occupies as a leading technology conglomerate *that some people also see as an omniscient purveyor of information.*

Instagram Wants to Uphold Its Terms of Use

Terms of Use (also known as "Terms" or "TOU," sometimes with "use" replaced by "service") documents have historically been so dense that the mandatory box-checking to continue signing up for or downloading a service is a running joke. But TOU violations form the basis of many major criminal cases and lawsuits. "I didn't read the terms" doesn't seem to be a valid excuse.

Ironically, the details of a TOU document give users ideas on how to misbehave. They can also point journalists to vectors of exploitation and platform-adjacent evildoing. Upholding terms of use is not done for sport —the terms get so much attention because there are significant consequences if a company doesn't cover its bases.

If a term of service prohibits posting more than a thousand times a day, suddenly there is widespread interest in *who* was posting so often and to gain what. If definitions are too broad, users decry a lack of freedom. If too specific, users decry that there is too much to read.

In 2022, when PayPal added a line to its terms to levy a twenty-five-hundred-dollar fine against those who spread "misinformation," the internet collectively said, "absolutely not."[9]

Compared to the pedantic documents of days past, Instagram's terms[10] are surprisingly legible. Succinct, useful, and agreeable, I'd argue there's no reason not to peruse the terms except that they constantly evolve, and staying up to date might require regular checks and comparisons.

Instagram defines four groups forbidden from accessing the platform.[11] In the Instagram TOU, these exclusions are listed under "Who Can Use Instagram." The list includes convicted sex offenders, children under the age of thirteen, users previously banned ("disabled") for TOU violation or committing crimes, and users prohibited from receiving the service or receiving payments from the service if they are on a "denied party" listing.

I have argued that sexual predators shouldn't be on any platform. If that requires checking *everyone's* ID, so be it. I also made the case that children shouldn't use social media at all. Thirteen, the age at which I started using social media, is imperfect but fair. I interpret the "denied party" group to be a catch-all that includes governments hostile to American tech companies. Perhaps it's Meta's way of discouraging users from flouting countries' laws.

The "How You Can't Use Instagram" section lists nine restricted behaviors.[12] This provides the ultimate definition of "black hat" activities and TOU violations by platform-adjacent services. I provide my take for each quoted term below:

1. **"You can't impersonate others or provide inaccurate information**." Users are not required to disclose their identities on Instagram. However, Instagram collects personal data at registration, which must be accurate. The year 2009 saw the origin of the impersonation problem on Twitter. The need for verification was spurred by a lawsuit filed by someone angry about a parody account. What makes "parody" tricky is that creators prefer not to plaster the "parody" label all over their content. Instagram provides guidelines on exactly how it should be done.[13]

2. **"You can't do anything unlawful, misleading, or fraudulent or for an illegal or unauthorized purpose."** Sure, don't use Instagram to break the law. "Misleading" is a loaded word these days though.

3. **"You can't violate (or help or encourage others to violate) these Terms or our policies, including in particular the Instagram Community Guidelines, Meta Platform Terms and Developer Policies, and Music Guidelines."** Although these sub-guidelines are more fluid and subjective, they often come down to decency, respect, and decorum. Posting, "Hey guys, here's a totally illicit way to grow your followers!" violates this rule.

4. **"You can't do anything to interfere with or impair the intended operation of the Service."** Impairing Instagram's service damages the bottom line. Every moment ads don't run properly and aren't served to the broadest and most optimal swath of users, Instagram loses money. This rule protects against service disruptions. It must include exploits or glitches that can affect service quality. It also covers abuse of reporting systems and general disruptive behavior.

5. **"You can't attempt to create accounts or access or collect information in unauthorized ways."** Automated account

creation is often the engine behind black hat activity on social media. Crafty operators can mitigate activity bans by switching to other accounts created automatically. If accounts are created automatically and *en masse*, the cost of risking burner accounts getting ban-hammered is quite low. The second part of this has to do with scraping Instagram. Instagram isn't entirely locked down to registered users, but most of it is. This is by design. Logging in to an account is required to collect detailed user and post information by automated means. Instagram disallows scraping its content, but scraping a site for non-commercial purposes is not illegal.

6. **"You can't sell, license, or purchase any account or data obtained from us or our Service".** This prohibition was the backbone of the Craigslist-RadPad lawsuit in "Punishing Crime." The data on Instagram has incomprehensible value. Anyone able to scrape it can store it, aggregate it, and sell it for profit. Data middleman businesses can transact huge dumps of illicitly scraped public user data on platforms like Instagram. It can be hard for Instagram to trace when and from where data was sourced or prove it, so much of the enforcement for this item happens within item number five. That handles the initial or continued data extraction, which is more damaging to the platform.

7. **"You can't post someone else's private or confidential information without permission or do anything that violates someone else's rights, including intellectual property rights (e.g., copyright infringement, trademark infringement, counterfeit, or pirated goods)."** This is an easily understood rule. This forbids "doxxing," posting someone's personal information on the internet, and reposting content without a user's permission. Instagram provides reporting tools to help facilitate copyright takedowns. It's imperfect but useful, and violated users surely appreciate when it works.

8. **"You can't modify, translate, create derivative works of, or reverse engineer our products or their components."** This is one of the most important rules and governs reverse

engineering Instagram's private API. The secret of most Instagram-adjacent services is that they use derivative works based on the reverse engineering of Instagram's private API. This is expressly forbidden for good reason. The internet used to be freer, but abuse of Instagram's private API is problematic. Users may erroneously suspect that this is meant to address copycats with the look and feel of Instagram.

9. **"You can't use a domain name or URL in your username without our prior written consent."** This may seem like minutiae, but Instagram must go to great lengths to police external links. The coupling of a link with an account identity suggests a relationship that may not exist. It could be considered another form of impersonation if my display name is Tim O'Hearn but my username is @wwwnissancom. Resolving ownership disputes or this type of derivative domain squatting[14] would be a waste of resources for Instagram. On top of that, they don't want the username to be used for external promotion that might send a user to an adult content website.

Re-reading these terms makes me blush. BlackHatWorld forums read like a rap sheet of terms of use transgressions. Anyone who used an Instagram growth service violated several of these terms. Businesses providing growth services violated as many as five of the nine terms.

Getting caught breaking the rules means account suspension. Industriously breaking rules could incur cease-and-desist notices and legal action. Breaking the rules surreptitiously means first understanding them. The terms' guardrails are lines in the sand beckoning daring platform-adjacent business owners to leap over them.

Check "I Agree" to Continue

Instagram users, Instagram-adjacent businesses, and Meta are interlocked in a perpetual sparring match.

There is ground to be ceded, ground to be captured, and battles to be fought. When it comes down to it, it's Meta's dojo. Meta has responsibilities to its shareholders. Entitled, snot-nosed script kiddies who disregard terms of use are flies on the windshield. Sometimes Meta makes corporate decisions that people like, sometimes it doesn't. Thousands of parasitic businesses hang in the balance.

Protecting interests may be synonymous with focusing on cold hard cash and shareholder appeasement. Thousands of words are devoted each quarter to outlooks and investor expectations. TOU changes are often newsworthy. Meta doesn't have unlimited resources, and knowing that the company spends millions snuffing out the *really bad stuff* so that companies like Shark Social could monkey around was a privilege, not an inconvenience. Still, *inconvenienced* parties were happy to pay Shark Social for growth services, even though the service violated the rules and, ultimately, shareholders.

6

FREE LUNCH

I n February 2019, near the zenith of the Instagram growth industry, a viral Medium post caught my attention: "How I Eat For Free in NYC Using Python, Automation, Artificial Intelligence, and Instagram."[1] It was published by Chris Buetti, a Wake Forest alumnus around my age. This caught my attention because, though I was paying full price for my meals, I was involved with a business that used the Python programming language to automate Instagram actions.

How I Eat For Free in NYC Using Python, Automation, Artificial Intelligence, and Instagram

Buetti complained about the costs of living in New York City and revealed how he harnessed a special *currency* to *finance* his dining. With a technical background and the knowledge that large Instagram followings could be monetized, he automated the operation of a popular Instagram page that could earn him free meals.[2]

From his Beautiful New York City account with twenty-five thousand followers, Chris Buetti messaged restaurants asking for free stuff. "Almost every" restaurant offered him a discount or a gift card in exchange for a promotion on his page. He had wielded a social media following to turn exposure to his audience into currency.[3]

Chris claimed to have automated every aspect of the operation aside from actually eating at the restaurants, which was a hilarious way to phrase his venture. He automated:

- Sourcing pictures and videos for the page (and crediting where they came from)
- Creating captions, adding hashtags, and posting the pictures
- Following and unfollowing other users to grow the account and gain exposure
- DMing and emailing restaurants requesting promotional partnerships

He claimed that human hands did not touch the account until a restaurant responded to offer a promotional deal. In a word: amazing.

Chris explained that trawling for the right content to repost was crucial. He scoured Instagram pages constantly, filtered for quality without using human eyes, and then reposted the best photos. Automation was the name of the game, and the workflow might have been a full-time job for a human. Consistent posting, Buetti explained, was rewarded by Instagram's algorithm.[4]

Chris introduced the first tool he had created: the scraper. The scraper was fed a list of fifty or so pages that posted pretty pictures of New York City. It crawled from there. It tagged and downloaded pictures.[5] That helped him build up an inventory of content that could be reposted.

The scraper needed a "cleaner" because even high-quality pages could contain low-quality content and sponsored posts.[6] If the Beautiful New York City account blindly and automatically posted all pictures, the audience might have noticed that no human was steering the ship. The cleaner performed basic text analysis to descriptions for spammy or advertising-related terms. That was smart. The cleaner also ignored posts with comments turned off and posts with multiple people tagged.

The advanced part of the cleaner applied machine learning to the post metadata using a classification model to decide whether each picture was good enough. There was no scoring, no complex training—it was just yes or no.[7] The training set was a group of pictures that Buetti himself sorted through. He used the following explanatory variables: vectorized caption, number of mentions, number of hashtags, caption length, whether the caption was edited, media type, video view ratio/video age, like ratio/content age, and comment ratio/content age.

This made sense! Altogether, these variables could be used to differentiate good content from bad. Buetti claimed it worked well. Having looked through the Beautiful New York City page's archives, I can say that the content is impressively high quality (though, of course, I can only take Chris' word that it was all automated).

Buetti then tackled the problem of creating captions despite not knowing what the sourced picture looked like. There are free algorithms that can classify images and better inspire captions (for example, an algorithm can definitely tell if there is a cat in a picture, and that's not a bad start). Buetti hardcoded a list of hashtags and captions that would fit most pictures generally classified as "New York City." His algorithm then assembled a caption from those two dimensions, which included a credit to the page or photographer who originally posted the picture.[8]

Putting it all together, Buetti hosted his code on an Amazon Web Services EC2 instance. There, he had his scraper, his cleaner, his caption generator, and a scheduled poster that would post photos at prime times: 8:00 am, 2:00 pm, and 7:30 pm Eastern time. He also had an auto-seller that sent DMs to restaurants using templates he created.[9]

When Buetti discovered that Instagram (at the time) limited users to four hundred follows and unfollows a day, he realized the importance of optimizing the account's crawling and following. He refined an "interaction script," which employed basic follow-unfollow and liking tactics, "in order to have the same be done back to me."[10] The bot should only follow accounts with the highest chance of following back and engaging.

Brilliantly, he tagged the results of interacting with targeted followers. He created another machine learning model to help reason through the problem. With the insights he gained from classifying accounts using his systems, he ensured that each follow resulted in more reciprocal actions. Because each account could only follow a maximum of seventy-five hundred people, space had to be regularly cleared, and his algorithm helped with that, too.

With Buetti's automation system, the account consistently grew by one to five hundred followers per day.[11] In an era with a limit of four hundred follows per day, the claim seemed feasible to me. And most restaurants were willing to trade food for promotion, not caring or knowing that the page was merely a robot curating pictures from other sources and spinning generic captions.

All of this harkens back to a central idea in the war between social media platforms and social media exploiters: there isn't—or shouldn't be—any "free lunch."

Instagram would have preferred that accounts grow by paying for Instagram ads. If it got there without paying, fair game. But how could it grow so large *without a human tapping on the phone all day and viewing feed ads*? Engineers like Chris, creative as they are, shouldn't be able to automate so much. If Chris really expended zero daily effort, what would stop him from operating ten accounts? One hundred accounts? Success breeds copycats, and thousands of imitators running bots while seeking free food would degrade the platform's integrity. Regardless of the required technical skills to pull it off, no social network is designed to reward inorganic activity.

So, what happened?

Chris' article was popular and shared widely across the nerdier parts of the internet. It was received well on Hacker News,[12] generated notoriety on reddit, and gained coverage in the tech blogosphere. Hell, even BlackHatWorld dwellers were impressed.[13]

In March 2019, Chris was featured on the business news site Cheddar, where two co-hosts live interviewed him. In their praise, they bestowed the new title of "influencer" on Chris. The interview video was titled, *Under the Influencer*.[14]

The seven-minute interview helped me understand what was really going on. Chris and I operated in the same world with the same rules (or lack thereof). Although beginning with a rough, misinformed question, the two interviewers posed surprisingly deep, thought-provoking inquiries that haven't often been followed by other pundits.

About two minutes in, the female interviewer was thinking about

A BHW user named xpolent commenting on Chris Buetti's invention

whether the type of activity that Chris was bragging about was compliant with Instagram's terms of service:

"And Instagram allows–"

"You told us before the show that you have, hundreds, of Instagram accounts that you manage?"[15]

Oh, my goodness. The guy who developed all of this wasn't just getting free food. He was running an Instagram growth service on the side!

At that point, Chris didn't admit to managing Instagram accounts for others.[16] He deflected and said he "delete[s] some and give[s] some away." That made no sense, and the darting of his eyes back-and-forth and up-and-down revealed a stretching of the truth. He then told the big fib—that Instagram put out a public API that "allows" automated actions, such as liking posts. He claimed that there was documentation on the website to that effect. That was true at one point but not in 2019.

The co-host continued, on the verge of a revelation, "To kind of, game the system..."

Chris responded, "It's all provided by Instagram right there."[17] He mentioned using Instagram's developer API which, again, didn't exist in 2019. A cached copy of the old documentation could have helped guide a private API discovery effort, but that's it.

At face value, Chris' defense was plausible. Anybody who remembered the "open" APIs of the early 2010s could have believed that Instagram still had an open API. Besides, anyone thinking that it probably wasn't allowed could be convinced that it was only accessible to elite programmers like Chris. The hosts hadn't done enough research to expose his lie. However, they continued their refreshingly deep questions.

"You say the followers are real, how do you know that they're real?"[18]

Good question! Intuition for how hard it might be to prove the authenticity of a universe of followers can be hard to come by. It's hard to be successful in the social media marketing space or be a journalist covering the space without having a natural understanding that legitimate services *can* attract unnatural results.

"I mean that I don't go out to some shady website [an SMM panel] and buy...X amount of followers for whatever price."[19]

Chris' redirection of the question revealed deeper knowledge of social media marketing, well beyond that of a programmer/data scientist who woke up in his small apartment one day and hatched a plan to get free food. Tellingly, it was not relevant to the question.

He mentioned that fake followers, who don't do actions, would not really *do anything* for him in any scenario where they needed to be converted.[20] This was a weak answer, and he wasn't prepared for the question. I don't think that the followers on his page needed to convert or do anything beyond bolstering his follower count.

He admitted that for the Beautiful New York City account, he probably could have gotten away with boosting the follower count with fake followers since follower count, not user engagement, was the reason restaurants gave him free food.[21] I agree. In February 2019, despite what March 2018's "Uncovering Instagram Bots With a New Kind of Detective Work" had said, a *restaurant owner* assessing a brand deal wouldn't scrutinize follower quality.

This essay is not meant to discredit Chris. In fact, at the time of this interview, Chris and his team were developing systems to help identify fake followers. These were systems that I later contributed to. Is it possible to prevent fake accounts from following an account one owns? **No!** But identifying fake accounts is immensely valuable and was central to "Uncovering Instagram Bots With a New Kind of Detective Work."

"How many more people out there, like you, do you think there are?"[22]

Oh, to relive the emotions felt while listening to the Cheddar interview. To remember what it was like to be on the cusp of relevancy and clout. Chris mentioned that there were more practitioners than one might think.[23] He hadn't even met me yet. The male host then mentioned earnings calls held by social media companies. He homed in on the important link between metrics touted by social media companies and the types of actions artificially boosted by people like Chris.

"Should they be taking these [automation-driven] numbers out every single quarter?"

Should they discount that, do you think? Chris said that he didn't think it mattered.[24] At the time, he knew that it *did* matter, but he was playing dumb. Publicly traded companies have a duty to report fake activity, especially if it's a non-trivial part of the stats reported to investors. That's what I think. This willful ignorance is part of a larger problem with corporate ethics.

"Do you think that Instagram should be making it harder for people to open up new accounts?"[25]

Creating accounts *en masse* was already tough by that point, so Chris could respond fairly honestly to that question. But what about those extra likes and follows? What about all that active user time? If any of it was automated, surely investors would like to know.

Chris concluded by saying that he didn't think social media influencing was going away anytime soon.[26] Chris was right.

Soon after his interview concluded, Chris promoted it with a LinkedIn post.[27] I congratulated him on the exposure and called out his fib. He deleted my comment. He messaged me to let me know that I was right and that he appreciated my analysis, but for obvious reasons, he had to delete the comment.

I spent hours speaking to Chris on the phone and learned that he ran an Instagram growth service just like Shark Social. We compared notes. Under the hood, we were doing pretty much the same thing. I had more customers, better systems, and better knowledge of Python. Chris had better knowledge of applied statistics and machine learning, a more versatile team, and a Rolodex of industry contacts.

Later, Chris pivoted and founded an influencer marketing startup, which was eventually named Lionize. Over the years, I've worked with Chris' team in various iterations of the company. Not only were they fun to work with, they thought *big*, and they were probably the only team to successfully pivot from black-hat social media growth to a venture-funded software startup.

When I finally moved to New York City, I met up with the Lionize team for lunch. They paid.

7

GITTING GUD

I n 2022, I toiled through a lengthy interview process at a hedge fund. I received an offer of employment. It was met with jubilance. I remember asking my would-be manager how the team approached self-improvement, especially considering the challenges in the business's domain.

"Tim, do you play videogames?" He responded.

"Yeah, sure," I said, not wanting to reveal that I had probably spent over five thousand hours playing *Runescape*.

"Git gud," he enunciated.

I smiled and nodded, hiding my perturbation that this barely complete sentence was uttered by a vice president at a prestigious hedge fund. I was also embarrassed that I, a seasoned gamer, only had a vague understanding of the phrase. I had to visit knowyourmeme.com to ensure the meaning wasn't lost.[1]

According to the meme site, "git gud" is a corruption of "get good," and it's a way of heckling an inexperienced player without providing any other specific instruction.[2] Git gud. In my defense, usage of this term skyrocketed around the time I graduated from college and started working. I wasn't playing video games then, so the usage had escaped me.

I guess the hedge fund guy was trying to tell me that the team was regularly humbled by the complexity of the problem space and that, to put it kindly, we would be dealing with tough losses and low scores.

I ended up rejecting the job offer as I thought back to my time at Shark Social. Unlike a hedge fund, Shark Social took *anybody's* money. We ran a promotion where the first month only cost one dollar! Like a hedge fund, Shark Social proudly displayed results (and even testimonials) alongside paragraphs of fine print warning that past performance was not an indicator of future returns.

Each year, millions of people pay for marketing services. It's now possible to pay ten dollars directly to a media platform for guaranteed digital exposure—an ad. It's possible to pay someone ten dollars to design the ad. Services are widely available and broadly useful. Instagram growth was a sliver of worldwide marketing spend.

Investment managers and promotional campaign managers alike want happy customers. However, there are awkward compensation arrangements in which some service providers don't necessarily benefit from their clients' success. They don't have their clients' best interests in mind. A glowing testimonial is awesome! What about selling someone a product they don't need or won't realistically help them reach their goals?

A growing segment of Americans who grew up immersed in social media has a vague goal of ascending to influencer status. At Shark Social, we encountered thousands of customers who expressed desires for followers, popularity, and prominence.

Every customer who signed up with Shark Social gained followers. However, when they didn't quickly snag brand deals, some asked us for advice. My recommendation, never actually forwarded, was that clients "git gud."

Yeah, sorry! Behind the branding of smiling models and luxurious lifestyles, Instagram marketing agencies only helped with marketing. I wasn't a personal trainer, photographer, or career coach. Shark Social didn't sell endgame success, though that's exactly what customers hoped they were buying. Most people don't have what it takes to be influential. Most never reach their goals on social media or in life. If this book doesn't sell one hundred copies, I'll probably have to call the hedge fund back and tell them I've reconsidered.

Focus on the Craft!

Gitting gud was not a service I offered. Coincidentally, I propose users can reach their goals on social media primarily by *getting better*, even when the climb feels insurmountable. This is good advice to anyone seeking short-cuts, evidenced by one funny exchange in the wake of the Instagress automation suite being shut down in 2017:[3]

> Can anyone recommend any alternative apps to Instagress?
>   → Good content and community management.
>   → Yea the "app" is called "*manual work*" :p

Getting better doesn't mean prematurely incurring marketing expenses for an underdeveloped or non-existent product. Post better content instead. Better content likely requires focusing on improving a craft. It also means facing failure, disappointment, the grind, and maybe ridicule—digital media meanies shouting, "GIT GUD!" when the like count is pathetic.

Getting better is hard. It involves uncomfortable truths. It doesn't feature a spigot of dopamine. Charting a course to self-improvement necessitates admitting that the account, and perhaps the person curating it, isn't currently worth jack shit.

I've talked about the wonderful opportunities brought on by the Information Age. I believe we live in a world where much is within reach of the average person. Unfortunately, social media success isn't within reach for the average person, especially when "success" is defined by beautiful, talented, top-tier influencers.

The quest for self-improvement is a brutal, demoralizing, daily routine of comparing oneself to the most well-constructed people. Why are people so sad scrolling on Instagram? When someone gets beat in a video game while someone spams "git gud," at least the loser got to *play the game*. Firing up social media and facing a perfection-filled feed is an implicit reminder both to "git gud" and that the scroller never even gets to play the "game." It's a futile beatdown.[4]

The best way to get what one wants on social media is, ironically, to spend as little time using or thinking about social media as possible. Social media businesses' continuous promotion of the dream along with feeds entirely composed of avatars of that dream make staying off difficult.

A *business* can set up conversion funnels and regularly post. The self-oriented "business" aspirant should not be thinking about social media. This can be difficult when the tastemaker of what a 2020s kid wants is an Instafamous supernova who attributes success to intangible skills or happenstance. Spending long hours on a platform as if it will backfill talent or be a substitute for dedicated practice can be dangerous. It can leave one stuck in a cycle of futile "learning."

Learning, or, the Preparation Trap

With any endeavor, participants should learn a bit before jumping in—get shown the ropes or watch a demonstration. See someone else make a mistake. Read the fucking manual.[5] The internet is an endless repository of new pursuits and how to pursue them. Free guides, how-to's, and demonstration videos are uploaded faster than they can be consumed.

The benefits of the internet are incalculable. What's unfortunate about this cornucopia of consumerism is that it's easy to get caught in what I call the "preparation trap" or the "expertise trap."

Let's say someone wants to learn how to throw a javelin. A regulation men's javelin is 260 centimeters long, weighs about two pounds, and, in the hands of a Roman warrior, could kill. A javelin is an implement of warfare.

Considering the risks and upfront investment involved, it makes sense that the would-be tosser might start by looking up videos and product reviews. What's the best starter javelin? How much should shipping cost? Where can it be thrown? How–how does one qualify for the Olympics? How was Jan Železný so good?

A brief inquiry can turn into a whole night of consuming javelin content, which could turn into a whole weekend. In the right niche, a curious novice could be submerged in the hobby without actively participating. The internet encourages the development of non-participative spectators. There might be enough podcasts and content creators that the anxious customer never actually buys a javelin or attempts a throw. These content creators and the algorithms that keep viewers consuming *may* incentivize someone to *buy* a javelin, but there is no profit when a consumer practices javelin throwing (just like most marketing businesses). This is the preparation trap.

The trap, the framework for preventing escape, starts with the instinct that *learning* is *good*.

Humans enjoy engaging from afar, consuming content in the guise of building expertise. But the catch is that expertise building, if not paired with participation, quickly reaches the point of diminishing returns.

Trying to do *anything*, whether paying taxes or homebrewing beer, can lead to reading, scrolling, and gazing at high-quality content that drains users of time, energy, and motivation without getting any closer to a tax refund check or tasting that first small batch pilsner.

Social media exacerbates this problem. Whenever social media success is associated with conventional success, the gears of nefarious machinery start spinning. **It's natural to be tricked into believing that ordinary social media usage translates to building a brand or expertise on social media**. The accumulation of knowledge is wonderful. Scrolling through social media and watching streamers does not help one accumulate knowledge beyond a rudimentary level. But, unfortunately, it *feels* good.

If a public relations agency wants to hire a junior-level social media manager, should the job description ask for candidates who spend "all day every day" on social media?

No, of course not! Yet, I've seen similar coquettish lines in real job descriptions for social media managers. There's a difference between expertise and overuse. If a casino manager was looking to hire a pit boss, a daily visitor to the one-armed bandits might not be the best candidate. If the pathological gambler shouldn't be hired, why should the pathological scroller?

I've hired a few social media assistants, all college kids or recent grads, and assessed the profiles of at least one hundred applicants and prospects. While I occasionally saw a benefit to the social-media-obsessed because they identified important things in a feed that could turn into story leads or new offerings, there wasn't a net positive, even at minimum wage.

The "social media" kids I hired tended to be terrible writers, unskilled at content curation, resistant to feedback, and, most notably, insufficiently independent.

I started to believe that these people were *so* used to scrolling and being told what to do by the creators they followed, their critical thinking was stunted. Moreover, they convinced themselves that "social media expertise" *was* a skill set. It came at the cost of developing tangible skills.

When someone tries to *get what they want* on social media, the "preparation trap" is ever-present. Imagine spending the majority of time *consuming* and thinking that it's providing a benefit and justifying it because the dopamine is real because, of course, legions do the same.

Elite influencers use social media to elevate their brands. "If it worked for them..." is a dangerous justification. Small victories may come and inconsequential goals might be reached as one's audience organically grows. It's a mirage. I've seen meager engagement attained a thousand times. Every Shark Social customer gained followers. While a bot was earning them exposure, their free time should have been spent on self-improvement. Gitting gud, not continuing to scroll.

Self-Promotion

Not everyone is a calculating miscreant. Ordinary people log in to social media platforms without thinking about business or accomplishment. They are the user's users, the mainstream screen tappers doing the subconscious scrolling, routine liking, and goaded commenting. They aren't the ones who signed up for Shark Social.

Basic usage patterns on social media are, plainly, **self-promotion**.

A user takes a visible action for self-promotion. Right? If Marlboro Cigarettes followed me on Instagram and liked my pictures, I'd remember that red label. Even if an employee at Marlboro genuinely appreciated my picture despite it having nothing to do with the Marlboro brand, the "like" submitted by that business would have a promotional element.

These actions, especially an unexpected "like" from a cigarette brand, induce elevated excitement—surprise. They're memorable and intriguing and blur the line between organic interactions and traditional "self-promotion."

Using social media as designed means self-promoting. Usage and promotion are tightly coupled. For example, why do we *really* leave comments on pictures of people we know? Surely, we could text them, DM them, or express kindness privately about a picture. We do it because of a social contract in which reciprocal actions between socializers are expected, which explains the evolution of *picture-comment-4-picture-comment* (PC4PC) on Myspace.[6] At times, though, commenters are overwhelmed by the desire to publicly express their feelings about a picture.

We're acutely aware that *others can see our comments.* Whatever we say is broadcast to everyone who likes, comments, or checks the comments. Leaving a public comment may be self-serving. The possibility of a friend's friend discovering my profile that way and following me is tantalizing.

What's the difference between a musician commenting, "Good stuff bro!" and "Check out my music fam!"?

Hm.

Variations on this comment should be familiar to any Instagram user. Sapna Maheshwari discussed these positive spam comments in "How Bots are Inflating Instagram Egos." Anyone who hasn't seen this brand of comment can find them under the pictures of any major musician. This is one of the oldest internet promotional techniques and probably goes back as far as Myspace. When I had a musical group in high school, I went to other groups' pages to comment, hoping to divert a little traffic.

There's no difference between the two hypothetical musician comments. Even the comment, "You're an idiot," *is self-promotion.* Although regular interactive usage won't result in massive metrics growth, the growth is often steady and reliable.

It's also worth noting that, since I started writing this book, Instagram added push notifications for when *certain users one follows post comments on others' content.*

Ads

Instagram would prefer users paid to run ads. It's easy. A user simply creates a new post or edits an old one and turns it into a promoted post. Users who do this become paying *customers.*

Plenty of users won't consider ads for two reasons:

1. They view running platform-native ads as inorganic and a threat to credibility.
2. They don't have well-designed content strategies or funnels to entice conversions.

From 2016 to 2020, my primary hobby was reading books and writing book reviews. I built a small following on Goodreads,[7] the book review site now owned by Amazon. Some of my reviews rose to be the most helpful reviews for popular titles. I cross-posted the reviews to my blog hoping to increase search engine traffic. I didn't get any.

In 2016, the year before I became involved with Shark Social, I read fifty-two books. I wrote a year-end summary post that was received warmly by friends and family.[8] In 2015, Tai Lopez posted his infamous "Here in My Garage" video connecting reading books to ownership of a Lamborghini and a house in the Hollywood Hills.[9] What it revealed, and what I found as my lowbrow book reviews gained viewership, was that books *were* cool, and reading *was* a respected hobby even with attention spans at an all-time shortness. I thought I could capitalize on my ability to read quickly and write insightful reviews.

I planned to run Instagram ads. I asked my mom to take a picture of me sitting on a bookshelf wearing tight-fitting, white J. Crew pants and a henley from UNIQLO. Below is the original picture and caption I ran in the ads, sourced from Facebook.

A social media advertisement that I ran in early 2017.

Yep, that's me, seated in front of my grandmother's library, its wooden shelves sagging under the weight of HarperCollins' finest hardcovers stored there for decades.

"I read a book every week in 2016. See what I have to say by clicking the link in my bio."

I had the content. I had the picture. I had the call to action. I spent a decent amount of money on Instagram ads, maybe two hundred and fifty dollars. I targeted book readers or a related interest group. I submitted my promoted post.

The estimated "impressions" were about what Instagram had promised. The engagement, though, was abysmal. I remember a comment on the post that read, "Who cares that he read these books?"

I spent the next few years continuing to read and write a similar volume before realizing that, beyond personal enrichment, it wasn't getting me anything. I was never going to be a book influencer (and that was before book influencers). Maybe it was the preparation trap after all.

Today, I'm willing to look at this picture and caption and say, "Yeah, nice try, but there's nothing compelling here." The call to action was based on hope and a dream. Expecting strangers to click through to my profile and *then* click the link to my post in my Instagram bio was asking too much. This doesn't mean that Instagram ads aren't viable. Tai Lopez became famous (and rich) after purportedly spending millions on his YouTube ad campaign. Social media platform ad spend is trending upward. Those who have better content, better marketing copy, and *things to sell* must be seeing success.

I paid a few hundred dollars to receive indirect feedback that my picture and ad copy weren't good enough. This is part of *gitting gud*—I needed to keep developing my craft even when the task seemed nebulous. All those years ago, I didn't snap to thinking about buying followers. I didn't spend hundreds of hours scrolling through other reviews. I focused on my craft —*for several more years*. No, it still hasn't led to internet fame. There are Instagram commenters who could ask the same question about my various pursuits: "Who cares what Tim does?" At the very least, I'd like to think that my adult life and, by extension, this book, are testaments to self-improvement, self-promotion, and gitting gud.

Those who run ads rarely find everything they want in platform promotion. In fact, spending money on ads may embolden users who are willing to consider black hat solutions.

Paid External Promotion

Users pursuing social media fame might pay others to promote them. "Shoutout marketing"—popular users on Instagram using Reels and other media to encourage their followers to follow other accounts—is widespread.

At its worst, buying a shoutout is renting a tiny space in a spammy Reel for twenty dollars hoping a few followers transfer. It's a progression of Myspace bulletin whore trains. At its best, a "shoutout" can be an advertising campaign in which an influencer pretends to have a real association with the account in question, potentially driving thousands of impressions. People have paid influencers, and outright famous people, to take pictures with them *and* post them, suggesting endorsement. Tai Lopez was alleged to have paid celebrities to boost his credibility. We call this "celebrity endorsement."

Hiring a Traditional Agency

In the first draft of this book, an entire section dealt with the inner workings of social media agencies. I collected hundreds of job descriptions. I perused hundreds of websites. I logged examples from working at an agency myself.

Ultimately, I decided that twenty or thirty pages about social media agencies that played by the rules weren't important.

I'll say that there was a big difference between "Hey, we'll design your website" agencies and fly-by-night "agencies" that specialized in Instagram growth and used bots to grow accounts. Tellingly, I encountered fewer than a handful of Instagram growth services or SMM panels that offered marketing agency services. Some agencies, however, did "white label" growth services. At Shark Social, we partnered with several agencies.

Social media agencies became big business in the late 2010s. So much so that in 2016 Tai Lopez, the Lamborghini-in-the-garage guy, started selling a course on how to profit from opening an agency.[10] He wasn't wrong—local businesses benefit from having a social media presence and enacting marketing strategies. The internet of today makes small-scale ad campaigns and launching websites widely feasible, so much so that I've known business owners who opted to launch websites or digital marketing campaigns before their businesses were ready to launch.

Although, again, there is a distinction between real businesses and internet denizens who think *they* are businesses. Hiring an agency can be a great idea or a step that brings a delusional person back to Earth. An agency can't guarantee that it will make a business *viable*. Just as I did when I purchased Instagram ads to be a book influencer, agency customers may realize that the money they've spent was useful because it necessitated a hard look at the underlying business and its viability.

Agencies help *customers* pursue *success* every day. Before I move on, I will list agencies' commonly provided services.

Web development: site design, integration of payment flows and e-commerce, and coupling of mailing lists.

Multimedia production: pictures, videos, written copy, and branding.

Social media management: content production, audience engagement, competitor analysis, and consistency across platforms.

Ads: strategy, placement, campaign design, analytics, and email marketing.

Public relations: crisis management, customer support, and press releases.

These digital media agency services help customers get what they want, though perhaps at high prices and without guarantees of end-game success. Users seeking cheaper solutions and more rapid gains may turn to the dark side—the black hat solution providers.

Black Hat

Black hat solutions, which violate a website's terms of use, are in demand because they're cheap, quantifiable, and guaranteed. Rather than "Pay $1000 for a marketing strategy and advertising campaign," how about, "Pay $40 for 5,000 more followers"?

Instagram users are tempted to try black hat growth methods, which led to standalone services that are essentially outgrowths of cheaper providers deep in those forums. Black hat growth methods are usually cheaper. They're advertised as low risk. It's exciting to find a cheat code and use it.

Specifically for Instagram, black hat services are usually used to boost social metrics, such as follower count, comments, and photo likes. I've also seen cunning users buy existing accounts preloaded with followers hoping to mold them to their intended niche or purpose.

Potentially, this farcical activity, sometimes provided by "SMM panels," could be used to quickly deliver bogus engagement and fool Instagram's algorithms or manipulate discussions.

Another Life

Gitting gud speaks to the futility of improvement when faced with a mature, experienced, player base. Imagine logging into a video game, creating a new character, leaving the safe zone, and immediately being slain by a level seventy opponent surrounded by a menacing aura.

"Git gud," the paladin says, as he teabags your corpse.

When the game asks if the player wants to "continue," what's the response? Logging into social media can incite similar feelings of hopelessness. There are thousands of more-experienced players out there in every niche! Some can be defeated after dedicated training, while others cannot. Players are constantly reminded that they aren't anywhere near the high score table. It's crushing.

As in a competitive video game, the respawning Instagram user has two choices: give up or give in. Giving up doesn't necessarily mean deleting one's account, though it can. It means tossing aside the ambitions of platform success and regressing to join the perpetually scrolling masses who periodically post a cute picture. It means settling down and growing comfortable with the audience one already has and the likers who reliably reciprocate.

Giving in means fully committing to the game, even if the path isn't well-defined or requires financial outlay. It means chasing the win condition. And that almost always means opening the wallet to whoever accepts the player's tokens. Giving in also means acknowledging that *there must be shortcuts and the competition must be using the shortcuts.* Users who want to play the game must be willing to break the rules. In a virtual world, maybe running a bot for two weeks gets a character close to defeating that paladin.

Having expended considerable stamina commenting on customer

psychology, terms of use, and a treasure chest full of other background material, this quest now enters its second phase: The Underworld. The waypoints include rule enforcement, rule-breaking, and the lengths Instagram users go to to git gud.

8

SAFEGUARDING AND SHADOWBANS PART I

On June 21, 2018, one of the Sharks sent an email titled, "!! Shadow Ban Dilemma !!"

It was a full-blown emergency. Both burner accounts and customers had issues with taking actions or having posts reach *anyone*. For some accounts, exposure and reciprocity were down ninety percent. However, there was no outward indication that the accounts had been restricted or banned. I was tasked with solving this problem. I had to start on the ground floor. I had to learn what a shadowban was.

By the summer of 2018, Shark Social was doing well. More customers meant multiplied revenue. It also meant multiplied stress and complaints when things went wrong. I had read about "shadow ban" long before June 2018, but it was always a fluid concept.

Cheating the system involved learning how the system worked. It also involved lengthy investigations into rulebreaking and enforcement across the internet. It involved subscribing to self-righteous newsletters and podcasters on the path to understanding platforms' efforts to keep users safe and enforce good behavior.

What's "Safe"?

Governments, interest groups, angry parents, and journalists leverage pressure to keep things "safe." Safety has been wielded to justify increased surveillance or decreased quality of service. Internet safety has myriad interpretations. What does safety mean?

It means being protected from harm. When I first saw it used to moderate virtual experiences, it felt like a stretch. In the aughts, safety and "security" meant the same thing. Whenever there is an account to log into, account *security* is a valid concern. If asking a fourteen-year-old playing *Runescape* in 2008 about "safety," the conversation would center around account login credentials. I polled friends, "What does internet safety mean to you?" and everyone mentioned not getting hacked.

Businesses avoid addressing what "safety" means. It's necessary to read between the lines. The MMORPG game *Runescape* has a "Staying Safe" section on its website.[1]

> What we do to keep your child safe
>
> We have a team dedicated to keeping players safe online. Although these situations are rare, highly-trained specialists review and take action on any concerning chat. As part of our commitment to safeguarding our players, we have built strong relations with law enforcement and child protection agencies worldwide.

"Situations" here refer to "concerning chat." But the guide introduces "law enforcement" and "child protection agencies" as the guardians without any explanation. Huh? If I read this in 2008, I would wonder why I needed help from a child protection agency while chatting with other players and chopping yew logs.

The player's guide to safety is opaque. "Please remember to be careful what personal information you are sharing online as you can't be sure everyone is who they say they are."[2]

Well, it's a medieval roleplaying game. I concede that I wasn't actually *who I said I was*, an archer named "Noble Aloof" with enough farming skills to grow palm trees. My read is that safety on the platform might mean "protection from physical, real-world harm initiated by real-life predators embedded in the game world who are fishing for victims' personal information."

If a player tells a predator their legal name, where they live, and how old they are, that maniac *just might* find and kidnap them. Be safe kids!

The crossover is addressed in a page titled, "Harassment."[3] There is an admission that internet harassment can potentially result in real-world harm—an affront to safety.

Real-World Harassment

If the harassment you are experiencing in game has crossed over into the real world, or if you are concerned about your safety, please do not hesitate to get in touch with your local law enforcement.

We work closely with many law enforcement agencies and we will co-operate fully with any official investigation.

What about cyberbullying? It's a concern, but there's a fine line between over-the-top gamesmanship and "bullying." Yes, I used to harass people when I slayed them. Using the "block" feature works well for temporal chat messages in *games*. Someone getting cyberbullied by real-life opponents can't entirely block their way out of virtual showdowns.

The concern with cyberbullying is twofold. First, cyberbullying threatens safety because the bullied person could be motivated to find the bully in the overworld and retaliate. The question about school shooters is often if they were bullied in person or online. Second, if unchecked, a *bully* could physically harm the victim at an in-person venue.

When I was in eighth grade, I was called to the guidance counselor's office. The counselor wanted to arbitrate a dispute between my friend James and me. I had been calling him a "noob" in *Runescape* and lured him to the wilderness to kill him, aided by my friend Carlos. Presumably, when James mentioned his avatar losing all of its life points, the counselor concluded that two gangly computer nerds might try to off each other in real life. I still think it was ridiculous and blown out of proportion.

Cyberbullying can cause a user to contemplate suicide, an extreme example of social-media-fueled depression and safety concerns. Over the past few years, this topic has been extensively covered.[4]

Another aspect of maintaining safety is reducing exposure to "harmful material." This doesn't usually manifest as direct physical harm but is nonetheless a threat.

Suggestions to "light nail polish remover on fire" or "try to huff compressed air" are also safety concerns. I've suggested that the disclaimer, "Don't try this at home" has become something of a joke. As someone who did dangerous things after reading about them on the internet (including lighting nail polish remover on fire), I can say that platforms can probably do more to warn against "dangerous thoughts," but the problem space is so nebulous that I don't see the point. It quickly becomes *thought control* and *censorship*.

Sharing illegal imagery worsens victims' suffering. Although there isn't necessarily further direct physical harm, moderating it aggressively is under the umbrella of safeguarding users.

It's hard to envy Instagram since it must manage safety and all its offshoots. When I last checked in 2024, Instagram's Help Center contained nine sections under the header, "Staying Safe":[5] "Sharing Photos Safely," "Safety Tips," "Tips for Parents," "Being your authentic self on Instagram," "Abuse and Spam," "Ways to deal with conflict or abuse on Instagram," "Self-Injury," "About Eating Disorders," "Information for Law Enforcement," and "Health & Safety Warnings for Meta Spark AR Walk Experiences."

Any business would prefer to not go on the record about abuse, self-injury, eating disorders, or anything piquing the interest of law enforcement. To address it at any level is light assent that a platform hosts, if not facilitates, harmful behaviors and actions.

The "Tips for Parents" section includes a 105-page guide[6] to help parents understand Instagram. It was developed in partnership with connectsafely.org and childmindinstitute.org. The Child Mind Institute "offers treatment for children and young adults with mental health and learning challenges."[7] ConnectSafely is a nonprofit "dedicated to educating people about online safety, privacy, security and digital wellness."[8] The existence of a 105-page guide does speak to the paradox of platforms needing to address bad things that are happening without drawing too much attention to them. The guide would be useful to any parent who cares enough to read it but is ineffective when parents discredit internet safety or are addicted to screens themselves.

Right out of the gate, Instagram (Meta) doesn't seem evil. The introduction from Larry Magid, CEO of the Child Mind Institute, clearly addresses the overlapping emotional experiences I've explored using Plutchik's wheel of emotions:[9]

> Like all human interaction, there will be times of joy, kindness and compassion. There will also be moments of drama and anxiety -- not necessarily because of the technology, but because that's the nature of relationships, online and off.

The guide recommends that parents encourage teens to make their accounts private. Page fifteen mentions "suspicious behavior" exhibited by users who may threaten the safety of vulnerable users.

> Instagram recently began exploring ways to make it more difficult for adults who have been exhibiting potentially suspicious behavior to interact with teens. This may include things like restricting these adults from seeing teen accounts in 'Suggested Users', preventing them from discovering teen content in Reels or Explore, and automatically hiding their comments on public posts by teens.[10]

The guide also recommends making some Reels available only to close friends and restricting who can send DMs. It introduces a new feature (one I wasn't familiar with) that displays a "Safety Notice" when adults send DMs to teenagers. The notice seems to encourage restricting, reporting, or blocking the user and includes the reminder, "Don't feel pressured to respond."

Pages 52 and 53 introduce comment filtering features that users can use to hide comments "that may be offensive" from their posted content. There's also a manual filter that a user can configure with specific words and phrases to help protect them from bullying, harassment, scams, or worse.

Instagram claims to have introduced automatic comment filters based on "comments that seem similar to others that have been reported."[11] When a user attempts to leave an inappropriate comment, the filter may show the "Keeping Instagram a Supportive Place" popup that asks users to "rethink" what they've typed.

Instagram seems to censor negativity under a broad definition of harassment. Writing "you're stupid" in a picture caption will be blocked by the filters. I understand the motivation. To me, this is too restrictive.

The guide addresses screen time. Although Instagram must be appreciated for enabling reminders for a daily, in-app screen time limit, it does little to address the ubiquity of screengrabbing.

At the end of the pamphlet are quotes from two teenage Instagram users (to imagined parents), Nancey, nineteen, and Riya, sixteen. Nancey says, "My advice is: Don't start a conversation with me by saying social media [is] bad for me. Instead, ask me why I use it and how it inspires me."[12] Riya says, "I want parents to know that it's possible to learn through Instagram. It's not just what we look at on our phones when we're bored!"

I say why not push for dumbphones? Teams of engineers are working tirelessly to get teens to spend *more* time using the app, not less. For each content moderator or safe-use evangelist employed by Meta, there are probably fifty engineers dedicated to making the app more "engaging."

User-Driven Feedback Systems

In conjunction with an automated system that detects *bad stuff* on a platform, the user-driven "report" feature is a useful, ubiquitous tool. Having a content integrity specialist review content reported by humans is more efficient than having someone assess each post.

People respect reporting features, and they are used widely. Unfortunately, especially on sites like reddit, people commonly report things *they don't agree with*, hoping to bias and pressure moderators into siding with them or looking at personal disputes. Speaking as someone who has moderated reddit communities and been reported because I was winning an argument, the amount of time and detail put into superfluous reports is frightening. On Instagram, there's a section of the safety guide called, "Ways to deal with conflict or abuse on Instagram," which, essentially, can be reduced to "stop wasting our time with bogus reporting."

Users expect their reports to be addressed in a timely manner. Instagram alerts users when their reports have been reviewed and asserts that showing report results enforces fairness.

Another user-driven feedback system gives users the ability to *downvote* or dislike content. Although users naturally downvote low-quality content and content they disagree with, they'll also downvote content for bad behavior. For example, a reddit comment with spammy links might be reportable (violating rules) and downvotable (low quality, disruptive). Highly downvoted comments (say, with scores below -20) might contain controversial opinions and be affected by brigading, but there would be clear rule-breaking patterns.

Objectionable content isn't always necessary to moderate or censor! Allowing users to downvote content naturally leads to safer platforms. Rather than removing or disallowing comments like, "you're stupid," a user-driven feedback system like reddit's can help new users learn what types of behavior aren't popular or socially acceptable.

YouTube hid public dislike counts in late 2021.[13] A high number of dislikes may motivate someone to leave a meritless dislike (brigading), but dislikes are *healthy*. I understand why Instagram adjusted its branding to include "positivity," but if everything is positive, nothing is. Some argue that a dislike is an inherently negative action and can worsen cases of harassment or smear campaigns against individuals or businesses.

YouTube, with fewer interactive social elements, faces less safety pressure. YouTube likely caved to pressure from content creators and ad partners by removing dislike displays. If an advertisement runs on a video that is thirty percent disliked (a bad rating), that reflects poorly on the advertiser.

However, dislikes are important to the platforms! They explicitly indicate that a user did not jive with a piece of content. As more websites take stances *against* downvotes, their engineers must design recommendation algorithms that more heavily weigh "implicit metrics" like viewing time and cursor position. Engineers want dislikes when building a recommendation feed.

Over a decade ago, there was a petition for Facebook to add a "dislike button" to posts, and rumors spread that it would be added. Although I can't find the old petition, I did find a group from 2009 that speaks to this desire and establishes a bridge between Myspace-style speech and Facebook's propriety:[14]

PETITION FOR FACEBOOK TO INSTALL A DISLIKE BUTTON...NEED 1,000,000 MEMBERS ASAP..INVITE EVERYONE YOU KNOW TO JOIN

So facebook has a LIKE button for those who like others status's [sic].

. .but what if you dislike them[?] If 1 million people join this group then facebook will officially install a DISLIKE button.

The dislike button never arrived. Eventually, the "crying laughing" emoji became a proxy for "I disagree with this."

On Instagram, there is no explicit feedback for negative ranking. The platform uses implicit feedback when deciding to promote posts. For example, if users look at one post less than another, the feed algorithm interprets that the post is low-quality but not necessarily that it breaks the rules. As I learned working at Cutlet, platforms know what users dislike even when they don't have a button to press to show it. The like button provides positive feedback.

Community Empowerment and Volunteer Moderation

Volunteer moderators used to be a big deal. Moderators were nominated by community members or hand-picked by site owners and were Web 2.0 demigods.

Moderators were often entrusted with admin privileges and could hand out bans and censor content. They wielded serious power in game worlds and message boards. In *Runescape*, Player Moderators had silver crowns next to their names in the "in-game chat." This conferred status akin to badging." They were the gentle, mature, and respected older cousins of adolescent gamers.

Community members upheld the sanctity of their communities. Because other players, users, and forum-dwellers wanted those special badges next to *their* usernames, people behaved a little better. Site owners got free labor, often from their most loyal users.

Reddit still utilizes the volunteer moderator system. *Runescape* probably does too, but I haven't played in a long time. It is decentralized on reddit. The mods are selected by whoever starts a given subreddit. reddit employees only step in for major disputes, allegations of corruption, or if all a community's moderators are inactive. Generally, it works well.

Social networks needed more firepower. Instagram's "moderators" are Meta employees (or temporary contractors). Moderator isn't a great term either since a lot of bad behavior on social networks is not people throwing tantrums in debates in need of *moderation* but rather behaviors that require *policing*.

The Social Network Police

According to a Meta Transparency Center article, "The people behind Meta's review teams,"[15] Meta employed over fifteen thousand content moderators as of January 2022. According to an explosive *Wall Street Journal* report from December 2017,[16] the company expected to employ seventy-five hundred by the end of that year. The doubled number of moderators in just over four years speaks to the immense task of what is described as *the* hardest technology job.

"Facebook and Instagram users create billions of pieces of content each day," according to Meta's "Reviewing high-impact content accurately via our cross-check system."[17] However, the hardest part of the job is not sorting through this sheer volume of data, it's that the moderators must view some of the most vile and disturbing content on the internet before deciding whether to intervene. I just finished criticizing the softness of nerfing the downvote feature. I'll admit that this job sounds upsetting and traumatic.

For human-driven moderation, user-driven reports and software-identified objectionable content are loaded into a queue. Moderators must quickly decide whether the flag has merit and if the offending content should be removed. Each contract worker must analyze thousands of pieces of content each day. Meta has implemented a cross-check system to control against false positives, one of many tools that augment the moderators' job function.

In January 2021, a reddit user named u/chrriihs posted, "I am a Facebook/Instagram content moderator AMA"[18] and claimed to have worked as a Facebook content moderator for a contracting agency in a third-world country. He said that the agencies sign NDAs with Meta, so, so employees don't know where they are working until their first day.

One user commented that the job must be "pretty rough." The OP responded:

All of us are desensitized to all of that. I personally went in already desensitized since i'm young and used to browse shock websites long before i started so nothing rattled me. There are still mandatory therapist sessions every 15 days unless someone requests for one and it will be provided right away (but no one asks anyways).

In "The Worst Job in Technology: Staring at Human Depravity to Keep It Off Facebook"[19] published by the *Wall Street Journal* in 2017, one former Google moderator also addressed the topic of desensitization:

…he became desensitized to pornography after reviewing content for pornographic images all day long. "The first disturbing thing was just burnout, like I've literally been staring at porn all day and I can't see a human body as anything except a possible [terms of service] violation," he says.

Moderators must see horrific things and become worn down. Despite the multiple lawsuits and complaints mentioned in the article, the dystopian truth is that a job is a job. For the right amount of money, there will always be willing moderators, but the title no longer includes the cachet of special badges held by volunteer forum moderators.

In 2019, Chris Gray, a former Facebook moderator, wrote an opinion piece for *The Guardian* titled, "As a Facebook moderator I saw the worst of humanity. We need to be valued."[20] He also mentioned that a lack of moderation can affect Facebook's ability to *earn advertising dollars*. He seemed to allege that the push for more moderation was borne out of a profit interest, not a moral high ground.

With billions of people on Facebook it only takes a tiny percentage to post "inappropriate" stuff, which often gets shared and re-posted endlessly, before you need an army of moderators—the specialists who keep your newsfeed clean, so you can continue to look at the ads Facebook makes billions out of.[21]

The topic of desensitization was raised again:

It's not just the gore and suffering, it's the insidious drip-drip-drip of half-truths and emotional arguments that make extremists start to make sense, and those racist memes look really funny.[22]

The author asked if emotionally disturbed people (the moderators) policing the internet is "good." Frankly, I don't think anyone wants to answer that question or provide further coverage.

My take is that this work is important, and none of the thousands of contractors are tackling Instagram growth service providers who have reverse-engineered Instagram's API.

Gatekeeping

The best way to keep undesirable folks out of the castle is to stop them at the gate. Once inside, finding and kicking them out can be onerous.

Outcomes are better if bad people are stopped from logging in at all. "Gatekeeping" has increasingly been used to describe insufferable people safeguarding their hobbies from newcomers. It also applies to social media platforms, as non-niche as they may seem.

These days, social media platforms don't want to be known for elitism or exclusivity. There are teams dedicated to getting new users up and running as quickly as possible. However, precautions are taken even if there is a dastardly incentive to welcome *everyone*, including bots, fake accounts, and other scoundrels.

Most platforms require users to log in to see most content and use discovery features. This is a small price for most users. Requiring a login is a typical funnel ("registration locking" content) for web-based businesses. For social media sites, the practice offers a veil of privacy from unsophisticated bad guys and data miners. A stalker or other predator would prefer not to log in to Instagram to stalk someone. Thankfully, Instagram's web client doesn't show much content to users who aren't logged in, and the app is only usable for logged-in users. It's not perfect, but if a dangerous person is forced to sign up and then commits a crime enabled by Instagram browsing, Instagram should have more information for law enforcement (likely including a phone number, IP address, and cohesive usage history). A web scraper mining data from Instagram profiles is similarly a terms-of-service-violating nuisance. By requiring those actors to create accounts (which can then be action-blocked and banned), Instagram can drive up the cost of unwanted automated activity on the platform.

The final frontier of gatekeeping is ID verification. The future of everything is ID verification. If we assume that government-issued identification documents can't be forged, then requiring IDs will surely help ensure "safety." Convicted sex offenders already aren't allowed on the platform. But how effective is that policy if a user's identity isn't confirmed? In 2009, the eye-popping headline was "MySpace removes 90,000 sex offenders."[23] On the other hand, verification is costly for the platform and makes signups languish. It leaves a bad taste in the mouth for those who have used the internet under screen names like CrazyEmoNinjaBoy4040 and reduces the chance of a user returning after being stymied by a request for official documentation.

Subscription Locking and Paywalls

"Subscription locking" and "paywall[ing]" describe when platforms take previously free (or, free elsewhere) features and place them behind a paywall.

Social media is free, right? What could be locked away behind anything other than a login?

This is not the place to debate the "cost" of social media. I will however wax about money changing hands. When it comes down to it, Instagram *growth* is behind a paywall: the Meta ads platform. Anyone who wants to meaningfully grow or promote themselves or their products must pay to promote posts on the platform.

Greater costs for users mean that the rule-breaking users will also incur greater costs. As the costs rise, the overall amount of activity tied to those costs should decrease. Channeling growth through an internal ads platform benefits platform integrity as a whole.

Mandating payment details does quite a bit to identify a person or entity to a business. Second, the platform will more closely scrutinize promoted posts for objectionable (rule-breaking) content. Users aren't usually happy to see integrated promoted content in their feeds, but if it's targeted properly, it's preferable to megacorp banner ads.

Niche social media sites do use paywalls, or "premium" subscriptions. For example, LinkedIn and Strava both "lock" substantial features and "premium" *badges* behind monthly fees. Of course, they still manage to extract value from their free users.

Like Instagram, they are still expected to safeguard their free users. They might use shadowbans to enforce platform integrity.

9

SAFEGUARDING AND
SHADOWBANS PART II

M eta has its hands full when keeping users "safe." Given the spectrum of wrongdoing on social networks, it's no wonder that fake accounts and bots might not be the top priority.

Abiding users are stuck in the middle. They are inconvenienced by restrictions meant for the bad guys, and their experiences are simultaneously sullied by the effects of illicit activities.

Users must undergo "continuing education" to understand how rules change and rule-breakers operate. There are always new nuisances and risks. Refreshing one's understanding of the forces at play is valuable.

Humans can perform a number of basic checks to identify malicious accounts. Those who have access to bespoke software can go further, and by thinking like a bot buster, we can understand the techniques that Instagram uses to safeguard the platform from bad intentions, including poorly understood enforcement actions such as the "shadowban."

Humans Assessing Bots

Profile picture

The classic test of a user's legitimacy is the profile picture. Reverse image search services can assess profile pictures to determine if it has been stolen. A profile picture that seems suspiciously professional (or attractive) but "off" might be AI-generated or purchased from a stock image provider. If a user has a professional-looking business headshot on Instagram but is enticing users to buy research chemicals from an online pharmacy, that doesn't make sense. The photo should match the theme of the profile. Pictures can be run through genAI detectors.

Post history and account age

The easiest way to catch fake profiles is by assessing their post histories —scrolling through the image gallery and seeing when content was first uploaded. No history or sparse history dramatically increases the chance that the account was created with bad intentions.

Instagram has existed for more than a decade. Although new people join every day, new users are viewed with suspicion. If it is a scammer or a bot, it's probably not the account overseer's first rodeo and will probably skip some steps to quickly return to nefariousness.

A gallery stuffed with recent content should be viewed with suspicion. Nobody is consistently posting five pictures per day. Anyone slamming content probably also has congruence problems. This is hard to detect programmatically, but a human can catch it. A bot could post poorly curated content to seem more legitimate, but human analysis would reveal inconsistencies. Figuring out how to scrape/post content congruent with a central theme was a major achievement of Chris Buetti's, whose *@beautiful.newyorkcity* account was a 2019 masterpiece of automation.[1]

An account's age has been rumored to be a primary metric used by Instagram to identify misbehavior and scrutinize account quality. An account created the same week it starts posting at a high rate has a basement-level "trust score." For this reason, account sellers will reserve "fresh" accounts for a while and later tout them as "aged" accounts because they supposedly fool this aspect of Instagram's trust classification system and better evade detection.

Engagement Rate

One of the most authoritative indicators of whether an account is "real" or regular is the "engagement rate." This refers to the number of users who interact with content relative to an account's total number of followers. This may be averaged across a full post history, the most recent nine posts, or on a picture-by-picture basis. It's usually just likes but can be a combination of likes and comments. Of course, a picture shown to an extended audience by the feed algorithm can have an engagement rate exceeding one hundred percent.

Low engagement means poor content quality. Near-zero or highly inconsistent engagement suggests shady activity.

Though not discussed often, a human can assess whether the account seems to have *any* engagements from genuine *friends*—people who express familiarity beyond cyberspace, including nicknames, inside jokes, and reciprocal engagements. No bot operator is faking detailed sidebars and two-sided relationships. I'd call this "network intimacy" or "real friend rate," the number of *commenters* who appear to be close friends with a user.

Followers, following

Followers and following form the foundation of reputation. The "follower-following" ratio is useful, but the raw number of followers or users followed is usually enough to judge reputation.

On Myspace, too many friends would make the chronological bulletin feed chaotic and unusable. This is less of a concern with algorithmic feeds, but generally, someone following more than a thousand accounts would have an unpleasant feed.

Many users pay a lot of money to increase their follower counts. "Too many" followers is subjective, but it's an important sense to develop. For example, my 5200 Twitter followers were "too many" for a college freshman. However, I now have friends with more than 5200 Twitter followers, and I'm not suspicious at all.

In my experience, SMM panel bot accounts within a cluster would follow each other to legitimize each account. Furthermore, finding accounts with "round" numbers (e.g., 988, 5010) of followers attracts special scrutiny. Numbers that hover around those marketed by follower sellers suggest purchased followers.

Investigating an account's following can elucidate its intentions. Who are these people? Is there a pattern? This becomes very hard for a non-technical user to approach, but for smaller accounts (say, two hundred followers or less), it's a viable check.

Display name – username parity

Gibberish display names and randomly generated usernames are usually indicative of bogus accounts. Creating an account is a prideful pursuit. It's expected that any account creator would want to personalize their handle or display name.

Consider the presence of numbers in the handle. Although numbers are increasingly necessary to create distinct usernames as new users flood the internet, everyone prefers as few and as meaningful numbers as possible. I prefer Tim1 or Tim1994 over Tim1029829. YouTube recently forced accounts to include numbers in their usernames, likely to prevent impersonation. Some YouTube accounts with names like "Jesus Christ" were leaving parody comments on videos where a comment from Jesus was absurdist humor. This merrimaking tended to be highly "liked," but it could have also been used for impersonation-based trust scams.

By "display name – username parity" I mean that some programmatically-generated accounts might have more structure to their names and usernames, but patterns may be obvious, either in the relationship between display name and username or between the networked accounts, because the accounts are created *en masse*. For example, the display name could be repeated in the username or the username is always a certain length.

I've observed bot farms mixing up given names and surnames in combinations that could be valid but look unnatural, like Carlos Fitzpatrick or Donatella Chang.

Reels

Although a page visitor can't easily assess how often a user posts ephemeral Reels or when the last one was posted, a history of coherent saved Reels helps establish that a profile is probably real. A profile with no saved or active Reels is more suspicious.

Links and redirects

Spam accounts have always infiltrated social media platforms to link users to external websites. The easiest way is to provide a link. Instagram allows users to include one link on their bio page, subject to some restrictions.

Controlling link spam is actually pretty easy. In the past, webmasters auto-rejected comments that contained hyperlinks or formed web addresses. Spammers navigated this by adding spaces or symbols or even posting links as photos.

Regardless, accounts that appear constructed to link users elsewhere will draw the ire of other users. Getting users to jump is lucrative, and it's feasible for scammers to continuously create (or buy) new accounts to draw in new marks.

With the explosion in web-based adult entertainment in the early

2020s, performers wanted to link to their "spicy" content from their Instagram bios. At least since 2021, Instagram has banned accounts for linking directly to so-called inappropriate content. Creators have switched to using external link aggregators, but those aggregated links may conceal links to dishonest websites.

If an account appears to be a funnel to somewhere else, people take it less seriously.

Bots Assessing Bots

Socialblade.com is a social media analytics website. It grabs data like views and likes from different social media platforms, plots it, and makes it searchable. Depending on the access methods and "commercial" applications of the data, this activity violates platforms' terms of use and potentially the current legal precedent on "scraping" for commercial gain.

However, last time I checked, Social Blade is permitted by Instagram, using some software integration with Instagram's APIs. Has it been permitted by every site it has evaluated since it started operating? I don't think so. "Grey hat" businesses like hiQ Labs provide immense value from scraping-driven analytics products. Someone could recreate Social Blade using scrapers, but that would violate Instagram's terms.

Social Blade and sites like it are used to analyze account metrics over time. The dashboards display the number of posts, followers/following, engagement rate, average likes, and average comments. They also display follower growth to identify users who have anomalous jumps in their metrics and might have bought followers.

IP addresses are unique identifiers on the internet. When a client sends a request that reaches Instagram, usually by way of Instagram's app, but also by use of Instagram's private API, Instagram's servers log the IP address. A cell phone has an IP address. A computer has an IP address. These addresses can be thought of as street addresses.

Internet location addressing works because IP addresses contain identifying information. This identifying information, supplemented by usage data from other IP addresses, contributes to "IP address quality."

An IP address in an Amazon datacenter, a so-called "datacenter IP," is lower quality than an address assigned to a home, called a "residential IP." Phones have "mobile IP" addresses. Bad guys rotate through data center IPs when they want to conceal the source of their traffic. Residential IPs, because they're significantly harder to obtain, tend to be the most trustworthy.

When someone layers another IP address to conceal their own, that's called a "proxy."

Instagram flags data center IPs at the gate. Instagram will flag any IP address whenever there is suspicious activity. If twenty accounts send tons of likes from the same high-trust residential IP address, something is likely amiss. Instagram will re-assess a proxy's trustworthiness on a case-by-case basis.

Flagging and assessment require computing power and applied statistics. If an outsider could view an account's IP (impossible unless a phone user is lured to click a link), they could discover an IP in an Amazon data center. Amazon publicizes its IP ranges. However, fine-grained IP "trust" lives within Instagram's systems.

To avoid detection, bot farm operators purchase or create proxies, which are sometimes "rotated" to keep sites from detecting that the traffic sent through does not conform to the terms of service. Addresses might change every ten requests. This may help bots stay ahead of the sliding reputation of (ranges of) proxies used for black hat activity.

Other pattern matching

When bot accounts are created *en masse* or clusters of accounts are manipulated to do bad things, zooming out can be helpful. The accounts usually will have some commonality, at least relative to each other. This is part of the "new kind of detective work" referenced in "Uncovering Instagram Bots With a New Kind of Detective Work"[2] from March 2018 regarding bot detection. The creation of a follower's account in April 2015 isn't cause for concern. Foul play is likely if sixty percent of an account's followers were created in April 2015.[3]

It's statistically improbable that so many followers were created around the same time unless the same person created them using illicit account creation software.

A group of accounts, typically from an account's followers, should be compared against one another because bots or suspicious accounts (like those that astroturf discussions in comments) don't typically act alone. Even if a user has a hundred thousand followers, interesting patterns can be found by analyzing all of them, even those that aren't obvious bots.

Account creation date, if available, is a useful metric. Any other statistical outliers are fair game; many are related to the checks outlined above. Other examples include username length or formatting, number of posts, bio text, or pictures copied between accounts.

The scale of this pattern matching is too large to be performed by hand. Ironically, scraping an account's followers requires a web scraper or private API access, which are both against Instagram's terms of service. So "new detective work" may mean violating terms of service to assess terms of service violations. Nobody is doing this for fun, they're earning money from it. From "Uncovering Instagram Bots With a New Kind of Detective Work":[4]

> Dovetale flagged one account that claimed to be someone named Meg Cragle because it was part of a group of profiles that had made one or two unrelated posts and contained similarly worded bios of exactly 99 characters that ended with ellipses.

If not made available by API access closely monitored by a platform provider, these deep investigations of any "group of profiles" are nigh impossible. For the layman, they'd require scraping Instagram and storing the results or employing an army from a country where cheap labor and smartphones are prevalent, therefore violating Instagram's terms of service. I can't know exactly what Dovetale was doing, but it's worth mentioning that the company seemed to pivot away from intensive Instagram analysis and into software-aided influence marketing before being acquired by Shopify in 2022.[5]

Instagram already owns the data and can query it seamlessly. This removes significant barriers, so Instagram's algorithms may be more advanced than this and definitely more advanced than Tim O'Hearn can blindly guess.

Instagram's Bot Busting

If botting, which is profitable, goes unchecked and if account creation can be done automatically and at a low cost, a platform will eventually reach a state in which the majority of active users are bots and the majority of activity is conducted by bots. This feeds into the "dead internet theory." This isn't desirable!

Instagram's content moderation is as expensive as it is imperfect. Why can't all bots be eliminated today? Why can't all rule-breakers be thrown out a window? Perfect enforcement means inconveniences for compliant users.

Consider the duality. What if a bot isn't *always* a bot? Those who purchase growth services are probably only botting part-time. Some scrolled while the bot ran in the cloud! A computer program can still control a real person's account. They aren't all blatant cluster accounts identifiable by "new kinds of detective work." What if a user automates *ten clicks per day*? How could that possibly be caught?

I'll provide an outsider's take on Instagram's methods for busting bots and ramrodding those with bad intentions.

Instagram Trust Score

There's a strong belief in the "Instagram Trust Score." Instagram assigns a score to each account at signup, and the score changes with a user's actions. The lower the trust score, the more likely an account ban. If the trust score is higher, the user may be granted broader exposure in the feed. People love keeping score. They're blissfully unaware of how closely their activities are being scrutinized.

On early social media sites, detailed behavior tracking wasn't necessary. Either a user had earned a ban, or they hadn't. Besides, it's expensive and complicated to track each action and constantly run calculations of quality or trustworthiness. Given unlimited resources, engineers, game publishers, and webmasters would love trust score systems that score and aggregate users' actions.

Like recommendation systems, trust score systems are hard to implement fairly and automate completely. Badly behaving users don't know their scores, so they can't give "feedback." The only "feedback" is whether a ban was justified or not. Volunteer moderators used to hand out bans in response to in-game transgressions. Instagram employs tens of thousands to manually assess content while implementing a sophisticated system for overall account trustworthiness—allegedly. It's never been officially addressed.

Malice prevention systems have broad notions of trust scores. It's more common to get a difficult CAPTCHA puzzle when browsing with a VPN. Cloudflare DDoS-mitigation queuing is also more sensitive when malicious behavior patterns are matched.

It makes sense that Instagram doesn't document this system for outsiders. Implementing a trust score helps Instagram better protect its interests. Admitting its existence invites unnecessary prying and, eventually, attempts to game the system.

My question is, why would Instagram *not* calculate an account's overall engagement ratio and use it to decide which accounts to closely monitor? Assuming 2020s technology costs, a company would *not* do it only if their software or data infrastructure was poorly designed or they had no use for it. Even Chris Buetti, the data scientist, was able to create classifiers for the quality, or *trust*, of pictures and accounts his scrapers evaluated.[6] Instagram's system is probably just Buetti's system times a hundred.

In the late 2010s, whispers of a "trust score" eventually turned to shouts. There are hundreds of mentions of this concept on BlackHatWorld dating back to December 2016, where G-S-T said: "The only thing I can attribute this level of engagement to is the fact that the accounts have got a decent trust score from their age and are getting preferential treatment in the hashtag search results."[7] The number of mentions through 2017 was meager. In mid-2018, as black hat automation attracted more participants and Instagram started hunting down bots, it was mentioned several times per week.

On a site not known for insightful comments, discussions referencing a "trust score" tended to be some of the most informative and thought-provoking. Consider this August 2019 comment: "Does anyone know if paid ads on Instagram help make the account trust score better?".[8] We still don't know the answer to this question, but it lends itself to the conspiracy that those who pay for Instagram ads may receive preferential treatment. It was a reasonable inquiry!

Fully reverse engineering trust scores was not feasible. However, operators could isolate some important aspects, such as the circumstances of an account's creation or daily actions, commonly referred to as "activity limits." Black hat engineers tracked the number of interactions their bots took before they got action blocked or banned and proposed thresholds for safe automation activity (such as "three hundred follows per day," a common rule of thumb). A few sophisticated users with enough burner accounts to sacrifice claimed they were able to tease out specifics. In January 2017, a user named Henry Cooper claimed, "The fancy stuff is about how having a mail.ru email on the account [a]ffects your trust score (supported with numbers)."[9]

I can't get too excited. Henry Cooper never provided those supporting numbers. Think about how hard it would be to isolate a specific email address extension as a relevant feature within the universe of all the features that could lead to an account ban.

Given unlimited resources to obtain new accounts and run botting scripts on them, a user could closely approximate a trust score threshold. However, it would mean months of breaking Instagram's terms of service and require sacrificing hundreds, if not thousands, of accounts along with valuable proxies. Until a ban or enforcement action is enacted, no conclusion can be drawn from the experiment (unless it goes on for long enough to conclude that it doesn't harm a trust score). The overall trust score wasn't the most important to black hat operators. The activity bounds, *a rough proxy for trust*, were largely considered good enough.

I feel pressure to speculate what *exactly* I think factors into the "trust score" and go beyond "beat the trust score" style blog posts and forum threads. I'm willing to do this with the admission that I personally proved few of these items—most are my intuition or suggestions from others in the space.

Tim's speculation on behaviors and "trust score"

Harmful:

- Account recently created
- Account created with a datacenter IP address (or other IP with a low "IP trust score")
- Account created with a low-quality email address
- Account created on a device with a low "device trust score"
- Account not phone-verified ("PVA")
- Device creation/device login disparity
- No profile picture
- Recently changed profile picture

- Low engagement rate/high proportion of "low trust" followers or engagers
- High following/follower ratio
- High rate of unfollowing accounts
- Content reported and removed by moderators
- Sending follow requests to private accounts that get denied
- High frequency of posts, comments, or DMs
- Low cooldown time between actions
- High number of received blocks
- Overuse of hashtags
- High proportion of users tagged in photos removing their tags
- Having a link in the bio
- Having an empty bio
- Logging in from multiple, distant locations (i.e., proxy hopping, account sharing)
- Having faced a previous enforcement action (a "permanent record")

Helpful:

- *The opposite of harmful behaviors, where applicable*
- Having linked accounts with other Meta products
- Becoming "verified"
- Buying ads
- Posting Reels
- Reciprocating actions with a user
- Higher "network intimacy"
- Regular daily logins

CAPTCHA

Instagram employs CAPTCHAs during certain login flows to determine if a user is human. They can be ridiculously challenging because bots have become better at solving them.

CAPTCHAs help prevent spam, denial of service attacks, scraping, and all automated bad behavior. However, if a user has to deal with a tricky challenge every login, that's no fun.

Both humans and computers can have trouble solving CAPTCHAs. I have failed at least fifty in my lifetime. When I started writing this book, computers could not reliably solve them without a significant budget allocated to image recognition. With generative AI, some people now consider CAPTCHAs obsolete—a small hurdle to make unwanted automation more expensive.

CAPTCHAs are usually delivered when certain risk factors have been identified. This is true across the internet, like in the Cloudflare example above. CAPTCHAs are often just trivial checkboxes. Whenever I use an incognito browser, I encounter more difficult ones. Whenever I leave my VPN connected to a low-quality data center IP address, my browsing experience is greatly degraded. Some sites are rendered unusable. It's common for scraping programs to use data center proxies and browsers with tracking features disabled. The software that delivers captures is pattern-matching users with bad guys encountered in training data.

CAPTCHAs can stop low-effort botting. There are costs to solving them, whether by human (owner), computer (image recognition or local AI), or outsourced (other humans or other computers via a "CAPTCHA solver" service). They no longer block bots reliably, but they increase the cost for malicious users to operate and safeguard against hapless script kiddies.

Yes, it's me

Rotating through proxies seems like a good idea. What if an Instagram account logs in from Baltimore in the morning and Brazil in the afternoon?

Though thought to be designed more for account security (like the original "I'm getting hacked" security), Instagram implemented an onerous login flow in 2019. Upon detecting "suspicious" activity—in Shark Social's case, a private API login from a data center IP different from a customer's usual IP—Instagram locked the account and required whoever had access to the account's email address to affirm, "Yes, it's me."

This system frustrated black hatters since it could be triggered regularly, requiring daily intervention.

This system was sneakily effective because it caused growth services customers, many of whom didn't think they were violating any rules, to think, "Oh, crap, could I lose my account here?" At least fifteen percent of

Shark Social's customers didn't realize that we would be logging into their accounts, even though they provided their passwords, and we made it clear during signup. Instagram's block-induced panic caused customers to ask for snap refunds. It made onboarding annoying because we often had to collaborate with customers to establish access. They'd miss our messages, become angry, and ask for refunds. At least fifty customers were lost this way.

The issue persisted even when using burner accounts, but solving it was easier since a burner account owner can access its email inbox. Advanced software engineers fully automated the process of receiving the login failure, checking the email, clicking the email (button or code), and proceeding with the login.

API Restrictions

In the good ole days, internet software companies, founded by nerds, gleefully promoted their public APIs. See what you can do! Happy hacking!

By the early 2020s, there were few public APIs left. Usage was conditioned upon thousands of words of user agreements. Hackathons, the student-run programming contests to "hack together" different APIs to create whacky apps, were degraded under these new restrictions.

There are many reasons for API restrictions or public API shutdowns, such as:

1. With unrestricted access to the voluminous data available on a social network, it's easy to "exfiltrate" data. With the data siphoned away, it was possible to create a data reselling service, perhaps one that resulted in user-provided contact mediums (public phone numbers and email addresses) getting spammed. Instagram gains nothing from these reselling services and wants to curtail them.
2. Competitors and enemies could harness data streams to gather valuable competitive intelligence.
3. API methods that allow programmatic actions (liking, commenting, following, DMing) can be used to mercilessly spam users and degrade the quality of interactions on the

platform. This was seen as far back as with the Myspace MyFriendBot.

However, I think that Instagram's sunsetting of its public API in 2018 resulted in a speed bump for black hat operators. Criticism aside, it was a reprieve from spam and unwanted activities.

Sophisticated programmers switched to using the private API. Others were scared away or forced to pause services while they regrouped. Instagram, in its own documentation, used to recommend using third-party services that utilized its public API for things like analyzing followers. It's hard to agree that the elimination of the public API was a net positive, but the safeguards borne out of it did guarantee a better experience for the "good" guys.

Action Limits/API Usage Restrictions

Instagram wants users to use the platform less *if*, that is, they approach a certain usage threshold.

Social media companies revel in user metrics, especially high-conviction actions, like commenting. Comparatively, typing and posting a comment takes *a lot* of effort. If a user leaves ten comments in a day, that's abnormal. Maybe it raises some eyebrows. But it boosts Instagram's cachet. That user is *more active*. In the aggregate, the shareholders will like that. What if a user leaves one hundred comments?

In the old days, Instagram was permissive of user actions. More user actions meant growth services could earn clients more followers. During the Instagress Era, daily actions could approach one thousand without fear of a ban.

Toward the end of my involvement with Instagram growth, the rule of thumb was three hundred follows per day, max.

According to Reddit user Instagram_Marketer,[10] the 2023 "action limits" were along the lines of:

- 20-25 follows per hour
- 160-200 follows per day
- 2-3 comments per hour
- 7-15 comments per day

- 10-15 likes per hour
- 100-120 likes per day

Recall that Instagram did provide "rate limits" for each endpoint while hosting its open API. Nowadays, users have to uncover them. It's an inexact science because these variables can't be fully isolated. There's never an explicit message like, "You followed 201 people, you're banned!" There are pages and pages of speculation on BlackHatWorld under titles like, "2017 automation guidelines," but there are so many trust factors that nobody can be sure. I believe it's so complex that there are developers on Instagram's anti-botting team who *would not be able* to state "limits" like those posted by reddit savants or the software rate limiters of days past. However, action limits were closely analyzed, and bot software providers, like Jarvee, constantly updated their default settings and guidelines to respect changes.

Still, accounts were disabled.

It's debated whether Instagram actually has "hard" limits on these actions or what some experienced automators have uncovered is merely a sidecar to a complex trust score. Having worked through the dog days of Instagram's bot busting, I admit that there were times when I doubted all conventional wisdom. I believe that there are more factors at play. I outlined them above, but I have enough data showing account bans converging around certain numbers within certain windows of time. Action limits are real.

How Instagram Punishes Bad Behavior

Users who behave badly often face consequences, ranging from a virtual slap on the wrist to being served with court papers. I'll provide an overview of the enforcement actions Instagram takes to ensure a more pleasant scrolling experience, and, indirectly, greater shareholder equity.

Auto-moderation is a newer tool. Rather than Instagram waiting for users to report objectionable text posts, like captions and comments, Instagram has trained systems to identify and censor words and phrases found to be offensive in past reports. According to Instagram, "you're stupid" may be prohibited language because it violates the community guidelines, and Instagram is a "positive" place.[11]

Any auto-moderated text is prevented from being posted. Instagram doesn't seem to penalize further if their filters catch future attempts. This is all sourced from the Instagram parents' guide.

Removal of inauthentic activity was first threatened on November 19, 2018.[12] Instagram announced that it built "machine learning tools" to find and eliminate activity "from accounts that use third-party apps to boost their popularity." This targeted organic growth providers, not fake follower farms. While there's no doubt that Instagram *did* identify these offending accounts and blanketed customers with scary in-app warning messages, I never saw evidence that the actions had been removed *en masse*. In discussions from the time, nobody presented evidence of the threat being carried out (however, researchers affiliated with Meta did "invent" this practice and enacted it during the course of their research).

Action Blocks are dispatched to users who take too many actions on the platform. Although Instagram doesn't publish guidelines for how *many* actions are allowed per window of time, the limit has been ratcheted down significantly since 2018. In 2018, only bots were getting action blocks. Today, hyperactive users get them too. "Actions" include anything that changes the platform, such as likes, comments, or follows. Action blocks don't stop users from navigating around the app. It's thought that activity limits are somewhat relative to an account's trust score. Guides available on BlackHatWorld recommend "ramp-up" periods for new accounts, which are generally considered to have lower scores.

Action blocks commonly expire at the end of the "window" during which a user has taken too many actions. These windows are usually twenty-four hours. However, severe action blocks, possibly for repeated infractions, can last longer. Users will be notified of specific dates and times when they can resume taking actions.

I've seen mentions that action blocks can be permanent (essentially, making an account read-only) but not seen evidence. My experience is that, for repeated violations, the account will be **banned**.

Account bans ("disables") and IP bans are two severe punishments. The terms say that anyone banned cannot sign up for another Instagram account. IP bans help enforce that rule more strictly, as a user's IP address and device ID can be prevented from signing up again. If a user has self-verified or re-used an email address, the platform can easily reference that and ban the user again or place the account in a type of permanent shadow-ban. I estimate that Instagram bans over ten thousand users per day.

Beyond a ban, Instagram has two options: **refer cases to local law enforcement** or **file a lawsuit** for violations that undermine the platform. A wide range of behaviors would fall under the jurisdiction of local law enforcement. Those that cause significant harm to Meta might be addressed in court.

Instagram's account decisions can be appealed once. Instagram provides users with an in-app form to "disagree with the decision," which is available thirty days after the account is disabled. Although this is new, the appeal process also encourages users to verify their identities by uploading photos of government-issued ID cards.

Instagram also enforces **content removal**. Moderation decisions are made by humans and AI and sometimes originate from user-submitted reports:

> Artificial intelligence (AI) technology is central to our content review process. AI can detect and remove content that goes against our Community Guidelines before anyone reports it. Other times, our technology sends content to human review teams to take a closer look and make a decision on it.[13]

Once content is in the moderation queue, moderators—those with *the worst job in technology*[14]—assess it. Users who reported content or had their content reported can request an appeal. In some cases, content decisions can be appealed to Meta's Oversight Board.[15]

Legal Action Against Private API Coders

Taking down publicly shared source code that facilitates rule-breaking is one method for bot eradication. Unfortunately, code spreads quickly as users clone and fork it.

Tim Grossman invented InstaPy. It was one of the earliest Instagram automation libraries and was shared on GitHub in September 2016. Tim was generous enough to answer dozens of my questions.

It took five years, but Instagram served Tim a cease-and-desist for the project that he earned no income from. This was captured in "Facebook goes after the creator of InstaPy, a tool that automates Instagram likes."[16] As a response, Tim "gave away 100% of the control of the repository and everything" but still ended up with lifetime bans from Meta's services.

Tim speculated that (the) two contemporaneous open-source libraries, Instabot and InstagramAPI, both helmed by a mysterious user with the screen name, LevPasha, were also "shut down" in Instagram's bot eradication effort. Those repositories disappeared years ago. Tim Grossman's, under new ownership, remains on GitHub. In his words, "Open-source projects like this can't be fully removed." Although the disappearance of original branches of peer libraries challenges this, Tim's perspective on how open-source works is right on, and much of what occurred in the black hat Instagram space bears the fingerprints of a talented software engineer who earned nothing from his creation.

Shadowbans and Algorithmic Interference

A "shadowban" is a stealthy account restriction in which a user can use a platform but is *secretly* disadvantaged or hidden. Although this has been defined on Urban Dictionary's site since 2007 and was known to me in 2017, I'd argue it only became mainstream due to Twitter controversies in 2018 and repeated allegations by TikTok content creators in the early 2020s.

I've seen claims that shadowbans also include users leaving likes and comments that don't persist *and* aren't visible to other users. This isn't well corroborated. The primary definition of "shadowban" is when a user is still *able* to post content, but the content is shown to very few users. In some cases, the content won't be shown to anyone, including followers. On Instagram, the content also won't appear on the Explore page, and the user's entire account and posts might not be visible on the search page.

To my surprise, Instagram actually acknowledged "Shadowbanning" in a June 8, 2021, blog post, "Shedding More Light on How Instagram Works."[17]

Well, kind of.

The most important quote from that post is "We also hear that people consider their posts getting fewer likes or comments as a form of 'shadowbanning.'"

The rest of the paragraph is a wordy non-explanation that invites further speculation. Instagram didn't come out and say that they shadowban or have an internal notion of a "trust score" that plugs into a shadowban formula. They didn't address algorithmic interference or how easily their algorithms could be altered to promote some topics while demoting others.

Consensus says that Instagram *must* design systems that punish users for posting spammy, harmful, or low-quality content. A shadowban, which may only be temporary, may precede an action block or actual ban. The advantage of shadowbanning is its invisibility. It happens covertly and casts the user's content into the shadows. There's a chance a user won't notice unless they ask their friends if they saw a post. Instagram doesn't have to deal with the support kerfuffle of users whose reach is restricted to the point that they are, effectively, not *on* the platform at all. A user can't appeal a shadowban because, as far as Instagram is concerned, shadowbans don't exist!

Urban Dictionary provides a glimpse into the evolution of the term from 2007 to 2019.[18]

The 2007 definition says, "Banning a user from a web forum in such a way that the banned user is unaware of the ban...Considered underhanded chicken-shit behavior."

The 2011 definition, seemingly *responding* to the 2007 definition, says, "A method of banning users where their posts are visible only to them. Created to prevent spammers, trolls, and flamers from realizing they have been banned and creating new accounts. *Considered underhanded chicken-shit behavior by trolls who hate being trolled.*"

When the 2007 definition was posted, the author absolutely meant "web forum" when he typed "web forum." The 2011 definition also indicated forums (a truncated portion including "the forum") rather than social networks, as further evidenced by the inclusion of the term "flamers," which means "someone who starts a flame war (argument)." This is antiquated in today's web language but, in my experience, was *more common* than "troll" in the late aughts.

The 2018 definition emerged when accusations of shadowbans proliferated on Twitter. It's logical that shadowbans re-emerged in text-based social networks rather than a less serious, picture-based platform, like Instagram. More serious, denser content is shared on Twitter. The author makes explicit the link between Twitter and shadowbans:

A Shadowban is an excuse trolls and sad people use to justify why no one bothers to read, reply or like the content that they post online. They assume that it must be because their content is hidden from public view, in fact they're just boring.

I know for sure I've been shadowbanned because hardly anyone comments or likes my posts on Twitter. It's definitely a shadowban conspiracy because I know, I'm like, genius, and everyone would be amazed by my super-radical views.[19]

On Twitter, shadowbans, or the belief in shadowbans, became so widespread that "Shadowban Test" services emerged to check an account's Tweet visibility from different test observer accounts. Although such tests couldn't measure *all* aspects of a shadowban (such as initial reach or expansion of reach), they could confirm whether Tweets were hidden from search. Similar practices can be applied to Instagram shadowban analyses, though, confirming that *initial reach* is brutally penalized because conducting such an experiment requires measurements of past reach, which would ultimately require login access to all an account's followers.

The definition submitted in 2019 is much darker. It suggests a metamorphosis of the idea from "chicken-shit" behavior to Orwellian censorship. The definition has shifted from "annoying users versus complying users" to "users expressing opinions versus users likely on the other side of those debates" to "the platforms versus the platform users, especially those expressing unpopular opinions."

ShadowBan:

When totalitarian entities use automated algorithms in social media to 'back page' or make content or users no longer findable

These bans are usually set in place to prevent quality content such as criticism, investigative methods or political commentating

Has anybody noticed that conservative and conspiracy media is being ShadowBanned?

I can tell by going to YouTube statistics sites that my views are not being shown for what they actually are, we're being ShadowBanned folks while van life gets artificial growth[20]

Proving that conservative media is systemically shadowbanned while "van life" (videos about people living in vans) is artificially boosted is diffi-cult. My personal experience described in "Influencers, Verifying Them" was that my "Trump Riot" livestream from 2016 did not appear when I searched the term "Trump" but did appear when I searched for "riot." I don't consider that a shadow*ban* because to me, a ban suggests action taken against a specific account. It was, however, clear evidence of *algorithmic interference,* which had nothing to do with purported "safety." The term "riot" is a dangerous search term, yet the term "Trump" was interfered with.

Acknowledging shadowbans means acknowledging shadow*boosting*. If a platform can and wants to disadvantage a post, then the opposite is also true. Posts may be artificially boosted while users remain unaware. Plat-forms could easily and secretly "shadowban" users who post criticisms of the platform while "shadowboosting" users who praise the platform. Pundits would be up in arms if the naysayers were banned and formally silenced; shadowbanning is an extremely effective Information Age propa-ganda tool.

You Can't Call Instagram

I don't envy Meta for being at the frontier of online safety. The costs of upholding "safety" are astronomical: employing moderators, supporting software systems, reviewing appeal decisions, pursuing legal actions, and navigating the fallout when things go wrong.

Instagram and all other social networks have an advantage over legacy enterprises in that they can't be reached by phone. There is no customer support line or email address. Once an appeal is denied, that's it. Read the docs for any other inquiry.

The internet is filled with frantic people with disabled accounts. These aren't Devumi-style bot farmers with thousands of accounts (though I'm sure those people were frantic too). These are everyday people, like the bread baker. Some deserved bans; others probably didn't. An account ban covers a wide swath of the wheel of emotions: *rage, loathing, grief, terror.* Witnessing a fresh ban is like witnessing someone get served with divorce papers. That social proof, that eternal commitment is violated.

When people get desperate on the internet, predators circle.

"Recovery scamming" is an emerging trend where scammers trawl social media sites (especially reddit and Facebook) for users complaining about having *lost* social media accounts, passwords, or keys for cryptocurrency wallets. I posted an inquiry about this book in the "Hackathon Hackers" Facebook group just to see comments left by bots mistaking my post for a complaint that my account was hacked.

The scammers assure users that their services are legit. They aren't. They collect thousands of dollars from users in emotional turmoil facing "big" losses in actual terms (cryptocurrency) or social-proof terms (social media profiles).

Users pursue alternative paths to recovery with varying levels of success. The tried and true "public appeal" on a different social network, which does tend to have success with customer-oriented businesses, doesn't seem to help users restore their social media accounts. The cases I reviewed seemed to only attract recovery scammers.

It turns out that Meta does have a customer support line, though it isn't well advertised, and the contact methods have changed multiple times as I've written this book. Essentially, Meta increasingly offers resources to *paying* customers, those who run ads through Meta Business. Scrappy users who want to "ask questions" have purchased small ad packages hoping to talk to "real people" known as "Meta Support Pros" because the lower-tiered support is outsourced and overburdened. Users on the internet report varying levels of success with this.

Intuitively, *some* level of ad spend must qualify users for dedicated U.S.-based support representatives. Meta has an interest in keeping fat cats happy. Usually, though, someone spending six figures on ads each month isn't going to get banned for running a bot or harassing people in the first place. The "support" needs will be totally different, quite a bit elevated from needing to reverse a ban for calling someone stupid.

No set number qualifies users for a Meta Business representative. Similar to what constitutes the curation of topics under the Explore page, users allege that there is randomness at play. In "Anyone know a spend amount that'll get the attention of an account manager at FB?"[21] *someone reported getting* a rep after $500k ad spend in a year. In the same discussion, someone else reported spending "around $500k" and getting "support" but that "Facebook still treat[s] me like I'm a fucking bozo."[22] Others said that the domain vertical and "overall brand awareness" is what matters. Nobody really knows. *I don't.* But it's clear that even with extravagant ad spend, people find Meta's support to be stingy.

A different reddit thread suggested that support, specifically for account bans, can be pursued using one final, desperate angle: legal action! Not lawyering up, exactly, but contacting a state Attorney General. In the thread, multiple users reported that various state A.G. offices were willing to forward their complaints and that account recovery was successful as a result.[23]

Although customer support leaves a lot to be desired, Instagram deserves credit for trying to keep users safe. It isn't known if Instagram has a phone number or if anyone is staffed to pick up the metonymic phone. A large segment of Instagram users sought popularity without picking up their phones, either.

PART II

THE UNDERWORLD

10

SOCIAL MEDIA MARKETING PANELS AND SOCKPUPPET BOTNETS

I n a January 2018 exposé titled, "The Follower Factory,"[1] reporters from the New York Times analyzed the scourge of fake Twitter followers. They homed in on the U.S.-based company Devumi, a reseller of fake activity. According to that investigation, Devumi was "drawing on an estimated stock of at least 3.5 million automated accounts, each sold many times over" and had "provided customers with more than 200 million Twitter followers."[2]

A year later, the company settled with the FTC for two and a half million dollars, establishing a precedent that selling fake followers was "illegal deception."[3]

I bought fake Twitter followers in 2012. Elon Musk was complaining about fake followers when he purchased Twitter in 2022. During the decade in between, I learned a lot about how fake accounts were created and the use of software programs to control them. Bots and botnets are still important. The foundation of Devumi is informative for understanding how "social media marketing" came to be seen as a catch-all for the shadowy practices that enveloped Instagram. These seemingly one-dimensional nuisances have dynamic consequences.

SMM Panels

Devumi and the sites it drew from to provide followers are known as "social media marketing (SMM) panels." They're called "panels" in that customers pay, click, and instantly see changes to social media metrics as if they were using the Control Panel on Microsoft Windows.

The panels offer instant—or at least relatively quick—gratification. SMM service providers, including the compliant ones, tend to focus on follower growth. How does one reach ten thousand followers? There's the expensive route of hiring a marketing agency, which doesn't come with any guarantee. Then there's the winding path of self-directed growth and microfame. Finally, there's "gitting gud," which involves spending years honing a craft to avoid feckless self-promotion on social media and not being afraid to quit social media.

When using an SMM panel, forty dollars for five thousand followers delivered within twenty-four hours is a dream come true. Not even paying for promoted posts will guarantee such follower growth. Such lofty goals would take a dedicated marketing team many months and thousands of dollars of ad spend.

There's a trade-off with the guaranteed followers pedaled by these services. The followers aren't real.

Behind every panel is automated control of a cluster of fake accounts. If I helm an SMM panel and sell a thousand followers, I'm selling a guarantee that I can direct a thousand bots to follow a customer's account. Some customers know they're getting fake followers that might one day disappear. They're okay with that. Others are deluded into thinking that the followers are real.

Marketing materials contain not-infrequent insistences that the followers are real or are "just as good" as real. The bots might be somewhat convincing to skeptics who manually audit other peoples' followings. The fact of the matter is that it's much cheaper for the provider to send over a bundle of fake love than it is to corral a thousand accounts belonging to living, breathing, active Instagram users. Why do people pay for the facade of popularity?

They have plenty of followers and stacks of social proof in general. On platforms like Instagram, you need to look popular to get popular. The more followers you have, the easier it becomes to get more new followers on board. A quick and easy way to set the wheels in motion is to buy Instagram followers, giving your profile an instant credibility boost. Detailed below, you'll find all the information you need on how to buy the safest and most authentic Instagram followers on the web – all 100% identical to the real thing.[4]

How does this work? Running a service that sells followers—a one-click follower boost—requires programmatic control of hundreds or thousands of Instagram accounts or reselling someone else's bots for a higher fee, which is what Devumi did.

These are Botnets

This "programmatic control" is akin to a botnet. Y'know, a robot network. The term "botnet" started to gain momentum in the late 2000s. Botnets infect devices with malware to send malicious web requests, and the user sees no indication that the device has been hijacked.

The botnets of the late 2000s were used to pull off massive distributed denial of service (DDoS) attacks. which disrupted popular services by sending huge volumes of bulky network requests to web servers. The "distributed" aspect was only made possible by a hacker controlling a network of systems with different, high-quality IP addresses. If all the requests came from the same data center, a rudimentary firewall could easily stop them and the requests might clog the attacker's bandwidth more than anything. DDoS attacks could implement synchronized web requests to overwhelm web servers with a flood of fake traffic.

Realizing how problematic this could be, the well-known DDoS Mitigation company Cloudflare was founded in 2009. This company's branding is shown alongside a temporary redirect while visiting high-traffic websites. Websites pay for Cloudflare's service to help prevent DDoS attacks from botnets. Sometimes, it results in a slight delay for the innocent user.

Although fake accounts on social media platforms don't *necessarily* require unique devices and rarely involve *compromised* devices, there is a strong similarity here. An SMM panel's force of bots is a botnet, minus the distributed compute aspect. The attack vector is *limited* to the social media platform, which is likely well-prepared for activity surges. A traditional botnet isn't necessarily used for destructive evil, but it *could* be used to boost views on a YouTube video.

Instagram botnets aren't built by infecting devices with malware; they are created the same way a regular user would sign up for the platform, just stripped down, streamlined, and automated. The most cunning villains have the know-how to programmatically create fake accounts. A long time ago, this was easy for programmers to do. I was able to automate account creation on several platforms.

Every app craves users. Companies have teams dedicated to making the signup as fast and efficient as possible. Adding robot deterrents wasn't a priority on early Instagram. Once an algorithm became functional for account creation, it could be scaled up to an absurd extent. Thousands of accounts could have been created by one industrious engineer every day. At some point, platforms took notice and added restrictions. The internet changed a lot.

One of the most well-known purveyors of bots, Rantic, claimed in a 2015 Vice interview to control over thirty-five million bot accounts.[5] That was ten times more than Devumi "controlled." Both companies were operating after the Instagram Rapture.

Instagram's Rapture of 2014

Now a distant memory, in December 2014, Instagram swept bots and other recently disabled accounts from the platform. Some celebrities lost more than twenty percent of their followers. Instagram's official account supposedly lost over nineteen million followers.[6]

My interpretation is not that millions of accounts were freshly banned on December 18, 2014, but that there was a longstanding bug in the mechanism for disabling infringing accounts that still counted those accounts as followers. An old Help Center archive page seems to confirm this.

Follower/Following count is not accurate.

There is a known issue where the follower/following count displayed on your profile does not match the number of followers/following you may see when you view the full list. This may be because you are following or being followed by recently disabled accounts. We are working to resolve this number discrepancy, but have no official time frame for when this will occur.

Please note that if your followers/followings exceed 200, we will only show the most recent 200 followers/followings in the list. If you have over 5,000 followers or are following more than 1,000 users and would like to view a complete list, we suggest visiting a third-party site that uses our API such as web.stagram.com or gramfeed.com.

— INSTAGRAM HELP DESK POST ARCHIVED
DECEMBER 7, 2013

This was awkward for Instagram because, even though the disabled accounts had apparently been excluded from recent user counts, the "rapture" attracted attention to the problem: how were there so many disabled accounts on Instagram and why?

I have two other notes to share. First, it's notable that this Help Center page *encouraged* users to browse third-party apps to check complete lists of followers! By April 2018, all these services would have been rendered obsolete by Instagram's shutdown of its public API.[7]

Next, since this comes up whenever there are fake follower purges, yes, A-list celebrities always seem to lose the most followers but not necessarily because they purchase fake followers. Rather, bot owners instruct their bots to engage with popular accounts to seem more authentic. Justin Bieber was heckled for losing tons of followers in December 2014. Many were probably nestled in his fanbase so that *they* seemed more legitimate. He didn't buy them.

Adding Restrictions

Believe it or not, there was a time when users could sign up for services without an email address. Eventually, Instagram started mandating email addresses at signup and later email verification to prove ownership of the email address used at signup. Other catches were added too, such as eliminating users' ability to add symbols to email addresses to make them seem unique. A symbol in an address is ignored when an email is sent but might count as a unique key in a registrar's system, so bobsmith@xyz.com could be the same as bob+smith@xyz.com and bob++smith@xyz.com. All the account registration emails would be sent to the same inbox, but Bob Smith could register thousands of accounts this way.

Regardless of the controls, creating a fake account is *never* completely impossible. One could create a "fake" account right now by hand—its purpose wouldn't be apparent during the registration process. People are always creating fake accounts, even if they must register them one by one on their personal computers or pay for temporary phone numbers.

It's hard to track the costs because there are still millions of fake accounts created during more permissive periods. The expertise needed to maintain a botnet is similar enough for all social networks that providers can level set their prices and accept lower profit margins for services on one network knowing they can execute actions and create accounts elsewhere at higher profit margins.

Buying one hundred phone-verified Instagram accounts (PVAs) in late 2019 cost about fifty dollars. At fifty cents each, it is plausible that, somewhere in the world, creating these accounts by hand was sufficiently profitable. I bought my PVAs from Pakistan.

Burner Accounts and SMM Panel Algorithms

Okay, so bot accounts are as numerous as grains of sand on the beach. People want to buy followers from SMM panels. How does that happen?

After accounts are created, their login details are stored in a database. Buyers of "burner" accounts might receive a spreadsheet with this information. The account information could be just the username and password. Later, it would include the IP address the account was created on, the phone number, and the account's email address, which could be accessed programmatically to help manage any trouble logging in. Service providers who expect to lose, or "burn," the accounts use "burner accounts." These aren't typical panel customers. They might be used for scraping. Instagram growth providers often purchased burner accounts for testing because buying them was cheaper than developing and maintaining account-creation scripts.

A non-burner account (or sold as a burner to a botnet controller) would be included in a botnet.

An account meant for SMM panel services will go through a makeover before interacting with customers. A name will be set, a profile picture will be chosen, a bio will be written, and perhaps posts will be created. The account will be "primed" to receive a passable "trust score" in Instagram's eyes and to be more passable in the eyes of customers—looking plausibly real or "premium" as some providers call it. The botnet may further prime the new account by allocating it a few followers so its follower count isn't a big fat zero.

When a new order comes in—let's say, for a thousand followers for @abcd123—actions are dispatched to fulfill that order. Each step and decision can be broken down in plain English and then coded using a programming language like Python. Well-known actions like "follow" are made possible by Instagram client libraries, like InstaPy and InstagramAPI, unapproved open-source projects once hosted on GitHub.

The algorithm might look like this:

1. Operator enters "*follow abcd123 1000*"
2. The system checks to see that abcd123 is a valid Instagram account.
3. The system checks the database and locates a thousand available healthy bot accounts not already following abcd123.
4. The system dispatches these accounts to follow abcd123. The system may implement an algorithm to gradually send followers. Sometimes they are sent instantly.
   a. The system logs in to each bot account.
      i. If the login fails, the account gets marked as "unhealthy" and excluded from future queries.
      ii. If the login fails, the system chooses a different account and returns to 4a.
   b. The system follows user abcd123 from the account logged into in 4a.
5. The system confirms that the followers "stuck" and are visible on the account abcd1234 and indicates that the order has been fulfilled.

That's all there is to it. It's easy to pull off because many of the functions for interfacing with Instagram are provided by libraries someone else created. Someone else "sniffed" the private API. This gave rise to "script-kiddies" who had rudimentary coding ability but bought scripts that facilitated actions like this, which they then wielded to operate their own businesses.

Easy as it might seem, selling fake followers is considered illegal deception, and it's a no-no according to Instagram's terms. SMM panel sites remain tangled in webs of lies.

SMM panels are also called "reseller" sites. Who *actually* owns or controls the bot accounts is not always known. The nicer, neater, or more Westernized a web storefront is, the less likely the site owner created or controls the botnet. Shrewd resellers list what they find on panel sites in their own deceiving product offerings.

Many of the largest botnets were created in countries like Pakistan or Russia cheaply. The original, spartan panels were advertised in lesser-known places like BlackHatWorld. They avoided the attention of the FTC.

As demand grew, companies like Devumi began catering to mainstream Western audiences.[8] Nobody wanted to peruse the ugly forums at BHW; they wanted popularity sold to them with glitzy marketing. Sites like Devumi up-sold cheaper services. They charged higher rates and prayed that the underlying service provider actually ran the algorithm specified above.

Following the Devumi settlement[9], all U.S.-based SMM panels disappeared. Instagram aggressively and effectively used this legal precedent to cull the practice. The U.S.-based operators moved into other social media marketing services, mainly Instagram Growth, which was never regulated in the same way. SMM panels popped up on top-level domains other than ".com," often run by foreign business owners considered beyond the reach of American enforcement.

There is a pyramid of sellers and resellers building businesses on top of the cheaper originators. Results might not be guaranteed until after forty-eight or seventy-two hours because of these layers. When I bought Twitter followers, they were delivered in less than one hour. Today, some customers wait days for currency to be transferred through different payment processors and for the lynchpin in India to press play on the algorithm.

There are two ways of thinking about the delays:

1. Longer waits indicate more complex reseller relationships and that the storefront owner does not ultimately control the accounts.

2. Longer waits indicate more sophisticated delivery systems in which followers appear more slowly to deter bot detection measures.

Surprisingly, services reliably deliver the advertised numbers, but the process is left to the imagination because an explanation would reveal that the followers are not real.

High Quality Followers
These are Followers with profile pictures but no further uploads on their account. Auto-refill is enabled within the warranty[10]

Active Followers
New Active followers are for those who are serious about their Instagram growth. These are guaranteed with very little to no drop![11]

The excerpt above is typical doublespeak found on an active reseller's page. Buzzoid.com sells two different types of Instagram followers.[12] Five thousand "high quality" followers cost $39.99. Five thousand "active" followers cost $84.99. The price of the five thousand basic followers ($39.99) is eerily similar to the price of $39.95 set by Instafollowers.co for the same quantity. The price similarity could suggest collusion, price fixing, aggressive competition, or that the services are provided by the same entity.

Ah, the illusion of choice.

It doesn't take a genius to see that "high quality followers" are not high-quality. The only guarantee is that they have profile pictures. Will they have plausible names or will the names be like axadsa1234? Do they have profile bios set? Will they all follow thousands of accounts while only being followed by other fake accounts? A software tool for bot detection could easily expose the accounts. A human combing through the followers would immediately identify them as fugazi.

"Auto-refill" means that the provider will monitor the customer's account for follower loss (deleted accounts) and send other bots to make up for the loss. Usually, refill policies are a bit strict. Buzzoid's policy doesn't specify a time limit. Are they going to be monitoring for a year? Of course not. Are they even monitoring it to begin with? No, probably not. The onus is likely on the customer to reach out if the followers drop.

"Drop" refers to "unfollowing" or dropping off. Why would a bot account meant to boost follower count unfollow someone? Usually because the bot account was banned. A banned account immediately disappears from follower count (at least, post *Instagram Rapture*). The second reason is more devious. Instagram accounts can only follow five thousand accounts. Many bot accounts *do* reach that limit. Then the botnet owner must make a decision. Do these bots get unplugged and laid to rest? Or should a first-in-first-out algorithm gradually unfollow old customers? It's probably worth the risk! As detection algorithms have become more advanced, it's also possible that savvy operators would prune following counts long before they reached five thousand, shedding old customers more quickly.

"Active followers" is a weird term. I would think "active" means "human" and "using the platform in some meaningful way." For SMM panels, it can mean slightly higher-quality fake accounts.

The earlier excerpt from Mediamister, an SMM panel, has some truth to it. More followers mean greater social proof. Having a larger base of followers makes attracting new followers easier. However, Mediamister's assertion that the provided bot followers are authentic and "100% identical to the real thing" is a bald-faced lie. Yes, each follower provides an identical "+1 to follower count," but they're fake accounts controlled by computer programs. They don't represent real people. It's just not possible. A third party can't guarantee actions from massive amounts of independent-thinking users unless they are directly incentivized. Even if such were the case, the followers wouldn't be "authentic."

Gradual Delivery

Our drip feed delivery system ensures followers are added to profiles safely. The slow adding of followers is essential to maintain discretion, as followers that stack up too fast can trigger Instagram's spam filters. The gradual delivery of followers over a few working days ensures the process looks 100% organic from start to finish. Some providers promise 'instant' delivery of social proof, which could get you kicked off Instagram permanently.[13]

Rapid Results

Buying high-quality followers from Media Mister can make it much quicker and easier to achieve your goals on Instagram. Whether looking to boost brand awareness, sell more products or simply get more organic followers on board, you'll be looking at measurable results in no time. Our social signals make it fast, easy, and cheap to gain a competitive edge on the world's biggest social platforms.[14]

Refill Guarantee

Last up, we're so confident in the quality and authenticity of our no-drop followers that all sales are covered by a 60-day refill guarantee. This means that if any of the followers you buy drop from your profile during this time, they will be replaced free of charge. But as the followers we provide are real and active members of the Instagram community, most of the followers added to your account will be permanent.[15]

"Drip Delivery" is a funny angle. Drip delivery is apparently how things are done when they are done "safely." Huh...if everything is being done legitimately, why is "safety" even mentioned? Because directing thousands of bots to follow someone isn't inherently safe. That followers are described as "look[ing] 100% organic" implies that they aren't organic! Drip delivery does help evade detections of obvious malicious behavior by sending the followers at a trickle but within a standard time window, like forty-eight hours.

Benefits: Instant Start (The fulfillment starts right after the payment.) → Instant Delivery (Your order will be delivered right after the payment.) → Normal Looking (The accounts are looking good.) → 0-180D Guarantee (You can choose to guarantee up to 180 days.)[16]

Not many active providers appear in Google search results, but some don't make much effort to hide what's going on. Consider this gem: "Normal Looking - The accounts are looking good."[17] I can't say that such a description builds confidence.

Superviral, Famoid, Gore Ad.io, and Viralyft are other modern sites that sell Instagram followers. If these awful names and eerily similar websites aren't big enough clues, the sources of these panels are likely found in BlackHatWorld.

When I was actively involved in the Instagram growth space, I regularly surveyed the competition. There were dozens of SMM panels, and almost all the websites were low-effort. The names and branding weren't memorable. They were shut down and restarted constantly due to legal threats and periodic interruptions from Instagram API changes. An observer could be fooled into thinking that any SMM panel *still operating* today is somehow superior or has some special secret. That isn't true. The panels operating likely found some protection from United States court orders and simply outlasted others unable to justify participating in the game of Whac-a-Mole.[18]

What of the Operator?

Operating an SMM panel might seem lucrative. The business plan might look something like this:

- Buy five thousand Instagram burner accounts for twenty-five hundred dollars.
- Start a website advertising batches of five hundred to five thousand Instagram followers with immediate delivery.
- Buy or acquire a Python script that allows bot accounts to be directed follow customers' accounts.
- Sell five hundred to five thousand follower packages on the website for forty dollars each.
- With sixty-two customers paying the full price of forty dollars, the business has broken even with its startup costs.

With a botnet, a reliable automation script, a payment processor, and the knowledge of how to build a panel website, this seems like a brilliant business idea. After just sixty-something customers, it's pure profit. Isn't this the beauty of running a software business?

No. Accounts used for this type of thing are often banned and blocked. Sometimes phone-verified account sellers pull a scam and don't deliver the accounts. Sometimes they deliver the accounts, but before a customer can change the passwords, the originator will log back in and sell them to someone else. This happened to me and some of my friends operating black hat businesses on Instagram. In any case, when depending on dishonest people to carry out dishonest activities, good luck getting money back if things go awry!

Furthermore, the cost to run such a business is not zero. Payment processing is expensive. There is a fixed rate and fees as high as four percent for each transaction. Then, any mainstream payment processor brings exposure to chargebacks, of which there are many in this space. In fact, by 2019, most payment gateways had explicitly forbidden social media growth services as high-risk businesses, since, in 2019, they were declared illegal deception.[19]

The cost of frequently replacing churned accounts and using proxies for the accounts' actions adds up. The proxies, alternative IP addresses, would need to be used with every action to mask the account actions' origins. Five thousand follow requests from five thousand different accounts at the same IP address are suspicious. So-called "rotating" proxy solutions might be cost-effective but could cost hundreds of dollars per month, based on total used bandwidth.

It makes sense that many entrepreneurs waded into this space in the late 2010s, regardless of whether they had automation programs or methods to create accounts. Unfortunately, many found that their investments had not paid off, often after receiving cease-and-desist notices from Instagram or waking up to find the burner accounts banned and customers demanding refunds.

The only viable operators know how to create the accounts and write more advanced automation programs. If a business owner could do that, the ever-present fear of getting sued would lead to starting a growth service instead. In most cases, that's what happened.

SMM Panels Fall Off

A distinction emerged between "organic" growth services and "fake" SMM panel services, which Chris Buetti offhandedly referenced in his live interview with Cheddar in early 2019 as he scoffed at the idea of botnet-driven fake followers.[20] Follower resellers felt increasing legal pressure. Would-be customers were becoming more aware of the overt fakeness of guaranteed followers. Growth service providers distanced themselves from the illegal deception. Entrepreneurs learned that organic growth scaled much better and had much higher profit margins than panel services.

Don't get me wrong, growth services, which log in to customer accounts and interact with others for reciprocal actions, still generate annoying, spammy behavior and violate terms of use. Social metrics are debased. The panel services actually operate more auspiciously. The fake-nice comments of growth services are highly *visible*. The results of SMM panel trickery are typically only discovered when investigating an account's followers. The average Instagram user doesn't see their operations because most of these botnets don't generate any activity except following customers.

Shark Social focused on growth and so many interesting personalities inhabited the growth space because the pressure from the news articles and court dockets was scary. Instagram was hawklike in its enforcement of the precedent. Any *U.S.-based* seller of fraudulent activity was shut down quickly. All these sites I later interacted with were based in foreign countries, often adversarial to the United States.

This provided a convenient cover for growth service operators claiming *their service wasn't dealing in fake followers*. This was in fact true. Growth services that logged in to customers' accounts didn't typically direct fake activity toward those accounts. Users became aware of these "obviously fake" accounts, so growth services built momentum by disassociating from their practices.

Botnets and the Algorithms

Fake followers are annoying, like mosquitos leaving bites. But are they actually *dangerous*?

Where there are fake Instagram followers, there is a botnet that controls those accounts.

Seeing a popular suggested photo on Instagram doesn't rouse suspicion. An Instagram algorithm highlights that content, and, we trust those algorithms. We trust the procedures governing ranking, especially if there is a visible testament to positive feedback, like a ton of likes or comments. Users don't think about and or have the tools to uncover what might be happening if those same thousand accounts used for fake liking were instead used to boost pictures and comments.

We trust those algorithms.

A small botnet could meaningfully alter the content and discourse on anyone's Instagram feed. Users trust effective recommendation algorithms. What's shown is rarely challenged. If content is highly off-putting, an unhappy user may check the likes or leave an angry comment. To expect users to become Sherlock Holmes to perform "a new kind of detective work"[21] is a fairytale.

This speaks to the trust users place in content platforms. It also speaks to the trust humans historically placed in newspapers and newscasters. Users realize the exposure algorithmic assistance can provide and therefore pay for promotion and do all sorts of things for placements on feature boards, like Instagram's Explore page.

The most crucial calculations within any ranking algorithm deal with velocity and decay. Viral videos on the early internet were sometimes discovered months after they were first uploaded and *then* popularized by grassroots momentum. Content discovery doesn't work that way anymore. Some early "viral" videos were manually pegged to the front page of sites, like YouTube in 2006, once curators realized their brilliance. Yes, although YouTube had a rich search function, it still used manual curation, a holdover from directory sites!

Now, reddit, which is at its core a link-sharing site, still regularly breathes fresh life into old content. However, Instagram and TikTok audiences favor *new*, original content. This means that the first few moments of life—those minutes and hours after a picture is *juuuust* posted—are the most important. Although it varies, the rule of thumb is that after the first day, a post's exposure increase will decline. The algorithm's decay function will start reducing its virality.

Early content interactions are extremely important. These aren't simple ranking algorithms; mind-numbingly complex personalization is used for distribution. Then, there are "gates" involved for audience size and targeting. If a user with two hundred followers posts a picture, is that picture shown to all followers? No. The feeds are algorithmically curated, unlike the dense, chronological messes that typified late Myspace and early Facebook. Content may be presented to all a user's followers if an initial segment of followers (say, fifty) strongly engage (by interacting or keeping it in the active window for a set amount of time at a rate, say, higher than five percent) with the content.

Once a piece of content exceeds a popularity threshold, a gate is unlocked, and the content is shown to a wider group of users. And so on and so on. With hashtags (and organic, credited, reposting), the sphere of exposure can greatly exceed one's existing following. Theoretically, a relatively small but determined group of sockpuppet promoters can push anything through the first few gates.

Sockpuppets

"Sockpuppets," social media accounts that exist solely to manipulate public opinion, have been around for a long time. With the anonymity of the internet, it's easy for a guy named Mike Smith to create a fake account and comment, "I've personally met Mr. Smith, and he's not so bad" on a video titled, "I hate Mike Smith." If Mike Smith was careful enough and scaled his operation to just ten accounts, he just might be able to drown out any negative sentiment. Using fake accounts talking to themselves, he could "astroturf" a discussion—orchestrate a conversation to drive public opinion in one direction.

I admit that I've sockpuppeted. I've been under fire on the internet, under both my real name and screen names, and I've fired up fake accounts to boost my cause. It's a defense mechanism—a virtual social cheat code. That's not to say that everyone's done it, but everyone on the receiving end of internet hate has considered it.

What if instead of two or three accounts in one specific thread, I used thousands? What if attempted to sway opinion on an important topic across a wide swath of the internet? What if I used an Instagram SMM panel botnet?

Biologist Here!

One of the most notable reddit users was u/Unidan, a charismatic biologist and ecologist who penned witty, thorough, and engaging answers to all sorts of questions. Unidan wasn't well known for posting threads of original content[22]. Rather, he crafted top-level comments and replies to comments embedded under other people's posts.

For me, Unidan's behavior exemplified what made reddit such an amazing place in the early 2010s. Many of his comments began with "Biologist Here!" Although this type of knowledge sharing might seem old-timey, he was *not* plagiarizing from Wikipedia or a textbook. He was a subject matter expert who rapidly gained a huge following on the site. A comment by u/Unidan:

Biologist here!

I just took a quick glance, but I believe this is probably a Tree of Heaven (Ailanthus altissima), but probably not due to the fruits and non-compound leaves! With the new information, I'd change my current guess to hackberry (Celtis occidentalis), which seems to fit the new photos showing leaf shape, branching, and "fruit" which may actually be galls on the tree, explaining the bark and hollowness, too!

...

Ideally, the content of any ranking algorithm—reddit's, Digg's, Myspace's, YouTube's, Instagram's—rises to the top based on merit. A great piece of content attracts strong engagement and organic promotion. A ranking algorithm must remain equitable and consistent while allowing new content to rise.

Link directory sites from the early internet featured static rankings of links to external websites. Some were alphabetical, others "top ten," but those lists only changed when the webmaster decided to change them. Notably, there was no user-driven aspect to the ranks. The only way a user could express displeasure with a site was simply not visiting that index site or emailing the webmaster. Webmasters were supreme overlords.

Reddit's algorithm allows users to express their like or dislike of content using the now common "upvote" and "downvote." These were crucial to my work at Cutlet, and the downvotes enable users to police bad behavior.

Unidan had millions of "Comment Karma," meaning he attracted millions of upvotes on his comments. Millions! Each karma point was equivalent to one click of the upvote arrow. His comment above or any others suggests that he was a meritorious poster, but what's the point?

Unidan wrote good comments. *Unidan used sockpuppet accounts to promote his comments and squash opposing views and comments.* On reddit, each comment starts with 1 karma, and the default comment sort order is by karma amount. If Unidan responded quickly enough in a thread rising in popularity, his small group of sockpuppet accounts could quickly render his comment one of the most visible while effectively hiding most other comments. His high-quality comments were guaranteed to rocket to the top of the sorted discussions.

Unidan hijacked the algorithm. His actions were eventually uncovered

—by Reddit admins, not users—and he was banned. A reddit administrator released a statement:[23]

> He was caught using a number of alternate accounts to downvote people he was arguing with, upvote his own submissions and comments, and downvote submissions made around the same time he posted his own so that he got even more of an artificial popularity boost.

This unfolded over a decade ago. Today, the inquiry in the wake of such a drama would probably be about how much money he made and what he was selling, which speaks to the purity of the internet at that time. Unidan, real name Ben Eisenkop, really was a charismatic ecology nerd. There might have been some long-term plan, but he was a motivated PhD student willing to take things far enough to establish himself on reddit. With that came power, influence, and brand value. He did get a Wikipedia page[24] out of the whole thing. The storyline strikes me as a hobby that happened to turn into a corrupt use of power. There is no account of Eisenkop profiting from his vote manipulation.

His downfall came on the heels of a July 2014 argument regarding the differences between jackdaws and crows. He ceased his upbeat, positive demeanor and adopted a snarky tone:

> Here's the thing. You said a "jackdaw is a crow."
>
> Is it in the same family? Yes. No one's arguing that.
>
> As someone who is a scientist who studies crows, I am telling you, specifically, in science, no one calls jackdaws crows. If you want to be "specific" like you said, then you shouldn't either. They're not the same thing.
>
> ...
>
> It's okay to just admit you're wrong, you know?[25]

After this tirade, during which he presumably used his sockpuppets to downvote anyone who opposed him, he was investigated and then banned. I include this comment to help illustrate that, whether or not money is extracted from the platform, power is power. Unidan had a lot of it, due in part to manipulating the platform.

Post-ban, Unidan used a new account named UnidanX to admit to his behavior in a comment that received thousands of downvotes. It had negative 2094 points, which indicates that even once his comment had been hidden for having such a low score, hundreds of users brigaded to continue downvoting him. "Completely true...I had five 'vote alts'...to vote on stuff."[26] If, instead of squabbling about crows, he wished to affect public perception of more serious issues, he could have done that.

Here's the thing. That's with just five alt accounts.

What makes this so scary is that Unidan didn't need to use any special computer program to fool reddit's algorithms into boosting his content. He didn't need to buy the fake accounts. He created them by hand. It didn't really require much savvy at all. Although reddit now claims to have safeguards against self-driven sockpuppeting, anyone who can make an account *appear* human can pull off similar vote and algorithm manipulation. With enough fake accounts and a way to programmatically control them, a bad actor on reddit could become an incredibly cost-effective propagandist. Anyone who controls a botnet can alter public opinion on social media.

As Unidan demonstrated, everyday users would be none the wiser.

Sockpuppet Botnets as Vehicles for Propaganda

Hometown rappers paying forty dollars for five thousand fake followers were never the problem. Maybe they terrorized their suburban communities, but they didn't move the needle of social media platforms' integrity.

However, concern arose when the botnets that delivered fake followers to the rappers were used to artificially boost content by fooling algorithms and at a fraction of the cost of buying advertisements. Moreover, when those botnets were turned into propaganda machines to astroturf discussions, leave comments, downvote dissent, and upvote shills, it became mainstream news.

And, still, there's no agreement on what happened, what's happening, or what will happen.

I was consuming unfiltered shit on the internet for over a decade. Nobody was looking out for me. I had to learn how to do my own research and realize when "hot singles" weren't actually in my area. I spent a lot of time thinking about fact, fiction, and, in later years, schisms borne out of America's culture wars. For example, to what extent do platforms need to fact-check and provide warning labels? Do they have a duty to do this?

While I was processing hoax news about Lil Wayne's death and getting fooled by Unidan's sockpuppeting, people smarter than me were taking notes and considering vectors for attack: vulnerabilities to viral networked propaganda.

Many (yes, especially Boomers) fail to differentiate between the trustworthiness of social media "news feeds" and old-school journalism. Many newsrooms spent over one hundred years building public trust, so when we now see websites formatted like newspapers, we unreasonably trust them. They abuse that trust by running chumbox ads.

Nonsense on Facebook gaining five thousand likes doesn't change the fact that it's nonsense. Hundreds of millions of content items posted on Facebook every day would never be shown to a TV audience or printed in a newspaper. A large group of users still treats newsfeed content as if it's vetted by a newsroom. Schism groups unhappy with political happenings now demand "transparency," "fact-checking," and even manual curation. At its core, Facebook's newsfeed is no different from Myspace's bulletin board where I witnessed a city-wide death hoax circulate in 2008.

Guess what? We eventually used our teenage reasoning skills to determine that "Tippy" DeNunzio hadn't died.

The newsroom theory, social networks, algorithms, botnets, and recommendation systems come together in the "filter bubble."

In a filter bubble, recommendation systems gradually isolate users within arenas of strong preferences and beliefs. Purportedly, users see content that is less centric, and, as they express preferences for one side or the other, the content may become more "extreme." They'll never see content related to an opposing viewpoint, interest, or hobby. They do not question why they're being shown the material—they trust the curation.

This isn't an allegation of platform-driven indoctrination. Users show up with (perhaps strong) preferences, so they're guiding the algorithms. The algorithms aren't manipulating them directly.

I don't opine on whether filter bubbles are good or bad. Given how SMM panels can drive propaganda, the issue is that bot farm owners can use bots to dictate what appears popular in *any* bubble. However, I will clarify that SMM panel bots aren't fungible—Instagram bots can't jump over to Facebook. However, filter bubbles exist in tandem with recommendation algorithms. With enough fake accounts on a platform, manipulators can create their own bubbles! They can provide platforms for ideas much more nefarious and harmful than Unidan's insistence that a jackdaw is not a crow.

I think Unidan's success with five sockpuppet accounts and the thousands of customer accounts I controlled at Shark Social. I think about Devumi's access to a purported three-and-a-half million sockpuppet accounts.[27] I think about Rantic's claim of over thirty-five million sockpuppet accounts.[28] I wonder if we've even scratched the surface.

It's easy for a botnet to hijack a ranking algorithm but difficult to determine if a feed has been interfered with. *Algorithmic transparency* is low. Although SMM panel owners' most lucrative pursuit is selling fake likes, the most dangerous applications have yet to be seen—or perhaps yet to be uncovered.

11

THE FIVE ERAS

E ight of the final ten chapters include a narrative that is (mostly) chronological. Important events have been arranged into the five eras I have defined below. This chapter is included for enhanced reference—it contains spoilers.

The Early Days (October 2010 - May 2013)

- October 6, 2010: Instagram is launched[1]
- November 29, 2010: Mislav Marohnić releases the first unofficial Instagram client[2]
- December 7, 2010: "Creating the missing Instagram web interface"[3]
- February 7, 2011: Instagram's official API is launched[4]
- July 8, 2011: Snapchat is launched (under a different name)[5]
- September 20, 2011: Instagram 2.0: live filters[6]
- April 3, 2012: Instagram app released on Android[7]
- April 9, 2012: Facebook acquires Instagram for $1.01B[8]
- May 18, 2012: Facebook goes public with an initial public stock offering (IPO)[9]
- June 25, 2012: Instagram 2.5: "popular" aggregation is switched to "explore"[10]

- September 2012: xGram Bot and Botstagram emerge on BlackHatWorld[11]
- October 8, 2012: An Instagram Bot thread is started on BlackHatWorld[12]
- November 2012: Botstagram shuts down and updates the site to "Sold Out!"[13]
- November 7, 2012: Hans Kullin complains about an increase in spam[14]
- November 12, 2012: Instagram is made available on web browsers[15]
- January 24, 2013: Vine, a short-form video sharing service, officially launches
- January 8, 2013: Instagram removes user count data from Developer API[16]
- February 26, 2013: Instagram hits 100M monthly active users[17]
- March 2013: xGram Bot has been shut down
- June 20, 2013: Instagram adds video sharing[18]
- May 30, 2013: FollowLiker launches with Instagram and Twitter growth apps[19]

Instagress Beta through Theta (September 2013 - May 2017)

- September 2013: Instagress Beta launches[20]
- November 1, 2013: Instagram runs its first ad, or sponsored post[21]
- July 31, 2014: BlackHatWorld launches dedicated Instagram forum[22]
- December 10, 2014: Instagram has 300M users (more than Twitter) and will start manually verifying accounts[23]
- December 18, 2014: The "Instagram Rapture," millions of disabled accounts are finally removed from follower counts[24]
- November 17, 2015: "Instagram Kills Off Feed Reading Apps"[25]
- March 15, 2016: Instagram announces that chronological feed will be replaced by an algorithmic feed[26]
- May 31, 2016: Instagram introduces business profiles and the ability for any post to be "boosted" on the platform[27]

- June 1, 2016: First round of API restrictions and branding enforcement[28]
- August 2016: Gram MultiTool (GMT1) appears[29]
- August 2, 2016: Instagram announces Stories
- September 2016: TikTok launches in the United States[30]
- September 26, 2016: Tim Grossman launches InstaPy[31]
- April 20, 2017: Instagress is shut down after legal action by Facebook[32]
- May 12, 2017: Mass Planner, PeerBoost, InstaPlus, and FanHarvest are shut down by Facebook[33]

Copycats (June 2017 - November 2018)

- June 6, 2017: "How Bots Are Inflating Instagram Egos" published by the *New York Times*[34]
- *July 2017: I start working with Shark Social*
- September 2017: Jarvee emerges on BlackHatWorld[35]
- October 17, 2017: Gram Multitool 2 (GMT2) emerges on BlackHatWorld[36]
- January 27, 2018: "The Follower Factory" published by *New York Times*[37]
- January 30, 2018: Instagram launches Graph API, old API deprecation is announced, to begin on July 31, 2018[38]
- February 20, 2018: Social Media Series Limited sent cease-and-desist letter[39]
- March 2018: *New York Times* article "Uncovering Instagram Bots with a New Kind of Detective Work"[40]
- March 2018: Cambridge Analytica Scandal breaks, leading to the #DeleteFacebook movement[41]
- April 2, 2018: Instagram begins to shut down its public API[42]
- June 2018: Instagram hits one billion monthly active users[43]
- August 2018: "It was me" verification loop begins to hamper automation efforts
- August 28, 2018: Instagram announces verification services[44]
- September 24, 2018: Instagram cofounders announce that they are stepping down[45]

- October 31, 2018: Facebook publishes a seminal research paper on "abuse from for-profit services that offer to artificially manipulate a user's social standing" called "Following Their Footsteps: Characterizing Account Automation Abuse and Defects"[46]
- November 2018: Organic growth services and bot farms added to Stripe's high-risk list
- November 19, 2018: Instagram announces measures to reduce inauthentic activity on the app[47]

Follower Factory Fallout (December 2018 - March 2020)

- Jan 30, 2019: Devumi settles with NYC AG for $2.5M[48]
- March 1, 2019: Facebook crackdown on fake likes[49]
- April 25, 2019: Facebook files lawsuit against Social Media Series Limited[50]
- April, 30, 2019: Instagram begins experimenting with hiding likes[51]
- May 30, 2019: The *actual* "Instagram Rapture," most providers crippled[52]
- August 2019: Instagram updates Terms and Data Policy to include details about device touches and gestures (which may be used to better distinguish humans from bots)
- September 11, 2019: Facebook's lawsuit against Social Media Series Limited settled[53]
- October 2019: GMT2 is declared dead, owner stops responding on BHW, thread is locked in December[54]
- October 16, 2019: *Shark Social pauses operations*

The Meta; Or, Late Stage Instagram (March 2020 - Present)

- May 1, 2020: *Shark Social reopens*
- August 5, 2020: Instagram releases Reels
- October 1, 2020: Meta takes legal action against scraping services[55]

- October 2020: TikTok surpasses Instagram for activity share amongst teenage users[56]
- December 20, 2020: Instagram forbids direct links to adult websites in user bios[57]
- May 26, 2021: Instagram releases like-hiding feature toggle to all users[58]
- June 17, 2021: Meta launches Reel Ads[59]
- August 13, 2021: AlgorithmWatch's Instagram monitoring project shuts down[60]
- October 28, 2021: Facebook rebrands to Meta Platforms[61]
- November 9, 2021: Legal action against InstaPy[62]
- *February 2, 2022: I sign a separation agreement with Shark Social*
- September 20, 2022: Jarvee officially shuts down[63]

12

BULBS AND FLOWERS

FIRST AND SECOND ERAS

I nstagram launched on October 6, 2010. That was an innocent time. The soil had been freshly tilled. The extent of my programming experience was creating cool Myspace layouts and copying and pasting "hacking" scripts that never worked. Less than two months after the app for "fast beautiful photo sharing" debuted, someone had sniffed and published client code to access its private API. One month after that, Instagram officially released a public version.

On November 29, 2010, Mislav Marohnić committed code to a GitHub project named "instagram."[1] Tagged as "reverse-engineering," it was a "lightweight API HTTP client" written in Ruby. It allowed programmers to more easily write software to access Instagram's functionality whether or not they installed the Instagram app.

Marohnić, who recently told me that his "days are spent surrounded by bulb flower farms in rural Netherlands," was a pioneer in an era in which stances on API openness were totally different.

Like others, he was not motivated by profit. He "flocked" to the app at launch not for immense profit but because he was "eager to share [his] low-resolution, over-filtered photo creations with the world." His motivation for creating his library was twofold: "To share [his] feed with non-iPhone owners, such as [his] mom" and "To solve [this problem] for everyone else [by uploading code] to a public code-sharing site."

After a "huge response on Twitter," Mislav wrote the blog post, "Creating the Missing Instagram Web Interface."[2] His choice of words was telling. He implied that the web interface *should have* existed. It was "missing," and it wasn't possible to "link to or browse your or other's photo streams." A November 2015 blog post from Instagram announcing major API changes admitted, "When we launched our first Instagram API in 2011, we were a very small team and knew we wouldn't be able to build all the features our community might want."[3] By comparison, in 2016, nobody encountered TikTok and felt entitled to an API to access and manipulate content.

Mislav claimed he sniffed and documented the API in "a single day." In his post, he provided something of a tutorial on how to use Charles Proxy, a "reverse proxy" operating as a "man-in-the-middle."[4] This application was used to "sniff" the API or, as Mislav put it, to "[break] down requests and responses in separate views for cookies, GET/POST params, JSON/XML structure, and more."

Once he thoroughly inspected the back-and-forth traffic, he coded his "library" to match Instagram's servers' expectations. He provided useful abstractions that non-technical users could understand—functions like "viewPhoto," "lookup_user," and "tag_search" and models like "Tag," "Timeline," "User," and "Media."

In his words, "Anyone with basic software development skills could make an alternative app or website for Instagram."

When Instagram's fully featured API launched in January 2011, Mislav updated his blog post and code repository to redirect users to that official alternative.[5]

Ditching Myspace

The early 2010s were a primordial ooze of competing Myspace successors that hadn't evolved into the attention-grabbing mobile apps of today. Instagram was mobile first. It launched right around the time I received my first smartphone. The proliferation of smartphones and social networks' rapid growth went hand-in-hand.

As Snapchat launched and Facebook acquired Instagram, mobile became more dominant. By 2012, even "Myspace Tom" was sharing square pictures on Instagram.

There was effectively no news coverage of bad behavior on Instagram. Black hat activity was ramping up. During the summer of 2012, I bought five thousand fake Twitter followers. Clues about Instagram wrongdoing emerged late that summer as I prepared to head to college.

The apps being pedaled were traditional desktop programs similar to MyFriendBot,[6] which was certainly the best Myspace bot. Evildoers navigated BlackHatWorld, paid the purchasing price, downloaded the application, input a license key, and started automating tasks.

Two of the first widely available Instagram bots were Botstagram and xGram Bot, which emerged in September 2012. xGram Bot's co-creator, zenoGlitch, posted about it on September 28, 2012, claiming, "We co-conspired in the creation of xGram."[7] Before xGram, zenoGlitch designed a popular Pinterest bot. Botstagram's creator, whom I managed to track down, got banned from BlackHatWorld and generally wasn't as active there leading up to his ban.

Other bots emerged, but consensus and recordkeeping favored xGram's breadth of features. Other players included InstaGet, Instadominate, Instagram Mega Bot, Ninjagram, and Insta*macro*. Shady software wasn't promoted by search engine marketing back then, so websites weren't always maintained and snapshots might not exist today. zenoGlitch addressed this:

...We do not have any videos on youtube etc for the same reason our website robots.txt is no follow no index, we mostly stick to private releases to our tight knit group of customers so have no real need for promo videos/seo.[8]

xGram Bot had a rich feature set. It facilitated scraping, liking, following, commenting, image uploading, and even *account creation*. Botstagram, which didn't feature account creation, put it differently, "Our offer: Maximize Your Traffic, Boost Your Earnings, Be Famous & Popular, Instagram Followers."[9]

xGram Bot is the most stable, and only multi-threaded Instagram bot that will run uninterrupted 24 hours a day, 7 days a week with advanced task scheduling...xGram Bot has successfully mastered the art of instagram account creation and actually operates as a real smart phone user.[10]

Upon hearing of Botsta' and xGram, loads of profiteers were attracted to Instagram with the sole intention of making money—a complete corruption of Mislav Marohnić's intentions on the platform and, unfortunately, of the same API routes that he had sniffed. xGram's vector for facilitating copious spam was the same Mislav used to show pictures to his mom.

Some of zenoGlitch's posts were previously in "SEO" subforums. On October 8, 2012, the legendary "Instagram Bot Discussion - Request / Begging / Ideas / Dreams"[11] thread was started on BlackHatWorld. The first reply addressed an important point: "The only thing I see is this big Xgrambot banner at the end of each thread about making money with instagram. Even when someone ask [sic] a question about instagram, 50% are giving good answers and the others are just here to show their banner."

MyFriendBot for Myspace was launched (and crushed by Myspace's legal team) before BlackHatWorld's creation. The only record on any surviving forum is a 2006 for-hire listing on webhostingtalk.com[12] in which someone wanted features "like myfriendbot.com" and was "only interested in qualified programmers with experience in myspace." A fellow with the title, "web hosting master" replied: "Just so you know, people HATE these things. It's not going to help you, and in fact, is a violation of Myspace's Terms and Conditionds [sic]. Be warned."

Myspace's downfall as a platform coincided with a new era in black hat activity.

The First Complaint

xGram Bot, something of a successor to MyFriendBot, bridged the early internet spam featured in the excellent book, *Spam Kings,* and the new battlefield of social media. Presumably, spammers quickly started spamming on Instagram.

There are no surviving accounts from this time besides one written by digital strategist Hans Kullin. On November 7, 2012, Kullin published "Instagram's increasing problem with spam."[13] He identified a "major push from spammers that use hashtags to find images to publish spam comments on" over the "last few weeks." The timeline aligned exactly with the release of xGram Bot, which industrialized the posting of spam comments on posts found in hashtag searches. It spawned so many threads on illicit Instagram money-making that a mega thread was created!

Kullin didn't know what was happening on BlackHatWorld back then. I recently messaged him to thank him and let him know that I found the culprit.

He noted that many spammers were suspiciously channeling attention to *links in their profile bios*. They were not farming for likes. Because spam filters weren't good back then, bots left links in comments, like for "igfame . com." Kullin also identified that the "accounts are completely fake" and "have fake followers" with names like "36alida732"[14] that any human would identify as probably generated by a computer program.

Spam was emerging on Instagram. Hans Kullin's post and readers' comments ("Agree the spam is a real issue; hopefully they'll address it soon because it's really out of control!"[15]) attested to the problem but didn't pry into the root cause—that spamming was becoming increasingly automated *and* targeted. Automatic account creation empowered individuals to massively scale up their botting operations at a rate that would have been dreamlike in any subsequent era. Eventually, "spam" became synonymous with "bots," but wasn't in 2012.

When asked about the Instagram community's descent into lawlessness, Marohnić said that he wasn't familiar with specific instances but had this to share about the role his library might have played: "Yes, a bad actor *could* have potentially used my work as a starting point for sniffing out private APIs to create fake accounts and post spam comments, but realistically, they would have so many new problems to solve on top of it that my work would have been a negligible boost."

Soon after Hans Kullin's blog post, zenoGlitch encountered some of those "many new problems." By the spring of 2013, his application was no longer being sold.

> Unfortunately we were attacked very aggressively in this situation (as were all instagram bots) by the power to be and were literally forced to shut down the last bot.[16]

Botstagram sent a closing message to customers in late October 2012, around the same time Kullin (and likely Instagram) noticed an emerging problem: "Due to big changes in Instagram's API, we've decided to stop selling Botstagram."[17] By January, BlackHatWorld banned the creator of Botstagram[18] for not refunding a customer for whom the app never worked. Amusingly, its website URL is now owned by Meta and redirects to a page titled, "Why you should not use apps that offer likes and followers on Instagram and Threads."

Onlookers might wonder, for those who weren't using these illicit programs to sell things, how many "organic" followers were they gaining?

One 2012 testimonial attests "First of all: lol. Second: I got 26k followers in 22 days by just liking with InstaGet. So a bit over 1k followers daily."[19]

Instagress takes root

In the "Instagress Era," Instagram reached critical momentum in America, and automation activity on the platform became endemic. Users started to imagine what they wanted from the platform. People hanging out on BlackHatWorld schemed easy ways to "make $20 per day on Instagram"[20] from spamming. Users who just wanted to be more popular realized they could use similar practices to grow their followings.

I propose that the Instagress Era lasted from September 2013 to May 2017. It had major implications for Instagram as a platform and social boosting as a cultural phenomenon. So many trends and behaviors emerged during this period that they're impossible to track. This was when I became a capable software engineer. Without the madness induced by Instagress, I don't know if I would ever have turned my attention to Instagram automation.

Instagress was a technical jump from xGram Bot. Also, in line with my arguments for the increased ease in conducting digital entrepreneurship, it embraced a new payment model: monthly subscriptions processed by Stripe. Licensing keys were *so 2012*. The year 2013 was all about cloud apps and SaaS.

Instagress attracted attention on BlackHatWorld but also broke from xGram Bot in that it had an alluring website. It wasn't meant for traditional profit-driven spammers. The same access methods pioneered by Mislav Marohnić and later distributed for free by Instagram were used primarily to earn followers for people seeking virtual fame. This violated Instagram's terms of use and community guidelines.

Instagress' original call to action said this:[21]

Twist your life on Instagram

Best way to get real followers and become incredibly popular
Sign In with Instagram

During its free beta period beginning in September 2013, the messaging was thus:[22]

Free beta

Join Instagress today and start enjoying your progress immediately. Over the next month our service will be absolutely free and you can use it unlimited [sic]. Be active even when you sleep!

...

No installation and no special skills are required. You just need the internet, your Instagram account and some fun!

...

We provide a full range of actions and tools to help you increase your Instagram followers, likes and comments. You can manage your activity [depending on] your individual needs at anytime!

Its broad appeal stemmed from cheap pricing (ten dollars a month), automated features, and excellent customer results. The website also contained a more comprehensive "About" section,[23] which I'll include in full because I believe it epitomizes everything I've written about Instagram growth.

About

Instagress is a service which will help you to attract attention to your Instagram account and get more followers, like [sic] and comments.

When we started Instagress, we built it around our personal needs. We want to get more Instagram followers without spending a lot of time on it! And we've developed some tools to make this process as simple and effective as possible.

Of course you can buy followers, but they won't be real! [That] way is good for those who are interested only in the quantity. [Meanwhile,] we create a real following and increase your popularity!

We work with celebrities, brands, start-ups - anyone who might benefit from having a large number of followers. If you also want to promote yourself or your business on Instagram we can help to get you going!

Instagress' early marketing materials spoke to crucial themes:

- Even in 2013, there was some awareness that fake followers were only good for "quantity" and that they would not engage.
- There was dissonance between growth service marketing materials and Instagram's terms of use or any respect for the general user experience.
- Growth providers were happy to sell services but not the end result. Instagress offered to "help to get you going" after mentioning "celebrities," which I think speaks to the delusions central to internet marketing services' success. Wannabes would rather pay for Instagress than improve their craft.
- Internet popularity had some equivalence to "the good life" roughly expressed by the call to "twist your life" and "become incredibly popular."

Instagress was in a league of its own throughout 2014, 2015, and most of 2016. Mass Planner and PeerBoost emerged with the same business model. They helped users grow on autopilot for a cheap rate. The omnibot provider FollowLiker launched with its Instagram automation solution in May 2013 but followed the "old" model of being a Windows application that required a one-time payment. Still, those running accounts preferred the fixed price. It added a subscription later in 2017.

Shark Social, launching just after Instagress's closure in 2017, started by using FollowLiker.

Graduation

During those in-between years when botting was still not a cultural touchpoint, a lot of things happened. Right after the Instagress beta launched, Instagram ran its first platform advertisement or "sponsored post." BlackHatWorld abandoned the megathread in favor of a dedicated Instagram forum in July 2014. Instagram surpassed Twitter's active user count, claiming three hundred million active users.[24]

By 2016, Instagress was, by my conservative estimate, generating over one million dollars per month from at least fifty thousand subscribers. That year shifted the impact of botting, responses to bots, and the composure of the social media space. Things started moving quickly. Also, I graduated from college, got my first programming job, and made a move of my own.

In March, Instagram ditched the chronological feed, a relic of early Web 2.0, which most would now consider unsuitable for a social media site.[25] It was replaced with an "algorithmic feed," which served several purposes. Intelligent feeds indisputably result in stickier users. They also make ad insertion easier while slightly disadvantaging the "reach" of most users, which in turn spurs them to consider purchasing ads (or, ironically, paying for Instagress-like services). *Also,* as users pushed beyond the sanity bound of four hundred "friends," roughly established by Myspace behaviors, the feed construction would still be reasonable, not obstructed by a few hyper-active posters.

Unsurprisingly, right after the new feed launched, Instagram introduced business profiles and "boosted" posts—turning posts into ads.[26] Meta wanted to generate some cash from its blockbuster acquisition. Because the Instagram app's resource *costs* were never consistently split from Meta's other businesses, it's unclear when Instagram "became profitable." I estimate this threshold was crossed by Q4 2017. With money on their minds, priorities changed.

In June 2016, Meta announced major restrictions to Instagram's public API.[27] Yes, it was functional and widely used before then. It's hard not to see the correlation. Many longtime third-party services were rendered inoperable without warning.

General issues:

Policy Violation (Ad network, Influencer network, Other related): Your app should not attempt to build an ad network on Instagram, nor transfer any data that you receive from us (including anonymous, aggregate, or derived data) to any ad network, data broker, influencer network, or other advertising or monetization-related service. In working to build a high quality platform, we ask that you comply with our platform policy.

This resulted in a splintering. The first wave of API developers and hackathon-style hackers were disillusioned and dissuaded from creating tools on top of public APIs. Mislav Marohnić had this to say:

> The volume of my feelings about the end of the era of public APIs could have been a book in and of itself...[this action is] suffocating the ecosystems around these platforms, and inevitably disadvantaging their users. I think that this happens because a growth-at-all-costs mentality of online businesses is fundamentally incompatible with consumer freedoms and free flows of information, especially because the dominant online business model seems to be advertising. You can't reliably send ads down an API payload nor track user behavior and ad performance when those users are spread out through a vast ecosystem. Therefore, the ecosystem must be sacrificed on the altar of investor returns.

As he enjoys his sabbatical in the rural Netherlands, perhaps he should write that book. I'd certainly buy it. On the other side of this split, rule breakers were forced to interact with Instagram's private API, if they weren't already. Instagress' operation hummed along. To satisfy the growing demand for access to like, follow, and comment operations, new open-source tools were committed to GitHub.

Tim Grossman published InstaPy,[28] a browser emulation library used to interact with Instagram's web UI. Like Mislav, he didn't care about profit. He had a basic use case, he was interested in technology, and when he learned about Selenium, he switched from his private API scripts to developing the enterprise-grade InstaPy for browser emulation. He gave it away for free.

Tim described the experience as "the best thing that could have happened." He described being shuttled to a private party in Las Vegas by a "guy that loved InstaPy."

Everybody loved InstaPy, "Tooling that automates your social media interactions to 'farm' Likes, Comments, and Followers on Instagram Implemented in Python using the Selenium module." While Mislav certainly gets credit for building the first private API client, Tim perhaps only formalized and publicized what Instagress and other profitable dependent apps might have already figured out.

By 2017, the most advanced players in the space were able to switch between browser emulation (called "embedded browser"[29]) and private API access. There were two main ways to interact with Instagram, and Tim Grossman generously provided the "embedded browser" part to the masses.

Tim said that he didn't know the exact number, but "seven publicly available platforms [...] used InstaPy as the tool behind [them]." He could have been talking about Instagress, Mass Planner, and PeerBoost. He could have been talking about FollowLiker (though I suspect it only used a private API).

This was on a different scale than the 2010 Ruby client. Tim claimed about one hundred thousand people "used" InstaPy. A little over seventeen thousand people "starred" the repository, and the package has been down-loaded over eight hundred thousand times.[30] He was well aware of the good and the bad. He was "aware of the money that was in the [black hat growth] industry" but said that his team "never built a service and never planned to."

Also on GitHub was the venerable InstagramAPI project by "Lev-Pasha" (I know his real name but couldn't contact him, so I won't mention it). InstagramAPI was a private API client written in Python. LevPasha also maintained Instabot, code that applied InstagramAPI to showcase basic botting workflows. These have both been erased from GitHub, though I still have some of the code kicking around somewhere as do thousands of others.

Today, the most prominent private API library on GitHub lists a description similar to Marohnić's "instagram" from fifteen years earlier: "the most recent version of the API from Instagram, *which was obtained using reverse-engineering with Charles Proxy*."[31] It facilitates violation of Instagram's terms of use just the same.

Oh, and the *new thing*, TikTok, launched in September 2016.

Meta continued applying pressure on violators of Instagram terms of use. During the spring of 2017, cease-and-desist letters were sent to Instagress,[32] Mass Planner, and PeerBoost.[33] They complied. The Insta-gram growth space became worthy of news coverage right around the time I was looking to start a side hustle.

"Sad news to all of you who fell in love with Instagress: by request of Instagram we've closed our web-service that helped you so much."[34]

In the shadow of the commercialization of social networks, the growth platforms flowered and wilted. In April and May of 2017, the keyword "Instagress alternative" became prominent. Now almost ten years later, businesses are still fighting over the traffic related to this search phrase. There are over twelve hundred results for the literal query and over eighteen thousand for the default fuzzy match. Instagress' influence as a "mother plant" cannot be overstated.

13

ORGANIC GROWTH

Instafame, Instagress, Instaforce, Combin, Stellation Media, The Millennial Marketers, Ampfluence, Kicksta, Tree Frog Social, Social Sensei, Social Envy, Upleap—these firms and dozens of others sold Instagram engagement as a service. Unlike botnet wranglers who sold fake likes, these providers offered no guarantees and instead logged into customers' accounts and sprayed actions to attract reciprocal engagement.

They generated tens of millions of dollars and untold billions of inorganic transactions.

Ironically, this segment of the Instagram underworld was called "organic growth."

As Instagram charted its growth path through the 2010s, there was no doubt that a massive follower count *of people one didn't know* was desirable and indicated social proof. Users wised up to the downsides of buying fake followers in multiples of thousands. The shills disappeared, dragged down engagement rates, and made the customer look like a sap.

The shutdown of Instagress in 2017 coupled with harsh enforcement actions against "like" resellers led to the emergence of gangs of profiteers providing organic growth services. They had millions of customers lined up.

I joined Shark Social that summer.

The Breakup

SMM panel activities didn't reliably lead to useful *exposure*. Theoretically, barrages of automatic sockpuppeting could fool algorithms, but Instagram seemed good at filtering that. A bulging follower count still meant *social proof*, but it did very little for post reach and may have hampered it due to lower engagement rates.

What if the faceless bot accounts were cut out of the picture? Forget swarms of pseudos. Wouldn't everyone prefer *real* people who *continued* engaging? Wasn't everyone holding out hope for real people when they bought those "guaranteed" packages?

I was when I bought my fake Twitter followers.

Organic growth tossed aside the follow-only robots. Organic agencies logged into customer accounts and automatically sent likes, followers, and comments to targeted users. The hopefully human receivers of these actions *organically* decided to send likes, follows, and comments *back* to the real-looking customer who just happened to be running a bot.

Nobody could tell the difference. As Sapna pointed out, people noticed, but the uplifting generic comments were a "flattering" type of spam and so nobody *complained*.[1] It was a departure from what Hans Kullin noticed in late 2012. It was a different world compared to what Brian McWilliams captured in *Spam Kings*.

Organic growth exposure cost significantly less than running platform ads or boosting posts.

Here's the algorithm. Anyone capable of encoding this in 2017 could have become a millionaire:

1. Log in to a customer's Instagram account
2. Discover accounts to follow with a high chance of following the customer back
3. Like, comment, and follow those accounts from the customer account
4. Unfollow some accounts as needed

I know millionaires who followed this simple formula. At Shark Social, we were trying to get our numbers up, trudging from our first customer, the baker, to our tenth, then fiftieth. It must have still been summer when we reached our fiftieth active subscriber because I posted a Snapchat story with a promotional message while sitting by my apartment's pool.

Interest was growing, and a few friends responded to my story. My business partners were teaching me to generate buzz, which requires exposure, reciprocity, and high-level solutions.

Exposure and Reciprocity

The most common social transaction on Instagram is the "like," tapping the heart under someone's content. It is a low-effort method of expressing light praise, interest, or agreement. The recipient is notified of who passed the digital love.

Users are notified when others like their content. Users who aren't outright celebrities are intimately familiar with others in their network who like their stuff. There is awareness of "top fans" as well as those who scroll past. Naturally, when someone sees a like from an unknown user or someone they *do* know but rarely engages, that incites curiosity. *Interest* and *anticipation* are emotions on Plutchik's diagram,[2] which I believe uniquely maps onto social media.

Receiving an interesting like or comment often incites a user to click on the profile of the person who initiated the interaction. Is this person a follower? Who are they and what do they want? A curious user might read the bio. They might start scrolling through the gallery.

This is the type of organic social interaction that Instagram streamlines and is exploited by organic growth providers' algorithms.

If a verified celebrity interacts with someone's content on Instagram, **that celebrity is going to receive a follow back**. As in real life, if I were walking around the West Village and a television actor stopped to compliment me, I'd take a few minutes to engage and offer a compliment in return, especially if he had an entourage with him providing *social proof*.

Hierarchies exist in social media, but I see interactions in less grandiose terms. If someone perceived as socially superior interacts with my content, there is a strong nudge to return the favor. I mean, not everyone abides by social contracts, but how people handle attention from the "popular kid" at school is universal. At times we reciprocate out of pity ("pitylikes"), but, the higher the person's social standing, the higher the likelihood of reciprocation.

The best way to find users outside of one's network is to madly click through Instagram's Explore page, since it's supposed to show pictures from accounts with no tie to the user. Let's say I navigated to the smaller content creators and "liked" one hundred of their pictures. Would I get a hundred likes in return? No. Some of those users wouldn't even see my action notification. Could I count on getting ten likes in return? Probably!

That's the magic. On Myspace, haters derided those who had friends *they didn't even know.* On Instagram, users are *more excited* to hear from people they don't know and want to reciprocate.

Liking content and following is free *exposure* for every user. It's free advertising. This is a fundamental feature of networked social engagement and self-promotion. Reliably, users check who is interacting with them. Influencers won't notice every peon in the comments section, but those with single-digit thousands of followers do. Those with single-digit hundreds of followers almost certainly will. Guess who was paying for organic growth?

Following someone might earn a follow back. Liking a picture might boomerang. Leaving a public comment is even juicer because it might signal to other users an *openness* to trade engagement. These subtle signals and nudges are a maturation of the reciprocal engagements on Myspace in the aughts: picture-comment-4-picture-comment, comment-4-comment, whore-4-whore.

Organic growth providers discovered and emulated this interaction flow to attract reciprocal actions and garner attention.

When first explained to me, it didn't make sense. I thought that it worked for the upper echelons of account quality, but sure there was a quality boundary below which that was no longer true. What if my profile sucked or I was ugly?

Remarkably, even with minimal targeting or tuning, a low-status user could reliably gain followers. It worked better for higher-status accounts, aesthetically consistent niche accounts, and conventionally attractive women, but it worked for *everybody*, especially in 2017 and 2018. Instagram simplified social assessment, presentation, and outreach while catering to the deepest desires of the emo kids on Myspace during the previous decade.

What happens when we get to the bottom of the totem pole? There is an entire class of internet users simply *happy to be on the internet.* They haven't been using the internet for twenty years. They don't know what Myspace was. They don't have Generation Z's high standards. During tests, mediocre accounts reliably accrued low-end followers.

I saw reciprocity rates as high as sixty percent when my American-themed test accounts interacted with accounts based in Southeast Asia and Africa. Less technologically literate and probably less proficient in English, they may have been less able to identify accounts that were fake, scams, or relying on automation.

If you follow someone, you might get a follow back. The rate at which actions are reciprocated has been surprisingly high, generally exceeding ten percent. If the captain of the football team compliments the shy loner girl, of course she'll return the compliment! She'll probably spend the next two years thinking about it. If the "captain of the football team" has a bot discovering and complimenting shy loner girls, he'll soon have an army of admirers. That's organic growth. It works if pursued by hand, and it's supercharged by software.

Methods of Interacting with Instagram

Actions, engagements, web clients, and APIs—I've touched on different methods of interacting with Instagram. For most users, interacting with Instagram means opening the app on a smartphone and tapping, swiping, and flicking.

For those operating Instagram-adjacent services, it's more complicated. Many references to methods of access are thus far unexplained. If this organic growth algorithm minted so many millionaires, how was it coded?

An API provides an abstraction of functionality, such as "like," "login," "follow," and "get followers." Every action, whether from a bot or human, is processed through a central API on Instagram's servers—a "private API." Translating an intention into a command that reaches the private API is seamless for mobile phone users—no understanding of programming jargon required. For someone running a bot farm, however, custom-made clients are everything, and comprehending the intricacies of how Instagram works is paramount.

Normal usage falls into two camps: apps and web browsers. Instagram provides richly featured apps on mobile platforms, iOS, and Android. Believe it or not, there is a desktop app for Instagram, but it's only available for Windows. Instagram is accessible via web browser, too. Social media apps tend to discourage browser access by limiting features (TikTok), while some are only accessible via mobile app.

Today, Instagram's web app is fully featured. Meta would still prefer that everyone use the mobile apps, since the tracking is better and push notifications and alert badges lead to more engagement. The tendency to passively scroll on a phone is stronger, which means that users view more advertisements. Finding usage stats on mobile app versus browser/desktop exclusivity proved very difficult. I estimate the split is ninety-five to five percent.

Did any growth services operate without using software programs?

Human-Driven Growth

Not every avenue of organic growth is executed by a computer. One growth service, Ampfluence, relied on human hands, like a traditional agency would. Ampfluence outsourced the tedious work of *spending all day on Instagram* to a team in the Philippines with a collection of smartphones. Those employees logged into client accounts and tapped and scrolled all day. This behavior wasn't caught by Instagram's bot controls because there was no automation! **The terms of use weren't being violated**. However, due to the hardware and labor costs, this service wasn't cheap.

In August 2019, I spoke to Ampfluence's founder on the phone for over an hour trying to poke holes in his business model. A serial entrepreneur, he knew what he was doing even though the profit margins were puny compared to services relying on bots. I spoke to his employee directing operations in the Philippines and even sent over a few clients to test the waters. It was totally legit—one of the most trustworthy businesses in the space.

I dug up an old email from Ampfluence with analytics for our accounts. In the summer of 2019, while software providers were struggling, Ampfluence provided fantastic results. I believe these numbers came after roughly two weeks. These are account results provided by Ampfluence, all without leaving comments and focusing on follow-unfollow.

@cust1 - 253 new followers - no comments requested in notes (exceeding goal by > 40%)

@*cust2* - 206 new followers - no comments requested in notes exceeding goal by > 15%

@*cust3* - 215 new followers - asked specifically not to comment in notes - exceeding by 20%

Further, Ampfluence provided detailed spreadsheets with "analysts'" logged daily activity and exported all relevant metrics by hand each day. Anyone using the service over a long period of time could enjoy the satisfaction of an upward-trending graph like that featured by Instagress until April 2017.

The business has pivoted since I started writing this book, but the cost of human-powered organic growth plans has increased to 250 dollars per month. Shark Social cost less than one fifth of that. Ideally, everyone wants "real humans" growing their accounts. Faced with the economic reality of paying for humans' time, would-be customers searched for cheaper options.

Other business owners relied on teams in countries known for tech outsourcing. Ultimately, this isn't a scalable or profitable business model. Each human can only handle so many accounts. Further, giving a human unfettered access to an Instagram account presents a privacy concern.

The growth service Emiiko launched in 2021. I posted an exposé on the business because it was similar to other services that made dishonest claims. Emiiko advertised humans growing accounts like Ampfluence did. I doubted this.

To my shock, the owner of Emiiko (who I've spoken to genially while writing this book but has asked to remain anonymous) reached out to me and provided extensive proof and explanation of his operation. He even sent me pictures of his office space, proof of having purchased and operated two dozen phones, and a treatise on how he transitioned from running a traditional growth service to one that utilized human hands. In June 2021, he had this to say:

> We are getting much better results than we used to do with automation. We went from guaranteeing 200 followers to at least 400 now. And this is mainly because it's so much easier to engage with people from the correct target audience. It's also more or less impossible to run automation now as IG detects the bot so fast.

The service cost ninety-seven dollars per month, and the website remained active until it vanished in September 2024.

The Private and Public APIs

Instgram's open API, documented and available to everybody, **included routes for liking, following, and commenting**. The daily action limit in each category was high—in some cases, in the thousands. These features were removed from the public API in June 2016, and the API was shut down entirely in 2018.

What remains of the "public" API has been funneled into two systems: the Instagram Graph API and the Instagram Basic Display API. They are both well documented, but usage is subject to approval and tight limits. I actually don't know a single person who has access to either service.

The private API is the one with the good stuff needed to write programs to robotically emulate user social behaviors. Where's the documentation? It's internal at Instagram. Only employees know for sure. The private API isn't meant to be used by outsiders. But, because it underpins all actions in the app, outsiders can interact with it. This is true for all apps that communicate with a server.

There are two ways to learn about a private API: sniff it or find open-source code written by people who have already sniffed it. Sniffing is essential for API hacking and involves inserting a "middleman" (man-in-the-middle proxy) between Instagram's servers and a mobile device. The sniffer then logs the precise API calls and payloads sent to and from a web service. With enough repetition, the investigator can map out API routes and different combinations of parameters.

This is tedious and time consuming. To sniff the route for uploading a picture, the engineer must actually upload a picture. To sniff the route for accepting a follow request, an account must be private, and another account must send a follow request. There are no developer release notes accompanying each change. Any changes are usually discovered from the reverse-engineered API failing. Then, the external developer needs to go back and debug again.

An API, public or private, is an "interface," a collection of building blocks. While "log into account X" and "follow customer account Y" are plausible operations, they don't make for a cohesive organic growth program. What if the login fails due to an invalid password? What if the login fails due to a disabled account? There needs to be extra logic for everything. In some scripts, actions can be dispatched sloppily with no logging, error handling, or robustness of any kind. Taking an API and developing an enterprise-grade program to farm likes and followers for thousands of customers takes thousands of lines of code.

Meta employs tens of thousands of software engineers. I haven't been able to verify that any Instagram growth service ever employed more than three. I was the only one at Shark Social. Mastering the complexity of Instagram meant making a lot of money. There were shortcuts. Much of the valuable client code was provided for free on GitHub. Further, for those who didn't know how to code, desktop applications like FollowLiker and Jarvee had features similar to Instagress and allowed boneheads to grow accounts in bulk.

Instagram, the "app of the 2010s" became the preferred playing field for the automation software of the 2010s.

Browser Emulation - InstaPy

Instagram is first and foremost a mobile app. Starting in 2012, some functionality was added to Instagram's web app, like an enhanced profile and feed view. Instagram's web app doesn't get much attention. Most people only browse it in desperation, and its feature set lags behind the mobile app's. Scrolling with a mouse isn't nearly as engrossing as swiping with a finger.

For some, including this author, building an interactive web scraper is more familiar than setting up a man-in-the-middle proxy for a private API. A web "scraper" program could navigate any page, mine the data, and click on whatever is necessary. Black hat developers who hunted treasure on other parts of the internet applied those techniques to Instagram's web app.

Remember, underneath those clicks are private API routes. Rather than a private API needing to be sniffed, web pages had to be explored and their HTML elements had to be analyzed. This has become more difficult. In the early days of chronological feeds without async updates, it was much easier. In the era of dynamic web pages with deeply nested content and tons of different types of content, it can be more frustrating to extract XPaths from a website than to map out private API routes.

XPath is the language used to construct and locate values in an XML document, like a webpage. Scraping XPaths and building code that interacts with website elements is a popular technique used in web scraping and browser automation.

An Instagram client that uses browser emulation (also known as an "embedded browser") would have most of the same functionality of Instagram's private API (like, follow, comment, etc), except instead of a web request being sent directly, a series of clicks to XPaths would be executed inside a web browser.

InstaPy, a library published by Tim Grossman on September 26, 2016,[3] is the best-known and most feature-rich browser emulation library. It uses Selenium, an open-source framework that can automate actions within web browsers to navigate, select elements, and click through Instagram's web app.

Tim answered a string of my long, rambling questions. For that, I am thankful. His motivation for creating InstaPy was similar to Chris Buetti's motivation for creating his private Instagram bot that earned him free meals.[4]

> I wanted to learn Python and was starting out as a vegan food creator on IG, trying to get free food. Since I'm a programmer at heart, what first thought would you have rather than automating all the annoying things.

There are competing opinions on whether Instagram can detect browser-based automation or an API better. There are advantages and disadvantages to each approach. Running a web browser, even in an "invisible" headless mode (no UI), requires more computing resources than dealing with API requests. Websites can detect that a browser is running "headless," so libraries have evolved to run clandestinely headless. There are layers and layers of trickery that go beyond what any independent engineer can develop. Anyone running a browser-based automation solution is beholden to third-party libraries to do the heavy lifting and avoid detection.

One persistent rumor was that the browser API differed from the mobile API and that some browser API routes weren't subject to Instagram's action limits or bot detection schemes. All I know is that the one supposedly limitless action, "Mass Story Viewing," was patched before I could test it.

One benefit of using the browser with Selenium is that the page load time helps dictate sane interaction intervals. Web request send/response times enable programmers to dispatch requests faster than a human ever would, which can cause activity to get flagged. In the web browser, there are sometimes dozens of requests behind each displayed page. A page can be accessible without fully loading. Waiting the extra few hundred milliseconds and then navigating the page flow like a human could avoid detection.

The real benefit of the browser is data mining in a way that is more resistant to API changes. If the API is changed but the browser view remains consistent, then the program will continue to work without any finagling.

A big disadvantage of browser-based workflows is that they're clunky and have interdependent steps. Spinning up the browser takes a non-zero amount of time. Waiting for content to load can take longer, and some workflows that involve multiple steps (compared to pure-HTTP workflows, which largely don't) can be undermined by lazy coding, small changes to the website, or bot-busting techniques.

Testing is a pain in the ass. What happens when an automated headless browser session crashes? It can be nigh impossible to recreate an error on a web page exactly. Without some type of harness to capture the page at the time of the crash, a developer might not have any insight into what happened.

Mobile devices offer better safeguards against scraping. Also, users tend to view more ads on their phones than in their browsers, so platforms have severely restricted what's possible on desktop browser apps. On Instagram, a full-featured web platform invites browser emulation, though it comes with unique challenges.

Tim's perspective on browser emulation versus API clients mostly aligned with mine. He said that using a private API client was good because it was "very sturdy once correctly implemented, fast, easily scalable, and easily deployed—basically the way advanced and better option." Some of the cons of using APIs were that they were complex, they required deeper tech knowledge, and bot detection more easily blocked traffic.

Further, he highlighted an interesting point: the visual aspect of InstaPy "controlling" a web browser helped non-technical users understand what was going on: "...nothing was as fun and broadly understandable as browser emulation. (Way more people were able to understand what's going on and how to get started + watch InstaPy work it's magic.)"

He said that emulation was generally simpler and easier to understand but an absolute nightmare when site composition changed. Testing took much longer, and deploying and scaling the code was harder, just as I experienced.

Phone Emulation

Nearly all organic growth services and SMM panels used reverse-engineered, private APIs and/or browser emulation. These methods were cheap to set up, monitor, and scale. They provided great results. This has always been the case. Whenever there has been a hitch with private APIs, engineers have found success with browser emulation. However, these two methods are susceptible to detection. Detection means disabled accounts. What if there were another way to automate activity?

What if human behavior could be emulated at the application level? What if taps, swipes, and other gestures could be executed undetected?

Emulator software, which can only be activated by connecting a phone to a computer, can be used to feed human actions and environmental data into the phone's sensors. This software, for iOS or Android, provides a sandbox environment meant to be used to test apps. This functionality is reserved for app developers. Unsurprisingly, some experienced app developers who wanted to build Instagram growth solutions exploited this technology.

Followyst was the only company that provided this service. It emerged in late 2020, well after many traditional growth services had thrown in the towel.

The Followyst team deserves applause for embracing this methodology and making their marketing materials transparent. Followyst provided a desktop application to control Android phones and execute typical organic automated growth actions. Later, they released an app on the Google Play store.

My respect for this company does not mean they were compliant with Instagram's rules. A customer could face disciplinary action from Instagram. However, users were less likely to get caught because they were using a high-quality IP address (from the laptop location), weren't taking many actions, and could pass any device ID or gesture-based tests.

While brilliant, the automation didn't scale well. It required a powered-on computer *and* would monopolize control of a phone. A customer or practitioner could see the actions taking place with a level of fidelity not seen in other growth methods. Where other methods could scale to hundreds of accounts from a few cheap cloud-based servers, this type of growth was hardware-hungry—one account per device.

Also, because the API wasn't used to bypass mundane and useless aspects of user activity, liking and commenting weren't optimized. A bot program could use the API to take shortcuts and avoid a lot of scrolling and clicking to scrape or interact with the highly reciprocal accounts. A program like Followyst's *could have* benefitted from insights from elsewhere, but it wouldn't be intelligent enough to consistently get better results than a human similarly using a phone. Perhaps a better solution is hiring people in the Philippines after all.

Unfortunately, I couldn't reconnect with Followyst's co-founder, Chris. The company seems to have vanished in 2024. Googling it returns very little, but I did uncover a believable claim the company made in 2020:[5]

> We're getting a [sic] really good feedback from people using our product, Followyst. They observed gains from +300 (micro) to +750 (influencer) followers per month. What's most important to them, though, is safety – it's extremely hard to block, even when running continuous[ly] for hours at top speeds.
>
> It relies on automatically liking posts with specific criteria, which is very effective in terms of finding new followers and increasing engagement.

What of the Sharks?

When the two DJs who started Shark Social first reached out to me in 2017, they already had *some* software and clients. They certainly weren't growing accounts by hand. They weren't social media savants. They also weren't software engineers. They were DJs. It's time to reveal Shark Social's original approach to organic Instagram growth.

Shark Social, and its precursory sole proprietorship, grew customer accounts using FollowLiker.

FollowLiker emerged around May 30, 2013, and became one of the most relied-upon and consistent black hat growth applications. It utilized Instagram's private API.

The desktop app originally sold for a one-time fee and allowed *unlimited* accounts to be run. Later versions included a subscription component. In the last iteration, the unlimited license was ninety-eight dollars with a $5.99 monthly subscription.

Promotional materials claimed, "Your follower and like counts will skyrocket with this amazing tool." It was a fully functional "follow-unfollow" bot along the lines of the four-step algorithm outlined above. Customer accounts were loaded in, targeting was set, and the program started mimicking human behavior on Instagram. The likes started pouring in. It was so easy that a DJ could do it.

FollowLiker's feature set was rich. According to the website,[6] it allowed customers to "follow users, unfollow users, share photos and videos, like photos, unlike photos, comment on photos, send direct messages, [search users], [search photos], blacklist users, white-list users, assign proxies, run multiple accounts, schedule tasks, and view account details."

It worked well, though superior alternatives emerged post-Instagress. Many operators, even those who knew how to program, kept programs like FollowLiker in reserve for emergencies when their custom applications broke. We would even send inquiries to their support staff while debugging issues with bespoke software just to see if "new" restrictions were afoot.

FollowLiker's impact was vast. It's hard to believe that an app used to generate millions of dollars for black hat agencies *never* appeared in a mainstream news article. To my knowledge, it never publicly faced legal action from any social media company. It lived and died in the shadows. The site is still up, but attempting to purchase its Instagram, Twitter, Pinterest, or Tumblr software produces the message, "Follow Liker is getting updated. Please check back later..."[7]

Someone complained about the software being "shut down" on May 4, 2023.[8] On November 27, 2023, one of the founders of Shark Social, who by that point owned a fitness studio, sent a screenshot of the same message with the caption, "I was bored and super curious to see if I could restart [Shark Social] [on my own] for [nth] time...Doesn't look like it."

. . .

So, why hire a code monkey like me?

14

BUILDING BOTS
THIRD ERA

*This is not an instruction manual on how to break Instagram's or any other platform's terms of use. This information should be considered outdated and hypothetical. It is provided only as commentary and to improve platform safety, and it draws from **publicly available information**, including research conducted by Facebook employees. I do not operate or distribute any software system that violates Instagram's TOU.*

"This is why you hire a programmer!! This is why you hire a programmer!!"

The CEO of Shark Social danced around the kitchen island in his code monkey's Chicago apartment. I was perched on a stool debugging the custom applications I had designed. To the CEO's untrained eye and his hundreds of Snapchat followers who received the video he filmed while shrieking, I was a savant, a hacker even. I was expected to solve a production issue as he bounced around. Undoubtedly, replacing our trusty copy of FollowLiker with custom software was a good idea.

In the "Copycat Era" immediately after Instagress, Mass Planner, and

PeerBoost were shut down in the spring of 2017, dozens of Instagram growth services emerged, including Shark Social.

That fall, new growth applications called Jarvee[1] and GramMultiTool (GMT2) emerged on BlackHatWorld. These graphical user interfaces controlling bulk account automation were heralded as "alternatives" to (replacements for) Instagress. Over four years after the first wave of growth apps, xGram Bot and Botstagram were almost completely forgotten.

With Jarvee and GMT2, any computer-literate person could build a follower-boosting "agency" and scale to a few dozen clients. That's what Shark had done with FollowLiker. Technical expertise wasn't needed, sales expertise was. Any bozo could have learned the ropes and started making 1,500 dollars per month. It was too easy—powerful spam tools were in the hands of everyone (who knew about BlackHatWorld).

So why hire a code monkey like me?

When I first signed on, there was no grand ambition. My orders were to set up the Wordpress website, integrate Stripe, help adjust SEO, and create a new customer signup flow that involved sending emails. Today, anyone can use a website builder and genAI, and hiring a programmer would be foolish.

I had the payment flow working in early July, and on August 24, 2017, we were accepting new customers with the "YEE HAW!" emails. I was paid five hundred dollars for that work. They had FollowLiker. They had a web storefront. They didn't need me.

Becoming a Shark

As I helped the Sharks start their new business, I was tempted by the vast opportunities on the dark side. I saw the competition. I saw the wild claims. I saw one of the founders of Instafame posted Stripe billing statements on his Instagram showing over 100,000 dollars per month of recurring revenue.

I thought to myself, "How many of these bozos are also just running FollowLiker? I could do that!"

Truly, this was a popular thought in late 2017 and early 2018 as dozens of growth services emerged using FollowLiker, Jarvee, and GMT2. Nobody was upfront about it—the websites all made the same over-the-top claims with the same branding. I couldn't just jump in though. One year into my first job, I knew nothing about sales, customers, or running a business.

As different as we were, I really liked the Sharks. I didn't withhold anything from them, and on July 2, 2017, I started the email thread, "Research and Findings."

Seeking job security, I fear mongered about one of the biggest threats—obtaining high-quality proxies to evade detection. My logic holds up more than seven years later:

> ...Let's say [CEO] is running 20 accounts [in FollowLiker] on relatively tight settings. All is well. Then, one day, one of the accounts gets banned. Immediately, all other accounts accessing instagram from [CEO's] computer['s IP address] will be scrutinized more heavily by Instagram.

Proxies are alternative IP addresses (stripped-down versions of VPNs) that can conceal the source of web traffic. Can't view a "region-locked" video? Use a proxy from a different region. TikTok is blocked in the United States? Use a proxy from a different country. Piping activities through proxies can evade bot detection systems. Running twenty accounts from the same IP address is risky. The rule of thumb is no more than three accounts per proxy.

Later in the email, I provided a ridiculous timeline with options for building "a cloud-based subscription-based application like what Mass-Planner and Instagress[2] did." I can't be blamed for being ambitious, but the endeavor was well beyond my technical abilities at the time. *No copycat* emerged to build the next-generation dashboard-based bot program.

It turned out that the immense technical investment required for a web or desktop app wasn't necessary. I didn't know it in August 2017, but thousands of customers were searching and signing up for organic growth providers daily. They wanted to "set it and forget it." Like the casual gamers of my generation who were supplanted by kids who *only watched games*, dashboards and desktop apps were ignored for the low-effort storefronts offering follower growth in a fully-managed setup (that didn't reference botting).

The Sharks liked my long-winded emails and my spaghetti code. We rolled the five-hundred-dollar payment into a continuous agreement that would go into effect once the systems were up and running. They were willing to pay me a generous double-digit percentage share of gross revenue. In addition to the technical aspect, my role specified that I would "Help with further business development, planning, and direction if needed."

I signed on as the code monkey. I ended up learning everything there was to know about the business.

Logging In

Instafame, like Instagress before it, had an "Instagram login" as part of its customer signup flow.

That feature built user trust, streamlined signups, and reduced complaints. However, these logins were dangerous and deceitful. I was asked to reverse engineer Instafame's login system and add it to the Shark Social website.

"So, if you follow these screenshots, you'll see that InstaFame is authenticating login passwords. Hmmmmm..." The next day, I responded, "I was able to do a basic login. I know when the login is successful and when it isn't."

When the APIs were open, finding "login-with..." features on websites was common. My 2014 website WhenDidMyParentsBang.com allowed users to connect to Facebook *without entering their passwords*. I extracted each user's date of birth from Facebook and used that to calculate a possible conception date.

Customers arrived at "Instagram growth" storefronts and assumed that the "login with your Instagram credentials" prompts were Instagram-sponsored programmatic logins. *They were not*. The password was never supposed to be exposed. The API integrations of the early 2010s specified that a "token" would have been safely passed. That was not happening. Users unaware of the distinction were getting "phished" by growth providers. They were sending their unencrypted usernames and passwords to the site owner, not Instagram.

What if the information was wrong? This is where programmers were separated from script kiddies. Anyone running Jarvee behind the scenes wouldn't have been able to validate logins during signup. We noticed that Instafame *was* validating logins on their website, which meant they were familiar with the private API for Instagram's login flow.

Instafame wouldn't allow users to continue signing up if their usernames or passwords didn't result in "successful logins" on their backend. I had to copy this for Shark Social.

I found the private API client on GitHub and the Instabot library. I wrote code on top of it to accept a username, password, and proxy and return a message based on whether the login was successful. After testing things locally, I wired up the code on our website (which used PHP—not my first choice).

Any website visitor who filled in the form to start the process would have their credentials sent to my server and validated with Instagram's private API. I entered bogus credentials on competitors' websites to map which ones had the functionality. I confirmed those using unvalidated forms and could only correct login information post-signup after communicating with their customers.

These login flows building "trust" was ironic considering customers were actually providing full access to their accounts.

I battled with temptation. When confirming login credentials, why not use the private API to send a few "likes" to Shark Social's Instagram? Why not send a follow to *my* Instagram? Why not download the user's DMs, posts, and profile metadata for further analysis or sale? I never did, but I could have, as a service provider entrusted with a customer's login credentials.

At Shark Social, customers who visited already had a strong inclination to make a purchase. More than eighty percent of visitors who passed through the login gate became paying customers. But we had the Instagram account names of those who dropped. We DMed some of them, "Hey, we noticed you didn't complete signup, what happened?" We coerced signups at a high rate. However, ultimately, this was a "dark pattern" because users didn't realize they were providing their Instagram names directly to Shark Social.

Customer Portals

Although customers were generally fine with viewing their follower growth inside the official app, some expressed a desire to "press buttons." They asked for a customer portal or "dashboard" to log into. Although I eventually created data analysis tools for the Sharks' internal use, we never provided this feature to customers. Fewer than ten percent asked.

While we were using FollowLiker, we couldn't make the stats broadly available. Providing a customer dashboard necessitated storing statistics that were accessible on the internet. None of the off-the-shelf tools from BlackHatWorld allowed that.

As for adjustments in targeting, we asked customers to submit a basic form. Most of our competitors did the same thing. For password changes, I designed a separate login validator that connected to my backend server.

Jarvee and GMT2

On May 12, 2017, the day that MassPlanner shut down, a user named "rtribe13" posted a wanted ad on BHW, "Hiring a developer - MP Replacement":[3]

> With the closing of MassPlanner I am looking to hire a developer to create
> an automation tool similar to what massplanner [sic] accomplished with
> Instagram. Other details and pricing can be negotiated. Pleave [sic] leave a
> reply or PM me if interested in the job.

rtribe13 must not have found his programmer because a year later, he was on a thread called, "What is the best Instagram bot"[4] and shared that he found Jarvee, which had entered the space in September 2017, to be "quite powerful." Jarvee ran on users' local machines like FollowLiker rather than in the cloud like Instagress.

The cloud had drawbacks. Instagress's demise revealed that trusting a cloud service is trusting a "single point of failure" that can disappear. The urgency expressed on BHW following shutdowns indicated many users had clients to lose. A standalone app on each agency owner's desktop could *technically* continue working even if the provider's servers had been shut down (only "technically" though, as they'd need to connect to a licensing server to prevent piracy).

The main benefit of desktop apps for small operators is that any computer naturally has a high-quality "residential" IP address. A web dashboard running bots in data centers has naturally *low* IP quality. Anybody running bots would have to pay for a residential proxy to run a small batch of accounts in the cloud to mitigate the risk of getting blocked.

Late 2017 was an exciting time for Shark Social as well as for those looking for the "new thing" on BlackHatWorld. Jarvee's November 2017 tagline promised, "With JARVEE you can reach over 100,000 new Instagram users each month."[5] It continued, "Only real and engaged Instagram users, that is! It is the way pros do it and if you want to beat them at their own game you will need to use Instagram marketing automation for sure."

Jarvee's features included post scheduling, auto re-post, auto-follow, follow-back, unfollow, auto-like, auto-comment, delete posts, contact prospects, DM management, hashtag research, block followers, find and extract targeted users, manage comments, delete comments, like comments, save posts, auto phone-verify accounts, import data from other tools, spin syntax, and proxy support.[6]

GMT2 came not long after Jarvee on October 17, 2017.[7] It was another Windows app, a successor to the original Gram MultiTool, which I believe was launched in August 2016 (though there is little remaining evidence).[8] The pitch was similar: "With GMT[2] you will be able to grow your follower base and engagement in a matter of weeks, without having to lift a finger!"[9]

The wording of the feature set suggested it was pitched more toward power users than those looking to grow one account (it did involve lifting "a finger" to set up and press play each time a computer was restarted). The features included a follow module, unfollow module, like module, comment module, advanced filtering, batch publisher, quick publisher, advanced analytics, user tracing, and unlimited accounts.[10]

These successors to the original xGram Bot and Botstagram combined with post-Instagress automated account services meant an increasingly crowded, spammy, Instagram experience as 2018 dawned.

Downhill

By January 2018, I was hanging on to my day job by a thread. A manager from a different team offered to bring me into his fold. The pressure was on. Meanwhile, Shark Social ascended in search results and appeared on the first page for certain high-value keywords, like "Instagram growth service." We never advertised or hired an SEO consultant. We were getting customers every day, it was only a question of how many.

As I built an alternative to FollowLiker and experimented on test accounts, the responsibilities of my day job and side hustle began to clash.

My time wasn't bifurcated into nine-to-five workdays versus nights and weekends. I loved the "YEE HAW!" emails. They helped me get through the stressful days. Increasingly, there were customer support requests and issues with everything from signup flows to proxies that meant more than just skipping happy hour.

Search traffic picked up, and we quickly reached one hundred active customers, a major milestone. That January, I returned from New Year's Eve in Miami to go skiing in Aspen the next weekend before traveling to Utah to ski Alta two weeks later. I felt like a jet-setter—like I was growing closer to the Instafame guy's Instagram feed with pictures of private planes. I was doing my part to sell the dream even while wracked with stress and living paycheck to paycheck.

It ended up being a tough winter. To start, on January 27, 2018, "The Follower Factory"[11] concerning Devumi and fake Twitter followers was published. On one hand, we didn't sell fake followers, and the increased awareness pushed more traffic to Instagram growth businesses with false branding as being compliant. On the other hand, the investigative work pressured platform owners and regulatory agencies to squash the problem.

In a view free of nuance, organic growth like Shark Social was as "bad" as Devumi's fake follower reselling. In actuality, its disruptive potential and scale were *different,* but the engagement was indeed based on a "fake," deceitful premise.

Three days later, Instagram announced major API changes, including a phase-out plan for the remaining public API functions as Instagram merged with Facebook's Graph API.[12] Although this likely didn't affect any major bot operators, it did threaten the ecosystem of hobbyist developers who had created apps based on Kevin Systrom's original vision of the developer program.

Regardless of the nuance between fake likes and fake-activity-generated likes, February 20, 2018, was a significant date in the Instagram growth timeline. Social Media Series Limited, the parent company of Social Envy and a major player in the growth space, was served with a cease-and-desist order from Facebook,[13] a digital "slap on the wrist."

There is no record of this from a primary news source. The Wayback Machine, however, indicates that by February 24, 2018, the Social Envy site was undergoing panicked maintenance. By the March 7, 2018, capture, the site had been updated: "FRIENDLY NOTE - Social Envy is no longer accepting clients."[14]

The planes had been grounded.

In short order, the Cambridge Analytica Scandal broke, on March 12, 2018; Sapna Maheshwari published "Uncovering Instagram Bots with a New Kind of Detective Work"[15]; and on April 2, 2018, Instagram unexpectedly accelerated the shutdown of its public API.[16] This was almost certainly due to the fallout from Cambridge Analytica more than the *New York Times* articles.

We read headlines and participated in discussions on BlackHatWorld and realized that our remaining time was limited. Yet, Shark Social was fielding more inquiries than ever. That spring, we started switching customers to the system I'd designed.

Mako

Off-the-shelf software was limited in many respects. Issues were compounded as the customer base grew from ten to one hundred to, eventually, one thousand! Scalability problems and the lack of a common interface between FollowLiker and other programs were an operational conundrum for anyone running a business. It also meant that testing hypotheses about specific sequences of actions and enforcement thresholds was nearly impossible.

I wanted to build a bot, which I thought could help Shark Social become a prominent provider in the space. In a swaggering summer 2017 email, I said, "I'd advocate for going all out from the start. Taking more time to get my automated, custom program working and then blowing the doors off the competition."

The evolution of my system was like that of any other in the space. At first, I only used it to verify logins. It was a thin "wrapper" around the private API functions for signing in. Then I started to use it for sporadic testing of proxy viability, likes, follows, and comments. From there, it was a matter of how much time and effort I wanted to put into coding a full-fledged program that could run all day, like FollowLiker ("FL") without the user interface.

The system I designed was known by different names—at one point, "Whitefish" because I believed it would earn me enough money to buy a house with a fireplace in Whitefish, Montana. However, since I'm already using a codename for the company and I never did buy that house, I'll name it "Mako." The shortfin mako is one of the fastest and smartest sharks.

The Sharks' primary concern was streamlining customer management. People signed up, their login details were sent to one server, their targeting details were emailed to us, and then FL was running on a gaming computer in the CEO's basement. The CEO, or someone with remote access, had to log in, manually enter the customer's details, and restart the app. Not only was this error-prone, but it was also time-consuming. There was no reason to have a human involved in the process. The same pain points existed when users wanted to update their targeting details—we had to do them in batches for our sanity.

The first thing Mako did was integrate with Shark Social's signup flow. Details came through and were pushed to Mako's database. Competitors asked for "24-48 hours" to get new customers up and running. Mako could get someone running in less than a minute. It was so fast that it scared people, and I had to implement delays and a ramp-up period.

When customers cancel, it could be painful. People would cancel in the middle of the night and then send angry emails because FL ran for a few extra hours. Nobody jumped out of bed to turn it off. Mako solved this by integrating with the cancellation process. The coding wasn't crazy, but, unlike FL, there was no support rep to message when things went wrong. It was just me. "Single point of value" as it might have been, we *could have* got everyone running on FL in an emergency if we were willing to trudge through it.

Proxies remained a crucial part of the operation. Switching them out in FL was brutal. We hired part-time help to manage miscellaneous customer support tasks *and* manage proxies. Every customer needed a proxy. We purchased them from an online provider. At first, we maintained an Excel sheet in which we arranged them by hand, which became ridiculously hard to manage.

I loaded the proxies into Mako's database (it's worth mentioning that most proxy providers offered API access for exporting newly purchased proxies). There, we could associate proxies with account records and track deactivated proxies. I added a feature to the customer signup flow that randomly selected a proxy to log in with. This proxy was then assigned to the customer record in Mako. Using one IP address during the signup and another while botting was a recipe for triggering an action block.

Although the work fell on me (since I didn't provide a user interface), it became easier to deal with proxies and run tests on them. Proxy types (data center, residential, mobile) and providers were also stored in the database.

Later, I created an AWS dashboard that a non-technical person could have used to spin up data center proxies in Amazon EC2. By then, those proxies had low trust scores, and they didn't work particularly well, but it was neat to say that Shark Social had become a low-budget proxy provider (for anyone who knew the password).

Next was the "event stream." I logged every event that occurred when interacting with Instagram: logins, likes, follows—not every *request* to the platform but those I thought would matter. This helped form a notion of activity limits beyond FL or the other apps and provided fine-grained stats for future analysis and "account status." If an account was blocked, banned, waiting for email/in-app verification, or just had its password changed, I'd mark that. We received immediate alerts for important stuff and daily summary emails for anything to be addressed with a customer. I don't know how anyone running an agency on top of someone else's desktop app could operate without sending alerts or exporting statistics.

Mako 2

Mako's initial buildout promised to save tons of human operational time. But if the targeting was the same, the scraping of targeted accounts/hashtags was the same, and it was just follow-unfollow, was there any reason to exclaim, "This is why you hire a programmer!!"?

Later in 2018, I developed advanced features, some that might be considered novel. Chris Buetti's February 24, 2019, Medium post[17] disclosing the system he built to get free meals in New York outlined aspects of the approach. Separating the "scraper" from the "follow-unfollow" flow was enormously efficient. FL appeared to do some scraping, then some liking, then who knows what. Crawling through targeted accounts and hashtags *using customer accounts* wasted valuable actions. We only cared about customer accounts taking actions that could be reciprocated.

If the scraping was a separate process:

1. It could be accomplished by burner accounts instead of valuable customer accounts.
2. Similarities between targeting sets could be identified to help prevent duplicate actions.

In FollowLiker, all customer bot threads were isolated. If five customers listed "Kim Kardashian" as a target account, all five would separately query Kim's followers and media to find accounts to interact with, which would have been a huge waste. What if one had "Kim Kardashian" and the other "Khloe Kardashian"? Surely, further analysis could create more intelligent targeting groups.

Burner accounts could be run *just* to scrape, which allowed customer accounts to be run just to like, follow, and comment. Any Mako instance with similar targeting could query and interact with the related accounts already in the database. This had a huge impact but required a distinct set of logic, more proxies, and a new maintenance burden. Beyond that, it required purchasing burner accounts from overseas providers. These were the same types of accounts used in bot farms that Devumi could have been reselling likes from. For my purposes, having one hundred active burners at any time was overkill. I needed to run one for every twenty customers or so.

Scraping required new database models and a fair bit of storage space (I never downloaded pictures). These were not particularly complicated, but arranging the data and collecting insights became an art form. This is why "data science" people make money from creating cute charts a few times per month. Mountains of data can be overwhelming. One thing Chris Buetti did,[18] which I also implemented, was find traits common to low-quality accounts and media that shouldn't be interacted with (e.g., low like or follower counts, too many people tagged in a photo). Chris's system was more advanced than the part of Mako that handled this.

Techniques were developed to guide accounts with low "trust scores." This was hard to get right since it was just an estimate and partially guided by unsubstantiated claims on BHW. Some accounts would be "warmed up," initially only taking small numbers of actions before approaching the "action limit." Accounts could also "backoff" after a block or warning and take fewer actions. Retrospectively, I'd love to claim to be a genius who ducked and countered every punch thrown by Instagram's anti-botting measures. That wasn't the case! People with FollowLiker were stuck chatting with support. Mako made running customer accounts safer and more efficient while providing a platform to test hypotheses but never solved problems for me.

Jarvee had added an option to switch between the private API and the browser emulation ("embedded browser") routes. This was heralded on BlackHatWorld. Painstakingly, I added the ability to switch between these two options in Mako, adding the InstaPy dependency for browser emulation. It was never completely fluid because I would have had to design tons of tests specific to the browser function, and debugging it was a pain in the ass. At times, I felt we had evaded bans by switching our interaction method, but I often wished I had hired a full-time software engineer to help me.

There were architectural concerns. I didn't want to keep the "What should I do next?" logic inside any scraper or engager (customer) thread. I used durable queues in the cloud (I know—stay with me) that allowed me to simplify logic inside a growing universe of "microservices" while making things much easier to test, observe, and scale.

The queuing also allowed me to implement crazy stuff like "reactive engagement." To my knowledge, nobody has gone on the record saying that they prodded, calculated, and force-pushed commands to interact with specific accounts seemingly guaranteed to reciprocate. *I did this.* When I showed the "Mako 2" system diagram to Chris Buetti in 2019, he immediately invited me to work with his team on special projects. Once I synced incoming engagements (received likes, follows, and comments) with the "event stream," I created a standalone app for identifying users that were either:

1. Very, very likely to be running auto-reciprocating bots; or
2. Staffed by humans with a high chance of engaging.

I couldn't just calculate it once; I had to keep testing before redirecting the engagers to the account. I created a "prodder" mode in which burner accounts were used to test reciprocal exchanges of actions. If one account quickly received a follow back, I'd send a few more. If they received follows back, I'd open the floodgates. If the base reciprocation rate was only ten percent, finding an account reciprocating eighty percent or more was a godsend! I added some reliably "reflective" accounts to what amounted to

Mako's "favorites" list. I continued prodding until I reached a conclusion either way (this was fully automated only in my dreams).

As the user count zoomed toward two hundred, I formalized the Mako API. It allowed for better interprocess communication and reporting. It also allowed me to do things like, "Send one hundred followers to @timothy_ohearn11231." It was like I had an SMM panel in my pocket. Because the queues were "prioritized," we could fluidly cut the line and insert a high-priority like or follow. There was an API that I could pass some parameters to...control my own botnet.

It made for a cool trick at bars and house parties.

The final step was the "circle jerk." Customers expected to see engagement—followers, likes, and comments. When the total number of daily actions was severely limited, each engagement became more valuable. To pad numbers for accounts that weren't doing so well, we had an "emergency" system, a closed loop in which *customers interacted with other customers*. These were guaranteed actions. While one account could spend weeks sending randomized picture likes, each customer was only good for a single "follow" to the account in need. I estimated that a system like this could become entirely self-sustaining (at a modest customer turnover rate) with around five thousand customers.

Shark Social never got there. Mako, though always in disrepair, was a superweapon that I believe could have established Shark Social as the indisputable "number one Instagram growth service." I spoke freely of its merits to any developer who would listen, but I never sent the code to anyone or contributed more than minor bug fixes to the underlying libraries on GitHub. Maybe that was for the better.

Following Their Footsteps

In September 2018, the Instagram co-founders stepped down from their roles at Facebook.[19] That month, I stepped into a new day job even though I didn't have to. My cut of Shark Social's revenue was paying my bills. The Sharks had been so impressed with Mako that we negotiated a richer contract. They hired support staff to help with basic operations. Although my weekends were usually packed with maintenance and research, I settled into my new job and happily checked my phone to see the "YEE HAW!'s" flowing in.

On October 31, 2018, a research paper titled, "Following Their Footsteps: Characterizing Account Automation Abuse and Defects"[20] was published. Two of the five authors worked at Facebook, and the other three were employed by UCSD.

As much as I envy anyone able to get paid to work on such cool research projects, I don't envy that the researchers had to create one hundred and fifty Instagram accounts by hand.[21]

But it was worth it. The study is groundbreaking.

The paper stated that "Hublaagram" had over one million active customers while Instazood and Instalex together had over one hundred thousand.[22] I thought it was cool that Mako executed maybe—maybe—one billion actions. Hublaagram could have been responsible for billions of actions *per week*.

The revenue estimates of the tested services were "$200k-$800k per month."[23] The money from Shark Social changed our lives, but we never sniffed six figures *per month*. We were small fish—not at the bottom of search rankings but drawing in a tiny share of the overall market. To us, that share was everything. I could only dream about how well Mako would have scaled with hundreds of thousands of customers.

The basis of the study was that like engagement resellers were "simple," so the researchers decided to "focus on the more sophisticated segment of this market, Account Automation Services (AASs) in which users provide their Instagram credentials to third party actors who, in turn, use those credentials to perform actions on the user's behalf in a manner that violates Instagram's Terms of Use."[24]

Batches of the researcher's accounts called "honeypots" were used to subscribe to the leading automation services.[25] After weeks of observation, the researchers managed to "[Use] our service characterizations...to identify all accounts used by customers of each service." This allowed them to estimate the size of each operation (along with revenue projections) and then institute countermeasures within Instagram's bot prevention system to conduct experiments.

They identified two primary activities undertaken by AASs: "Reciprocity Abuse" and "Collusion Networks."[26] Collusion Networks are the same as the "circle jerk" but with academic language. These networks only became self-sustaining as customer counts grew to thousands. The profiled services had sufficient volume to sustain collusion. For Mako, the "collusion" was utilized in times of drought.

Reciprocity Abuse—"This 'you follow me, I follow you' behavior is an organic response taken by some subset of Instagram users. Reciprocity Abuse AASs abuse this behavior by automating large numbers of (outbound) actions from their customer's Instagram account in the hope that a subset of users receiving an action will return the favor in kind—thus providing their customer with inbound actions, such as follows."

With a statistically significant sample size, the researchers elucidated what drew customers and operatives into the business—the big secret. Even "empty" accounts received reciprocal (inbound) follows at a rate exceeding ten percent![27] Honeypot accounts that appeared real ("lived-in") attracted reciprocal engagements at rates of 12.0%, 13.7%, and 16.1%, depending on the service provider. Account quality had a minimal (0.9%-3.1%) impact on reciprocation.[28] When I was testing "lived-in" burners in specific niches, I observed rates above twenty percent (approaching thirty percent for "babe" accounts). The researchers' numbers aligned with what we observed at Shark Social.

The enforcement actions, or countermeasures, were equally compelling. During the observation period, accounts controlled by one provider were following a median of 350 accounts per day.[29] This matched the rule of thumb at the time, three hundred follows per day. After the researchers implemented an immediate ("strong signal") countermeasure block, it took only about three days for the bot to adapt to the new "control" threshold of 150 follows per day. It's unknown whether the bot itself adapted (using exponential backoffs and ramp-ups) or if a manager guessed a lower threshold of actions and turned the dial manually.

One of the biggest findings was that a "delayed removal of follows" "one day later" elicited no reaction from service providers. "The services *do not* react to the delayed removal of follows."[30] At Mako, it only would have been obvious if we graphed followers from an hourly sampling (daily might not have been good enough) and if customers started complaining. We never observed this. However, shortly after "Following Their Footsteps" was published, Instagram started serving an in-app popup threatening the removal of fake actions.

End of the Era

If researchers at Facebook could blow the lid off growth providers—if they were willing to pierce the marketing veil of "compliance" by signing up for the automation services—the immensely profitable industry would be reduced to a game of cat and mouse. If they were willing to send cease and desist letters to the largest players, tighten the screws on action limits, blacklist proxy networks, and retroactively remove followers gained illicitly, the end of 2018 would have a much different vibe than the end of 2017.

By November 2018, Stripe had added organic growth services and fake-like resellers to its high-risk, restricted businesses list. Shark Social was grandfathered in (or so we believed). We tried to create backup accounts just in case, and not a single one was approved on *any* payment processor. Social media software businesses were, in a way, "deplatformed" months after losing public API access because of Cambridge Analytica.

On November 19, 2018, Instagram announced measures to reduce inauthentic activity in the app.[31] Although the paper published three weeks earlier wasn't referenced, it likely influenced that swift announcement. There is no doubt that Instagram was able to identify and remove ill-gotten followers, but we never observed it, and there is no evidence provided on BHW (maybe it was so sneaky that nobody ever noticed, as mentioned in the paper).

Shark Social and Mako were holding up just fine. I didn't read "Following Their Footsteps" until people on BlackHatWorld started talking about it in the face of new sanctions in June 2019. The researchers suggested that the characterizations resulted from checking for patterns in the "IP address," "Autonomous System Number," and "additional signals produced within Instagram."[32] They admitted that an AAS "going so far as to use an extensive proxy network to drastically increase IP diversity" was "out of reach of the blocking countermeasure we employed." My initial fear-mongering was prescient. It ended up being *all about proxies*.

Other adaptive tactics could be encoded into advanced bots to help AASs make their footsteps harder to follow. By mid-2019, automation providers, including Shark Social, would find themselves not taking many footsteps at all.

15

THEY CAN'T ALL BE NUMBER ONE!

Exasperated, I raced through the list of Shark Social's competitors. I analyzed keywords, offerings, search position, branding, and even customer reviews. Had there been a mistake? An errant copy and paste? Never has the superlative "number one" been as overused as it was in the 2018 Instagram growth space. "They can't all be *number one*! They can't all be *the best*!" I spit as I lashed out in my empty apartment.

"Faked: The Headquarters. The Followers. The Influence?"[1] a *New York Times* article about Devumi from January 27, 2018, captured problems with services like mine. Black hat service providers not only operated on shaky legal ground,[2] but nearly every aspect of their business conduct was misleading, shady, and dishonest. Some growth services still employ such tactics. However, what emerged during the 2010s foreshadowed the refined approaches across the internet today, including in social engineering scams.

While writing this chapter, I revised and expanded the old spreadsheet, aided by my longtime "intern" who is now one year from graduating law school. We analyzed *over two hundred* SMM panels and growth services. The look and feel of the classic growth sites were borne out of a game of follow-the-leader. Each successive business copied *everything* from the leaders in the space—signup flows, website text, sales pitches, motifs of smiling female influencers, terms and conditions, and pricing plans.

In early 2018 as I turned competitor analysis into feature development, I was a bit shady myself. I added "Number One Instagram Growth Service" to Shark Social's website title and metadata. There was money to be made. It was time to *get this bread.*

Company Naming

Many growth providers and SMM panels used "Insta" in their names, including Easy Get Insta, Insta Captain, Instaboostgram, Instafame, Instafollowers, Instaforce, Instagooo, Instagram Bot Follower, Instagram-followersfree, Instagrampromotions, Instagress, Instamber, Instanobel, InstaPlus, Instapromoteme, Instaquiire, Instarazzo, Instato, Instazood, and Mr. Insta.

"Insta" was a smooth, flowing prefix. It also suggested an association with Instagram, which was a no-no. "Instagram Cracks Down On Connected Apps Using 'Insta' And 'Gram,'"[3] detailed early enforcement actions. This "crackdown" occurred years before Instagram growth services proliferated and while there were still a healthy number of "connected apps" using the (now-closed) public API.

Though less attractive than "Insta," "Gram" was also commonly used by providers like Gram Multi Tool (GMT), Gram Growing, Grameity, Gramista, GramSeed, GramTo, and NinjaGram.

Unscrupulous providers hijacked the name to convince potential customers of their authority, perhaps even that they were official offshoots. This is why trademarks exist. Instagram started strictly enforcing its trademarks. There was a rumor that Instagress had been targeted just as much for its name as for the millions of transactions it automated daily.

Fake Numbers

In a revelation that will stun no one, companies known for maliciously boosting social audiences were lying about their metrics.

Shady providers *loved* to boast how many customers they had and how many followers they'd acquired for their clients. This was the evolution of the "hit counter" from days past, a tally that some Myspace "friend adder" software providers seemed to legitimately implement.[4] Using the Wayback Machine, I found cached websites that showed *believable* growth of a "friends gained" metric between monthly captures on Infinite Adds in the aughts. Ten years later, not a single Instagram growth service provided a believable externally facing "hit counter" indicating total customers or cumulative results. But they provided plenty of hastily penned claims to manipulate visitors: "thousands" of satisfied customers and "millions" of followers gained.

I also discovered that sites had *launched* displaying text that quantified their already massive success! Fake it until you make it, comrades.

At Shark Social, there *was* a precursor business with maybe twenty satisfied customers. When we launched the website, what were we supposed to say? That we had ten customers so far apart from family friends? Of course not. We just made up nice round numbers.

Providers also "primed" their social media accounts by purchasing bulk fake followers. This made the services appear more successful. To my trained eye, 9,950 or 10,014 followers are highly suspicious. Anything close to a nice round number suggests that the vast majority of followers are fake because the chances are slim that the growth naturally stagnated at that number. If the number is just under, it means that fake followers have started to get banned at a rate faster than real followers could attach themselves. Because of a perceived "crackdown" in 2018, many services (over sixty percent on my list) avoided maintaining active Instagram accounts. Yes, supposed "Instagram experts" were scared to operate Instagram accounts for their businesses.

Shark Social did have an Instagram account with an audience built using our product. Although the company no longer operates, that page had over eight thousand followers.

Product Claims

It has been established that:

1. Instagram growth services could (pretty much) guarantee that followers would be human but not specific numbers.
2. Instagram "bot like" resellers could guarantee specific numbers of followers but not that they would be human.

Despite these facts, growth services freely posted numerical guarantees while SMM panels insisted that the followers were "not bots" or were human.

Although the core products *worked*, there were many faulty claims. Almost every growth service operated a follow-unfollow bot. Every SMM panel had access to a botnet. They couldn't admit to that for fear of being shut down. Claims of human hands and Instagram compliance were lies. Almost every SMM panel mystified customers with tiers of service to conceal that they were catapulting hordes of fake accounts to their customers from overseas.

When it came to guaranteeing specific numbers, growth services got creative. "Followers" became "impressions" and "reach." Although digital advertising platforms standardized these concepts, the switcheroos were sneaky. At Shark Social, we used "reach" and "exposure" instead of "followers or "likes." Some customers still misinterpreted this as guaranteed "followers," and they complained via fiery hate mail.

Almost every growth website had a frequently asked questions page. Again, each new player in the space tended to copy the top players. These FAQs attempted to placate users concerned that their accounts could get action-blocked or shadow banned. There were dozens if not hundreds of false assurances. Action blocks and shadow bans were widespread.

The companies that did "guarantee" followers masked guarantees behind another layer of deception: they didn't answer customer support requests.

Wanton Copying

Black hat service providers had a problem with the large-scale lifting of branding materials. All the website copy was eerily similar, as if sourced from the same genAI model. In a way, it had been! In early 2019, we ran Shark Social's site through a comprehensive plagiarism checker. I received an email from a cofounder with the subject line, "We have 2 plagiarism issues." We were furious, even though we had probably "borrowed" phrasing from our peers. We drafted cease-and-desist letters but resolved the issue by contacting the two sites that had "plagiarized" ours.

Testimonials and Fake Authority Sites

Just like a high follower count can boost a profile's authority, high-quality testimonials can boost a business's authority. They can be featured in a Google business profile, business aggregator sites, industry-specific blogs, or on a business's website.

The testimonial game evolved *significantly* between 2017 and the early 2020s. What started as rudimentary, faked, internal testimonials grew into a web of complicated, debased "truth" that proved hard to unravel. On BlackHatWorld, providers emerged to write fake reviews.

Just as early Web 2.0 visitors trusted websites as if they were news authorities, embedded testimonials were trusted and became popular. It took a long time for regulation to emerge to dissuade false, fake testimonials. The ruling on paid or fake testimonials didn't go into effect until October 2024![5] What happened before then?

A 2017 testimonial[6] on the now-defunct site SocialEnvy.co contained a thumbnail and handle of a female's Instagram page with the text: "Gained over 3000 followers, people who actually comment! Can vouch these followers are real."

This doesn't immediately strike me as a *fake* testimonial, especially considering the account still has over three thousand followers. These testimonials worked well when linked to live Instagram pages. However, the text is a bit suspicious in how well it fits into a terse blurb. It's impossible to confirm that all three thousand followers left comments. The non-technical customer couldn't prove that the followers were *all* real.

Some businesses posted fake testimonials for real accounts with hundreds of thousands of followers, claiming account holders were customers. They weren't. At Shark, we posted purely statistical testimonials ("from 500 to 5000!") but sometimes without asking for customers' permission.

By 2018, "trust" came to mean something different. Customers started asking about our "Trustpilot reviews." Trustpilot[7] is an independent authority that provides unbiased reviews. At launch, it suffered from the same problems as Yelp. Trustpilot and Yelp's business models both depend on *payments* from listees. Platforms are naturally biased toward and reward businesses that pay. An unbiased directory or review site is impossible when some clients pay and others don't. For business owners who could be crushed by one angry customer's negative review campaign, the lack of support could be a nightmare.

Yelp is great at screening abuse. I rarely see a non-filtered review that needs to be removed. By contrast, the same people gaming Instagram gamed business reviews on Trustpilot.

Yelp review distributions are usually predictable. People create accounts to write a single one-star review. Overall, the reviews are somewhat evenly distributed. On Trustpilot, the positive-negative review distribution for every Instagram growth site was comically bifurcated. Today, Upleap's site has 141 reviews. Forty-six percent are five-star, and forty-four percent are one-star.[8]

Presumably, the one-star reviews are from angry customers, some probably justified, while the five-star reviews are from incentivized customers or a purveyor of fake reviews. Charmed customers don't rush to leave five-star reviews. It isn't human nature. But extremely detailed one-star reviews are believable.

I prefer reviews from external sites, not a business's site, but my overall experience with Trustpilot was negative. Responding to potential customers who had *read something on Trustpilot* was exhausting and a drain on resources, but we did it *every time* someone asked. Seeing competitors' fake Trustpilot reviews was a huge drain on motivation.

Private blogs with meaningful search authority writing fake, negative reviews emerged alongside black hat Instagram activity. Bloggers collected affiliate revenue from an elite group of leading Instagram growth services. I call these "fake review sites."

They attracted so much web traffic that, like web directory sites of the aughts, they dictated *what* the popular Instagram growth sites were. Behind the "careful research" was...nothing! "Reviewers" (almost) never had proof of purchasing services from the providers in question. There were hundreds if not thousands of templated fake reviews.

Impressionable customers were fooled. The sites appeared to be impartial, even hosting comment sections, but they filtered the comments and only allowed negative ones for non-selected sites and positive ones for those paying affiliate kickbacks.

Every review was short and followed a templated format with maybe five minutes of research. *Every non-paying service* was deemed a scam between redirects to the partnered affiliate sites (which would also be labeled scams if they weren't paying).

Don't get me started on Jonathan Spire. If he were a real person, I would challenge him to a duel. That's how much I dislike him and his stock photo shit-eating grin. JonathonSpire.com was perhaps the most dominant Instagram "review" blog. "Since 1998" was an obviously false claim, but the creator excluded it from the Wayback Machine so it's hard to know when he started it.

This website gained major search traction in 2019, employing all types of SEO strategies, such as article auto-updating. It ranked extremely highly for most queries related to growth services.

Although the reviews were written decently well, they didn't represent real consumer experiences. Useful information was limited. Predictably, there were always several templated plugs for sites with good affiliate programs.

In the late 2010s, it seemed like every search for "Is <service> a scam?" and "<service> reviews" led to sites like JonathanSpire.com. I estimate that Shark Social lost over twenty-five thousand dollars in gross revenue due to the fake review sites. People messaged us about the fake reviews and asked us to rebut every point. Unfortunately, Shark *was* an automated growth service, so, there *were* inherent risks. It was a poker game rife with bluffing. We were losing chips. All the major providers stealing our traffic were breaking the same rules! We were getting crushed in the SEO oligarchy. We started sending templated responses to potential customers. Several competitors wrote responses and published them on their sites.

Customers scammed by sites recommended by the fictitious persona created a Trustpilot page for Jonathan Spire's "business" to warn others.[9]

Understanding how the thievery worked, we started an affiliate program and attempted to bribe the blog owners to post our affiliate link! None of the major, interlinked fake review blogs responded, but one of the largest independent operators did. He ranked us highly, and we probably made over six thousand dollars from customers he referred. He probably made a thousand dollars from sliding us into his top ten list!

One service provider fought back admirably.

In September 2022, QQTube.com wrote a blog post titled, "Jonathon-Spire & EarthWeb Scam Exposed,"[10] which detailed the madness of the fake blog network. This site and blog post emerged years after Instagram growth services' peak and well after I stopped updating my list. The article was an admirable piece of investigative journalism written by an ownership team that had been wronged.

The article is no longer live, and a representative from QQTube refused to comment and asked me not to quote the article further.

QQTube's owners may have suffered defamation or general financial harm based on the false criticism levied onto their business (if it *was* false). The author identified clear links between the top review sites of the period and showed that the same Instagram service providers were ranked highly by them all. The businesses mentioned in the article included Social10x, Social Envy (a reboot I *think*), Magic Social, Rize Social, SurgeSocial, TweSocial, Phoenix Social, and LikeSocial.[11]

The conspiracy was that the reviewed companies, or their close associates, *also* owned the review sites. Extreme marketing tactics (fake review blog networks) were used to funnel customers toward extreme marketing tactics (follower growth services using bots). All's fair, I guess. Sublime Directory's pay-to-play adult content network in the early aughts was not much different.

The article's analysis corroborated what I had noticed: the writing style, site structure, templated language, and external links were nearly identical.[12] The web of deceit was like nothing I had seen at Shark. It's unfortunate that this blog appeared so late. The review sites gradually lost rank, and the FTC judgement scared some people off, but I regret not forwarding this article to a "real" journalist when I first found it. It really could have provided insight into algorithmic manipulation, fake testimonials, and black hat SEO.

The Roach Motel Model

The rise of social media growth in 2017 was predicated on the new ease of running internet businesses. Stripe made *subscriptions* simple. I don't think that anybody knows how to set up a subscription in PayPal.

What's well known today but wasn't in 2017 is that digital subscriptions guarantee *way more* money from average customers. People forget they're signed up, and people who don't have the money are lured in by promotional discounts. Worst of all, some companies do everything they can to discourage cancellations.

Gyms notoriously practice this tactic, which new-age payment processors then leveraged.

Because of *subscriptions*, Instagram growth enjoyed substantially higher lifetime customer values than SMM panels. My "lifetime" customer value at the panel where I bought my Twitter followers was *maybe* twenty dollars —my single purchase. Shark Social, a budget provider of Instagram growth, had an average customer value of something like 175 dollars. Other providers had customers generate an average of three hundred dollars before bouncing.

Subscription models were *so new* in 2017 that a huge portion of customers, even when faced with the "this is a subscription service" disclaimer, would become outraged at the second month's charge, arguing that they "didn't know." At Shark Social, we naively believed every excuse and offered refunds for months. Eventually we instituted a no-refund policy for those who forgot to cancel before renewal, just like Netflix.

If Netflix made it hard to cancel, though, there would be a massive lawsuit. California passed a law that cancelling a subscription has to be "at least as easy" as starting a new one. Unfortunately, with dozens of operators (many claiming to be number one), ethics weren't enforced. It wasn't possible to cancel a subscription directly in Stripe. Users were bound by roundabout, opaque cancellation flows on providers' websites that were almost *never* as easy as signing up.

I demoed competitors' services, intending to only use each for one month. Frustration abounded. I encountered businesses that didn't detail cancellation policies anywhere on the website. I sent emails. I sent emails and received "confirmations" just to find that I was still being charged. "Terms" sometimes specified a forty-eight-hour cancellation process—how convenient! I felt violated.

I experimented with the darker practice of setting the "anchor" of each customer's subscription to the first of the month. They'd receive a prorated discount at signup but were charged again on the first of the next month. This was within my legal right. Unfortunately, it worked *too* well. It squeezed a bit more money out of customers who intended to cancel after the first month, but they were irate, so I discontinued the practice.

Other operators changed from monthly to weekly renewals. They lured customers in with the "cheapest" prices attached to plans that were renewed every six days, which were, of course, more expensive compared to monthly plans. Companies probably didn't shift to daily renewals because the billing statement spam would result in more cancellations and disputes. Weekly was devious.

What of the "roach motel"? If roadtrippers find a motel, they'll pay and stay the night, even after discovering that the room contains cockroaches. It's too much effort to find a different motel or demand a refund. This idea translated well to the Instagram growth space. Services calculated that the affronts (service interruptions, crappy results) were not bad enough for customers to complain or take action. Any abject scam was bound to be investigated and shut down by Stripe based on dispute activity (charge-backs).[13] Absent a "high" dispute rate, businesses had free reign.

I wouldn't have called Shark Social a roach motel. Late in the game, however, I did implement a cancellation flow that I'm not proud of. We added a "Tell us why you're canceling" box; filling it in was a prerequisite for cancellation. That was bad enough, but after hundreds of cancellations, we distilled the themes and built an FAQ *into* our cancellation process.

Instead of a one-click cancel, customers had to click through options, some of which led them *away* from the cancellation flow and to our knowledge documents or contact information. Of course, people complained about that too, but the cancellation rate did drop a bit. Ultimately, the increased rate of support requests made it a net negative.

Phone Support

Businesses claiming years of expertise in social media and connectedness were hard to contact. Once you know to search for it, it's a ubiquitous, easy-to-recognize omission.

The main "tell" of a disreputable growth service was not having a functioning phone. Social media marketing agencies list their numbers front and center. It's not just for existing customers; it's an important sales tool. I only found *seven* Instagram growth services that listed phone numbers. I called each one. Nobody ever answered.

At Shark, we set up a phone service, which was *way more* trouble than it was worth. I fielded a few phone calls, though I don't think I was ever officially cleared to speak on the phone. Every caller paused in amazement when somebody picked up, even if it was the programmer. "I can't believe somebody answered the phone! I'm definitely signing up!"

Social media adjacent businesses without phone numbers weren't reliable or planning to communicate much.

Fake...People?

Newbies building their first websites spend significant time on the "About Us" page. They write third-person testaments to their greatness, accompanied by headshots. Team pages are commonplace. They build trust. I couldn't imagine hiring a traditional marketing agency that didn't have one. It's pretty weird then that fewer than ten percent of Instagram growth businesses identified their teams on their websites. Of those, at least half were fake. The people weren't real!

As I built my competitor analysis sheet, my investigation into who was behind businesses and whether they were real took me to some weird places. It was awkward to learn that some identities I had discussed with my teammates had been fabricated—imaginary friends peddling imaginary businesses where "humans" grew accounts for thirty-nine dollars per month.

A growth service called Upleap, referenced above, claims "thousands of happy customers"[14] against a 3.5/5.0 average review on Trustpilot.[15] The Trustpilot page has a pattern of negative reviews quickly followed by positive reviews. It's almost like the positivity is throttled to avoid alerting Trustpilot to the fakeness of the supportive reviews. Speaking of fake, Upleap was one of the earliest hirers of fake employees. Upleap created the personas, "Emily Trevino" and "Kate Fernandez" with LinkedIn profiles to match. Emily was the "co-founder." Kate was an "account manager." Their pictures were high quality, the names were relatively common, and at least fifteen minutes were spent constructing each professional backstory.

These attractive females posed as "experts" on other platforms, like Quora, to drive traffic to Upleap. Almost *one million people* have seen Emily Trevino's beautiful face on Quora.[16] She isn't a real person.

LinkedIn was a major help to me. Anonymous owners gleefully shared their success numbers on a website where clients and jilted competitors weren't looking. Some provided precise customer numbers and revenue. For example, one founder retrospectively stated that they "...helped 4,000+ clients across 80+ countries, reached $200K monthly recurring revenue, and provided flexible employment for a remote team that spanned 10+ countries. Shut down in late 2019 due to Instagram algorithm changes."

No, that wasn't Tim O'Hearn's page. Everything feels much more trustworthy on LinkedIn, but I had to add a column to my sheet titled, "real?"

I found success in checking business registrations. This is easy to overlook in a page's footer, checkout page, or even terms of use. Business names led me to directories where I could pilfer *real* names or continue my investigation.

Upleap lists "SocialGrowth LLC FZ" in its footer. A Google search shows that it is a business registered in Dubai.[17] Scrolling down in the search results reveals more. *As I write this*, the following websites list that same LLC on their sites: Social Growth Pay, Upleap, Flock Social, Aimfox, Stim Social, Nitreo, HeyRank, Kenji, and SocialFollow.

Almost all these websites offer *well-known* Instagram growth services. The branding is excellent. Pricing plans—beginning with the thirty-nine-dollar offering—are identical across almost all the sites—the illusion of choice.

This group likely has a stranglehold on what's left of the demand for automated Instagram growth. If these services are all under the same ownership umbrella, how can they all be superlative?

16

TAPPING OUT
FOURTH ERA

Subject: Finishing up the month

Hey [Tim],

Thank you for everything you have done for [Shark Social] over the last few years. Unfortunately, the time has come where we need to terminate your contract after this month as we are unable to hold up our end of the bargain. Due to Stripe's most recent decision on our funds, it appears we will not receive anything else for at least a month, if ever again at all. We are officially operating at a loss and [co-founder] or I will probably never see another dollar from the business.

S hark Social's CEO sent me that email in October 2019 which bookended a turbulent summer for the Sharks.

In 2019, the fallout from "The Follower Factory" and other social media exposés was met with meaningful action. Weak players cowered under emphatic shouts of "git gud" and perhaps even "boom! headshot!"

This "era" kicked off with "game over" for Devumi on January 30, 2019.[1]

Letitia James, the attorney general of New York, announced a settlement on Wednesday with Devumi, a company that sold hundreds of millions of fake followers on Twitter and other social media platforms before going out of business last year.

The settlement is one of the first major efforts by regulators and law enforcement officials to investigate the shadowy market of social media fraud, where armies of fake accounts are sold to businesses, politicians and celebrities seeking the appearance of influence.

New York Attorney General Letitia James' announcement was crystal clear: "Settlement is First in the Country to Find that Selling Fake Followers and 'Likes' Is Illegal Deception and that Fake Activity Using Stolen Identities Is Illegal Impersonation."[2]

As much as readers must appreciate journalists who take risks to conduct investigations that result in legal precedents and consumer protections, *I was farming for friends on Myspace when I was thirteen*. I was inflating my Myspace band's fan count when I was fifteen. I found the strongly worded announcement overblown because it covered a dubious need. Remember? When Biz Stone announced the "blue checkmark" experiment in 2009, he insinuated that everyone should have been able to figure out without verification which accounts were fake.

Acknowledging that the "Illegal Deception" was widespread and difficult to understand insulted the intelligence of anyone able to use a web browser. Of course the followers were fake! The value proposition didn't make any sense! It was a twenty-dollar lesson for me (and millions of others).

The *impersonation* aspect was pretty scary and deserved attention, but today, people are still searching for, buying, and being "deceived" by SMM panels that peddle wholesale fake activity. The only big difference is that those storefronts aren't connected to businesses operating in the United States.

In 2018, the "like" resellers fell out of favor, paving the way for automated account growth providers, like Shark Social. In early 2019, a few were still competing for similar search keywords. They faded away under the legal threat. Everyone who managed to get linked up with a payment processor that would process payments from the United States piled into organic growth, especially on Instagram.

In early 2019, Shark Social benefitted from more people equating fake followers with fraud—it meant they sought out Instagram growth services. The business attracted tons of customers, attained modest results, and sometimes cracked the top ten results for the industry's most valuable search terms. Organic first-time visitors to the site converted at a peak rate of *fifteen percent*!

For almost every month of its existence, Shark Social's number of customers and average customer value *increased*. We never raised prices. We never charged as little as Instagress's ten dollars per month, but in 2019, I believe Shark Social became the lowest-cost player in the space. The money coming in was unbelievable: tens of thousands per month. Competitors who outranked us in searches, many of whom were quite transparent if contacted over the right channel, were making over one hundred thousand dollars per month. Most of that was profit.

During that spring we noticed an increase in disputes on Stripe. For whatever reason, it became more common for American consumers to abuse "fraud" chargebacks on their credit cards to express dissatisfaction. Buyer's remorse doesn't indicate a merchant committed fraud. However, thinking back to PayPal on eBay, e-commerce payment processors have always seemed to side with the customer. Stripe fined businesses for chargebacks and implemented an onerous review process in which each side had to submit mountains of evidence.

Shark Social's service offering, which involved my Mako system, was one of the best in the business. Customers were getting great results. Yet, as we solidified our position serving the "budget" market, our customers filed chargebacks with frightening frequency. And they were winning about half of the disputes. Customers would submit chargebacks when they forgot to cancel and win! Eventually, we hired a lawyer, rewrote our terms, and created incident response templates. We stemmed the flow of new disputes and "beat" many of the chargebacks.

We understood why Stripe updated the restricted businesses list to include social media automation services. We were a pain in the ass for the payment processor because we catered to the most pain-in-the-ass segment of customers.

On April 25, 2019, Meta filed a lawsuit against Social Media Series Limited,[3] alleging the owners only superficially complied with the cease-and-desist letter from February 20, 2018: "Defendants stopped offering fake engagement services on Socialenvy.co and IGFamous.net but began selling fake engagement services on other websites, including Likesocial.co."[4] Activities continued and were traced back to the owners of the parent company based in New Zealand.

A few days later, Instagram initiated the "like hiding" experiment.[5] This was something of a come-to-Jesus moment because it was an awkward admission that people cared way too much about "likes." Although followers reigned supreme in new account evaluations, likes were the main metric for a user's relative popularity (and engagement rate, which could have exposed that followers were fake). Those in the business of selling services that grew like and follower counts panicked.

These two events happening in such a short period of time was probably coincidental—I doubt Meta's legal team collaborates with its front-end visionaries—but it showed how futile the whole exercise was for automation agencies. The players in that virtual arena were close to running out of lives and remaining credits.

May 30, 2019, was the actual "Instagram Rapture." It's been memorialized by the BlackHatWorld thread, "Instagram follow Action Blocks from this morning 30 May."[6]

Summer 2019 brought an end to most automation services. The restrictions were crushing—customer accounts were getting action blocked at high rates. They continued to face blocks even when executing scaled-down workflows. They continued to face blocks when rotating proxies.

Shark Social's Mako system was just a lot of the color red and error messages. However, I never had to "adapt" the system in dealing with "iceberg" events. Mako wasn't advanced enough to "identify" a rogue wave of action blocks (the "above the water" portion) and scale down unaffected accounts (the larger, "below the water" portion of the iceberg). Ironically, when we were monitoring FollowLiker on a gaming PC, shutting everything down at any sign of trouble was a knee-jerk reaction. Unfortunately, when the system became distributed and "efficient," I never found the time to implement advanced defensive strategies.

The first post on the BHW thread said it all: "It seems Instagram has once again tried to stop our botting activities and business. This morning I woke up to all my client's accounts having temporarily been follow blocked. I am using the same setting which I have used for the past few months without issues being following up to 350 per day with human like Intervals."[7]

Some operators were *still* approaching 350 follows per day! That was in the ballpark of what the major services had executed according to "Following Their Footsteps,"[8] published in November 2018. If the BHW post was to be believed, for 2018 and the first four months of 2019, Instagram had not made a significant change to daily limits for action blocks. The business tightened the screws elsewhere with legal action, proxy changes, "like hiding" experiments, and even reversing activity it deemed fake.

The thread is a real-time ledger of Instagram miscreants realizing that their businesses were probably toast. In terms of post frequency relative to total volume, this was the most popular Instagram thread on the forum, even more subscribed to than the original "megathread."

One of the early theories, provided by a well-known proxy distributor, was: "IG made a new feature update in their API, and when they did this it mostly reset the 'trust score' for accounts. Working at ground zero on trust, bots will always have more suspicion than normal users - therefore, blocks happened widespread [sic]."[9]

I agreed with this (ahem, everybody *wanted* this to be true)—we were able to get some burners and customer accounts back up and running in early June. However, nobody could figure out the root cause. Every experiment failed. After more than a week, customers filled our support inbox with concerned questions. There was also an uptick in "Your Account Was Compromised" popups inside the Instagram app that forced users to change their passwords after sharing them with "a service to help you get more likes or followers." It was well known that forcing a password update would interrupt service because the customer had to send the new password to the service provider. We had an automated system for password changes, but panicked users tended to submit support tickets and leave it to us to update the system by hand.

Growing desperate, we purchased Jarvee and GMT2 and booted up FollowLiker to see if any "commercial" developers had figured it out. Jarvee sent an email in mid-June. It didn't build much confidence because it started with: "If you're doing Instagram I know that you've probably had a few bad weeks. After their latest changes, we all had [sic]." The email only provided basic suggestions—no guarantees. It repeated the new rule of thumb of only two hundred followers per day, extremely prolonged ramp-up periods after blocks, and switching away from follow-unfollow (presumably to "Mass Story Viewing"). Jarvee published "What to Do About the Latest Instagram Action Blocks"[10] on June 14, which provided more detail, including ways to build trust scores in the wake of new scrutiny. The comments section was a collection of hopelessness.

I thought that by creating my own software tool, the swiftly swimming Mako, Shark Social would be better protected in worst-case scenarios. One well-respected member of the black hat community had said as much: "Been preaching for years now – LEARN TO CODE PEOPLE. goddammit. Can't stress this enough. Programming skills are a savior when shit hits the fan in IM. Come on..."[11]

"Programming skills" built my initial confidence, but each test and new feature required tons of time. Constant failures eroded my confidence. Burner accounts became so unreliable that I began flippantly running experiments on customer accounts. My nights and weekends were miserable. I was working a full-time job. I couldn't just run home and test a new hypothesis. As I tested new scenarios and saw that nothing was working, I started to realize that we were in way too deep. It wasn't twenty customers who would "understand," it was nearly two orders of magnitude more. Some of the customers had purchased premium plans, and we spoke with them on the phone. They trusted us. Shark Social was still onboarding new customers through June.

We had to change course. We started processing "pauses," "credits," refunds, and whatever else placated customers. We didn't want them to quit Shark Social. We *were* working on keeping the business running. We no longer concealed that we were operating in direct opposition to Instagram and that the overlords could have just as easily banned the accounts instead of dishing out temporary blocks. The business wasn't running properly. A service established as a "solution" to the "fraud" inherent to fake like resellers had—perhaps—become just as big of a disappointment to customers.

I was not involved in dispute resolutions, credits, or refunds, but the disputes came rolling in. Whatever decisions *were* made during that time, they were the wrong choices. I stood to benefit from greed and so I was greedy too. I feel bad about it. In the SaaS space, the desire to keep the customer signed up at any cost meant ethical failings.

As we became buried in disputes, Stripe promptly shut off payments, *stopped sending collected money into the business checking account,* and levied some fines. To continue accepting deposits, we'd have to lower the dispute rate. I thought the process was fair, it was just that the business seemed completely lost at that point. The only reason it was hanging on was the classic SaaS feature—so many people had forgotten they were signed up that they weren't complaining about crappy results.

It was time to put things on pause. Shark Social stopped accepting new customers, and the founders worked through the disputes and support cases to see what they could salvage and to what extent they could cover expenses. Watching the payments dry up was harrowing. But we deserved it. We couldn't provide sufficient new followers, and we were causing regular interruptions to their accounts.

It's worth mentioning that not a single customer got banned, and, because we communicated often during the prolonged outages, we were probably still one of the most "well-liked" providers. Our reviews were comparatively good. GMT2 couldn't figure it out and was the subject of vitriol, and the service was declared dead in October.[12]

In my October 17, 2019, reply to the "Finishing up the month" email, I said:

This business that I told you was a stupid idea helped pull me up from [nearly getting fired and feeling worthless]. For that, for the memories, for the experience, even for the clout--I will always be grateful.

17

"INSTAGRESS ALTERNATIVE" ALTERNATIVES

From xGram Bot to FollowLiker to Mako, the "follow-unfollow" algorithm generated tens of millions of dollars for automated growth services. Whether executed by hand, a program, or phone emulation software, "f-uf" was the gold standard method. The reciprocation rates were reliable. That linear path through the eras was intersected by a winding road of alternative growth methods that attracted new participants whenever anti-bot enforcement ramped up—whenever users sought an alternative to the "Instagress alternative."

Instagram users can see who views their stories but not who visits their Reels. An alternative path to gaining followers was automating the viewing of stories. An unpopular account owner seeing a brand-new viewer might be tempted to follow that user. Bots that exploited this impulse were called "Mass Story Viewers." Jarvee included this as an alternative growth method. I noticed when the private API functions were added to the libraries on GitHub, but I never desired to try it myself.

In 2019, I saw claims that there was *no limit* to how many Instagram stories could be viewed per day. People on BHW were *claiming* to be able to view over one million stories daily. The claimed following rate that I saw was .005%. One million views netted fifty followers. At some point, the daily limit was ratcheted down, and Jarvee imposed a limit of ten thousand stories viewed per day.

The "Mother-Child" method was another that I never tried to implement. The premise was cunning. The "main" account that needed traffic was designated the "mother." Then burner accounts, called "children," were loaded with pictures and content from the mother, effectively impersonating the mother.

Those children took all the risks. They were used as crash test dummies for automation while containing links and calls to action: "Follow my main account!" They would brazenly send DMs to targeted accounts, which has been considered reckless since 2017.

Brilliantly, Mother-Child *should* absolve the "mother" account, which has something to lose, from any terms of use violations. The burner accounts do the bidding. The main account gets some traffic. These take more effort to set up and maintain, and the engagement is *usually* worse than pure f-uf, but BHW is stuffed with claims that this works. It's challenging to scale, so it isn't offered by agencies. Users usually have a singular purpose and are directing traffic to a mother account meant to convert traffic to *sales* (usually in a traditionally spammy niche, like adult content).

A more advanced approach that wouldn't involve rule breaking is using the child accounts to explore more specific niches or to A/B test how "the algorithm" treats content posted at different times of the day (or even different types of content). I wouldn't say it's traditional Mother-Child, but influencers seem more apt to split niche or "not-as-professional" content into multiple "child" accounts. This is common for adult content creators who live in fear of their main accounts being banned and having to start from scratch.

"Shout Out Marketing" is a practice in which influential users sell "ad space" in the form of their stories, Reels, or posted media to promote other accounts. The message will be as simple as "Follow →this← account!" There are underground marketplaces where people buy shoutouts. People buy followers believing the "investment" can be recouped by selling shout-outs. In my experience, these are low-quality and sometimes feature posted lists of usernames. I don't want a shout-out—unless you want to promote this book, in which case, email me.

"Growth pods" and "engagement groups" are basically the same thing. Instagram cautioned against these in its API terms: "Don't participate in any 'like,' 'share,' 'comment,' or 'follower' exchange programs."[1] But groups of like-minded individuals still get together in group chats and demand, "LIKE MY LATEST PICTURE FOR THE ALGORITHM!" Small bunches of friends commonly do this, usually to exchange "likes" for new content since they already follow each other. The reciprocation doesn't scale...without software. It's hard to brand as harmful. Social contracts similar to "growth pod" expectations underpin regular friendships.

However, like Myspace "whore train" activity, larger groups *do* get together and collude on massive, inorganic, mutual boosting. Whereas it was previously difficult to keep whore trains on the tracks, engagement pods of today use simple bots to promote content and loosely enforce manual engagement. I have seen bots in Telegram group chats tracking activities and holding participants accountable. Just like Myspace whore trains that turned into "adder services," some of the "Instagram like exchange services" were monetized by offering participants increased exposure for a price.

"Coin Apps," also known as "coin-based apps," were the next step. Engagement groups needed bots to enforce proper etiquette, just as the Myspace adder services were built to facilitate whore trains. As the groups grew and the bots became more advanced, attention was commoditized, and standalone apps were developed. Unfortunately, records are hard to search for now because the word "coin" is used in every crypto promotional scheme ever to exist.

These apps used Instagram's private API to show participants a stripped-down version of Instagram. Users would log in and see a balance of zero "coins" or whatever the currency was. Coins accrued as the user sent "likes" or "follows" to users shown to them within the app. Because the activity was piped through the coin app's interface, it was tracked in a more sophisticated implementation of what the "adder" sites had done ten years prior.

Coins were "spent" when a user's profile was shown to others inside the app. Users could spend more coins for even higher placements. Those users would like and follow in a massive software-assisted engagement pod. Some apps required users to watch ads to earn more coins. Some replenished a small amount each day. *All* allowed users to purchase coins.

One app in the Google Play store, *Follow4Follow - Get Followers,* was released in 2020 but was removed before I finalized this chapter. The app description read, "You want to become [sic] influencer and reach some of your dreams? Get more visibility on your profile."

It had 100,000+ verified downloads and 26.9 thousand ratings resulting in a 4.6-star average review. One of the most "helpful" reviews was, "Other reviews are fake. It used to work perfectly, until they started putting too many ads. Now you can't even use the app, it's just ads."

Coin apps were advanced engagement pods that used software to ensure all users were doing their fair share of promotion. Due to flaws with the business model and the difficulties of running an Instagram client app so blatantly infringing on Instagram's terms and conditions, this app class has effectively been erased.

"Giveaway Marketing" and "Loop Giveaways" were the best ways to grow an Instagram account. Although giveaways require collaboration between different parties and can cost a decent amount of money to set up, they're one of the only growth "hacks" not explicitly forbidden by Instagram. They also scale better than all other methods.

Giveaway marketing started to take off in 2019 once it became clear that automation services wouldn't prevail over Instagram. Additionally, growth from f-uf and derivative methods was widely known to become menial after twenty thousand followers. Those with significant followings won't benefit much from reciprocal actions, which is why many conventionally famous people from stories like "The Follower Factory" purchased massive amounts of fake followers.

Giveaway growth combines organic growth aspects with the guarantees of SMM panels and the enforcement of the coin apps. In practice, these are commonly called "loop giveaways." The organizers of loop giveaways solicit customers who want to grow their followings and are willing to pay hundreds if not thousands of dollars for guaranteed followers.

Cash in hand, the giveaway organizers contact extremely popular accounts on Instagram, often those with five million followers or more. The giveaway organizers offer large sums of money, into the five figures, for influencers to make one post advertising the giveaway (essentially a shout-out). Once the giveaway is over, the user can delete the post.

The giveaway is *typical*: a prize valued at thousands of dollars, like a new Macbook, is offered to a participant who follows the instructions. To participate, users are funneled to a different Instagram account, the loop redirect account, that instructs them to follow a list of accounts (the "loop" of accounts) to be eligible.

Because so much traffic streams from these accounts, the loop organizers can direct *thousands* of guaranteed followers to the "loop" accounts (those paying for followers). Once a customer has grown by the prescribed number of followers (ten, fifty, or a hundred thousand), the account name is subbed out by the redirecting account for another customer. Each loop might have only ten usernames displayed at one time. Names cycle out once they've gained the guaranteed number of followers.

This process is almost foolproof because if a customer doesn't reach the followers in the initial giveaway or complains about follower loss, a loop organizer can briefly rotate the account name into a different (or later) giveaway loop until the prescribed number is reached.

Once the giveaway has concluded, software tools called "comment pickers" are used to locate entrants, whose conformance to entry standards may be verified in part by hand. The giveaway prizes are then shipped to the winners. Many giveaway tools and comment pickers are on the market now, and many are used for giveaways on other platforms.

I never ran a giveaway myself, but Shark Social did collaborate with a major giveaway service for a few months. I spoke extensively to its owner on the phone at the time. He originally agreed to be interviewed but never answered the questions I sent.

Giveaway marketing is (or was) the best way for accounts to grow by large margins. In a September 9, 2020, case study by *SocialMedia Examiner*, the author estimated "a 71% probability that more than 50% of new followers an account gains during a giveaway will abandon it within 2 weeks."[2] Many service providers have disappeared, and Instagram's messaging around "inauthentic" sources of followers likely refers to numbers boosted by giveaways. In a reversion to the hushed tones of xGram Bot early in BlackHatWorld's Instagram escapade, these services are not traditionally advertised, and the implementation details are concealed. I believe there are large companies in the United States funneling tens of thousands of dollars into giveaway growth, but I've been advised not to present specific allegations in this book.

18

BROKEN-HEARTED

FIFTH ERA

"I know where you live, my friend."

"I am not so far away, my friend."

The phone crackled as if his sinister tongue left his mouth and tickled the microphone with each word. I couldn't believe this message that sounded like a horror movie trailer came from the Shark Social voicemail.

As our team of three exchanged frightened text messages, our top priority was identifying the crackling voice and which of us this deranged individual considered his "friend."

I ribbed, "Hey, maybe the crackling is his N95 mask rubbing against his phone? Maybe he's not a well-rehearsed villain but rather a dork taking precautions against COVID-19 while calling us from his bedroom?"

Nobody laughed. Things were different in 2020. We were older, more cynical, and resigned to the fact that Shark Social, despite featuring an apex predator, never ascended to the top of the Instagram growth food chain. More than six months after our "pause" in October 2019, the Shark Social team had given "growth" another go. The pandemic had impacted us, and we had time to experiment with fixes to issues that had led to the shutdown. We cleaned up billing issues, issued mass refunds, and got the green light from Stripe. I designed new web interfaces so the whole team (including any helpers) could manage customer accounts. Somebody handled proxies. Somebody handled marketing and hat-in-hand emails beckoning customers to return.

On June 1, 2020, Shark Social started over with zero subscribers. The CEO sent a familiar battle cry, "Let's get it!!!"

Surprisingly, customers kept showing up. Aside from the huge conglomerates, most had called it quits. Visitors to the site converted into paying customers at a high rate, sometimes exceeding ten percent. However, the "safe" number of actions the bots could take was depressingly low, likely fewer than one hundred per day. That was down massively from the near-unlimited 24/7 nature of xGram Bot almost ten years earlier and the three-hundred-ish recommendation when Shark Social first launched in 2017.

Regrettably, customers were impacted, too. We figured that the caller was a disgruntled subscriber. However, we were dealing with so many complaints about blocks, possible shadowbans, and "meh"-quality results that we didn't even have a lineup of suspects. In fact, we had hired part-time help to deal with tickets in Zendesk,[1] so the original team was less familiar with individual customer complaints.

I felt the squeeze. Testing was more expensive and took longer. Proxies were more expensive. Burner accounts were more expensive. Proxy "theory" was becoming increasingly difficult to follow. All my past "phone-a-friend" collaborators had moved on, and even BlackHatWorld was filled with doomsaying. Ironically, I was a better programmer than ever, but the anti-botting overlords were toying with me. My assessment of a "trust score" was not accurate. As I gradually lost faith in Mako for API and embedded browser access, I ran tests with Jarvee, GMT2, and even FollowLiker!

After a day or two, we believed we had identified the caller. He had submitted a support ticket, and we gave him credit for a full month because he had forgotten he had subscribed (or something), but he wanted a full refund. I went through Stripe to check his billing address—Florida.

Oh—one of the Sharks had moved on from DJing and relocated to Florida to expand his niche social media agency. I looked more closely at my partner's home address, which was likely listed on his business page. I looked at the customer's billing address. I entered the two addresses into Google Maps. They lived fifteen minutes apart.

"I am not so far away" indeed.

Our next team phone call was perhaps the closest we ever got to "life or death." Our only relief was that we hadn't received another call or a knock at the door. We were shocked that our trusted partner—by far the most likable character in our group—now faced a threat to his safety. We decided against calling the police unless we received another threat. That customer sure as hell didn't get his refund.

I was ordered to shut down the company phone service.

That was the theme of the last eighteen months I spent in the Instagram growth space. *Things shut down.* The partner who received the threat exited. It was just me, the Shark CEO, the new customer support guy, and some blog writing interns. Competitors cleared out. Meta pushed more ads.[2] TikTok surpassed Instagram's activity share among teenage users.[3]

Meta served cease-and-desist letters to developers, hitting Tim Grossman with one in November 2021, five years after he launched InstaPy.[4] Tim complied. He told me, "I gave away 100% of the control of the repository and everything." He also received a lifetime ban from all Meta services.

Although processing increased the volume of refunds and disputes, Shark Social clawed back up to provide nice supplemental income, exceeding one hundred thousand dollars per year gross. Demand was still *insanely* high, but it was much more stressful. I found solace in managing a small team of college-aged writers pushing out blog posts to increase search traffic.

Toward the end of 2021, we disagreed about the ethics of continuing and "faith" in the business. I wasn't entirely fulfilling my responsibilities. I would think I figured something out and implemented it for a small set of customers, but then everybody would get action blocked. Then we extended credits to the impacted users. The universe of potential variables factoring into the "trust score" was too much for me to manage. I didn't think that it was fair to customers.

I sent out inquiries to people from the past, but I heard what I also later gathered in interviews: "not worth it," "no longer worth it," "not worth it," "f*ck that."

How did so many people accept walking away from businesses earning six or seven figures in annual revenue?

At Shark Social, we prepared to do exactly that. We were browbeaten. We went from being Sharks to swimming with the sharks. My path had arced from using GameShark to cheat on my PS2 to helping thousands of people "cheat" on Instagram to being stuck in a game I couldn't win. But we made one last gambit.

Shark Social was a software business with excellent profit margins. Revenue was substantial. Though a distant memory by late 2021, in the best of times, it *kind of* ran itself. The business sounds cool and is easy to understand. We hatched a cockamamie plan to sell Shark Social as if it were a software startup. At that point, the CEO had one hundred percent of the company shares. He offered me a finder's fee to push through a sale.

I tried to make a call from our virtual number to make it seem more official but was reminded that we shut down the phone after the incident with the unhinged Floridian.

Undeterred, I developed a pitch deck. I arranged our numbers. I wondered which numbers people would care about. Our profit margin, calculated for the first time, was...eighty-six percent? I also thought about the historical impact. How many button presses did we automate?

I came up with a number in the hundreds of millions. Some of these stats had been stored in Mako, but not all, so I had to extrapolate and estimate for periods when we used FollowLiker or other applications. For those times, multiplying the monthly customer count against a discounted "safe" number of activities was fine. At our peak, I calculate twenty-five hundred customers with three hundred actions per day. That's almost three hundred million actions in a year—and that's just customer "actions" governed by activity limits, not including navigation activity, logins, or anything from burners.

Maybe the stats would attract a buyer. I visited two platforms built to help business owners sell websites, e-commerce stores, and SaaS products. I found that a SaaS social media growth business had never been sold. I was willing to admit the risks: we violated Instagram's terms of use and our niche had been included on Stripe's restricted business list since 2018.[5] However, the business existed since 2017 and had a...decent...track record.

One curator responded within thirty minutes to tell me that it was "an interesting case" and that we could *try* to submit the listing with our disclosures and an appropriately reduced asking price.

Neither platform accepted our listing. I grew desperate and asked my contacts if they wanted to buy the business *and all supporting software* at a favorable multiple. It was nowhere near a "standard" thirty-times monthly revenue. They knew why we were selling. They weren't interested. I ran out of leads.

The Shark Social CEO, who was preparing to open a DJ-driven boutique fitness studio, thanked me for my years of dedication. When he called me, I knew it was the breakup call. Surprisingly, he offered me a severance package. I didn't need one. I was a contractor. He sent me the document, and I signed it, effective February 1, 2022. My time as a Shark ended.

Looking at that final deposit in my bank account was sobering. It felt like wired earbuds being yanked out of both ears at the same time—the music stopped. I thought about my failed sales pitches. I remembered mentioning Shark Social at a hometown bar in 2018 to a woman who smiled and nodded as she ran away. By the time I was twenty-seven years old, I was entrusted with leading the sale of the business itself. But I didn't really make it to the finish line.

Sure, this story of "growth" was a story of personal growth. I was born in 1994, and my parents probably never imagined this outcome when they bought me my computer and placed no usage restrictions. Yes, I was a Myspace "whore." Forced exchanges of social engagement on Myspace led to a "cottage industry"[6] that ended up being worth over a hundred million dollars. Yes, I was a screen addict. Shark Social bit off a large customer base from the millions of baitfish like me. I finally ran my own "whore train," and all those dispatched actions led to millions of followers and over *one billion* impressions.

I fondly recall attending my first hackathon and the first time I felt like a "hacker." I remember everyone I admired from the tech scenes at the hometown, collegiate, and even industry levels, and I remember feeling that "cracking the code" with Shark Social increased my worth as a professional. But I was actually generating activity that everyone hated. I sat for job interviews and eagerly awaited a chance to talk about Shark Social. I found my experiences applied to pretty much every generic interview question. If social media comprised the full wheel of emotions, then what about running a social media growth service?

"How close are you to your career goals?"

"I am not so far away, my friend."

How long would it have taken a human or even a team of humans to reach three hundred million likes? I thought about tapping that cute little heart icon with my thumb. I acted it out, twitching like a kid mashing a PS2 controller button. Emblematic of digital assent or support or favor, that heart became Shark Social's profit center. We sure as hell did our part to turn digital love into fake love. We broke and shattered that heart. We didn't have much time to reflect on it then, but we were part of the force in the post-Instagress world that changed the dynamics of an internet community and developers' relationships with social media platforms.

19

BLOOD IN THE WATER

A qualified professional advised me that this essay was a "guaranteed lawsuit." One lawyer deemed it a "hard hitter." "Blood in the Water" was my investigation of a well-funded private company with a CEO obsessed with social media. I argued that the company's Instagram follower growth was unrealistic, based on the techniques I've disclosed so far. I suggested that knowingly using investor money on fake or incentivized growth constituted a form of fraud.

This was a standalone essay. Its removal is not meant to provide an excuse for plot holes or poorly developed theses. If you're enjoying *Framed* and think you could help ensure that fiercer critiques make it into a future edition, please contact me.

20

THE PUPPETEER PART II

"I was free to manipulate the app's small audience without anyone knowing who I was, what I was doing, or what I was trying to accomplish."[1]

As previously discussed, I led a team at a company with the alias "Cutlet." It never got off the ground and claimed just a few thousand users by the time I was fired, but it was one of the most rewarding experiences of my career.

Cutlet provided the perfect setup for a technocratic villain, a digitally cloaked deity. A rogue engineer at Instagram would have been subject to layers of supervision and access controls. But no one at Cutlet reviewed my work to ensure it was ethically or legally compliant. I had the supreme authority to deploy changes to the app's content feed or push notifications. At any time, I could have changed the composition of any user's feed. I could have sent a push notification with the text, "Tim says hi!"

My employers and business partners would describe me as having roguish tendencies. But I didn't do anything immoral while working at Cutlet except beckon users to return to an app and spend as much time on it as possible, which may be a "negative sum game"[2] (the overall negatives outweigh the positives) but not unethical. It was my job description *and* the investor edict: apps must provide compelling, immersive, intuitive user experiences.

There were actions I could have taken to really, you know, pull the strings. I could have committed offenses with push notifications. I could have sold user data. More than anything, though, algorithmically curated feeds provide their stewards the power to influence the hearts and minds of consumers. If done subtly, mellow users would never question it. Personalized feeds are much more powerful and less transparent than the previous generation's go-to: advertisements and messages displayed on cable TV channels.

"Though rooted in conspiracy, there are accusations that some websites have special algorithms just for dealing with content related to elections. The conspiracy is that some of the algorithms may favor one candidate, or one belief system, over another. Because the feed is "intelligent" and impossible to audit, it's extremely hard to investigate layered manipulation."[3]

At the end of my chronicle detailing my involvement in social media manipulation driven by third-party software developers, I declare that it's not just the platform owners who have power. There are also "power users,"[4] those not affiliated with social media companies but who create nuisance automation systems to manipulate algorithms and extract profit.

There are two types of puppeteers:

1. Those who write the software that powers black-box recommendation and curation algorithms (Instagram employees, Google employees, me at Cutlet).
2. Those who create (often illicit) software to emulate human interaction with social media platforms (state-sponsored propaganda teams, Instagram growth services, me at Shark Social.)

This deviant can claim to have been on both sides. This deviant decided to write a book about it. The relevance of my experience is bolstered by the thousands of hours spent as a puppet, a willing participant in the same types of systems that I designed and exploited.

If social media platforms are becoming better at manipulating humans and the bots are better at acting human, where does the path to technological singularity[5] leave humans? Where does that leave the internet?

Will Instagram ever fade?

I once wrote a blog post titled, "What Will Replace Instagram?" because in 2018 that specific search query was trending, and I wanted to splice that traffic stream toward Shark Social. I wanted to predict the rise of a TikTok-like app while feigning ignorance of TikTok being Instagram's likely successor.

My post was not received well. One comment read, "I can't believe how bad of a writer this guy is." Despite that feedback, I had a new idea, "What if *nothing* replaces Instagram?" Furthermore, what if Instagram goes from being an app synonymous with fun, friends, and photo-sharing to one known for cruelty and oppression?

I started tossing around the term, "late-stage Instagram." It was a riff on a theory, hotly discussed on reddit in the late 2010s, called "late-stage capitalism" or "late capitalism."[6] "Late capitalism" hypothesizes that eventually, without meaningful controls (by government regulation, benevolent barons, or disruptive forces), capitalistic societies regress until competition is low, wealth is highly concentrated, and the humongous underclass is abjectly miserable. reddit folks[7] asserted that we were already living in that gloomy "late" state. The front page was filled with supposed examples of how capitalism was failing developed societies.

I started thinking that commercial social media platforms might become proxies for capitalism's bleak "win condition"?[8] Isn't it likely that late capitalism will play out on Facebook and Instagram? Maybe they'll never fade. Meta will face investor pressure to generate as much money as possible from the user base, which coincides with eroding the quality of the user experience. Meta's servers will keep humming, the advertisements will be intrusive and ubiquitous, and the enjoyment of the early Web 2.0 will be forgotten. In this theory, "late-stage Instagram" entails the same bleakness and near-full reversal of founding principles.

I operated an Instagram organic growth service between 2017 and 2022, in which a computer program controlled each customer's account to garner more engagement. Savvy customers asked questions like, "What if this 'organic' growth is just another customer's bot interacting with my account?" "What if it's all a circular pattern of software-aided grab-ass with no human element?"

Years after I wrote that crappy blog post pondering late-stage Instagram, I became aware of the "dead internet theory"[9] and wrestled with its thesis and the role I might have played in advancing it.

Dead Internet Theory

The "dead internet theory"[10] posits that most of the internet is non-human:

1. Content is heavily augmented by algorithms or entirely created by generative AI.
2. Profiles and avatars are largely fake—facsimiles of real people or digital imposters. Computers control their actions.
3. Content is moderated, filtered, and served by feed algorithms, search engines, and black-box curation systems that can be tuned by platform owners or exploited by savvy bot farmers.

The nefarious angle is that this enriches platform owners, a late-game development with an apparent connection to late-stage capitalism. Even more hotly contested is the dead internet theory's suggestion of a far-reaching conspiracy to control and manipulate humans, not just by tech companies but also by governments and special interest groups.

These conspiratorial manipulators first keep users entertained (distracted) in perpetuity, stymy users' efforts to distinguish, create, and distribute original content, and finally curate material to push an agenda and potentially augment truth.

Anecdotes have fueled "dead-internet" ruminations in fringe communities since the mid-2010s. For those who have been using the internet for a long time, it sure does seem like the quality of content, communities, and interactions are decaying even as corporate revenue grows. In his 2022 writings,[11] Cory Doctorow[12] coins the term, "enshittification"[13] to describe this decay.

The erosion of trust in black-box algorithms aligns with my musings on late-stage Instagram. Absent a catchy label, most people nonetheless summarize their experiences using the internet today as, "Yeah, well, the internet is worse now because...".

Denizens of the internet are unhappy and frustrated. Those who remember the delight of early Web 2.0 can latch onto any postulations of the dead internet theory and bask in self-confirmation.

Since late 2022, generative AI and large language models have completely changed digital content, breathing new life into the dead internet theory. These models have been "trained"[14] on enough human-created content such that the algorithms can create pretty much anything —convincingly. ChatGPT[15] and derivatives can write textual content, conduct believable conversations, fabricate images, and make videos.

Before genAI, the internet experience was in decline because of "content recycling," a trend that emerged in popular reddit communities where users regularly re-used generic discussion titles like, "What's a secret you'll never tell your significant other?" and "What happened to the loner kid from high school?"

I'm not saying these post titles aren't alluring or clickable, but I can attest to the triviality of designing an algorithm to analyze popular thread titles from the previous six months and selectively repost them. If it only happened a few times, a user could potentially have organically thought to post the topic without realizing it had already been posted. Executed on a larger scale, it's called "karma farming."[16] With a coordinated effort, recurring content becomes a pillar of the dead internet theory.

If bot-recycled or bot-generated content rises to the front page, it disadvantages original content. There is limited space at the top. If the masses have memories too short to remember the last appearance of regularly recurring content (and thus do not downvote it), then whoever is pushing it is also minimizing the reach of truly original or controversial thought.

There are other types of content recycling. In the mid-2010s Instagram bots scraped and reposted high-quality pictures, sometimes without crediting creators. YouTube accounts curated video mashups, which were just outgrowths of *America's Funniest Home Videos*. In the blogosphere, it was common to copy keywords from popular articles to attract search traffic.

On the black hat side of things, "content spinning,"[17] a primitive precursor to genAI, allowed non-technical users to "spin" the text of a web article by creating a new article with basic changes (starting with synonymic replacements) to fool Google's search algorithms into not classifying it as duplicate plagiarized content. The resulting corpus was usually low quality, and the fact that most have probably never encountered a "spun" site indicates that the perpetrators of this method were not particularly good at fooling search engines.

GenAI became an existential problem for content platforms because it took "spinning" to the extreme. ChatGPT creates all types of content, even from outlandish prompts like, "Pen me a poem about Count Dracula as if it was written by Tupac Shakur."

I don't know if I have permission to print the generated poem. I'm terrified by it, and not because it uses ghoulish imagery. I am so impressed by it because I am sure if I posted it on reddit back in 2012 with the title, "A poem about Count Dracula while channeling the voice of Tupac Shakur," it would have been a smash hit.

The dead internet theory is a reminder that the content we upvote, like, share, or admire could be created by a computer program. How do we know it's not *all* non-human? Of course, text is much easier to generate than images, and images are much easier to generate than videos, but generated images are already so good that the dead internet theory has gone from fringy and weird to entirely plausible and frightening.

In early 2023, I showed my grandmother a picture of Pope Francis with an AI-generated white puffer jacket.[18] After laughing and asking to see it again, she declared that "people have too much time on their hands." News outlets latched onto this image as an example of a harmless but "oh-my-goodness-what's-happening?" event in the developing generative AI plot. Perhaps, the epoch event of mainstream realization that *anybody* could be generating such images and that *they didn't need much time on their hands at all.*

When I browse YouTube, I have a pretty good sense of what's original content, recycled content, and AI-generated content (including "deepfakes").[19] However, when scrolling through Instagram, I have less confidence that any *picture* is human or original, even if it features humans! I would also be unsure about comments and text posts on reddit without checking users' comment histories unless the text seemed particularly eerie. I admit I'm still developing my sense for "detecting" AI (it's worth mentioning that there are web tools that assess this, LLM-trained programs finger-pointing at LLM-trained content).

While researching for an essay I wrote about Myspace, I posted a reddit thread asking about user experiences with a peculiar aspect of Myspace. I used the slang, "Myspace whore"[20] in the post. A posted reply seemed to be responding to my request but made no sense. The comment belonged to an account with a history of posts that vaguely responded to newly posted threads but had no real depth. Someone had created a bot that used generative AI to write plausible reddit comments—to farm karma.[21]

My response convinced moderators to remove the comment:

This is really interesting--your entire comment history is you leaving Chat-GPT-generated comments on recently-created threads. This is one that is a clear miss and goes to show how poorly trained LLMs are on internet jargon from twenty years ago.

These occurrences corroborate the dead internet theory and the cheapening of digital content creation. What does it mean for networks to be "social"? The cheaper and *easier* it is to deploy automation programs that act human, the more that will be deployed. If the benefits of deploying the programs outweigh the cost, then there is an incentive to scale infinitely, and humans would be outnumbered by bots and computer-generated content overnight.

The fact that there are so many fake profiles, bots, and questionable content means there are rewards to be pilfered. Because of the possible vast payout, there is the potential for clandestine lone-wolf operators to evolve into organized bot farms, to government-sponsored and corporation-funded working groups.

The dead internet theory doesn't exactly state that there are no humans on the internet because the theory is regularly reinterpreted. I define it as humans being outnumbered, outsmarted, and outcompeted by bots and bot jockeys in all facets of the digital experience. While this might not yet be absolutely true, opposing ideas sound ridiculous:

In the "thriving internet theory," the internet fortifies human bonds while increasing participation, productivity, and knowledge sharing. Humans' growing mastery of the internet helps eliminate inorganic content, bots, and bad behavior faster than negative behaviors can proliferate.

Keeping the internet *majority human* involves walking a tightrope.

External Puppeteers

Both types of puppeteers—employees of the platforms and the power users, the external participants—use *software* to wield godlike influence in the digital world. Both parties are driving forces behind the surging public decrying of the desecration of the internet.

The external puppeteers are innumerable, but their influence is often uneven, uncertain, and inconsistent. They don't *control* platforms like Instagram, reddit, and TikTok. Badly-behaving operators can face restrictions, account bans, and legal action. There is always a *cost* to their puppeteering.

I can't recall how many of my accounts have been banned for botting. Clearly, if there was a conspiracy to kill the internet, the platforms that banned me didn't want me joining in.

At Shark Social, I ran engagement bots on the Instagram accounts of thousands of customers. Including scraping activity and miscellaneous actions by my sockpuppet accounts,[22] I might have been responsible for between one and two billion queries to Instagram's private API over four years. Realistically, I think the number of likes, comments, and follows was around four hundred million. That's certainly enough actions to move the needle on *something—some* meaningful influence—right? Meh. Since campaigns centered on each customer's goal of gaining followers, I mostly exploited follow-unfollow mechanics, which contributed to the degradation in overall engagement quality.

There are potentially *hundreds of millions* of Instagram accounts that received at least one inorganic, bot-driven "poke"[23] from Tim O'Hearn's software. As botting software was distributed to non-technical users, there were thousands of Tims. Lone wolves only grow their own accounts. Entrepreneurs build businesses. I don't have access to data on average daily actions taken on Instagram in the 2010s, but I can estimate how much activity was driven by bots.

During the prime "post-Instagress" era in 2018, I'd say that as much as thirty percent of everything on Instagram (following, liking, and commenting) was driven by bots. Based on what we know about reciprocity, at least another five percent of actions were probably spurred by bot actions (I liked a bot's picture because it had liked mine first, and so on). Both the dead internet theory and my estimates suggest that bots are rampant.

As long as there is an incentive, people will continue to automate, even if that means breaking the rules! Cost-benefit analysis, supply and demand, and predator-prey[24] may curb extreme or bizarre automation. There are costs involved, and platforms have been making it harder for external puppeteers to interfere with operations.

On the other hand, if the platforms truly wanted to encourage all aspects of botting, they wouldn't ban thousands of rulebreakers a day. When xGram Bot emerged on BlackHatWorld in September 2012, it gave users the ability to automate *account creation* and spam comments.

In November 2012, blogger Hans Kullin bemoaned the sharp increase in spam.[25] While Instagram's "very small" team[26] was certainly caught by surprise, it was account creation that made xGram Bot so problematic. Banning spam accounts is insufficient when script kiddies can create new spam accounts at low costs. As Instagram made creating accounts more difficult and cheaper, certain forms of spam tapered off. Black hat software developers never again offered auto-account creation. For the modern puppeteer, the cost of a banned burner account is not negligible.

Yet, some insist that platforms *do* welcome external rule-breaking puppeteers. It is a gray area and varies widely between platforms. It's worth describing how third-party automators, software engineers, and script kiddies affect user experiences on the internet. I've split this into four sections: content, personas, interaction/socializing, and algorithmic gaming.

Content

"Content" is a rapidly advancing space in which I am not an expert. When I worked with a creative agency coupled with Shark Social, a customer willing to pay for "content services" was usually looking for a blend of in-person photography and editing, a bit of writing, and graphic design for promotional filler pictures. They also sometimes looked for creative advice.

Content—blogs, TikTok videos, and Instagram pictures—is the center-piece of the internet. User-generated content puts power in users' hands, not platform owners'. Unless the content itself concerns content creation, viewers don't get an inside look into the team or tools behind it. Is it a solo operation or is there a creative group fine-tuning each release? The dead internet theory treats this secrecy with suspicion. What if what we see is created by genAI? What if it's part of a carefully crafted, government-run psychological operation?[27] Who, exactly, is the puppeteer, and what do they want?

Where the authenticity of content is harder to glean, there's a higher chance of it being non-human or, indirectly, part of a conspiracy to harness technology to control the populace. Before ChatGPT, an April 11, 2019, *Wall Street Journal* article captured the growing concern about the anonymity of animated content creation: "Kids Love These YouTube Channels. Who Creates Them Is a Mystery."[28] It continued: "Almost anyone can upload videos to YouTube—but the difficulty identifying kids content creators fosters a 'lack of accountability,' a critic says."

Separately, bots were used to scrape content throughout the 2010s. Programmers aggregated and reposted what they scraped. This still happens today, including individuals who cross-post and share others' work. This is what Chris Buetti did to "eat for free" in 2019.[29] Humans recycling content drives the dead internet theory. Seeing the same material, perhaps a meme, posted by multiple sources across multiple platforms creates a "glitch in the Matrix" type moment. Like, "Woah, I *just* saw that! That's not original (why did I get a dopamine hit anyway?)!" These instances inspired an early interest in this theory.

With the proliferation of copied and derivative creations, it's no wonder that well-received memes and pictures of beautiful women displace the weightier, boring topics. I think this is partly the reason my four-year quest to become a book review influencer failed.

A Roman visionary proclaimed, "If you give people bread and circuses, they'll never revolt."[30]

Social media is that circus. It's caused a hell of a lot of headaches for the ruling class over the past decade, but the more the population embraces zombie-like consumption of low-brow distractions, the lesser the chances of a revolution. Authoritarian governments simply shut their internet connections off whenever there is too much heat. It is reasonable to allege that America's government really, really, really, wants to leave social media *on*, implicitly supporting the long-term, late-stage continuity of certain American-made apps, particularly Instagram.

AI-generated content is changing everything. ChatGPT has debased the bread-and-butter services that hometown social media agencies were built upon. Using AI to generate images and text and reason through prompts is now cheap. Unlike purely disruptive behaviors, such as spam messaging, most platforms don't attach strict consequences to posting AI-generated content. StackOverflow.com, a knowledge-sharing platform, shows its disapproval with a policy that begins, "Generative artificial intelligence (a.k.a. GPT, LLM, generative AI, genAI) tools may not be used to generate content for Stack Overflow."[31]

Other platforms have done next to nothing. StackOverflow must preserve the human aspect of its high-quality technical discussions, but reddit and Facebook don't care. In fact, when users either use AI to create or mold content or don't post at all, platforms can acquire a taste for AI. If allowing computer-generated content means more users are posting something and higher user engagement numbers, a platform may welcome AI, even if not intentionally. While broad swaths of industries will be annihilated by generative AI, social media platforms stand to benefit. It makes the effort of low-effort posting even lower, as users only have to engineer prompts rather than write posts or take pictures themselves.

As long as users upvote and interact with the AI-generated content, the late stage becomes one in which fewer people care about what's real and what's fake. If non-human content continues to gain prominence, other low-skill puppeteers will seek software to generate their own content. There will be less vigilance.

How many skilled photographers with professional-grade cameras are there? Probably over one million. How many are located in or can travel to an area where the aurora borealis is visible? We can train new photographers and travel to northern Siberia all we want, but I could generate tens of thousands of beautiful aurora borealis pictures by the time the sun rises tomorrow. Once a photo is digitized, it's really hard to discern whether or not it's real.

If people prove uninterested or unable to discern real from not real, then the death of the human-generated internet is nigh.

Personas

The AI onslaught, the viability of the dead internet theory, and external puppeteers struggle when it comes to building online personas, especially on-camera personalities.

The January 27, 2018, *New York Times* article, "The Follower Factory,"[32] detailed the practice of seeding fake Twitter accounts with real peoples' profile pictures—digital identity theft. A face is trusted, whereas faceless accounts are untrustworthy.

More than six years have passed since that article. With generative AI, human faces don't need to be lifted from other profiles. They can be generated. However, building a persona is difficult when an account pursues a content niche that requires a human body, face, and voice to star in pictures or videos.

Yes, of course, there is AI-for-this and AI-for-that. It has yet to be seen whether any AI campaign can achieve a sustained intimacy commensurate with modern influencers. Live streams would be difficult with nonhumans.

The presence of camera-facing influencers with well-developed post histories and who have been seen in real life is a safeguard against the dead internet. Faceless accounts can no longer be trusted. Platform-designated identity verification—paying for a blue checkmark—is of utmost importance.

This is a haunting resurrection of parents' advice to nineties kids when they first started browsing the internet: "You never know who is on the other side of the screen." Now, if an account is not verified with a full post history and convincing persona, it definitely isn't real, and the internet is dead.

The silver lining is that platforms have made account creation costly enough to curb automated account creation. The lawless days of xGram Bot are in the past on most platforms.

Interaction and Socializing

At Shark Social, we might have thought of ourselves as big fish, but we weren't the first people to write code that used the private API of a social network to facilitate interactions. The first program we used was written by somebody else. Interaction and socialization on the internet are pretty much as old as the internet. Although a modern take on this topic involves the horror of AI, we're also talking about traditional spam.

The dead internet theory hangs on this. If the interactions are real, the internet isn't dead. Unfortunately, many interactions aren't real, and there is still an underground economy built upon robo-likes, follows, comments, and all types of social transactions. As long as using bots to generate activity outweighs the cost, fake socialization will be rife.

When assessing the results of the earlier iterations of the bots I built, I wondered, "What if I'm optimizing for reciprocal actions from other bots rather than other humans?" That was back in 2017. As Shark Social acquired customers and I accumulated more test dummies, I found that a troubling amount of the "reciprocal" activity came via "flattering spam,"[33] the same generic, positive comments I was dishing out!

"Nice pic!"

By building bots that generated fake socialization from real accounts, I contributed to the death of the internet. There was a facade of activity, being online, growth, and participation. It was fake but nobody cared since it was sourced from real accounts. It wasn't weird at all that an independent ski manufacturer commented on my picture taken on the beach in Mexico. Users didn't, and still don't, have the tools to assess whether interactions are real. So, unless an account is obviously a spam account, users gleefully accept the compliments.

Unless a platform is under pressure to clean up bot accounts, they're happy to tally the interactions in their quarterly reported user metrics.

Algorithmic Gaming

For external puppeteers, the name of the game may be fooling the algorithms and exploiting ranking systems. The connotation of "gaming" makes it sound dirty, but it's important to remember that practices like search engine optimization (SEO) are based on gaming Google's search algorithms. Google even provides tips on how to do this. Maybe instead of gaming, it can be called polite compliance; instead of puppeteering, mere "participation."

Yes, I do see those who practice algorithmic SEO as a band of external puppeteers, though a strait-laced sect. PageRank is just another algorithm, and every platform has puppeteers trying to reverse engineer and exploit them, which can bring havoc and disruption. This is the plane on which external puppeteers are most at odds with the platform operators, the ranking and retrieval algorithm designers.

One distinction to make is that follow-unfollow bots on Instagram didn't interfere with Instagram's ranking algorithms. At least, that wasn't the purpose. Software-driven likes and comments could have been used to boost posts since Instagram's feed algorithm relies on measuring users who saw the post against users who liked the post to determine audience scoping. However, Instagram is thought to protect against fake activity influencing its algorithms, so services claiming they could reliably boost reach never gained a foothold. By contrast, using alt accounts[34] on reddit to increase initial upvotes can still have a major impact on the reach of comments and posts, more than ten years after u/Unidan's high-profile ban[35] for sockpuppeting.[36]

The importance of discussing algorithmic gaming in the context of the dead internet puppet users is that those with more resources and more knowledge eventually form strangleholds over the ranking algorithms that are supposed to favor organic, original content.

Try to publish a recipe and get ranked in the first fifty results in a Google search. Try to create a reddit thread that makes it to the *front page*. Try to get featured on Instagram's Explore page. Try to go viral.

The layman is powerless against the puppeteers who have spent years reverse engineering rank algorithms and perfecting how to court them. The idea of reaching the coveted "top" is no longer realistic. This reality, strung by puppeteers who have studied the algorithms, means that users' enthusiasm for sharing wide-reaching content has deflated. The quirky, unpolished stuff—the beloved kernel of the internet—is too often buried or filtered, if would-be creators even bother posting at all.

Internal Puppeteers

The engineers who build social media platforms exert influence over much of humankind. Instagram has over two billion monthly active users.[37] People no longer ask what will replace Instagram.

I designed systems at Cutlet to manipulate user behavior—they were nothing novel. I implemented the same wiles that had stolen thousands of hours of my own attention during the previous decade.

In the dead internet theory, social media platforms are dystopian control systems. Those helming the systems have supreme authority. As technology companies fixate on profit, the user experience degrades, while the benefits of bot activity and AI-driven content can incentivize more botting.

One controversial allegation is that companies that sell ad impressions benefit from bot traffic because bots view ads but never click them. Bots purportedly boost the projected reach of ads. This was a conspiracy theory that I read way back in 2015. I can't find the source now. All I remember is that in the spring of 2015, I was enrolled in a college entrepreneurship class, and we discussed startups' paths to monetization.

In one of many polemics I delivered to the class, I stated that fifteen percent of Facebook traffic in 2015 was allegedly fake. Nobody took me seriously, which was a central theme of my college experience. I found it plausible that a social media company could have its own bot farm to cheat the scale under the guide of crawling its own site for other purposes.

All puppeteers face a moral dilemma: access, influence, and power come with responsibilities. As social media platforms grow into all-encompassing bastions of human socialization, how can they be audited? They can't without exposing trade secrets and incurring major expenses. Might it be that *regulation* is the only remedy for this "late stage" doom cycle?

Can the Government Help?

In a book filled with "conspiratorial diatribes," I don't accuse the federal government of being nefarious. The idea that a government agency is undertaking a massive psyop without a clear end goal is preposterous. Still, I acknowledge that people have accused the United States government of "killing" the internet.[38]

Following the money, the government isn't cozying up to Meta, Meta is cozying up to the government. There is no escaping the scrutiny of Uncle Sam. The idea that there is a behind-the-scenes, historic, collaborative effort to exploit Meta's platforms and advance secretive government agendas is pretty silly, especially considering everyone seemed totally blindsided by the "election interference" campaigns of 2016.[39]

Do I think that the CIA and NSA have excellent cyberspace monitoring? Yes. Through that monitoring, is it likely that they've identified novel routes for manipulation and propaganda? Absolutely. Generative AI has also necessitated developing methods to check fake activity, such as fake upvotes or articles not written by humans. Parties previously inconvenienced by print journalism (including all levels of government) may celebrate that investigative reporting is headed toward extinction and that televised news has lost its teeth.

Do I think that branches of the federal government are sponsoring internet propaganda campaigns? Maybe. Could the government be working with content creators or platform owners to propagate its messaging? Maybe, but it'd be a big risk, a big effort, and for what?

A government figure may one day demand an "explainable artificial intelligence."[40] It could help mitigate the manipulative aspect of the dead internet theory but not the botting or fake content. Even with that, a tech company providing layered explanations of "why?" content is shown in order to "explain" it could increase a platform's data transfer, computer, and storage costs by two orders of magnitude. That'll never happen.

Apart from authoritarian rule—shutting off the internet—solving all three aspects of the dead internet theory is now out of any government's hands.

As for barreling toward a future where nothing is real—but filled with puppeteers and braindead buffoons—I declare that our "bread and circuses" have been working just fine. We've lost the internet I loved, but it's not dead yet.

21

UNFOLLOWED

"Do you have Instagram?" is a pretty bad pickup line. "What if I told you that I could get you more Instagram followers?" is equally cringeworthy, but both worked surprisingly well during the period of my life when I could pull out my phone and use Mako to direct one hundred followers to the Instagram of a woman I had just met.

At Shark Social, we all carried cute business cards with our one-dollar-for-the-first-month promotion. My secret weapon was my special API route that I could use to direct customers to immediately follow an Instagram account that I dictated. On the not-infrequent occasion that it didn't work, I sulked.

As demand swelled, my partners taught me how to sell our product. I found myself in Miami nightclubs pitching an Instagram growth service. I watched our CEO dash through traffic on LaSalle Street in Chicago to interrupt what I remember as an engagement photoshoot in the shadow of the Board of Trade building. We dined at Swift & Sons that night, and I was angry that they didn't print special menus to celebrate Shark Social eclipsing five hundred active customers.

Instagram growth became part of my identity and, to be honest, a bit of a social crutch. It's easier to face rejection in the dating world when you can write off a "no" as a declination of business services. It was a convenient barrier. However, people may primarily see you as a conduit for gaining Instagram fame if you associate with an Instagram growth business.

In May 2018, I ended up quitting the job I was supposed to get fired from. My bizarre 2017 year-end had motivated me to focus on the side hustle. My side hustle not only grew to new heights, it also helped me get a new job at an elite firm.

On the day I gave my two weeks' notice, I found myself at my buddy's sprawling apartment in the River North neighborhood of Chicago. He asked me and one of my coworkers to "entertain" a female guest while he resolved a dispute with a different female guest he was dating.

I quickly launched into my organic growth sales pitch.

"Oh, I do Instagram growth, too! I use Telegram group bots, but I'm thinking about switching to FollowLiker!"

The night that I met Britt, I didn't even try the follower trick. She talked about e-commerce, growth hacking, and *having clients*. It was like an angel came down from heaven and stopped at this penthouse across the street from the Rock Bottom Restaurant & Brewery.

It took every ounce of confidence I had to sit on the couch next to her and challenge her to show me one of her client accounts. She pulled one up. The account was selling gray-area pharmaceutical supplements, also known as "research chemicals," which was a big business on social media in 2018. The account had over twenty thousand followers.

I gleefully showed her my clients without admitting that some of them had signed up with a hundred thousand followers already. Smitten and distracted, I didn't think to exchange Instagrams. I didn't thrust a business card into her lap. I didn't even ask for her phone number. As my coworker and I waved to the doorman and departed, he commented, "Dude, down in Texas girls like that only go for guys with—"

I shrugged it off.

As my two weeks' notice ticked toward my last day, I planned a quitting party. My buddy with the big-ass apartment texted that Britt wanted to come. I responded, "Surely" within five seconds.

On the big night, the VIPs arrived at my apartment. Britt refused a pickle-back shot. All the guys were wearing the same blue chambray shirt. As the pregame ended, two of my henchmen, who happened to be under-classmen in my college fraternity and were interning in Chicago that summer, draped trash bags over all my electronics, books, and other valuables.

We popped six bottles of cheap Prosecco and sprayed down the 765-square-foot apartment.

At that moment, I was living the life of the influencer. At a nightclub called The Bassment, I reserved a space for thirty people. A picture with Britt and all the blue shirts ended up being the most liked picture I ever posted to Instagram. One of my online friends who I knew only from my book reviews commented, "Congrats Tim! You famous"

I had attained Insta-fame. It was a peak as high as my triumphant emo transition on Myspace in 2008.

Britt and I went on a couple of dates. I'm not going to lie, we pillow-talked about Shark Social. I didn't think it was that weird. It was at least fifty percent of my life. I didn't have much time to reflect on it because I soon left for a month-long vacation. Britt and I texted often. I wanted her to be my girlfriend. Sometimes it was too businesslike, sometimes it was just kids in their early twenties figuring things out.

When I returned to Chicago and began my new job, Britt became squirrely, offering weird excuses and uncharacteristic deferrals. I never saw her again and accepted that we had both moved on.

But a month later, she texted to ask if I had deleted one of her Instagram accounts. How could I have done that? Oh, she had "signed up" one of her clients with Shark Social and not told me.

It was the pill pusher account that she had shown me in May. Yeah, it turned out that it had been signed up for Shark Social's service for several months. Yeah, it had disappeared! She demanded a refund and added, "My client is extremely upset and wants to blast your company on the internet."

Well, if the New York Times had taught me nothing else, it was that getting blasted on the internet always meant more business.

Contacting a former lover to say, "Hey sorry I know it's been a while," before revealing sneaky patronizing of his business is awkward. I actually didn't understand what was going on because I never had seen a client's account disappear. I refused the refund, avoided mentioning my growing suspicion that she had "used" me, and didn't engage further.

Months later, she texted me more refund requests. She told me, "It's been nothing but hell with [Shark Social]" and that I would be "hearing from [her] cousin who is a lawyer." In her emails to the whole team, she revealed that I had shared trade secrets. Her main revelation was that we used "follow-unfollow," just like pretty much everyone else. My partners wondered how this irate customer understood, and I was forced to provide context. They weren't happy. I wasn't happy either. Under the veil of a romantic relationship, Britt had been extracting secrets about organic growth from the guy who would go on to write a hundred thousand words about it.

Obviously, she didn't extract them well enough to implement them herself because she ended up white-labeling[1] Shark Social. Her "clients" had gradually become *our* clients. She made money because she upsold our service to her people, who had no idea that Shark Social was growing their accounts. Mako was better than her Telegram groups or whatever. She was precariously and completely powerless if things went wrong. When they did go wrong, she directed her anger at me, the lover boy she took advantage of.

We did end up following each other on Instagram. She liked my photo from the club and probably a few others.

Transitioning a burgeoning (or, in my case, fraying) romance to Instagram can be tricky. The policy for dishing out likes might be austere. Not liking a partner's *every* picture indicates strife. Liking *every* picture of a paramour is creepy. Scenarios are questioned and discussed with friends at brunch. As things become more serious, one might expect the other to like pictures of the opposite sex less frequently. And, yes, obsessives do traverse the follower list and check.

I've had friends under strict orders to like their significant other's new photos within the first five minutes they are posted, "for the algorithm." I've had friends deal with the fallout of "failed" posts and shoulder blame for not engaging enough, quickly enough, as the posts were deleted to hide unflattering like counts. Friends have told their girlfriends to "just sign up for Tim O'Hearn's thing."

Staying connected on Instagram is so much more than a feeble attempt to just be friends. It means frequent reminders of what the other person is doing. It means subtle competition and the alluring spectrum of emotions unique to modern social media. It means leaving the door open.

In 2018, the term "gatsbying"[2] emerged to capture the complexity of Instagram-as-a-dating-app. A picture or string of pictures, usually with specific captions, could be designed to further a romantic agenda and mount a PR campaign to target one specific person as Jay Gatsby had with Daisy in *The Great Gatsby*.[3]

Gatsbying required an impregnable belief in the reach of Instagram and an assumption that posts would reach the targeted person, at least by way of their social circle. The *group* would discuss the extravagant parties and draw in the romantic target. The goal was to provoke that red badge indicating an unread DM, the type that makes the heart leap.

I've already opined that *everything* is self-promotion, so what difference is there between gatsbying and just regularly using Instagram for dating? That is, what's the difference between gatsbying poorly and gatsbying well? The goal of any post would be grabbing a valentine's attention. If that failed, it shouldn't convey desperation or anything near the severity of being "stalkerish" or a "thirst trap."[4]

For example, if I posted a picture from The Bassment with a *different* woman, that might have gotten Britt's attention. But, if I captioned it with, "This could be you, Britt!" the coyness of the practice would be violated, and my followers would think I was a weirdo. If my caption was a quote from a song that Britt and I had enjoyed together, that would have conformed to the subtlety of the practice. The target would almost certainly know and feel that emotional pulse, but something would be left to the imagination.

There were three potential responses to gatsbying. The first and perhaps most desirable was the target reaching out to rekindle things. The next was that the person would notice and consider further action but either do nothing or halfheartedly respond with their own gatsbying, thus placing the onus on the original poster to interpret the message and consider the next move.

Finally, there was the possibility of getting unfollowed. Daisy skipping town and leaving no forwarding address.[5]

Instagram doesn't send a notification when a follower unfollows. It has to be investigated and confirmed. The realization that the targeted audience might not have seen the posts or had any interest in seeing them to begin with was a gut punch.

To be honest, I don't think that I gatsbied Britt, but I thought about it. For months, I scanned my profiles to check specific interactors; I was looking for her name.

I did successfully gatsby one woman. She reconnected with me after seeing *targeted* posts on my Instagram; we reached a point where she posted a picture of us. The next day, I noticed her obsessively scrolling through her Snapchat story viewers and Instagram picture likers. I feared I had been used to Gatsby someone else! She deleted the picture soon after, and we stopped talking.

Instagram growth might have given me a bit more confidence and social clout, but it didn't change that I was a hopeless romantic.

Britt did unfollow me. Unfollowing is a final act, a closing of the door, a casting away, a breaking of a social contract—torn pages, blotched ink, frayed binding, and smudged gilding of the books in Jay Gatsby's library.

My journey through Instagram growth and social media wrongdoing never felt particularly *wrong*. It's not like I was selling dangerous chemicals to teenagers.[6] My journey ended in 2022, and, however exciting it had been, the reader might be surprised to learn that I had stopped using my personal Instagram account by 2020. Coincidentally, part of the motivation was noticing a different love interest had unfollowed me.

In a way, I quit. That's what the caption to my Insta-famous picture at The Bassment had said: "I quit." I limited my own Instagram use, unfollowed the growth industry, and neatly placed my black hat into a hatbox. Now, people ask *me,* "Do you have Instagram?" and I don't know where to start. I went on to work a regular job and started a blog in which I tried to expose the deception inherent in the Instagram growth industry.

I considered buying fake followers to make it appear more authoritative.

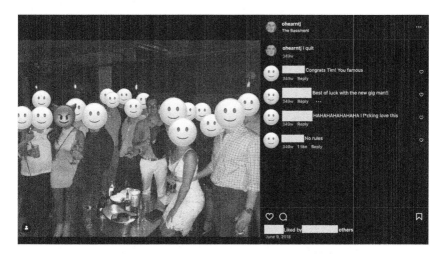

EPILOGUE

Framed is my confrontation with the Internet Age. These essays cover the wonders of growing up with the internet, the thrill of profiting from breaking the rules, and the tragicomic state of social media today. I've been a participant, puppet, pest, pawn, programmer, puppeteer, perpetrator, and, maybe, finally, pariah.

My perspective is not that of the richest or most-followed player in this game, but it cannot be replicated in terms of originality, regardless of how many tokens the machine is fed. My rap sheet of wanton violations and exploitation has led to my unshakeable belief that technology companies should stop the violation and exploitation of users. This book is a response to the mainstream mocking of seriousness, originality, and diverging from what the influencers are saying. Writing a book means producing a work of substance in a society that rewards groupthink.

I've spent most of my life chasing the highs manufactured by the internet—the dopamine hits I used to achieve refreshing the Myspace homepage to find that a pretty girl from the other side of town had sent me a friend request, the intellectual satisfaction of encountering u/Unidan's comments on early reddit, and the thrill of gaming without anything competing for my attention—the comfort and companionship the internet provides to an only child.

It all went so wrong. My attention span is warped; I'm a digital burnout. Sometimes I find myself struggling to differentiate between real and computer-generated. But I relish in the memories of the past. That pretty girl from across town is now the mother of a child who has never known anything other than social media as the primary source of entertainment, news, communication, and self-expression. Maybe one day he'll read this book and understand.

Villainy is hard to define. I can postulate violators against violated and exploiters against exploited. I broke the rules. I made money. I followed a path that hundreds of millions of Instagram users are now vaguely familiar with but that only a few dozen operatives have traversed with longevity and success. I'm left wondering which side of the conflict I'm really on.

In my journey with automation on Instagram, I used my skills in a way that my nerdy seventeen-year-old self could only dream of when coding my first computer program. In my journey writing this book, I again appeased a younger version of myself and spent an ungodly amount of time pursuing a lost art form as I imagined myself an avatar of a generation losing its way.

In the introduction, I wrote that I bought a few thousand fake Twitter followers and then learned how to program. I hoped to interlace my early internet memoir with my tour of duty in the digital underworld. Now, with my final few characters, I humbly thank you for following along and considering this villain's perspective.

Tim O'Hearn

ABOUT THE AUTHOR

Tim O'Hearn is a software engineer who works in quantitative finance. He is also an entrepreneur and freelance writer.

As a sports journalist, he covered the 2024 World Athletics Cross Country Championships in Belgrade, Serbia. As a prolific creator of user-generated content, he has written hundreds of book reviews and thousands of other entries such as restaurant reviews, product reviews, blog posts, and comments-section polemics.

Framed: A Villain's Perspective on Social Media is his first book.

Tim lives alone in the West Village.

MORE BY THE AUTHOR

Want to read more from Tim O'Hearn?

Yes!

Visit http://tjohearn.com/links

NOTES

2. They Shut Off TikTok. Now What?

1. CNN Business, "TikTok Shuts Down in the U.S. After Federal Ban Takes Effect," *CNN*, January 18, 2025, https://www.cnn.com/2025/01/18/business/trump-tiktok-ban/index.html.
2. Maheshwari, Sapna. "How Bots Are Inflating Instagram Egos." *The New York Times*, June 6, 2017. Accessed February 15, 2025. https://web.archive.org/web/20250217042425/https://www.nytimes.com/2017/06/06/business/media/instagram-bots.html.
3. Ibid.
4. Ibid.
5. Ibid.
6. Ibid.
7. Wilson, Calder. "I Spent Two Years Botting on Instagram – Here's What I Learned." *PetaPixel*, April 6, 2017. Accessed February 18, 2025. https://web.archive.org/web/20190509221830/https://petapixel.com/2017/04/06/spent-two-years-botting-instagram-heres-learned/.
8. Confessore, Nicholas, Gabriel J. X. Dance, Mark Hansen, and Richard Harris. "The Follower Factory." *New York Times*, January 27, 2018. Accessed February 15, 2025. https://web.archive.org/web/20250112143607/https://www.nytimes.com/interactive/2018/01/27/technology/social-media-bots.html.
9. Ibid.
10. Ibid.
11. Ibid.
12. Ibid.
13. Ibid.
14. O'Brien, Matt. "Elon Musk's Twitter Troubles Could Have Big Impact on Media." *AP News*, October 31, 2022. Accessed February 15, 2025. https://web.archive.org/web/20250129030026/https://apnews.com/article/elon-musk-twitter-inc-technology-business-12632270af1547933d41ffc50f3012ba.
15. New York State Attorney General. "Attorney General James Announces Groundbreaking Settlement with Sellers of Fake Followers." *New York State Attorney General*, January 30, 2019. Accessed February 15, 2025. https://web.archive.org/web/20250213223749/https://ag.ny.gov/press-release/2019/attorney-general-james-announces-groundbreaking-settlement-sellers-fake-followers.
16. Maheshwari, Sapna. "Uncovering Instagram Bots With a New Kind of Detective Work." *The New York Times*, March 12, 2018. Accessed February 15, 2025. https://web.archive.org/web/20241231201828/https://www.nytimes.com/2018/03/12/business/media/instagram-bots.html.
17. Ibid.
18. Ibid.
19. Ibid.
20. Ibid.

3. A Place for Friends, Pimps, and Whores

1. Challand, Skylar. "No Longer a Place for Friends." *IDSGN*, July 6, 2009. Accessed February 15, 2025. https://web.archive.org/web/20250216024419/http://idsgn.org/posts/no-longer-a-place-for-friends/.
2. *Urban Dictionary*. "Myspace Whores." *Urban Dictionary*, accessed August 1, 2024. https://web.archive.org/web/20240801144047/https://www.urbandictionary.com/define.php?term=myspace+whores.
3. Russell, Amanda. "The Beauty of the Ugly Internet." *Medium*, October 1, 2022. Accessed February 15, 2025. https://web.archive.org/web/20221001162230/https://medium.com/@amandagrussell/the-beauty-of-the-ugly-internet-6cd59cbba94a.
4. Hern, Alex. "Myspace Loses All Content Uploaded Before 2016." *The Guardian*, March 18, 2019. Accessed February 15, 2025. https://web.archive.org/web/20250121101426/https://www.theguardian.com/technology/2019/mar/18/myspace-loses-all-content-uploaded-before-2016.
5. Pedro D. Flores, *The Kings of Myspace - Myspace Rap Video*, September 11, 2006, YouTube, accessed February 15, 2025, https://www.youtube.com/watch?v=kS87r0YZJb8&ab_channel=PedroD.Flores.
6. Ibid.
7. *Wikipedia contributors*, "Pageview," *Wikipedia*, last modified February 15, 2025, accessed February 15, 2025, https://en.wikipedia.org/wiki/Pageview.
8. Google Trends™ tool is a trademark of Google LLC and this book is not endorsed by or affiliated with Google in any way.
9. Poulsen, Kevin. "'Y2K Pimp' Gets 12 Years for Recruiting Minor on MySpace." *Wired*, November 8, 2010. Accessed February 15, 2025. https://web.archive.org/web/20240805104926/https://www.wired.com/2010/11/epps/.
10. Poulsen, Kevin. "Pimps Go Online to Lure Kids Into Prostitution." *Wired*, February 25, 2009. Accessed February 15, 2025. https://web.archive.org/web/20231009091756/https://www.wired.com/2009/02/pimping/.
11. United States Courts. *USA v. Epps, 21-355*. United States Courts Opinions. Accessed February 15, 2025. https://www.govinfo.gov/app/details/USCOURTS-cand-3_21-cr-00355/USCOURTS-cand-3_21-cr-00355-0.
12. Epps, Marvin. "Marvin Epps - Male Prison Pen Pals." *Goodprisoner.com*, [no date]. Accessed February 15, 2025. https://web.archive.org/web/20161020005156/https://goodprisoner.com/male_prison_pen_pals/MarvinEpps/.
13. Ibid.
14. Urban Dictionary. "Myspace Pimp." Accessed February 15, 2025. https://web.archive.org/web/20250216031558/https://www.urbandictionary.com/define.php?term=myspace%20pimp.
15. Howcast. "How to Pimp Your Myspace Page." *Howcast*, March 3, 2008. Archived at Wayback Machine. Accessed February 16, 2025. https://web.archive.org/web/20220926030318/https://www.howcast.com/videos/2247-how-to-pimp-your-myspace-page.
16. Fall Out Boy. "Alternative Press (AP) Magazine." February 2007, no. 223.
17. Urban Dictionary. "Myspace Whores." *Urban Dictionary*, August 1, 2024. Archived at Wayback Machine. Accessed February 16, 2025. https://web.archive.org/web/20240801144047/https://www.urbandictionary.com/define.php?term=myspace+whores.

18. MyspaceGens.com. "Whore Me." *MyspaceGens*, n.d. Archived at Wayback Machine. Accessed February 16, 2025. https://web.archive.org/web/20250130140309/https://www.myspacegens.com/handler.php?gen=whoreme.

19. Urban Dictionary. "PC4PC." *Urban Dictionary*, August 10, 2024. Archived at Wayback Machine. Accessed February 16, 2025. https://web.archive.org/web/20240810080510/https://www.urbandictionary.com/define.php?term=PC4PC.

20. Urban Dictionary. "C4C." *Urban Dictionary*, January 14, 2024. Archived at Wayback Machine. Accessed February 16, 2025. https://web.archive.org/web/20240114110603/https://www.urbandictionary.com/define.php?term=c4c.

21. Urban Dictionary. "W4W." *Urban Dictionary*, August 8, 2024. Archived at Wayback Machine. Accessed February 16, 2025. https://web.archive.org/web/20240808073101/https://www.urbandictionary.com/define.php?term=w4w.

22. Urban Dictionary. "F4F." *Urban Dictionary*, May 25, 2010. Accessed February 16, 2025. https://www.urbandictionary.com/define.php?term=F4F.

23. Urban Dictionary. "Whore Train." *Urban Dictionary*, June 7, 2007. Archived at Wayback Machine. Accessed February 16, 2025. https://web.archive.org/web/20230819105139/https://www.urbandictionary.com/define.php?term=whore%20train.

24. *Urban Dictionary.* "Myspace Whores." *Urban Dictionary*, accessed August 1, 2024. https://web.archive.org/web/20240801144047/https://www.urbandictionary.com/define.php?term=myspace+whores.

25. Know Your Meme. "MySpace Angles." July 2, 2009. Accessed February 18, 2025. https://knowyourmeme.com/memes/myspace-angles.

26. Urban Dictionary. "Myspace Train." *Urban Dictionary*, August 10, 2023. Archived at Wayback Machine. Accessed February 16, 2025. https://web.archive.org/web/20230810014137/https://www.urbandictionary.com/define.php?term=myspace%20train.

27. Wikipedia contributors. "Samy (computer worm)." *Wikipedia*, last modified February 14, 2025. https://en.wikipedia.org/wiki/Samy_(computer_worm).

28. Ibid.

29. Ibid.

30. Friendstorm. "Help." *Friendstorm*, August 30, 2009. Archived at Wayback Machine. Accessed February 16, 2025. https://web.archive.org/web/20090830024654/http://www.friendstorm.net/help.aspx.

31. Friendstorm. "Featured Profile." *Friendstorm*, December 17, 2008. Archived at Wayback Machine. Accessed February 16, 2025. https://web.archive.org/web/20081217065203/http://www.friendstorm.net/featured.aspx.

32. Hern, Alex. "Myspace Loses All Content Uploaded Before 2016." *The Guardian*, March 18, 2019. Accessed February 15, 2025. https://web.archive.org/web/20250121101426/https://www.theguardian.com/technology/2019/mar/18/myspace-loses-all-content-uploaded-before-2016.

33. Friendpulse. "Top 50 Users." *Friendpulse*, July 24, 2008. Archived at Wayback Machine. Accessed February 16, 2025. https://web.archive.org/web/20080724171442/http://www.friendpulse.com/top-50-overall-today.html.

34. Maxadds. "Index." *Maxadds*, May 19, 2011. Archived at Wayback Machine. Accessed February 16, 2025. https://web.archive.org/web/20110519014247/http://maxadds.com/index.php?fid=.

35. MyFriendBot. "Homepage." *MyFriendBot*, November 2, 2005. Archived at Wayback Machine. Accessed February 16, 2025. https://web.archive.org/web/20051102042930/http://www.myfriendbot.com/.

36. Lineberry, Anthony. "Anthony Lineberry's MySpace Profile." *MySpace*, February 7, 2025. Archived at Wayback Machine. Accessed February 16, 2025. https://web.archive.org/web/20250207062252/https://myspace.com/anthonymckay.

37. "MyFriendBot." *MyFriendBot*, July 1, 2006. Archived at Wayback Machine. Accessed February 16, 2025. https://web.archive.org/web/20060701195509/http://www.myfriendbot.com/index.php.

38. *MySpace, Inc. v. Anthony Lineberry*. Case no. 2:2006cv02620, Central District of California. April 28, 2006. Archived at Wayback Machine. Accessed February 16, 2025. https://web.archive.org/web/20250207210437/https://dockets.justia.com/docket/california/cacdce/2:2006cv02620/367699.

39. *MyFriendBot*. "Down until further notice." Archived July 18, 2006. Accessed February 16, 2025. https://web.archive.org/web/20060718175047/http://www.myfriendbot.com/.

40. McWilliams, Brian. "MyFriendBot Author Threatened with Lawsuit." *Spam Kings*, January 31, 2006. Archived January 31, 2006. Accessed February 16, 2025. https://web.archive.org/web/20061230041227/http://spamkings.oreilly.com/archives/2006/01/myfriendbot_author_threatened.html.

41. Ibid.

42. Ibid.

43. McWilliams, Brian. "Author of MySpace Bot Denies Wrongdoing." *Spam Kings*, January 31, 2006. Archived October 5, 2022. Accessed February 16, 2025. https://web.archive.org/web/20221005094245/https://www.oreilly.com/spamkings/archives/2006/01/author_of_myspace_bot_denies_w_1.html.

44. McWilliams, Brian S. "Moving On." *Spam Kings Blog*, April 19, 2006. Archived at https://web.archive.org/web/20061230133400/http://spamkings.oreilly.com/.

45. Lineberry, Anthony. "Me..." *Dtors*, June 9, 2007. Archived at https://web.archive.org/web/20070609104259/http://dtors.ath.cx/index/me.

4. Algorithms and Truth

1. "Death Clock." Last modified February 1, 2003. Accessed February 15, 2025. https://web.archive.org/web/20030201212915/http://deathclock.com/.

2. "Algorithm," Wikipedia, last modified February 15, 2025, https://en.wikipedia.org/wiki/Algorithm.

3. Norman, Joshua. "Boomers Joining Social Media at Record Rate." *CBS News*, November 15, 2010. https://web.archive.org/web/20250216062213/https://www.cbsnews.com/news/boomers-joining-social-media-at-record-rate/.

4. Editorial Staff. "20 Best Newspaper WordPress Themes." *WPBeginner*, January 15, 2025. Accessed February 16, 2025. https://web.archive.org/web/20250216062420/https://www.wpbeginner.com/showcase/best-wordpress-newspaper-themes/.

5. "PEACE! IT'S OVER." *The Charlotte Observer*, August 15, 1945. Accessed February

16, 2025. https://web.archive.org/web/20250206054245/https://d3h6k4k-fl8m9p0.cloudfront.net/stories/A1OxV.B3-RpG5CKOFH8BRw.jpg.

6. "User Experience." *Wikipedia*, last modified January 15, 2025. Accessed February 16, 2025. https://en.wikipedia.org/wiki/User_experience.

7. Wikipedia. "Chumbox." Last modified date unavailable. Accessed February 18, 2025. https://en.wikipedia.org/wiki/Chumbox.

8. "Owners of Scranton Times-Tribune, 3 Other Pennsylvania Dailies Sell to Publishing Giant." *AP News*, updated August 31, 2023, 4:49 PM EST. Accessed February 16, 2025. https://web.archive.org/web/20231125051101/https://apnews.com/article/timesshamrock-scranton-sale-alden-medianews-37611ba0f46097f2a8553a6b35f406a2.

9. "Web Portal." Wikipedia, last modified November 10, 2024. https://en.wikipedia.org/wiki/Web_portal.

10. "Yahoo Sports." Last modified November 28, 1996. https://web.archive.org/web/19961128071513/http://www8.yahoo.com/Recreation/Sports/.

11. "Boomerang." *Yahoo Sports*. Last modified November 28, 1996.https://web.archive.org/web/19961128112252/http://www8.yahoo.com/Recreation/Sports/Boomerang/.

12. *Yahoo Sports*. "Recreation/Sports." Last modified August 5, 1997. https://web.archive.org/web/19970805071425/http://www10.yahoo.com:80/Recreation/Sports/.

13. *Yahoo Sports*. "Recreation/Sports." Last modified October 7, 1997. https://web.archive.org/web/19971007021731/http://www9.yahoo.com:80/Recreation/Sports/.

14. *Yahoo Sports*. "Recreation/Sports." Last modified June 30, 1998. https://web.archive.org/web/19980630073107/http://www.yahoo.com/Recreation/Sports/.

15. Sublime Directory. "The Basement." Last modified July 31, 2005. https://web.archive.org/web/20050731231954/http://www.sublimedirectory.com/basement/.

16. IMDb. "414 - (Icey) Mike Imber (Reality Kings & Kimbo Slice's Manager)." *Tangentially Speaking with Christopher Ryan*. Episode 414, 2020. 1h 32m. IMDbPro. Accessed February 15, 2025. https://www.imdb.com/title/tt26129152/.

17. Sublime Directory. *Sublime Directory Homepage*. August 1, 2005. Accessed February 15, 2025. https://web.archive.org/web/20050801010709/http://sublimedirectory.com/.

18. GPSiteCentral.com. "Submission Page For TGPSiteCentral.com and its Affiliates!" *TGPSiteCentral.com*. Accessed February 15, 2025. https://web.archive.org/web/20050811004502/http://www.tgpsitecentral.com/.

19. "PageRank." *Wikipedia*. Accessed February 15, 2025. https://en.wikipedia.org/wiki/PageRank.

20. Ibid.

21. Ibid.

22. Ibid.

23. Brabant, Romain. "How to Increase Your Domain Authority?" *SEO Buddy*, May 27, 2022. https://web.archive.org/web/20241012072612/https://seobuddy.com/blog/how-to-increase-your-domain-authority/.

24. "Black box." *Wikipedia*. Accessed February 15, 2025. https://en.wikipedia.org/wiki/Black_box.

25. Anderson, Keith. "SEO and Reverse Engineering Search Engines." *SEO Hermit*, December 17, 2024. Accessed February 16, 2025. https://web.archive.org/web/20250216064744/https://www.seohermit.com/articles/seo-and-reverse-engineering-search-engines/.

26. Bianchi, Tiago. "Google: Annual Advertising Revenue 2001-2024." *Statista*, February 5, 2025. https://web.archive.org/web/20250216064925/https://www.statista.com/statistics/266249/advertising-revenue-of-google/.

27. Wikipedia contributors. "Wikipedia:Fundraising/2023 banners." *Wikipedia*, 2023, https://en.wikipedia.org/wiki/Wikipedia:Fundraising/2023_banners.

28. Ibid.

29. almightybob1. "Comment on 'Let's talk content. AMA.'" *Reddit*, July 16, 2015, https://www.reddit.com/r/announcements/comments/3djjxw/comment/ct5r0ch/?utm_source=share&utm_medium=web3x&utm_name=web3xcss&utm_term=1&utm_content=share_button. Accessed February 16, 2025.

30. "Reddit Co-Founder Admits to Editing User's Pro-Trump Comments." *WBALTV*, updated November 28, 2016, https://web.archive.org/web/20220128184121/https://wbaltv.com/article/reddit-co-founder-admits-to-editing-users-pro-trump-comments/8372556. Accessed February 16, 2025.

31. Wikipedia contributors. "Censorship by Google." *Wikipedia, The Free Encyclopedia*. Last modified February 10, 2025. https://en.wikipedia.org/wiki/Censorship_by_Google.

32. "Google SafeSearch for Kids." *KidsSearch*. Accessed February 16, 2025. https://www.kidssearch.com/Safe-Search-Kids.php.

33. Wikipedia contributors. "Feed (Facebook)." *Wikipedia, The Free Encyclopedia*. Last modified February 10, 2025. https://en.wikipedia.org/wiki/Feed_(Facebook).

34. Kemp, Simon. "Digital 2024: Deep Dive – The Time We Spend on Social Media." *Datareportal*, January 31, 2024. https://web.archive.org/web/20250216070243/https://datareportal.com/reports/digital-2024-deep-dive-the-time-we-spend-on-social-media

35. Eidosmedia. "Is Social Media Traffic Essential to Online News?" *Eidosmedia*, May 30, 2024. https://web.archive.org/web/20250216070528/https://www.eidosmedia.com/updater/technology/is-social-media-traffic-essential-to-online-news

36. Bains, Callum. "The Chatbot Optimisation Game: Can We Trust AI Web Searches?" *The Guardian*, November 3, 2024. https://www.theguardian.com/technology/2024/nov/03/the-chatbot-optimisation-game-can-we-trust-ai-web-searches.

5. Hackathon Hackers

1. PennApps. "About." *PennApps*, accessed February 16, 2025.https://web.archive.org/web/20250216071618/https://pennapps.com/about/.

2. Wikipedia contributors. "Hackathon." *Wikipedia, The Free Encyclopedia*. Last modified February 14, 2025. https://en.wikipedia.org/wiki/Hackathon.

3. "PennApps XXIII: Sustainability." *Devpost*. September 2, 2022. Accessed March 3, 2024. https://web.archive.org/web/20240303062359/https://pennapps-xxiii.devpost.com/.

4. Broussard, Meredith. "The Secret Lives of Hackathon Junkies." *The Atlantic*, July 8, 2015. https://web.archive.org/web/20250216072014/https://www.theatlantic.com/technology/archive/2015/07/the-secret-lives-of-hackathon-junkies/397895/.

5. Conley, Kevin. "Preventing Cheating at Hackathons." *Kevin Technology*, September 15, 2013. https://kevintechnology.com/2013/09/15/preventing-cheating-at-hackathons.html.

6. "PennApps 2015 Winter." *Devpost*, accessed March 1, 2024. https://pennapps2015w.devpost.com/.

7. Cameron McKenzie. "What Is Open API (Public API)?" *TechTarget*, accessed February 16, 2025. https://www.techtarget.com/searchapparchitecture/definition/open-API-public-API.

8. Instagram. "Instagram Platform Update." *Instagram Developer Blog*, March 12, 2017. https://web.archive.org/web/20170312194745/https://developers.instagram.-com/post/133424514006/instagram-platform-update.

9. Parecki, Aaron. *November 18, 2015.* https://web.archive.org/web/20240912053044/https://aaronparecki.com/2015/11/18/5/instagram.

10. Devpost. "Deez Nuts." Last modified September 26, 2023. https://web.archive.org/web/20230926034710/https://devpost.com/software/deez-nuts-3b6uls.

11. Wikipedia contributors. "Create, read, update and delete." *Wikipedia*, last modified February 13, 2025. https://en.wikipedia.org/wiki/Create,_read,_update_and_delete.

12. Swagger contributors. "OpenAPI Specification." *Swagger*, last modified February 16, 2025. https://swagger.io/specification.

13. Neoteroi. "OpenAPI." *Neoteroi*, last modified December 30, 2024. https://www.-neoteroi.dev/blacksheep/openapi.

14. Neoteroi.dev. *BlackSheep OpenAPI Documentation*. Archived December 30, 2024. Accessed March 1, 2025. https://web.archive.org/web/20241230174726/https://www.neoteroi.dev/blacksheep/openapi/.

15. Ball, Corey. *Hacking APIs: Breaking Web Application Programming Interfaces*. July 2022.

16. Eduonix. "Ethical Hacking vs Malicious Hacking: Understanding the Key Differences." *Eduonix Blog*, September 27, 2024. https://web.archive.org/web/20250216073924/https://blog.eduonix.com/2024/09/ethical-hacking-vs-malicious-hacking-understanding-the-key-differences/

17. "PennApps Spring 2013." *PennApps*, 2013. https://web.archive.org/web/20130110071924/http://2013s.pennapps.com/.

18. "Sparktab." *Sparktab*, 2013. https://web.archive.org/web/20130511003312/http://sparktab.net/.

19. Biggs, John. "PennApps 2013 Hackathon Runner-Up Sparktab Could Be Your New Browser Start Page." *TechCrunch*, January 21, 2013, 3:37 PM PST. https://techcrunch.com/2013/01/21/pennapps-2013-hackathon-runner-up-sparktab-could-be-your-new-browser-start-page/?guccounter=1.

20. "About." *Major League Hacking (MLH)*, January 14, 2025. https://web.archive.org/web/20250114055053/https://mlh.io/about.

21. "Hackathon Rules." *Reality Virtually Hack*, June 24, 2024. https://web.archive.org/web/20240624072639/https://realityvirtuallyhack.com/hackathon-rules/.

6. Screengrabbing

1. "Adobe Flash." *Wikipedia*, Web. Accessed 16 Feb. 2025. https://en.wikipedia.org/wiki/Adobe_Flash.

2. Wikipedia. "Massively Multiplayer Online Role-Playing Game." Last modified [date unavailable]. Accessed February 18, 2025. https://en.wikipedia.org/wiki/Massively_multiplayer_online_role-playing_game.

3. Wikipedia. "Web Banner." Last modified date unavailable. Accessed February 18, 2025. https://en.wikipedia.org/wiki/Web_banner.

4. "Seventh Generation of Video Game Consoles." *Wikipedia*, Web. Accessed 16 Feb. 2025. https://en.wikipedia.org/wiki/Seventh_generation_of_video_game_consoles.

5. "Achievement (Video Games)." *Wikipedia*, Web. Accessed 16 Feb. 2025. https://en.wikipedia.org/wiki/Achievement_(video_games).

6. [deleted user]. "What Exactly Is Gamerscore?" *Reddit*, 10 Feb. 2021, https://www.reddit.com/r/xboxone/comments/lh2qso/comment/gmuvr5g/?utm_source=share&utm_medium=web3x&utm_name=web3xcss&utm_term=1&utm_content=share_button.

7. "Xbox Network." *Wikipedia*, 16 Feb. 2025, https://en.wikipedia.org/wiki/Xbox_network.

8. Wikipedia. "Mobile Marketing." Last modified date unavailable. Accessed February 18, 2025. https://en.wikipedia.org/wiki/Mobile_marketing#Push_notifications.

9. Baadsgaard, Jacob. "Pop-up Ads: Why Everyone Hates Them and Why They'll Never Die." *MarTech*, 30 Dec. 2019, https://web.archive.org/web/20250209021525/https://martech.org/pop-up-ads-why-everyone-hates-them-and-why-theyll-never-die/.

10. "Classical Conditioning." *Wikipedia*, https://en.wikipedia.org/wiki/Classical_conditioning. Accessed 16 Feb. 2025.

11. Ward, Adrian F., Kristen Duke, Ayelet Gneezy, and Maarten W. Bos. "Brain Drain: The Mere Presence of One's Own Smartphone Reduces Available Cognitive Capacity." *The Journal of Consumer Research*, vol. 44, no. 5, Apr. 2017, https://www.journals.uchicago.edu/doi/full/10.1086/691462. Accessed 16 Feb. 2025.

12. George Bush000. "Boom Headshot." *YouTube*, uploaded February 17, 2008. https://www.youtube.com/watch?v=olm7xC-gBMY&t=90s&ab_channel=georgebush000.

13. Ibid.

14. "Boom Headshot." *TV Tropes*, https://tvtropes.org/pmwiki/pmwiki.php/Main/BoomHeadshot. Accessed 16 Feb. 2025.

15. George Bush000. "Boom Headshot." *YouTube*, uploaded February 17, 2008. https://www.youtube.com/watch?v=olm7xC-gBMY&t=90s&ab_channel=georgebush000.

16. Parker, Trey, and Matt Stone, creators. "Make Love, Not Warcraft." *South Park*, season 10, episode 8. Aired October 4, 2006. Comedy Central.

17. "Classical Conditioning." *Wikipedia*, https://en.wikipedia.org/wiki/Classical_conditioning. Accessed 16 Feb. 2025.

18. "App Store (Apple)." *Wikipedia*, https://en.wikipedia.org/wiki/App_Store_(Apple). Accessed 16 Feb. 2025.

19. "Hottrix." *Wikipedia*, https://en.wikipedia.org/wiki/Hottrix#iBeer. Accessed 16 Feb. 2025.

20. Sheraton, Steve. *Steve Sheraton*. https://www.stevesheraton.com/. Accessed 16 Feb. 2025.

21. "Pocket God." *Wikipedia*, https://en.wikipedia.org/wiki/Pocket_God. Accessed 16 Feb. 2025.

22. "Tamagotchi." *Wikipedia*, https://en.wikipedia.org/wiki/Tamagotchi. Accessed 16 Feb. 2025.

23. "God game." *Wikipedia*, https://en.wikipedia.org/wiki/God_game. Accessed 16 Feb. 2025.

24. Takahashi, Dean. "After 6M Paid Downloads, Mobile Hit Pocket God Wraps Up with Its Final, Apocalyptic Update." *VentureBeat*, December 19, 2012. Accessed February 16, 2025. https://web.archive.org/web/20250211034956/https://venturebeat.com/2012/12/19/after-6m-paid-downloads-pocket-god-final-update/

25. Wikipedia. "First-Class Citizen." Last modified date unavailable. Accessed February 18, 2025. https://en.wikipedia.org/wiki/First-class_citizen.
26. "Pocket God." *Wikipedia*, https://en.wikipedia.org/wiki/Pocket_God. Accessed 16 Feb. 2025.
27. TechCrunch. "Twitter Officially Launches Its Mobile App for Android 2.1." *Tech-Crunch*, April 30, 2010. https://techcrunch.com/2010/04/30/official-twitter-app-launched-for-android-2-1
28. "Tamagotchi Effect." *Wikipedia*, last modified February 15, 2025. https://en.wikipedia.org/wiki/Tamagotchi_effect
29. "wut." *Urban Dictionary*, last modified February 9, 2025. https://www.urbandictionary.com/define.php?term=wut
30. "risky text." *Urban Dictionary*, last modified February 9, 2025. https://www.urbandictionary.com/define.php?term=risky%20text
31. 9to5 Staff. "Standard Emoji Keyboard Arrives to iOS 5, Here's How to Enable It." *9to5Mac*, June 8, 2011. Archived at https://web.archive.org/web/20241012232628/https://9to5mac.com/2011/06/08/standard-emoji-keyboard-arrives-to-ios-5-heres-how-to-enable-it/.
32. "Social Network Game." *Wikipedia*, last modified February 15, 2025. https://en.wikipedia.org/wiki/Social_network_game.
33. "Mafia Wars." *Wikipedia*, last modified February 15, 2025. https://en.wikipedia.org/wiki/Mafia_Wars.
34. "Incremental game." *Wikipedia*, last modified February 15, 2025. https://en.wikipedia.org/wiki/Incremental_game.
35. "Loot (video games)." *Wikipedia*, last modified February 15, 2025. https://en.wikipedia.org/wiki/Loot_(video_games).
36. "Choose Your Own Adventure." *Wikipedia*, last modified February 15, 2025. https://en.wikipedia.org/wiki/Choose_Your_Own_Adventure.
37. "TikTok." *Wikipedia*, last modified January 14, 2025. https://en.wikipedia.org/wiki/TikTok.
38. "Most Popular Games on Twitch Worldwide as of June 2024, by All-Time Views." *Statista*, June 2024. https://www.statista.com/statistics/1133004/twitch-all-time-viewers-games/.
39. GTA Wiki. "Wasted." Accessed February 18, 2025. https://gta.fandom.com/wiki/Wasted.
40. "Open World." *Wikipedia*, https://en.wikipedia.org/wiki/Open_world. Accessed February 16, 2025.
41. [Redacted]. "No Cellphone Policy." *Reddit*, July 24, 2023, comment on *Teachers* subreddit, https://www.reddit.com/r/Teachers/comments/1582z84/comment/jt8v4db/?utm_source=share&utm_medium=web3x&utm_name=web3xcss&utm_term=1&utm_content=share_button. Accessed February 16, 2025.
42. *Teachers* subreddit. *Reddit*. Accessed February 16, 2025. https://www.reddit.com/r/Teachers/
43. [deleted]. "CMV: Cellphones should be banned in all schools." *Teachers* subreddit. Reddit, January 26, 2022. https://www.reddit.com/r/Teachers/comments/sddvmt/comment/hucti1f/
44. [redacted]. "CMV: Cellphones should be banned in all schools." *Teachers* subreddit. Reddit, January 26, 2022. https://www.reddit.com/r/Teachers/comments/sddvmt/comment/hucfqft/
45. "Feature phone." *Wikipedia*, last modified February 15, 2025. https://en.wikipedia.org/wiki/Feature_phone.

46. Weatherbed, Jess. "China Proposes Severe Rules for Internet-Addicted Minors." *The Verge*, August 2, 2023. https://web.archive.org/web/20241225212922/https://www.theverge.com/2023/8/2/23817035/china-internet-smartphone-regulations-minors-curfew-addiction.

7. The Puppeteer Part I

1. "Stardew Valley." *Wikipedia*, last modified February 2025. https://en.wikipedia.org/wiki/Stardew_Valley.
2. "A/B testing." *Wikipedia*, last modified February 2025. https://en.wikipedia.org/wiki/A/B_testing.
3. "Push technology." *Wikipedia*, last modified February 2025. https://en.wikipedia.org/wiki/Push_technology.
4. "Apple Push Notification Service." *Wikipedia*, last modified February 2025. https://en.wikipedia.org/wiki/Apple_Push_Notification_service.
5. "List of Pop-up Blocking Software." *Wikipedia*, last modified February 2025. https://en.wikipedia.org/wiki/List_of_pop-up_blocking_software.
6. "Apple Push Notification Service." *Wikipedia*, last modified February 2025. https://en.wikipedia.org/wiki/Apple_Push_Notification_service.
7. "Blowing up my phone." *Urban Dictionary*, last modified February 2025. https://www.urbandictionary.com/define.php?term=Blowing%20up%20my%20phone.
8. OneSignal. "About." OneSignal, https://onesignal.com/about. Accessed February 17, 2025.
9. "Analytics." *OneSignal Documentation*, accessed January 29, 2025. https://documentation.onesignal.com/docs/analytics.
10. Wikipedia contributors. "Feed (Facebook)." *Wikipedia, The Free Encyclopedia*. Last modified February 10, 2025. https://en.wikipedia.org/wiki/Feed_(Facebook).
11. "API Documentation." *Reddit*, accessed December 25, 2022. https://web.archive.org/web/20221225105046/https://www.reddit.com/dev/api/.
12. "Apollo (app)." *Wikipedia*, last modified February 14, 2025. https://en.wikipedia.org/wiki/Apollo_(app).
13. Ibid.
14. "R/wallstreetbets." *Wikipedia*, last modified February 14, 2025. https://en.wikipedia.org/wiki/R/wallstreetbets.
15. Wikipedia contributors. "Clubhouse (app)." *Wikipedia, The Free Encyclopedia*. Accessed February 2025. https://en.wikipedia.org/wiki/Clubhouse_(app).
16. Falk, Kim. *Practical Recommender Systems*. Manning Publications, February 2, 2019.
17. Ibid.
18. "Reddit Co-Founder Admits to Editing User's Pro-Trump Comments." *WBALTV*, updated November 28, 2016, https://web.archive.org/web/20220128184121/https://wbaltv.com/article/reddit-co-founder-admits-to-editing-users-pro-trump-comments/8372556. Accessed February 16, 2025.
19. Orlowski, Jeff, director. *The Social Dilemma*. Exposure Labs, Argent Pictures, and The Space Program. Distributed by Netflix, 2020.
20. University of Texas at Austin. "First Findings Shed Light on Role of Social Media Algorithms in 2020 Election." *University of Texas News*, Jul 27, 2023. https://news.utexas.e-

du/2023/07/27/first-findings-shed-light-on-role-of-social-media-algorithms-in-2020-election/.

8. Influencers, Verifying Them

1. Ahmed, Arooj. "New Survey Shows How Many Children Want to Become Influencers." *Digital Information World*, December 15, 2024. https://www.digitalinformationworld.com/2024/12/new-survey-shows-how-many-children-want.html.
2. Dopson, Elise. "28 Important Influencer Marketing Statistics To Know in 2025." *Shopify Blog*, 11 Nov. 2024, https://www.shopify.com/blog/influencer-marketing-statistics. Accessed 17 Feb. 2025.
3. Issagholian, Aleh. "The Dark Side of the Screen: The Negative Impact of Influencers in Society." Clark Chronicle, 16 May 2024. https://clarkchronicle.com/uncategorized/2024/05/16/the-dark-side-of-the-screen-the-negative-impact-of-influencers-in-society/.
4. "Sanyo Xacti 2." *ElloVision*, 13 July 2009, https://www.youtube.com/watch?v=O5j63WkEpTU&ab_channel=ElloVision. Compilation includes content from ShayCarl. Accessed 17 Feb. 2025.
5. Morrissey, Brian. "Sanyo Enlists YouTube Stars." *Adweek*, 30 Mar. 2009, https://web.archive.org/web/20181214143855/https://www.adweek.com/brand-marketing/sanyo-enlists-youtube-stars-105513/. Accessed 17 Feb. 2025.
6. Geebee Micro. "Sanyo Uses YouTube A-Listers to Promote 'Xacti HD' Dig." *Trend Hunter*, 30 Mar. 2009, https://web.archive.org/web/20210413022148/https://www.trendhunter.com/trends/sanyo-xacti-hd-digital-camera-youtube. Accessed 17 Feb. 2025.
7. Morrissey, Brian. "Sanyo Enlists YouTube Stars." *Adweek*, 30 Mar. 2009, https://web.archive.org/web/20181214143855/https://www.adweek.com/brand-marketing/sanyo-enlists-youtube-stars-105513/. Accessed 17 Feb. 2025.
8. brianvidguy. "Sanyo Xacti CG10 HD Camcorder Unboxing (test footage inside)." *YouTube*, Aug 19, 2009, https://www.youtube.com/watch?v=M-bpRiisNLg&ab_channel=brianvidguy.
9. Morrissey, Brian. "Sanyo Enlists YouTube Stars." *Adweek*, 30 Mar. 2009, https://web.archive.org/web/20181214143855/https://www.adweek.com/brand-marketing/sanyo-enlists-youtube-stars-105513/. Accessed 17 Feb. 2025.
10. iJustine. "VIDEO BLOGGER: HOW-TO MUSIC VIDEO!" *YouTube*, Mar 24, 2009, https://www.youtube.com/watch?v=82aZZraeSxk&ab_channel=iJustine.
11. "Batch Renaming," *Wikipedia*, last modified February 16, 2025, https://en.wikipedia.org/wiki/Batch_renaming.
12. "Affiliate Marketing," *Wikipedia*, last modified February 16, 2025, https://en.wikipedia.org/wiki/Affiliate_marketing.
13. Culter35, "The Sanyo Xacti (Ft. ShaneDawsonTV, ShayCarl, and LisaNova)," *YouTube*, July 17, 2009, https://www.youtube.com/watch?v=O5j63WkEpTU&ab_channel=ElloVision.
14. Brian Morrissey, "Carl's Jr. Makes New Kind of Network Buy–Burger Promo Leans on Vast Reach of YouTube Content Creators," *Adweek*, June 1, 2009, https://web.archive.org/web/20090607074759/http://www.adweek.com/aw/content_display/news/digital/e3ic0507728e66c92e31aee680ca93bb623.
15. Ibid.
16. Ibid.

17. See this requirement for internet advertising: Federal Trade Commission, "Advertising and Marketing on the Internet: Rules of the Road," *Federal Trade Commission*, https://www.ftc.gov/business-guidance/resources/advertising-marketing-internet-rules-road.

18. "Internet Celebrity." *Wikipedia*, en.wikipedia.org/wiki/Internet_celebrity. Accessed February 17, 2025.

19. Pedro D. Flores, *The Kings of Myspace - Myspace Rap Video*, September 11, 2006, YouTube, accessed February 15, 2025, https://www.youtube.com/watch?v=kS87r0YZJb8&ab_channel=PedroD.Flores.

20. "AOL Entertainment." *Kim Kardashian's 2006 Pink Princess MySpace Page Unearthed.* AOL, May 9, 2019, aol.com/entertainment/kim-kardashians-2006-pink-princess-115300345.html. Accessed February 17, 2025.

21. "Jagex Moderator." RuneScape Wiki, https://runescape.wiki/w/Jagex_Moderator. Accessed 17 Feb. 2025.

22. Nadaraja, Nish. "The Fascinating Psychology Behind the Yelp Elite Program." *CMX Hub*, date unknown, https://www.cmxhub.com/blog/yelp-elite-nish-nadaraja-psychology.

23. "Twitter." *Wikipedia*, https://en.wikipedia.org/wiki/Twitter. Accessed 17 February 2025.

24. Stone, Biz. "Not Playing Ball." *X.com Blog*, 6 June 2009, https://web.archive.org/web/20240413171145/https://blog.x.com/en_us/a/2009/not-playing-ball. Accessed 17 February 2025.

25. Associated Press. "La Russa Sues Twitter Over Fake Page." *ESPN*, 4 June 2009, https://web.archive.org/web/20240922025504/https://www.espn.com/mlb/news/story?id=4230602. Accessed 17 February 2025.

26. Stone, Biz. "Not Playing Ball." *X.com Blog*, 6 June 2009, https://web.archive.org/web/20240413171145/https://blog.x.com/en_us/a/2009/not-playing-ball. Accessed 17 February 2025.

27. Ibid.

28. Ibid.

29. Ibid.

30. Ibid.

31. Dustin Penner, "@Dustinpenner25," X, accessed February 17, 2025. https://x.com/Dustinpenner25.

32. Etherington, Darrell. "Facebook Unveils Verified Pages And Profiles, Takes A Page From Twitter's Playbook." TechCrunch, May 29, 2013. Archived at https://web.archive.org/web/20241007160729/https://techcrunch.com/2013/05/29/facebook-unveils-verified-pages-and-profiles-takes-a-page-from-twitters-playbook/.

33. Mlot, Stephanie. "Instagram Celebrates 300M Users With Verified Accounts." PCMag, December 10, 2014. Archived at https://web.archive.org/web/20240615105412/https://www.pcmag.com/news/instagram-celebrates-300m-users-with-verified-accounts.

34. Confessore, Nicholas, Gabriel J. X. Dance, Mark Hansen, and Richard Harris. "The Follower Factory." *New York Times*, January 27, 2018. Accessed February 15, 2025. https://web.archive.org/web/20250112143607/https://www.nytimes.com/interactive/2018/01/27/technology/social-media-bots.html.

35. Flynn, Kerry. "Inside the Black Market Where People Pay Thousands of Dollars for Instagram Verification." *Mashable*, September 1, 2017. https://mashable.com/article/instagram-verification-paid-black-market-facebook.

36. "White-label Product," *Wikipedia*, last modified February 16, 2025, https://en.wikipedia.org/wiki/White-label_product.
37. Flynn, Kerry. "Inside the Black Market Where People Pay Thousands of Dollars for Instagram Verification." *Mashable*, September 1, 2017. https://mashable.com/article/instagram-verification-paid-black-market-facebook.
38. Ibid.
39. Ibid.
40. Ibid.
41. Wikipedia contributors, "Wikipedia: Notability," *Wikipedia*, last modified February 17, 2025, https://en.wikipedia.org/wiki/Wikipedia%3ANotability.
42. One example low-quality blog that I believe may be used for skirting notability requirements: "Global Money World," *GlobalMoneyWorld.com*, accessed February 17, 2025, https://globalmoneyworld.com/.
43. Ibid.
44. Google Search, "Spam policies for Google web search," accessed February 17, 2025, https://developers.google.com/search/docs/essentials/spam-policies.
45. Note "Difficulty 2": Zlatin, George. "Most Valuable Media Placements." *Digital Third Coast*, https://www.digitalthirdcoast.com/blog/most-valuable-media-placements. Accessed February 17, 2025.
46. buglight. "Swapd Blue Check Scam?" *Black Hat World*, September 2, 2022, https://www.blackhatworld.com/seo/swapd-blue-check-scam.1434729/. Accessed February 17, 2025.
47. Otter PR. "Instagram Verification." *Otter PR*, accessed February 17, 2025, https://web.archive.org/web/20241013131501/https://otterpr.com/social-media-verification/.
48. West, Chloe. "How to Get Verified on Instagram in 2025." *Hootsuite Blog*, February 7, 2025, https://blog.hootsuite.com/get-verified-on-instagram/#:~:text=These%20days%2C%20users%20can%20also,their%20Instagram%20or%20Facebook%20accounts.
49. "Netflix Crackdown on Password Sharing: Why Are Biometrics Better Than Passwords?" *iProov Blog*, June 16, 2022, https://www.iproov.com/blog/netflix-password-sharing-crackdown-biometric-authentication-solution.
50. "How to Safely Drive or Deliver Without Account Sharing." *Uber Blog*, October 13, 2022, https://www.uber.com/en-AU/blog/how-to-safely-drive-or-deliver-without-account-sharing/.
51. "Accessing Someone Else's Account with Their Permission." *Bogleheads Forum*, December 22, 2021, https://www.bogleheads.org/forum/viewtopic.php?t=365412.
52. Charming-Ice-7039. "Dasher Accounts for Rent or Sale?" *Reddit*, July 9, 2023, https://www.reddit.com/r/doordash/comments/14vdh19/dasher_accounts_for_rent_or_sale/.
53. Wikipedia contributors. "CAPTCHA." *Wikipedia*, last modified February 16, 2025, https://en.wikipedia.org/wiki/CAPTCHA.
54. Anura. "How CAPTCHAs Hurt the User Experience and Conversion Rate." *Anura*, December 6, 2023, https://www.anura.io/blog/captchas-hurt-user-experience-seamless-ad-fraud-detection.
55. CTV News. "Teen Burned in Popular Body Spray Stunt." *CTV Toronto*, September 28, 2007. Archived April 6, 2012. https://web.archive.org/web/20120406211600/http://toronto.ctv.ca/servlet/an/local/CTVNews/20070928/axe_spray_070928?hub=EdmontonHome.
56. Megatron_overlord, "Please Explain Why Logan Paul and Other Viners..." *Reddit*, June 9, 2021, https://www.reddit.com/r/answers/comments/nvraw7/please_explain_why_logan_paul_and_other_viners/.

57. Henry Belot, "'Suddenly it's cool': Children Believe Use of Influencers in Gambling Ads Makes It Seem Fun," *The Guardian*, February 11, 2024, https://www.the-guardian.com/australia-news/2024/feb/12/influencers-gambling-ads-children-cool-research-data-government-inquiry.

9. Punishing Crime

1. Wikipedia, "Black hat (computer security)," accessed February 17, 2025, https://en.wikipedia.org/wiki/Black_hat_(computer_security).
2. Wikipedia, "White hat (computer security)," accessed February 17, 2025, https://en.wikipedia.org/wiki/White_hat_(computer_security).
3. Wikipedia, "Penetration test," accessed February 17, 2025, https://en.wikipedia.org/wiki/Penetration_test.
4. Reddit, randomladyaj, "Instagram health/trust score," November 19, 2019, accessed February 17, 2025, https://www.reddit.com/r/Instagram/comments/dysfn3/instagram_healthtrust_score/.
5. BlackHatWorld, "Advertise on BlackHatWorld," accessed February 17, 2025, https://www.blackhatworld.com/pages/advertising/.
6. Wikipedia, s.v. "BlackHatWorld," accessed February 17, 2025, https://en.wikipedia.org/wiki/BlackHatWorld.
7. "Terms and Rules," BlackHatWorld, accessed February 17, 2025, https://www.blackhatworld.com/help/terms/.
8. New York State Attorney General. "Attorney General James Announces Groundbreaking Settlement with Sellers of Fake Followers." *New York State Attorney General*, January 30, 2019. Accessed February 15, 2025. https://web.archive.org/web/20250213223749/https://ag.ny.gov/press-release/2019/attorney-general-james-announces-groundbreaking-settlement-sellers-fake-followers.
9. Anura. "How CAPTCHAs Hurt the User Experience and Conversion Rate." *Anura*, December 6, 2023, https://www.anura.io/blog/captchas-hurt-user-experience-seamless-ad-fraud-detection.
10. Neuburger, Jeffrey. "Craigslist Garners $60 Million Judgment against Radpad in Scraping Dispute." *New Media and Technology Law Blog*, Proskauer Rose LLP, April 17, 2017. Accessed February 17, 2025. https://web.archive.org/web/20240619045337/https://newmedialaw.proskauer.com/2017/04/17/craigslist-garners-60-million-judgment-against-radpad-in-scraping-dispute/.
11. Ibid.
12. "Grey Hat." *Wikipedia*, last modified February 17, 2025. https://en.wikipedia.org/wiki/Grey_hat.
13. "A-Z Lyrics Homepage." *AZLyrics*, accessed February 17, 2025. https://web.archive.org/web/20060629051239/http://www.azlyrics.com/.
14. "Genius (company)." *Wikipedia*, last modified February 16, 2025. https://en.wikipedia.org/wiki/Genius_(company).
15. Greenburg, Zack O'Malley. "Inside Andreessen Horowitz's $15 Million Investment In Rap Genius." *Forbes*, October 3, 2012. Updated October 22, 2012. https://web.archive.org/web/20250207231853/https://www.forbes.com/sites/zackomalleygreenburg/2012/10/03/inside-andreessen-horowitz-15-million-investment-in-rap-genius/.
16. Dale, Brady. "The tech behind Rap Genius and its goal to annotate the web." *Techni-*

cal.ly, December 16, 2013. https://web.archive.org/web/20250207232004/https://technical.ly/uncategorized/rap-genius/.

17. Frizell, Sam. "Google Is Putting Song Lyrics Right in Search Results Now." *Time*, December 23, 2014. https://web.archive.org/web/20250207232049/https://time.com/3645526/google-song-lyrics-search/.

18. The Seobility Wiki team, "Google OneBox," *Seobility*, accessed February 17, 2025,https://web.archive.org/web/20250207232223/
    https://www.seobility.net/en/wiki/Google_OneBox.

19. Michael Kan, "Genius: We Caught Google 'Red Handed' Stealing Lyrics Data," *PCMag*, June 17, 2019, accessed February 17, 2025, https://web.archive.org/web/20250207232529/https://www.pcmag.com/news/genius-we-caught-google-red-handed-stealing-lyrics-data.

20. Andrew Liptak, "Genius.com Accuses Google of Copying Its Song Lyrics," *The Verge*, June 16, 2019, accessed February 17, 2025, https://web.archive.org/web/20250207232658/https://www.theverge.com/2019/6/16/18681225/genius-com-accused-google-copying-song-rap-lyrics.

21. Devin Coldewey, "Court Dismisses Genius Lawsuit Over Lyrics-Scraping by Google," *TechCrunch*, August 11, 2020, accessed February 17, 2025, https://web.archive.org/web/20250207232821/https://techcrunch.com/2020/08/11/court-dismisses-genius-lawsuit-over-lyrics-scraping-by-google/?guccounter=1.

22. Blake Brittain, "US Supreme Court Lets Google Win Stand Against Genius Suit Over Song Lyrics," *Reuters*, June 26, 2023, accessed February 17, 2025, https://web.archive.org/web/20250207232745/https://www.reuters.com/legal/us-supreme-court-lets-google-win-stand-against-genius-suit-over-song-lyrics-2023-06-26/.

23. Ibid.

24. "HiQ Labs v. LinkedIn," *Wikipedia*, accessed February 17, 2025, https://en.wikipedia.org/wiki/HiQ_Labs_v._LinkedIn.

25. hiQ Labs, "Data-Driven Talent Management," accessed February 17, 2025, https://web.archive.org/web/20161125124531/https://www.hiqlabs.com/.

26. "HiQ Labs v. LinkedIn," *Wikipedia*, accessed February 17, 2025, https://en.wikipedia.org/wiki/HiQ_Labs_v._LinkedIn.

27. Ibid.

28. Jennifer Oliver, "Ninth Circuit Holds Data Scraping Is Legal in hiQ v. LinkedIn," *California Lawyers Association*, May 2022, accessed February 17, 2025, https://web.archive.org/web/20250207233447/
    https://calawyers.org/privacy-law/ninth-circuit-holds-data-scraping-is-legal-in-hiq-v-linkedin/
    #:~:text=hiQ%20Labs%2C%20Inc.,scraping%20data%20from%20their%20websites.

29. Jeffrey D. Neuburger, "hiQ and LinkedIn Reach Proposed Settlement in Landmark Scraping Case," *New Media and Technology Law Blog*, Proskauer Rose LLP, December 8, 2022, accessed February 17, 2025, https://web.archive.org/web/20250207233528/https://natlawreview.com/article/hiq-and-linkedin-reach-proposed-settlement-landmark-scraping-case.

30. "Automate Ads." *Wikipedia*, https://en.wikipedia.org/wiki/Automate_Ads. Accessed February 17, 2025.

31. "Kuhcoon Homepage." *Kuhcoon*, https://web.archive.org/web/20140919074121/http://www.kuhcoon.com:80/. Accessed February 17, 2025.

32. "Kuhcoon Homepage." *Kuhcoon*, https://we-

b.archive.org/web/20140810223314/http://www.kuhcoon.com/index.html. Archived August 10, 2014. Accessed February 17, 2025.

33. "Automate Ads." *OpenCorporates*, https://archive.ph/20210208024310/https://open-corporates.com/companies/us_pa/4365645. Archived February 8, 2021. Accessed February 17, 2025.

34. "Gab (social network)." *Wikipedia*, https://en.wikipedia.org/wiki/Gab_(social_net-work). Accessed February 17, 2025.

35. I originally sourced another article that was more neutral in tone. Kantrowitz, Alex. "This New Social Network Promises Almost-Total Free Speech To Its Users." *BuzzFeed News*, September 9, 2016. https://web.archive.org/web/20250207234452/
https://www.buzzfeednews.com/article/alexkantrowitz/new-social-network-gab-growing-fast-free-speech.

36. "Who is Gab Founder Andrew Torba?" Gab News, November 24, 2020. https://news.-gab.com/2020/11/who-is-gab-founder-andrew-torba/.

37. Thompson, Nicholas. "Goodbye Gab, a Haven for the Far Right." *Wired*, October 29, 2018. https://web.archive.org/web/20250207235022/https://www.wired.com/sto-ry/gab-offline-free-speech-alt-right/.

38. Ha, Anthony. "Pro-Trump CEO Gets Booted from Y Combinator Over Harassment Concerns." *TechCrunch*, November 12, 2016. https://we-b.archive.org/web/20250207235145/https://techcrunch.com/2016/11/12/pro-trump-ceo-gets-booted-from-y-combinator/.

39. Kingdon, Ashton. "The Gift of the Gab: The Utilisation of COVID-19 for Neo-Nazi Recruitment." *GNet Research*, May 7, 2020. https://we-b.archive.org/web/20250207235504/https://gnet-research.org/2020/05/07/the-gift-of-the-gab-the-utilisation-of-covid-19-for-neo-nazi-recruitment/.

40. almightybob1. "Comment on 'Let's talk content. AMA.'" *Reddit*, July 16, 2015, https://www.reddit.com/r/announcements/comments/3djjxw/comment/ct5r0ch/?utm_source=share&utm_medium=web3x&utm_name=web3xcss&utm_term=1&ut-m_content=share_button. Accessed February 16, 2025.

41. "Gunman Used Social Media to Attack Jews Before Deadly Pittsburgh Synagogue Shooting, Jurors Learn." *Associated Press*, June 13, 2023, https://we-b.archive.org/web/20250207235921/https://apnews.com/article/pittsburgh-syna-gogue-shooting-death-penalty-trial-6d4eb2d14ffdc11ddc40f805b4131e83.

42. Hansen, Claire. "Tech Companies Drop Gab After Shooting." *U.S. News & World Report*, October 30, 2018, https://we-b.archive.org/web/20250208000528/https://www.usnews.com/news/national-news/articles/2018-10-30/tech-companies-drop-gab-after-pittsburgh-synagogue-shooting.

43. "Deplatforming," Wikipedia, https://en.wikipedia.org/wiki/Deplatform-ing#:~:text=Deplatforming%2C%20also%20known%20as%20no,commonly%20associ-ated%20with%20social%20media.

44. "Who is Gab Founder Andrew Torba?" Gab News, November 24, 2020. https://news.-gab.com/2020/11/who-is-gab-founder-andrew-torba/.

45. "Stripe Restricted Businesses." Stripe, accessed February 8, 2025. https://we-b.archive.org/web/20250208000814/https://stripe.com/legal/restricted-businesses.

46. "Gab Help Guides - Moderation and Reporting Features on Gab." Last updated January 12, 2021. https://web.archive.org/web/20250208001108/https://help.gab.-com/article/gab-social-moderation.

47. Torba, Andrew. "Social Credit Score Is In America: Visa Blacklisted My Business and My Family for Building Gab." *Gab News*, June 26, 2020. https://we-

b.archive.org/web/20250101115949/https://news.gab.com/2020/06/social-credit-score-is-in-america-visa-blacklisted-my-business-and-my-family-for-building-gab/.

48. Fox, Mira. "This Social Media Site Is Ready to Fund a Christian Nationalist America." *The Forward*, October 14, 2022. https://web.archive.org/web/20250208001526/https://forward.com/culture/521336/gab-gabbpay-paypal-andrew-torba-christian-nationalist/.

49. Washington Post. "PayPal Faces Backlash After Floating Fines for Sharing Misinformation." *The Washington Post*, October 10, 2022. https://web.archive.org/web/20250208001604/
    https://www.washingtonpost.com/politics/2022/10/10/paypal-faces-backlash-after-floating-fines-sharing-misinformation/.

50. Reuters. "PayPal Says Policy to Fine Customers for 'Misinformation' Was an 'Error.'" *Reuters*, October 10, 2022. https://www.reuters.com/business/finance/paypal-says-it-never-intended-fine-users-misinformation-bloomberg-news-2022-10-10/.

51. Rodriguez, Salvador. "Rejected Again by Apple, Gab Says It's a Victim of Anti-Trump Bias." *Inc.*, January 23, 2017. https://web.archive.org/web/20250208001955/https://www.inc.com/salvador-rodriguez/gab-apple-inauguration.html.

52. Coldewey, Devin. "Alt-social network Gab booted from Google Play Store for hate speech." *TechCrunch*, August 17, 2017. https://web.archive.org/web/20250208001843/https://techcrunch.com/2017/08/17/alt-social-network-gab-booted-from-google-play-store-for-hate-speech/.

53. Torba, Andrew. "Gab.com's Offer To Elon Musk." *Gab News*, April 14, 2022. https://news.gab.com/2022/04/gab-coms-offer-to-elon-musk/.

54. Ibid.

55. Saillant, Catherine. "Testing the Bounds of MySpace." *Los Angeles Times*, April 8, 2006. https://web.archive.org/web/20250208002249/https://www.latimes.com/archives/la-xpm-2006-apr-08-me-myspace8-story.html.

56. Andross. "First." *BlackHatWorld*, Jul. 31, 2014, https://www.blackhatworld.com/seo/first.693142/.

57. *Urban Dictionary*. "Myspace Whores." *Urban Dictionary*, accessed August 1, 2024.https://web.archive.org/web/20240801144047/https://www.urbandictionary.com/define.php?term=myspace+whores.

58. Dostoevsky, Fyodor. *Crime and Punishment*. Translated by Frederick Whishaw, 1866.

1. Introduction

1. "Overworld." Wikipedia, The Free Encyclopedia. https://en.wikipedia.org/wiki/Overworld. Accessed February 15, 2025.

2. Why Instagram?

1. Jumper Media. "Homepage." Last modified October 28, 2018. Accessed February 15, 2025. https://web.archive.org/web/20181028121244/https://jumpermedia.co/.

2. "Instagram." Wikipedia. Last modified February 14, 2025. Accessed February 15, 2025. https://en.wikipedia.org/wiki/Instagram.

3. Mui, Chunka. "Why Facebook or Anyone Else Might Never Crack the Code on Mobile Advertising." *Forbes*, June 15, 2012. Accessed February 18, 2025. Archived on February 9, 2025. https://web.archive.org/web/20250209231114/https://www.

forbes.com/sites/chunkamui/2012/06/15/why-facebook-or-anyone-else-might-never-crack-the-code-on-mobile-advertising/.

4. *Urban Dictionary*. "Myspace Whores." *Urban Dictionary*, accessed August 1, 2024. https://web.archive.org/web/20240801144047/https://www.urbandictionary.com/define.php?term=myspace+whores.

5. MyFriendBot. "Homepage." *MyFriendBot*, November 2, 2005. Archived at Wayback Machine. Accessed February 16, 2025. https://web.archive.org/web/20051102042930/http://www.myfriendbot.com/.

6. Constine, Josh. "Instagram Hits 1 Billion Monthly Users, Up from 800M in September." TechCrunch, June 20, 2018. Accessed February 15, 2025. https://web.archive.org/web/20250122044148/https://techcrunch.com/2018/06/20/instagram-1-billion-users/.

7. "Dan Bilzerian." *Wikipedia*, last modified December 7, 2024. https://en.wikipedia.org/wiki/Dan_Bilzerian.

8. "Instagram Launches API." *API Evangelist*, February 8, 2011. Accessed February 1, 2025. https://web.archive.org/web/20190316051303/https://apievangelist.com/2011/02/08/instagram-launches-api/.

9. "Instagram Developer Documentation." *Instagram*, September 2, 2012. Accessed February 1, 2025. https://web.archive.org/web/20120902060923/http://instagram.com/developer/.

10. Ibid.

11. "Instagram API Endpoints." *Instagram*, September 3, 2013. Accessed February 1, 2025. https://web.archive.org/web/20130903234111/http://instagram.com/developer/endpoints/.

12. "Instagram Developer." *Instagram*, September 1, 2016. Accessed February 1, 2025. https://web.archive.org/web/20160901080610/https://www.instagram.com/developer/.

13. Ibid.

14. "Instagram Developer." *Instagram*, September 1, 2016. Accessed February 1, 2025. https://web.archive.org/web/20160901080610/https://www.instagram.com/developer/.

15. Ibid.

16. Archibong, Ime. "API and Other Platform Product Changes." *Facebook Developers Blog*, April 4, 2018. Accessed February 1, 2025. https://web.archive.org/web/20241224053512/https://developers.facebook.com/blog/post/2018/04/04/facebook-api-platform-product-changes/.

17. Constine, Josh. "Instagram Suddenly Chokes Off Developers as Facebook Chases Privacy." *TechCrunch*, April 2, 2018. Accessed February 1, 2025. https://web.archive.org/web/20250115012520/https://techcrunch.com/2018/04/02/instagram-api-limit/.

18. Instagram. "Platform Changelog." *Instagram Developer Documentation*, April 4, 2018. Accessed February 1, 2025. https://web.archive.org/web/20180605182531/https://instagram.com/developer/changelog/.

3. Sharks

1. *"Gary's Hood Auto Clicker."* Gary's Hood. Archived December 11, 2024. https://web.archive.org/web/20241211194805/https://www.garyshood.com/rsclient/.

2. Cade, DL. "Instagram Shuts Down Popular Botting Service Instagress." *PetaPixel*, April 20, 2017. Accessed February 16, 2025. https://we-

b.archive.org/web/20250210034157/https://petapixel.com/2017/04/20/instagram-shuts-popular-botting-service-instagress/.

3. Victoria O'Meara. "The Threat the Bot Brings." *Notes from Below*, June 8, 2019. Accessed February 16, 2025. https://web.archive.org/web/20250210035702/https://notesfrombelow.org/article/threat-bot-brings.

4. Instagram. "Terms of Use." Last modified December 26, 2024. Accessed February 15, 2025. https://web.archive.org/web/20241226053342/
https://help.instagram.com/581066165581870/.

4. Say Hello to My New Gangster Friend

1. Quinones, Sam. *Dreamland: The True Tale of America's Opiate Epidemic*. New York: Bloomsbury Publishing, 2015.

2. Plutchik, Robert. "Robert Plutchik." *Wikipedia*. Last modified February 14, 2025. https://en.wikipedia.org/wiki/Robert_Plutchik#Wheel_of_Emotions.

3. George Bush000. "Boom Headshot." *YouTube*, uploaded February 17, 2008. https://www.youtube.com/watch?v=olm7xC-gBMY&t=90s&ab_channel=george-bush000.

4. George Bush000. "Boom Headshot." *YouTube*, uploaded February 17, 2008. https://www.youtube.com/watch?v=olm7xC-gBMY&t=90s&ab_channel=george-bush000.

5. Instagram. "A Parents' Guide to Instagram." *Instagram Help Center*. Accessed February 15, 2025. https://help.instagram.com/299484113584685?ref=ig_about.

6. "Glossary of Video Game Terms." *Wikipedia*. Last modified February 15, 2025. https://en.wikipedia.org/wiki/Glossary_of_video_game_terms#toxic.

7. "Griefer." *Glossary of Video Game Terms*. Last modified February 14, 2025. https://en.wikipedia.org/wiki/Glossary_of_video_game_terms#griefer.

8. "Studio Gangster." *Urban Dictionary*. Last modified February 16, 2025. https://web.archive.org/web/20250216055644/https://www.urbandictionary.com/define.php?term=Studio%20Gangster.

9. "Pull Up." *Urban Dictionary*. Last modified November 21, 2016. https://web.archive.org/web/20250216055531/https://www.urbandictionary.com/define.php?term=pull%20up.

10. internetbasedghosts. "Myspace-Era Electronics - Digigrind, Speednoise, Spazzpop, Trashcore." *Rate Your Music*. Last modified February 16, 2025. https://rateyourmusic.com/list/internetbasedghosts/myspace-era-electronics-digigrind-speednoise-spazzpop-trashcore/.

5. Terms and Term Sheets

1. *"Short-termism."* Wikipedia. Last modified January 2025. Accessed February 1, 2025. https://en.wikipedia.org/wiki/Short-termism.

2. Shontell, Alyson. "Jack Dorsey Was 'Heartbroken' When Instagram Sold to Facebook." *Business Insider*, May 6, 2013, 11:34 a.m. ET. Archived February 16, 2025. https://web.archive.org/web/20250216175953/https://www.businessinsider.com/jack-dorsey-was-heartbroken-when-instagram-sold-to-facebook-2013-5.

3. "Meta Reports Fourth Quarter and Full Year 2023 Results; Initiates Quarterly Dividend," *PR Newswire*, February 1, 2024, https://www.prnewswire.com/news-releases/

meta-reports-fourth-quarter-and-full-year-2023-results-initiates-quarterly-dividend-302051285.html.
4. Ibid.
5. Ibid.
6. "Meta Platforms Inc. Lobbying Profile," *OpenSecrets*, accessed February 16, 2025, https://www.opensecrets.org/federal-lobbying/clients/summary?id=D000033563.
7. "Client Profile: Philip Morris International," *OpenSecrets*, archived February 11, 2024, https://web.archive.org/web/20240211151431/https://www.opensecrets.org/federal-lobbying/clients/summary?id=D000055403.
8. "EU Reassesses Tech Probes into Apple, Google, Meta, FT Reports," *Reuters*, January 14, 2025,https://www.reuters.com/technology/eu-reassesses-tech-probes-into-apple-google-meta-ft-reports-2025-01-14/.
9. "PayPal Says It Never Intended to Fine Users for Misinformation," *Reuters*, October 10, 2022,https://www.reuters.com/business/finance/paypal-says-it-never-intended-fine-users-misinformation-bloomberg-news-2022-10-10/.
10. "Instagram Community Guidelines," *Instagram Help Center*, archived December 26, 2024,https://web.archive.org/web/20241226182722/https://help.instagram.com/581066165581870/.
11. Ibid.
12. Ibid.
13. "Why Am I Being Asked to Select a Category for My Instagram Account?" *Instagram Help Center*, archived September 25, 2021, https://web.archive.org/web/20210925035902/https://help.instagram.com/401142933819111?helpref=related.
14. "Cybersquatting," *Wikipedia*, last modified February 16, 2025, https://en.wikipedia.org/wiki/Cybersquatting.

6. Free Lunch

1. Chris Buetti, "How I Eat for Free in NYC Using Python, Automation, Artificial Intelligence, and Instagram," *Medium*, archived February 24, 2019, https://web.archive.org/web/20240829062747/https://medium.com/@chrisbuetti/how-i-eat-for-free-in-nyc-using-python-automation-artificial-intelligence-and-instagram-a5ed8a1e2a10.
2. Ibid.
3. Ibid.
4. Ibid.
5. Ibid.
6. Ibid.
7. Ibid.
8. Ibid.
9. Ibid.
10. Cheddar. "Data Scientist Created Automated Instagram Account to Score Free Food in NYC." *Cheddar*, September 23, 2020. Accessed February 15, 2025. https://web.archive.org/web/20200923164706/https://www.cheddar.com/media/data-scientist-created-automated-instagram-account-to-score-free-food-in-nyc/.
11. Ibid.
12. dlgeek, comment on "The Impact of Artificial Intelligence on Digital Marketing," *Hacker News*, April 2, 2019, https://news.ycombinator.com/item?id=19554425.

13. Xpolent, comment on "Machine Learning Instagram Bot," *BlackHatWorld*, accessed February 16, 2025, https://www.blackhatworld.com/seo/machine-learning-instagram-bot.1109101/.
14. Cheddar. "Data Scientist Created Automated Instagram Account to Score Free Food in NYC." *Cheddar*, September 23, 2020. Accessed February 15, 2025. https://web.archive.org/web/20200923164706/https://www.cheddar.com/media/data-scientist-created-automated-instagram-account-to-score-free-food-in-nyc/.
15. Ibid.
16. Ibid.
17. Ibid.
18. Ibid.
19. Ibid.
20. Ibid.
21. Ibid.
22. Ibid.
23. Ibid.
24. Ibid.
25. Ibid.
26. Ibid.
27. Chris Buetti, "Under the Influencer," *LinkedIn*, accessed February 16, 2025, https://www.linkedin.com/posts/chris-buetti_socialmedia-instagram-automation-activity-6515668873289703424-Twyc?utm_source=share&utm_medium=member_desktop&rcm=ACoAAAvPs44BnprjW-EGfk5uxn0-YPvUx6RiVJE.

7. Gitting Gud

1. *Know Your Meme*. "Git Gud." Added by MScratch 11 years ago. Accessed 16 February 2025. https://knowyourmeme.com/memes/git-gud.
2. Ibid.
3. Cade, DL. "Instagram Shuts Down Popular Botting Service Instagress." *PetaPixel*, April 20, 2017. Accessed February 16, 2025. https://web.archive.org/web/20250210034157/https://petapixel.com/2017/04/20/instagram-shuts-popular-botting-service-instagress/.
4. Issagholian, Aleh. "The Dark Side of the Screen: The Negative Impact of Influencers in Society." *Clark Chronicle*, 16 May 2024. https://clarkchronicle.com/uncategorized/2024/05/16/the-dark-side-of-the-screen-the-negative-impact-of-influencers-in-society/.
5. *Know Your Meme*. "RTFM." Added by Chris Menning 15 years ago. Accessed 16 February 2025. https://knowyourmeme.com/memes/rtfm.
6. Urban Dictionary. "PC4PC." *Urban Dictionary*, August 10, 2024. Archived at Wayback Machine. Accessed February 16, 2025. https://web.archive.org/web/20240810080510/https://www.urbandictionary.com/define.php?term=PC4PC.
7. Over one thousand followers
8. Tim O'Hearn. "52 Books in 2016." *Tim O'Hearn's Blog*, December 31, 2016. Accessed 16 February 2025. https://www.tjohearn.com/2016/12/31/52-books-in-2016/.
9. *Know Your Meme*. "Here in My Garage." Added by Don Caldwell 9 years ago. Accessed 16 February 2025. https://knowyourmeme.com/memes/here-in-my-garage.

10. *tmoney12*, "Tai Lopez Social Media Marketing Course," *Reddit*, December 3, 2016, https://www.reddit.com/r/DigitalMarketing/comments/5q8sh9/tai_lopez_social_media_marketing_course/.

8. Safeguarding and Shadowbans Part I

1. Jagex. *Parents' Guide*. May 18, 2024. Archived at the Wayback Machine. https://web.archive.org/web/20240518202015/https://support.runescape.com/hc/en-gb/articles/206747519-Parents-guide.
2. Ibid.
3. Jagex. *Harassment*. February 10, 2025. Archived at the Wayback Machine. https://web.archive.org/web/20250210060831/https://support.runescape.com/hc/en-gb/articles/360001155998-Harassment.
4. Memon, Aksha M., Shiva G. Sharma, Satyajit S. Mohite, and Shailesh Jain. "The Role of Online Social Networking on Deliberate Self-Harm and Suicidality in Adolescents: A Systematized Review of Literature." *Indian Journal of Psychiatry* 60, no. 4 (2018): 384–392. https://doi.org/10.4103/psychiatry.IndianJPsychiatry_414_17.
5. Instagram. *Staying Safe – Instagram Help Center*. January 12, 2024. Archived. https://web.archive.org/web/20240112021132/https://help.instagram.com/1502695926736394.
6. Instagram. "A Parents' Guide to Instagram." *Instagram Help Center*. Accessed February 15, 2025. https://help.instagram.com/299484113584685?ref=ig_about.
7. Child Mind Institute. *About Us*. Archived January 23, 2025. https://web.archive.org/web/20250123185308/https://childmind.org/about-us.
8. ConnectSafely.org. *About Us*. Archived April 21, 2024. https://web.archive.org/web/20240421112527/https://connectsafely.org/about-us/.
9. Instagram. "A Parents' Guide to Instagram." *Instagram Help Center*. Accessed February 15, 2025. https://help.instagram.com/299484113584685?ref=ig_about.
10. Ibid.
11. Ibid.
12. Ibid.
13. The YouTube Team. *Update to YouTube*. November 10, 2021. Archived February 2, 2025. https://web.archive.org/web/20250202153658/https://blog.youtube/news-and-events/update-to-youtube/.
14. Facebook user. *PETITION FOR FACEBOOK....* Created October 26, 2009. https://www.facebook.com/groups/72419683550/.
15. Meta. *The People Behind Meta's Review Teams*. Archived January 8, 2025. https://web.archive.org/web/20250108155340/https://transparency.meta.com/enforcement/detecting-violations/people-behind-our-review-teams/.
16. Weber, Lauren, and Deepa Seetharaman. "The Worst Job in Technology: Staring at Human Depravity to Keep It Off Facebook." *The Wall Street Journal*, December 27, 2017, 1:13 p.m. ET. Archived December 27, 2017. https://web.archive.org/web/20171227194836/https://www.wsj.com/articles/the-worst-job-in-technology-staring-at-human-depravity-to-keep-it-off-facebook-1514398398.
17. Meta. *Reviewing High-Impact Content Accurately via Our Cross-Check System*. Updated November 12, 2024. Archived December 27, 2024. https://web.archive.org/web/20241227021533/https://transparency.meta.com/enforcement/detecting-violations/reviewing-high-visibility-content-accurately/.

18. chrriihs. "I Am a Facebook/Instagram Content Moderator AMA." *Reddit*, January 21, 2021. https://www.reddit.com/r/AMA/comments/ktf8td/i_am_a_facebookinstagram_content_moderator_ama/.

19. Weber, Lauren, and Deepa Seetharaman. "The Worst Job in Technology: Staring at Human Depravity to Keep It Off Facebook." *The Wall Street Journal*, December 27, 2017, 1:13 p.m. ET. Archived December 27, 2017. https://web.archive.org/web/20171227194836/https://www.wsj.com/articles/the-worst-job-in-technology-staring-at-human-depravity-to-keep-it-off-facebook-1514398398.

20. Gray, Chris. "As a Facebook Moderator I Saw the Worst of Humanity. We Need to Be Valued." *The Guardian*, December 9, 2019. Archived November 22, 2024. https://web.archive.org/web/20241122063749/https://www.theguardian.com/commentisfree/2019/dec/09/facebook-moderator-worst-of-humanity-valued.

21. Ibid.

22. Ibid.

23. Jones, Sam, and agencies. "MySpace Removes 90,000 Sex Offenders." *The Guardian*, February 4, 2009, 10:01 EST. https://www.theguardian.com/technology/2009/feb/04/myspace-social-networking-sex-offenders.

9. Safeguarding and Shadowbans Part II

1. Chris Buetti, "How I Eat for Free in NYC Using Python, Automation, Artificial Intelligence, and Instagram," *Medium*, archived February 24, 2019, https://web.archive.org/web/20240829062747/https://medium.com/@chrisbuetti/how-i-eat-for-free-in-nyc-using-python-automation-artificial-intelligence-and-instagram-a5ed8a1e2a10.

2. Maheshwari, Sapna. "Uncovering Instagram Bots With a New Kind of Detective Work." *The New York Times*, March 12, 2018. Accessed February 15, 2025. https://web.archive.org/web/20241231201828/https://www.nytimes.com/2018/03/12/business/media/instagram-bots.html.

3. Ibid.

4. Ibid.

5. "Shopify Acquires Influencer Marketing Startup Dovetale." *Ecommerce News*, April 13, 2022. Accessed February 15, 2025. https://ecommercenews.eu/shopify-acquires-influencer-marketing-startup-dovetale/.

6. Chris Buetti, "How I Eat for Free in NYC Using Python, Automation, Artificial Intelligence, and Instagram," *Medium*, archived February 24, 2019, https://web.archive.org/web/20240829062747/https://medium.com/@chrisbuetti/how-i-eat-for-free-in-nyc-using-python-automation-artificial-intelligence-and-instagram-a5ed8a1e2a10.

7. G-S-T. "Excellent Results Using Well Aged Instagram Accounts." *BlackHatWorld*, December 5, 2016. Accessed February 15, 2025. https://www.blackhatworld.com/seo/excellent-results-using-well-aged-instagram-accounts.897959/.

8. mdtanos. Comment on "Instagram Cracking Down ?¿." *BlackHatWorld*, August 25, 2019. Accessed February 15, 2025. https://www.blackhatworld.com/seo/instagram-cracking-down.1155389/#post-12388662.

9. Henry Cooper. Comment on "2017 Instagram Daily Limits" by coda281. *BlackHatWorld*, January 9, 2017. Accessed February 15, 2025. https://www.blackhatworld.com/seo/2017-instagram-daily-limits.906495/#post-9630676.

10. Instagram_Marketer. "Instagram Action Limits in 2023." *Reddit*, June 10, 2023. Accessed February 15, 2025. https://www.reddit.com/r/InstagramMarketing/comments/145t1gu/instagram_action_limits_in_2023.
11. Instagram. "A Parents' Guide to Instagram." *Instagram Help Center*. Accessed February 15, 2025. https://help.instagram.com/299484113584685?ref=ig_about.
12. "Reducing Inauthentic Activity on Instagram." *Instagram Blog*, November 19, 2018. Accessed February 15, 2025. https://web.archive.org/web/20250119063012/https://about.instagram.com/blog/announcements/reducing-inauthentic-activity-on-instagram.
13. Meta. "How Facebook Uses Artificial Intelligence to Moderate Content." *Facebook Help Center*. Accessed February 15, 2025. https://www.facebook.com/help/1584908458516247/.
14. Weber, Lauren, and Deepa Seetharaman. "The Worst Job in Technology: Staring at Human Depravity to Keep It Off Facebook." *The Wall Street Journal*, December 27, 2017, 1:13 p.m. ET. Archived December 27, 2017. https://web.archive.org/web/20171227194836/https://www.wsj.com/articles/the-worst-job-in-technology-staring-at-human-depravity-to-keep-it-off-facebook-1514398398.
15. Meta. "About Meta's Oversight Board." *Instagram Help Center*. Accessed February 15, 2025. https://help.instagram.com/185474462526094/?helpref=related_articles.
16. Kayser-Bril, Nicolas. "Facebook Goes After the Creator of InstaPy, a Tool That Automates Instagram Likes." *AlgorithmWatch*, November 16, 2021. Accessed February 15, 2025. https://web.archive.org/web/20250121133344/https://algorithmwatch.org/en/facebook-goes-after-instapy/.
17. Instagram. "Shedding More Light on How Instagram Works." *Instagram Blog*, June 8, 2021. Accessed February 15, 2025. https://web.archive.org/web/20250106152854/https://about.instagram.com/blog/announcements/shedding-more-light-on-how-instagram-works.
18. "Shadow Ban." *Urban Dictionary*, accessed February 15, 2025. https://web.archive.org/web/20250110221022/https://www.urbandictionary.com/define.php?term=shadowban.
19. Ibid.
20. Ibid.
21. OldKingHamlet. "Anyone Know a Spend Amount That'll Get the Attention of an Account Manager at FB?" *Reddit*, August 30, 2023. Accessed February 15, 2025. https://www.reddit.com/r/FacebookAds/comments/165m3f9/comment/jymhkvg/?utm_source=share&utm_medium=web3x&utm_name=web3xcss&utm_term=1&utm_content=share_button.
22. Ibid.
23. samanthahah. "Instagram Disabled - How I Got My Account Back." *Reddit*, April 13, 2023. Accessed February 15, 2025. https://www.reddit.com/r/Instagram/comments/12las7u/instagram_disabled_how_i_got_my_account_back/.

10. Social Media Marketing Panels and Sockpuppet Botnets

1. Confessore, Nicholas, Gabriel J. X. Dance, Mark Hansen, and Richard Harris. "The Follower Factory." *New York Times*, January 27, 2018. Accessed February 15, 2025. https://web.archive.org/web/20250112143607/https://www.nytimes.com/interactive/2018/01/27/technology/social-media-bots.html.

2. Ibid.
3. New York State Attorney General. "Attorney General James Announces Ground-breaking Settlement with Sellers of Fake Followers." *New York State Attorney General*, January 30, 2019. Accessed February 15, 2025. https://web.archive.org/web/20250213223749/https://ag.ny.gov/press-release/2019/attorney-general-james-announces-groundbreaking-settlement-sellers-fake-followers.
4. *Media Mister*. "Buy Instagram Followers." *Media Mister*. Accessed February 15, 2025. https://web.archive.org/web/20250209111800/https://www.mediamister.com/buy-instagram-followers.
5. Eordogh, Fruzsina. "Inside an Instagram Bot Farm." *Vice*, August 10, 2015. Accessed February 15, 2025. https://web.archive.org/web/20230712141134/https://www.vice.com/en/article/4x3zy9/inside-an-instagram-bot-farm.
6. Global News. "Bieber Loses 3.5 Million Followers as Instagram Deletes Bogus Accounts." *Global News*, February 22, 2014. Accessed February 15, 2025. https://web.archive.org/web/20210222053534/https://globalnews.ca/news/1735984/bieber-loses-3-5-million-followers-as-instagram-deletes-bogus-accounts/.
7. Smith, Matt. "The Instagram API: Everything You Need to Know." *Later*, updated April 8, 2018. Accessed February 15, 2025. https://web.archive.org/web/20250103205217/https://later.com/blog/instagram-api/.
8. Confessore, Nicholas, Gabriel J. X. Dance, Mark Hansen, and Richard Harris. "The Follower Factory." *New York Times*, January 27, 2018. Accessed February 15, 2025. https://web.archive.org/web/20250112143607/https://www.nytimes.com/interactive/2018/01/27/technology/social-media-bots.html.
9. New York State Attorney General. "Attorney General James Announces Ground-breaking Settlement with Sellers of Fake Followers." *New York State Attorney General*, January 30, 2019. Accessed February 15, 2025. https://web.archive.org/web/20250213223749/https://ag.ny.gov/press-release/2019/attorney-general-ames-announces-groundbreaking-settlement-sellers-fake-followers.
10. *Explanations of instant followers by Buzzoid.com retrieved in 2024. This page has not been archived.*
11. Ibid.
12. There are now three types, including "Exclusive/VIP"
13. *Media Mister*. "Buy Instagram Followers." *Media Mister*. Accessed February 15, 2025. https://web.archive.org/web/20250209111800/https://www.mediamister.com/buy-instagram-followers.
14. Ibid.
15. Ibid.
16. *Poprey*. "Homepage." *Poprey*, 2024. Accessed February 15, 2025. https://web.archive.org/web/20240415063455/https://poprey.com/.
17. Ibid.
18. Maheshwari, Sapna. "Instagram Bots Are Inflating Instagram Egos." *The New York Times*, June 6, 2017. Accessed February 15, 2025. https://web.archive.org/web/20241207222636/https://www.nytimes.com/2017/06/06/business/media/instagram-bots.html.
19. New York State Attorney General. "Attorney General James Announces Ground-breaking Settlement with Sellers of Fake Followers." *New York State Attorney General*, January 30, 2019. Accessed February 15, 2025. https://web.archive.org/web/20250213223749/https://ag.ny.gov/press-release/2019/attorney-general-james-announces-groundbreaking-settlement-sellers-fake-followers.

20. Cheddar. "Data Scientist Created Automated Instagram Account to Score Free Food in NYC." *Cheddar*, September 23, 2020. Accessed February 15, 2025. https://web.archive.org/web/20200923164706/https://www.cheddar.com/media/data-scientist-created-automated-instagram-account-to-score-free-food-in-nyc/.

21. Maheshwari, Sapna. "Uncovering Instagram Bots With a New Kind of Detective Work." *The New York Times*, March 12, 2018. Accessed February 15, 2025. https://web.archive.org/web/20241231201828/https://www.nytimes.com/2018/03/12/business/media/instagram-bots.html.

22. Although he did have significant post karma

23. maciballz. "A Feast for Crows: The Fall of /u/Unidan." *r/MuseumOfReddit*, November 5, 2014. https://www.reddit.com/r/MuseumOfReddit/comments/2m5q11/a_feast_for_crows_the_fall_of_uunidan/.

24. *Wikipedia contributors.* "Unidan." *Wikipedia*, last modified February 15, 2025. Accessed February 15, 2025. https://en.wikipedia.org/wiki/Unidan.

25. sgtmum. "Jackdaws Aren't Crows." *r/copypasta*, January 7, 2020. https://www.reddit.com/r/copypasta/comments/ektjhq/jackdaws_arent_crows/.

26. maciballz. "A Feast for Crows: The Fall of /u/Unidan." *r/MuseumOfReddit*, November 5, 2014. https://www.reddit.com/r/MuseumOfReddit/comments/2m5q11/a_feast_for_crows_the_fall_of_uunidan/.

27. Confessore, Nicholas, Gabriel J. X. Dance, Mark Hansen, and Richard Harris. "The Follower Factory." *New York Times*, January 27, 2018. Accessed February 15, 2025. https://web.archive.org/web/20250112143607/https://www.nytimes.com/interactive/2018/01/27/technology/social-media-bots.html.

28. Eordogh, Fruzsina. "Inside an Instagram Bot Farm." *Vice*, August 10, 2015. Accessed February 15, 2025. https://web.archive.org/web/20230712141134/https://www.vice.com/en/article/4x3zy9/inside-an-instagram-bot-farm.

11. The Five Eras

1. "Instagram," *Wikipedia*, last modified February 16, 2025, https://en.wikipedia.org/wiki/Instagram.

2. Mislav Marohnić, "mislav/Instagram," GitHub, last modified February 16, 2025, https://github.com/mislav/instagram/commits/master/?after=9a21c94de154c2bae-b7c241f2780ae4afbeb6bb7+104.

3. Mislav Marohnić, "Creating the Missing Instagram Web Interface," *Mislav.net*, December 7, 2010, https://web.archive.org/web/20240305005509/https://mislav.net/2010/12/instagram-web/.

4. Kevin Systrom, "A More Open Platform: The Instagram API," *Instagram Blog*, February 7, 2011, 10:25 p.m., https://web.archive.org/web/20110804220514/https://instagr.am/blog/40/instagram-api.

5. "Snapchat," *Wikipedia*, last modified February 16, 2025, https://en.wikipedia.org/wiki/Snapchat.

6. Federico Viticci, "Instagram 2.0 Now Available: Live Filters, New Camera UI, Faster Engine," *MacStories*, September 20, 2011, 18:31 CUT, https://web.archive.org/web/20250123105944/https://www.macstories.net/reviews/instagram-2-0-now-available-live-filters-new-camera-ui-faster-engine/.

7. "Introducing Instagram for Android," *Instagram Blog*, April 3, 2012, https://web.archive.org/web/20241005144801/https://about.instagram.com/blog/announcements/introducing-instagram-for-android.

8. "Facebook," *Wikipedia*, last modified February 14, 2025, accessed February 16, 2025, https://en.wikipedia.org/wiki/Facebook.

9. Ibid.

10. Lum, Jessica. "Instagram Update Scraps Popularity for Explore Tab." *PetaPixel*, June 26, 2012, accessed February 16, 2025. https://web.archive.org/web/20210515152601/https://petapixel.com/2012/06/26/instagram-update-scraps-popularity-for-explore-tab/.

11. Knopper. "Who is Making Good Money with Instagram These Days." *BlackHatWorld*, September 27, 2012. https://www.blackhatworld.com/seo/who-is-making-good-money-with-instagram-this-days.486903/.

12. JackMorris. "Instagram Bot Discussion/Request: Begging, Ideas, Dreams." *BlackHatWorld*, October 8, 2012. https://www.blackhatworld.com/seo/instagram-bot-discussion-request-begging-ideas-dreams.551752/.

13. "Botstagram Sold Out." *Botstagram*, archived December 9, 2012. https://web.archive.org/web/20121209025500/http://botstagram.com/.

14. Kullin, Hans. "Instagram's Increasing Problem with Spam," *Media Culpa*, November 7, 2012, archived September 13, 2024, https://web.archive.org/web/20240913010244/https://www.kullin.net/2012/11/instagram-spam/.

15. Soci.ai. "The Evolution of Instagram Ads." *Soci.ai*, October 16, 2017, archived September 18, 2024. https://web.archive.org/web/20240918191409/https://www.soci.ai/blog/infographic-evolution-instagram-ads/.

16. Cade, DL. "Facebook Removes Member Counts from Instagram API After Rumors Hit Stock." *Petapixel*, January 8, 2013, archived May 15, 2021. https://web.archive.org/web/20210515031507/https://petapixel.com/2013/01/08/facebook-removes-member-counts-from-instagram-api-after-rumors-hit-stock/.

17. Constine, Josh. "Instagram Hits 100 Million Monthly Users 28 Months After Launch." *TechCrunch*, February 26, 2013, archived January 22, 2025. https://web.archive.org/web/20250122152850/https://techcrunch.com/2013/02/26/instagram-100-million/.

18. Taylor, Colleen. "Facebook Announces Instagram Video: 15-Second Clips with Filters, Facebook Sharing, and More." *TechCrunch*, June 20, 2013, archived January 1, 2025. https://web.archive.org/web/20250101114612/https://techcrunch.com/2013/06/20/facebook-instagram-video/.

19. "FollowLiker." *FollowLiker*, archived June 1, 2013. https://web.archive.org/web/20130601003014/http://followliker.com/.

20. "Instagress Beta." *Instagress*, archived September 8, 2013. https://web.archive.org/web/20130908191944/http://instagress.com/.

21. Kelly, Meghan. "Here's the first Instagram ad — thanks, Michael Kors." VentureBeat, November 1, 2013, 11:36 AM. https://venturebeat.com/business/heres-the-first-instagram-ad-thanks-michael-kors/.

22. Andross. "First." *BlackHatWorld*, Jul. 31, 2014, https://www.blackhatworld.com/seo/first.693142/.

23. Constine, Josh. "Instagram Hits 300 Million Monthly Users To Surpass Twitter, Keeps It Real With Verified Badges." *TechCrunch*, Dec. 10, 2014, https://web.archive.org/web/20250115020920/https://techcrunch.com/2014/12/10/not-a-fad/.

24. Kennedy, John R. "Bieber Loses 3.5 Million Followers as Instagram Deletes Bogus Accounts." *Global News*, Dec. 19, 2014, https://web.archive.org/web/20210222053534/https://globalnews.ca/news/1735984/bieber-

loses-3-5-million-followers-as-instagram-deletes-bogus-accounts/. Accessed Feb. 15, 2025.

25. Constine, Josh. "Instagram Kills Off Feed Reading Apps." *TechCrunch*, Nov. 17, 2015, https://web.archive.org/web/20250104005503/https://techcrunch.-com/2015/11/17/just-instagram/. Accessed Feb. 15, 2025.

26. "See Posts You Care About First in Your Feed." *Instagram Blog*, Mar. 15, 2016, https://web.archive.org/web/20241212224401/https://about.instagram.com/blog/an-nouncements/see-posts-you-care-about-first-in-your-feed. Accessed Feb. 15, 2025.

27. Perez, Sarah. "Instagram Officially Announces Its New Business Tools." *TechCrunch*, May 31, 2016. https://web.archive.org/web/20250214052129/https://techcrunch.-com/2016/05/31/instagram-officially-announces-its-new-business-tools/.

28. This, Emerson. "Everything You Need to Know About Instagram API Integration." *CSS-Tricks*, August 8, 2016 (Updated May 13, 2019). https://we-b.archive.org/web/20240625023240/https://css-tricks.com/everything-need-know-instagram-api-integration/#instagram-api-part-one-understanding.

29. "Portfolio." *Gram MultiTool*, accessed August 20, 2016. https://we-b.archive.org/web/20160820141920/http://grammultitool.com/#portfolio.

30. "TikTok." *Wikipedia*, last modified January 14, 2025. https://en.wikipedia.org/wiki/TikTok.

31. Grossman, Tim. "Initial Commit." *InstaPy/InstaPy*, GitHub, 26 Sept. 2016, https://github.com/InstaPy/InstaPy/commit/3bf011adf4c225f1fc0d428d8c5d-c7b103867d9f.

32. Cade, DL. "Instagram Shuts Down Popular Botting Service Instagress." *PetaPixel*, April 20, 2017. Accessed February 16, 2025. https://we-b.archive.org/web/20250210034157/https://petapixel.com/2017/04/20/instagram-shuts-popular-botting-service-instagress/.

33. Grigonis, Hillary. "Four More Programs Bite the Dust in Instagram's Quiet Battle Against the Bots." *Digital Trends*, 15 May 2017, 2:11 PM PST, https://we-b.archive.org/web/20190210234355/https://www.digitaltrends.com/social-media/in-stagram-shuts-down-four-more-bots/.

34. Maheshwari, Sapna. "How Bots Are Inflating Instagram Egos." *The New York Times*, June 6, 2017. Accessed February 15, 2025. https://we-b.archive.org/web/20250217042425/https://www.nytimes.com/2017/06/06/busi-ness/media/instagram-bots.htmll.

35. Stiletto. "JARVEE - Social Media Automation Tool for: Facebook, Instagram, Twitter, Pinterest, LinkedIn, Tumblr." *Black Hat World*, 4 Sept. 2017, https://www.blackhat-world.com/seo/jarvee-social-media-automation-tool-for-facebook-instagram-twitter-pinterest-linkedin-tumblr.969615/.

36. JJJackson. "[GMT2] Gram Multitool 2 | Instagram Automation Software." *Black Hat World*, 17 Oct. 2017, https://www.blackhatworld.com/seo/gmt2-gram-multitool-2-instagram-automation-software.980622/.

37. Confessore, Nicholas, Gabriel J. X. Dance, Mark Hansen, and Richard Harris. "The Follower Factory." *New York Times*, January 27, 2018. Accessed February 15, 2025. https://web.archive.org/web/20250112143607/https://www.nytimes.com/interac tive/2018/01/27/technology/social-media-bots.html.

38. Gummadi, Ravi. "Instagram Graph API Launches and Instagram API Platform Depre-cation." *Facebook Developers*, 30 Jan. 2018,https://web.archive.org/web/ 20250104030923/
https://developers.facebook.com/blog/post/2018/01/30/instagram-graph-api-updates/.

39. Facebook Inc., Instagram, LLC. *Complaint against Leon Hedges, Arend Nollen, David Pasanen, Social Media Series Limited*. 3:2019cv02262, Justia, https://docs.justia.com/cases/federal/district-courts/california/candce/3:2019cv02262/341343/1/.

40. Maheshwari, Sapna. "Uncovering Instagram Bots With a New Kind of Detective Work." *The New York Times*, March 12, 2018. Accessed February 15, 2025. https://web.archive.org/web/20241231201828/https://www.nytimes.com/2018/03/12/business/media/instagram-bots.html.

41. "Facebook–Cambridge Analytica data scandal." *Wikipedia*, last modified February 15, 2025. https://en.wikipedia.org/wiki/Facebook%E2%80%93Cambridge_Analytica_data_scandal.

42. Constine, Josh. "Instagram Suddenly Chokes off Developers as Facebook Chases Privacy." *TechCrunch*, April 2, 2018. Accessed February 15, 2025. https://web.archive.org/web/20250115012520/https://techcrunch.com/2018/04/02/instagram-api-limit/.

43. Constine, Josh. "Instagram Hits 1 Billion Monthly Users, Up from 800M in September." TechCrunch, June 20, 2018. Accessed February 15, 2025. https://web.archive.org/web/20250122044148/https://techcrunch.com/2018/06/20/instagram-1-billion-users/.

44. Hatmaker, Taylor. "Instagram Announces Verification Requests, Transparency Tools and Stronger 2FA." *TechCrunch*, August 28, 2018. Accessed February 15, 2025. https://techcrunch.com/2018/08/28/instagram-request-verification-2fa-about-this-account/.

45. Isaac, Mike. "Instagram's Co-Founders to Step Down From Company." *The New York Times*, September 24, 2018. Accessed February 15, 2025. https://web.archive.org/web/20250211163958/https://www.nytimes.com/2018/09/24/technology/instagram-cofounders-resign.html.

46. DeKoven, Louis F., Trevor Pottinger, Stefan Savage, Geoffrey M. Voelker, and Nektarios Leontiadis. "Following Their Footsteps: Characterizing Account Automation Abuse and Defenses." *Facebook Research*, October 31, 2018. Accessed February 15, 2025. https://research.facebook.com/publications/following-their-footsteps-characterizing-account-automation-abuse-and-defenses/.

47. "Reducing Inauthentic Activity on Instagram." *Instagram Blog*, November 19, 2018. Accessed February 15, 2025. https://web.archive.org/web/20250119063012/https://about.instagram.com/blog/announcements/reducing-inauthentic-activity-on-instagram.

48. New York State Attorney General. "Attorney General James Announces Groundbreaking Settlement with Sellers of Fake Followers." *New York State Attorney General*, January 30, 2019. Accessed February 15, 2025. https://web.archive.org/web/20250213223749/https://ag.ny.gov/press-release/2019/attorney-general-james-announces-groundbreaking-settlement-sellers-fake-followers.

49. Grewal, Paul. "Cracking Down on the Sale of Fake Accounts, Likes and Followers." *Facebook News*, March 1, 2019. Accessed February 15, 2025. https://about.fb.com/news/2019/03/sale-of-fake-accounts-likes-and-followers/.

50. Facebook Inc., Instagram, LLC. *Complaint against Leon Hedges, Arend Nollen, David Pasanen, Social Media Series Limited*. 3:2019cv02262, Justia, https://docs.justia.com/cases/federal/district-courts/california/candce/3:2019cv02262/341343/1/.

51. Constine, Josh. "Instagram Officially Tests Hiding Like Counts." *TechCrunch*, April 30, 2019. Accessed February 15, 2025. https://web.archive.org/web/20250120094156/https://techcrunch.com/2019/04/30/instagram-hidden-like-counter/.

52. "Instagram Follow Action Blocks from This Morning 30 May." *BlackHatWorld*, May 30, 2019. Accessed February 15, 2025. https://www.blackhatworld.com/seo/insta-gram-follow-action-blocks-from-this-morning-30-may.1124826/page-17#post-12151911.

53. Robertson, Adi. "Facebook Is Settling One of Its Lawsuits Over Fake Likes." *The Verge*, September 12, 2019. Accessed February 15, 2025. https://we-b.archive.org/web/20250214050922/https://www.theverge.-com/2019/9/12/20862620/facebook-instagram-new-zealand-bot-fake-like-company-lawsuit-settlement.

54. Milenkowich, Alex. "[GMT2] Gram Multitool 2 | Instagram Automation Software." *BlackHatWorld*, December 17, 2019. Accessed February 15, 2025. https://www.black-hatworld.com/seo/gmt2-gram-multitool-2-instagram-automation-soft-ware.980622/page-148.

55. Romero, Jessica. "Taking Legal Action Against Data Scraping." *Facebook News*, October 1, 2020. Accessed February 15, 2025. https://about.fb.-com/news/2020/10/taking-legal-action-against-data-scraping/.

56. Rodriguez, Salvador. "TikTok Passes Instagram as Second-Most Popular Social App for U.S. Teens." *CNBC*, October 6, 2020. Accessed February 15, 2025. https://we-b.archive.org/web/20250127200703/https://www.cnbc.com/2020/10/06/tiktok-passes-instagram-as-second-most-popular-social-app-for-us-teens.html.

57. Rimm, Hannah. "Instagram's New Ad Guidelines Could Have a Major Impact on OnlyFans." *Refinery29*, January 23, 2021. Accessed February 15, 2025. https://www.refinery29.com/en-gb/2021/01/10275667/instagram-ad-guidelines-onlyfans.

58. Perez, Sarah. "Facebook and Instagram Will Now Allow Users to Hide 'Like' Counts on Posts." *TechCrunch*, May 26, 2021. Accessed February 15, 2025. https://we-b.archive.org/web/20240513020529/https://techcrunch.com/2021/05/26/facebook-and-instagram-will-now-allow-users-to-hide-like-counts-on-posts/.

59. "Meta's 2021 Updates to Guide Your Advertising Efforts Through 2022." *Responsival*, March 2022. Accessed February 15, 2025. https://we-b.archive.org/web/20241205032521/https://www.responsival.com/post/metas-2021-updates-to-guide-your-advertising-efforts-through-2022.

60. Kayser-Bril, Nicolas. "AlgorithmWatch Forced to Shut Down Instagram Monitoring Project After Threats from Facebook." *AlgorithmWatch*, August 13, 2021. Accessed February 15, 2025. https://web.archive.org/web/20250214045937/https://algo-rithmwatch.org/en/instagram-research-shut-down-by-facebook/.

61. "Facebook," *Wikipedia*, last modified February 14, 2025, accessed February 16, 2025, https://en.wikipedia.org/wiki/Facebook.

62. Kayser-Bril, Nicolas. "Facebook Goes After the Creator of InstaPy, a Tool That Auto-mates Instagram Likes." *AlgorithmWatch*, November 16, 2021. Accessed February 15, 2025. https://web.archive.org/web/20250121133344/https://algo-rithmwatch.org/en/facebook-goes-after-instapy/.

63. Jarvee. "Service Permanently Closed." *Jarvee*, Web. 1 Oct. 2022. https://we-b.archive.org/web/20221001021020/https://jarvee.com/.

12. Bulbs and Flowers

1. Mislav Marohnić, "mislav/Instagram," GitHub, last modified February 16, 2025,

https://github.com/mislav/instagram/commits/master/?after=9a21c94de154c2bae-b7c241f2780ae4afbeb6bb7+104.

2. Mislav Marohnić, "Creating the Missing Instagram Web Interface," *Mislav.net*, December 7, 2010, https://web.archive.org/web/20240305005509/https://mislav.net/2010/12/instagram-web/.

3. "Instagram Platform Update," *Instagram Developers*, November 17, 2015, archived February 16, 2025, https://web.archive.org/web/20170312194745/https://developers.instagram.com/post/133424514006/instagram-platform-update.

4. Mislav Marohnić, "Creating the Missing Instagram Web Interface," *Mislav.net*, December 7, 2010, https://web.archive.org/web/20240305005509/https://mislav.net/2010/12/instagram-web/.

5. Ibid.

6. MyFriendBot. "Homepage." *MyFriendBot*, November 2, 2005. Archived at Wayback Machine. Accessed February 16, 2025.

7. Knopper. "Who is Making Good Money with Instagram These Days." *BlackHatWorld*, September 27, 2012. https://www.blackhatworld.com/seo/who-is-making-good-money-with-instagram-this-days.486903/.

8. zenoGlitch. Comment on "Which is the Best Tumblr Bot." *Black Hat World*, March 7, 2013. In "Which is the Best Tumblr Bot" thread. Accessed February 18, 2025. https://www.blackhatworld.com/seo/which-is-the-best-tumblr-bot.539720/page-2.

9. Botstagram. "Botstagram Homepage." Accessed February 18, 2025. https://web.archive.org/web/20121106185011/http://botstagram.com/.

10. BoomInfo. "xGram 1.0.3.6: Bot for Creating and Managing Instagram Accounts." Accessed February 18, 2025. https://boominfo.org/threads/xgram-1-0-3-6-bot-dlja-sozdanija-i-upravlenija-akauntami-v-instagram.25780/?utm_referrer=https%3A%2F%2Fwww.google.com%2F.

11. JackMorris. "Instagram Bot Discussion/Request: Begging, Ideas, Dreams." *BlackHatWorld*, October 8, 2012. https://www.blackhatworld.com/seo/instagram-bot-discussion-request-begging-ideas-dreams.551752/.

12. kmizt. "[Looking to Hire] Make MySpace Message Bot." *Web Hosting Talk*, February 20, 2006. Accessed February 18, 2025. https://web.archive.org/web/20250203004620/https://www.webhostingtalk.com/showthread.php?t=488728&p=3693101#post3693101.

13. Kullin, Hans. "Instagram's Increasing Problem with Spam," *Media Culpa*, November 7, 2012, archived September 13, 2024, https://web.archive.org/web/20240913010244/https://www.kullin.net/2012/11/instagram-spam/.

14. Ibid.

15. Ibid.

16. zenoGlitch. "Which is the Best Tumblr Bot." *Black Hat World*, March 6, 2013. In "Which is the Best Tumblr Bot" thread by juanpopo. Accessed February 18, 2025. https://www.blackhatworld.com/seo/which-is-the-best-tumblr-bot.539720/page-2.

17. HoNeYBiRD. Comment on "xGram Bot Website Down." *Black Hat World*, November 16, 2012. In "xGram Bot Website Down???" thread by HeRBaR. Accessed February 18, 2025. https://www.blackhatworld.com/seo/xgram-bot-website-down.502125/page-2#post-4895904.

18. Jongsumatra. "Botstagram Owner Scam Me $200." *Black Hat World*, January 23, 2013. Accessed February 18, 2025. https://web.archive.org/web/20250204014029/https://www.blackhatworld.com/seo/botstagram-owner-scam-me-200.524997/.

19. artiee. Comment on "Instagram Bot Discussion - Request / Begging / Ideas / Dreams." *Black Hat World*, March 27, 2013. In "Instagram Bot Discussion - Request / Begging / Ideas / Dreams" thread. Accessed February 18, 2025. https://www.blackhatworld.com/seo/instagram-bot-discussion-request-begging-ideas-dreams.551752/page-7.

20. vilcakurt. "[METHOD] My Instagram Method To Making $20+ A Day!" *Black Hat World*, May 22, 2017. Accessed February 18, 2025. https://www.blackhatworld.com/seo/method-my-instagram-method-to-making-20-a-day.941615/.

21. Instagress. "Instagress Homepage." Accessed February 18, 2025. Archived on September 8, 2013. https://web.archive.org/web/20130908191944/http://instagress.com/.

22. Ibid.

23. Instagress. "About." Accessed February 18, 2025. Archived on September 9, 2013. https://web.archive.org/web/20130909233927/http://instagress.com/about.

24. Mlot, Stephanie. "Instagram Celebrates 300M Users With Verified Accounts." PCMag, December 10, 2014. Archived at https://web.archive.org/web/20240615105412/https://www.pcmag.com/news/instagram-celebrates-300m-users-with-verified-accounts.

25. "See Posts You Care About First in Your Feed." *Instagram Blog*, Mar. 15, 2016, https://web.archive.org/web/20241212224401/https://about.instagram.com/blog/announcements/see-posts-you-care-about-first-in-your-feed. Accessed Feb. 15, 2025.

26. Perez, Sarah. "Instagram Officially Announces Its New Business Tools." *TechCrunch*, May 31, 2016. https://web.archive.org/web/20250214052129/https://techcrunch.com/2016/05/31/instagram-officially-announces-its-new-business-tools/.

27. This, Emerson. "Everything You Need to Know About Instagram API Integration." *CSS-Tricks*, August 8, 2016 (Updated May 13, 2019). https://web.archive.org/web/20240625023240/https://css-tricks.com/everything-need-know-instagram-api-integration/#instagram-api-part-one-understanding.

28. Grossman, Tim. "Initial Commit." *InstaPy/InstaPy*, GitHub, 26 Sept. 2016, https://github.com/InstaPy/InstaPy/commit/3bf011adf4c225f1fc0d428d8c5d-c7b103867d9f.

29. Wikipedia. "Headless Browser." Last modified date unavailable. Accessed February 18, 2025. https://en.wikipedia.org/wiki/Headless_browser.

30. InstaPy. "InstaPy Downloads." Accessed February 18, 2025. https://pepy.tech/projects/instapy?timeRange=threeMonths&category=version&includeCIDownloads=true&granularity=daily&viewType=chart&versions=0.6.16%2C0.6.15%2C0.6.14.

31. subzeroid. "instagrapi." *GitHub*. Accessed February 18, 2025. https://github.com/subzeroid/instagrapi.

32. Cade, DL. "Instagram Shuts Down Popular Botting Service Instagress." *PetaPixel*, April 20, 2017. Accessed February 16, 2025. https://web.archive.org/web/20250210034157/https://petapixel.com/2017/04/20/instagram-shuts-popular-botting-service-instagress/.

33. Grigonis, Hillary. "Four More Programs Bite the Dust in Instagram's Quiet Battle Against the Bots." *Digital Trends*, 15 May 2017, 2:11 PM PST, https://web.archive.org/web/20190210234355/https://www.digitaltrends.com/social-media/instagram-shuts-down-four-more-bots/.

34. Chong, Justine. "The Intriguing Case of Instagress." *Naytev*, 2017. Accessed February 18, 2025. https://www.naytev.com/insights/the-intriguing-case-of-instagress.

13. Organic Growth

1. Maheshwari, Sapna. "How Bots Are Inflating Instagram Egos." *The New York Times*, June 6, 2017. Accessed February 15, 2025. https://web.archive.org/web/20250217042425/https://www.nytimes.com/2017/06/06/business/media/instagram-bots.html.
2. Plutchik, Robert. "Robert Plutchik." *Wikipedia*. Last modified February 14, 2025. https://en.wikipedia.org/wiki/Robert_Plutchik#Wheel_of_Emotions.
3. Grossman, Tim. "Initial Commit." *InstaPy/InstaPy*, GitHub, 26 Sept. 2016, https://github.com/InstaPy/InstaPy/commit/3bf011adf4c225f1fc0d428d8c5d-c7b103867d9f.
4. Chris Buetti, "How I Eat for Free in NYC Using Python, Automation, Artificial Intelligence, and Instagram," *Medium*, archived February 24, 2019, https://web.archive.org/web/20240829062747/https://medium.com/@chrisbuetti/how-i-eat-for-free-in-nyc-using-python-automation-artificial-intelligence-and-instagram-a5ed8a1e2a10.
5. Followyst. Comment on "Instagram Follower Growth - Need to Grow Account to 50k - Best Automation Bots/Account Managers? (Nitreo, Kicksta, Kenji, Upleap)." *Reddit*, November 25, 2020. https://www.reddit.com/r/InstagramMarketing/comments/i52c-n7/comment/g17t1nz/?utm_source=share&utm_medium=web3x&utm_name=we-b3xcss&utm_term=1&utm_content=share_button.
6. FollowLiker. "Instagram Bot." *FollowLiker*, Accessed February 18, 2025. Archived on August 13, 2024. https://web.archive.org/web/20240813174340/https://www.follow-liker.com/instagram-bot.html.
7. FollowLiker. "Blocked Checkout." *FollowLiker*, Accessed February 18, 2025. Archived on September 13, 2024. https://web.archive.org/web/20240913074654/https://fol-lowliker.com/order/order.php?id=506305.
8. BlackHatWorld. "FollowLiker Not Working." *BlackHatWorld*, Accessed February 18, 2025. https://www.blackhatworld.com/seo/followliker-not-working.1495821/.

14. Building Bots

1. Stiletto. "JARVEE - Social Media Automation Tool for: Facebook, Instagram, Twitter, Pinterest, LinkedIn, Tumblr." *Black Hat World*, 4 Sept. 2017, https://www.blackhat-world.com/seo/jarvee-social-media-automation-tool-for-facebook-instagram-twitter-pinterest-linkedin-tumblr.969615/.
2. Instagress Beta." *Instagress*, archived September 8, 2013. https://web.archive.org/web/20130908191944/http://instagress.com/.
3. rtribe13. "Hiring a Developer - MP Replacement." *BlackHatWorld*, February 10, 2025. Archived on February 10, 2025. https://web.archive.org/web/20250210185023/https://www.blackhatworld.com/seo/hiring-a-developer-mp-replacement.939015/#post-10030096.
4. BlackHatWorld. "What Is the Best Instagram Bot." *BlackHatWorld*, Accessed February 18, 2025. https://www.blackhatworld.com/seo/what-is-the-best-instagram-bot.1031629/page-3#post-11097158.
5. Jarvee. *Jarvee*, Accessed February 18, 2025. Archived on October 27, 2018. https://web.archive.org/web/20181027065515/https://jarvee.com/.
6. Jarvee. "Instagram Marketing Automation Features." *Jarvee*, Accessed February 18, 2025. Archived on November 26, 2017. https://we-

b.archive.org/web/20171126151530/http://jarvee.com/instagram-marketing-automation-features/.

7. BlackHatWorld. "GMT2 - Gram Multitool 2 Instagram Automation Software." *Black-HatWorld*, Accessed February 18, 2025. https://www.blackhatworld.com/seo/gmt2-gram-multitool-2-instagram-automation-software.980622/.

8. GramMultitool. "GMT1." *GramMultitool*, Accessed February 18, 2025. Archived on August 20, 2016. https://web.archive.org/web/20160820141920/http://grammulti-tool.com/#portfolio.

9. BlackHatWorld. "GMT2 - Gram Multitool 2 Instagram Automation Software." *Black-HatWorld*, Accessed February 18, 2025. https://www.blackhatworld.com/seo/gmt2-gram-multitool-2-instagram-automation-software.980622/.

10. Ibid.

11. Confessore, Nicholas, Gabriel J.X. Dance, Shalini Ramachandran, and Michael H. Keller. "The Follower Factory." *The New York Times*, January 27, 2018. Accessed February 15, 2025. https://web.archive.org/web/20250112143607/https://www.ny-times.com/interactive/2018/01/27/technology/social-media-bots.html.

12. Gummadi, Ravi. "Instagram Graph API Launches and Instagram API Platform Depre-cation." *Facebook Developers*, 30 Jan. 2018, https://web.archive.org/web/20250104030923/https://developers.facebook.com/blog/post/2018/01/30/insta gram-graph-api-updates/.

13. Facebook Inc., Instagram, LLC. *Complaint against Leon Hedges, Arend Nollen, David Pasanen, Social Media Series Limited*. 3:2019cv02262, Justia, https://docs.justia.-com/cases/federal/district-courts/california/candce/3:2019cv02262/341343/1/.

14. SocialEnvy.co. "FRIENDLY NOTE." *SocialEnvy*, Accessed February 18, 2025. https://web.archive.org/web/20180120070621/https://www.socialenvy.co/.

15. Maheshwari, Sapna. "Uncovering Instagram Bots With a New Kind of Detective Work." *The New York Times*, March 12, 2018. Accessed February 15, 2025. https://we-b.archive.org/web/20241231201828/https://www.nytimes.com/2018/03/12/busi-ness/media/instagram-bots.html.

16. Constine, Josh. "Instagram Suddenly Chokes off Developers as Facebook Chases Priva-cy." *TechCrunch*, April 2, 2018. Accessed February 15, 2025. https://we-b.archive.org/web/20250115012520/https://techcrunch.com/2018/04/02/instagram-api-limit/.

17. Chris Buetti, "How I Eat for Free in NYC Using Python, Automation, Artificial Intel-ligence, and Instagram," *Medium*, archived February 24, 2019, https://we-b.archive.org/web/20240829062747/https://medium.com/@chrisbuetti/how-i-eat-for-free-in-nyc-using-python-automation-artificial-intelligence-and-instagram-a5ed8a1e2a10.

18. Chris Buetti, "How I Eat for Free in NYC Using Python, Automation, Artificial Intel-ligence, and Instagram," *Medium*, archived February 24, 2019, https://we-b.archive.org/web/20240829062747/https://medium.com/@chrisbuetti/how-i-eat-for-free-in-nyc-using-python-automation-artificial-intelligence-and-instagram-a5ed8a1e2a10.

19. Isaac, Mike. "Instagram's Co-Founders to Step Down From Company." *The New York Times*, September 24, 2018. Accessed February 15, 2025. https://we-b.archive.org/web/20250211163958/https://www.nytimes.com/2018/09/24/technol-ogy/instagram-cofounders-resign.html.

20. DeKoven, Louis F., Trevor Pottinger, Stefan Savage, Geoffrey M. Voelker, and Nektarios Leontiadis. "Following Their Footsteps: Characterizing Account Automation Abuse and Defenses." *Facebook Research*, October 31, 2018. Accessed

February 15, 2025. https://research.facebook.com/publications/following-their-foot-steps-characterizing-account-automation-abuse-and-defenses/.

21. Ibid.
22. Ibid.
23. Ibid.
24. Ibid.
25. Ibid.
26. Ibid.
27. Ibid.
28. Ibid.
29. Ibid.
30. Ibid.
31. "Reducing Inauthentic Activity on Instagram." *Instagram Blog*, November 19, 2018. Accessed February 15, 2025. https://we-b.archive.org/web/20250119063012/https://about.instagram.com/blog/announce-ments/reducing-inauthentic-activity-on-instagram.
32. DeKoven, Louis F., Trevor Pottinger, Stefan Savage, Geoffrey M. Voelker, and Nektarios Leontiadis. "Following Their Footsteps: Characterizing Account Automation Abuse and Defenses." *Facebook Research*, October 31, 2018. Accessed February 15, 2025. https://research.facebook.com/publications/following-their-foot-steps-characterizing-account-automation-abuse-and-defenses/.

15. They Can't All Be Number One!

1. Winstead, Ed. "Faked: The Headquarters. The Followers. The Influence?" *The New York Times*, January 27, 2018. Accessed February 15, 2025. https://we-b.archive.org/web/20250117022856/https://www.nytimes.com/2018/01/27/insid-er/twitter-buy-followers-bots-investigation-devumi.html.
2. Federal Trade Commission (FTC). "Devumi, LLC." Accessed February 18, 2025. https://www.ftc.gov/legal-library/browse/cases-proceedings/182-3066-devumi-llc.
3. Panzarino, Matthew. "Instagram Cracks Down On Connected Apps Using 'Insta' And 'Gram.'" *TechCrunch*, August 19, 2013. Accessed February 18, 2025. https://techcrunch.com/2013/08/19/instagram-cracks-down-on-connected-apps-using-insta-and-gram/.
4. InfiniteAdds. "Traffic Stats." *L2RVB*, Accessed February 18, 2025. Archived on April 1, 2009. https://web.archive.org/web/20090401184949/http://www.l2rvb.com/apps/index.php.
5. Federal Trade Commission (FTC). "Federal Trade Commission Announces Final Rule Banning Fake Reviews and Testimonials." *Federal Trade Commission*, August 14, 2024. Accessed February 18, 2025. https://we-b.archive.org/web/20250208021240/https://www.ftc.gov/news-events/news/press-releases/2024/08/federal-trade-commission-announces-final-rule-banning-fake-reviews-testimonials.
6. SocialEnvy.co. "Customer Testimonial on Homepage." Accessed February 18, 2025. Archived on January 20, 2018. https://we-b.archive.org/web/20180120070621/https://www.socialenvy.co/.
7. Trustpilot. Accessed February 18, 2025. Archived on January 30, 2025. https://we-b.archive.org/web/20250130100209/https://www.trustpilot.com/.

8. Upleap.com. "Trustpilot Reviews." Accessed February 18, 2025. Archived on February 8, 2025. https://web.archive.org/web/20250208023656/https://www.trustpilot.com/review/upleap.com.
9. Jonathanspire.com. "Trustpilot Reviews." Accessed February 18, 2025. Archived on February 2, 2025. https://web.archive.org/web/20250202151247/https://ie.trustpilot.com/review/jonathonspire.com.
10. QQTube. "JonathonSpire, EarthWeb, UseViral, StormViews, SidesMedia Scam Exposed." *QQTube Blog*, Accessed February 18, 2025. Archived on August 12, 2024. https://web.archive.org/web/20240812193143/https://www.qqtube.com/blog/jonathonspire-earthweb-useviral-stormviews-sidesmedia-scam-exposed.
11. Ibid.
12. Ibid.
13. Stripe. "Disputes." *Stripe Docs*, Accessed February 18, 2025. Archived on February 8, 2025. https://web.archive.org/web/20250208022518/https://docs.stripe.com/disputes/measuring.
14. Upleap. "Pricing." *Upleap*, Accessed February 18, 2025. Archived on November 17, 2024. https://web.archive.org/web/20241117235955/https://upleap.com/pricing/.
15. Trustpilot. "Upleap." Accessed February 18, 2025. Archived on February 8, 2025. https://web.archive.org/web/20250208023656/ https://www.trustpilot.com/review/upleap.com.
16. Trevino, Emily. *Quora Profile*. Accessed February 18, 2025. https://www.quora.com/profile/Emily-Trevino-4.
17. SocialGrowth LLC. *D&B Business Directory*. Accessed February 18, 2025. https://www.dnb.com/business-directory/company-profiles.socialgrowth_llc-fz.099852362b1fdeb22e3903916e774e24.html.

16. Tapping Out

1. Confessore, Nicholas. "Firm That Sold Social Media Bots Settles With New York Attorney General." *The New York Times*, January 30, 2019. Accessed February 18, 2025. https://web.archive.org/web/20240117052529/https://www.nytimes.com/2019/01/30/technology/letitia-james-social-media-bots.html.
2. New York State Attorney General. "Attorney General James Announces Groundbreaking Settlement with Sellers of Fake Followers." *New York State Attorney General*, January 30, 2019. Accessed February 15, 2025. https://web.archive.org/web/20250213223749/https://ag.ny.gov/press-release/2019/attorney-general-james-announces-groundbreaking-settlement-sellers-fake-followers.
3. Facebook Inc., Instagram, LLC. *Complaint against Leon Hedges, Arend Nollen, David Pasanen, Social Media Series Limited*. 3:2019cv02262, Justia, https://docs.justia.com/cases/federal/district-courts/california/candce/3:2019cv02262/341343/1/.
4. Ibid.
5. Constine, Josh. "Instagram Officially Tests Hiding Like Counts." *TechCrunch*, April 30, 2019. Accessed February 15, 2025. https://web.archive.org/web/20250120094156/https://techcrunch.com/2019/04/30/instagram-hidden-like-counter/.
6. "Instagram Follow Action Blocks from This Morning 30 May." *BlackHatWorld*, May 30, 2019. Accessed February 15, 2025. https://www.blackhatworld.com/seo/instagram-follow-action-blocks-from-this-morning-30-may.1124826/page-17#post-12151911.

Notes

7. Ibid.
8. DeKoven, Louis F., Trevor Pottinger, Stefan Savage, Geoffrey M. Voelker, and Nektarios Leontiadis. "Following Their Footsteps: Characterizing Account Automation Abuse and Defenses." *Facebook Research*, October 31, 2018. Accessed February 15, 2025. https://research.facebook.com/publications/following-their-footsteps-characterizing-account-automation-abuse-and-defenses/.
9. "Instagram Follow Action Blocks from This Morning 30 May." *BlackHatWorld*, May 30, 2019. Accessed February 15, 2025. https://www.blackhatworld.com/seo/instagram-follow-action-blocks-from-this-morning-30-may.1124826/page-17#post-12151911.
10. Adam. "What to Do About the Latest Instagram Action Blocks." *Jarvee*, June 14, 2019. Accessed February 18, 2025. https://web.archive.org/web/20240613002514/https://jarvee.com/what-to-do-about-the-latest-instagram-action-blocks/.
11. "Instagram Follow Action Blocks from This Morning 30 May." *BlackHatWorld*, May 30, 2019. Accessed February 15, 2025. https://www.blackhatworld.com/seo/instagram-follow-action-blocks-from-this-morning-30-may.1124826/page-17#post-12151911.
12. Milenkowich, Alex. "[GMT2] Gram Multitool 2 | Instagram Automation Software." *BlackHatWorld*, December 17, 2019. Accessed February 15, 2025. https://www.blackhatworld.com/seo/gmt2-gram-multitool-2-instagram-automation-software.980622/page-148.

17. "Instagress Alternative" Alternatives

1. Instagram. "Platform Policy." Accessed February 18, 2025. https://web.archive.org/web/20160901080704/https://www.instagram.com/about/legal/terms/api/.
2. Varnavski, Masha. "Do Sponsored Instagram Contests Really Work? Case Study." *Social Media Examiner*, September 8, 2020. Accessed February 18, 2025. https://web.archive.org/web/20240908093646/https://www.socialmediaexaminer.com/do-sponsored-instagram-contests-really-work-case-study/.

18. Broken-Hearted

1. Wikipedia. "Zendesk." Last modified date unavailable. Accessed February 18, 2025. https://en.wikipedia.org/wiki/Zendesk.
2. Bails, Victoria. "Meta Reel Ads." *Responsival*, March 2022. Accessed February 18, 2025. https://web.archive.org/web/20250208171919/https://www.responsival.com/post/metas-2021-updates-to-guide-your-advertising-efforts-through-2022.
3. Rodriguez, Salvador. "TikTok Passes Instagram as Second-Most Popular Social App for U.S. Teens." *CNBC*, October 6, 2020. Accessed February 15, 2025. https://web.archive.org/web/20250127200703/https://www.cnbc.com/2020/10/06/tiktok-passes-instagram-as-second-most-popular-social-app-for-us-teens.html.
4. Kayser-Bril, Nicolas. "Facebook Goes After the Creator of InstaPy, a Tool That Automates Instagram Likes." *AlgorithmWatch*, November 16, 2021. Accessed February 15, 2025. https://web.archive.org/web/20250121133344/https://algorithmwatch.org/en/facebook-goes-after-instapy/.
5. "Stripe Restricted Businesses." Stripe, accessed February 8, 2025. https://web.archive.org/web/20250208000814/https://stripe.com/legal/restricted-businesses.

6. Maheshwari, Sapna. "How Bots Are Inflating Instagram Egos." *The New York Times*, June 6, 2017. Accessed February 15, 2025. https://web.archive.org/web/20250217042425/https://www.nytimes.com/2017/06/06/business/media/instagram-bots.html.

20. The Puppeteer Part II

1. See "The Puppeteer Part I" for my claim.
2. "Negative-Sum Game," *Nontortion Wiki*, accessed February 16, 2025, https://nontortion.miraheze.org/wiki/Negative-sum_game.
3. See "The Puppeteer Part I" for my claim.
4. "Power User," *Wikipedia*, last modified November 24, 2024, https://en.wikipedia.org/wiki/Power_user.
5. "Technological Singularity," *Wikipedia*, last modified February 16, 2025, accessed February 16, 2025, https://en.wikipedia.org/wiki/Technological_singularity.
6. "Late Capitalism," *Wikipedia*, last modified February 13, 2025, accessed February 16, 2025, https://en.wikipedia.org/wiki/Late_capitalism.
7. r/LateStageCapitalism, *Reddit*, accessed February 16, 2025, https://www.reddit.com/r/LateStageCapitalism/.
8. "Game Mechanics," *Wikipedia*, last modified February 16, 2025, accessed February 16, 2025, https://en.wikipedia.org/wiki/Game_mechanics#Victory_conditions.
9. "Dead Internet Theory," *Wikipedia*, last modified February 16, 2025, accessed February 16, 2025, https://en.wikipedia.org/wiki/Dead_Internet_theory.
10. Ibid.
11. Cory Doctorow, "CRAPHOUND," *Craphound*, archived February 16, 2025, https://web.archive.org/web/20250216213446/https://craphound.com/.
12. "Cory Doctorow," *Wikipedia*, last modified February 16, 2025, accessed February 16, 2025, https://en.wikipedia.org/wiki/Cory_Doctorow."
13. "Enshittification," *Wikipedia*, last modified February 16, 2025, accessed February 16, 2025, https://en.wikipedia.org/wiki/Enshittification.
14. "Oden.io Glossary: Model Training," *Oden.io*, archived February 8, 2025, https://web.archive.org/web/20250208212524/https://oden.io/glossary/model-training/.
15. "ChatGPT," *Wikipedia*, last modified February 16, 2025, accessed February 16, 2025, https://en.wikipedia.org/wiki/ChatGPT.
16. "Karma Farming," *Encyclopaedia of Reddit*, last modified February 16, 2025, accessed February 16, 2025, https://www.reddit.com/r/EncyclopaediaOfReddit/wiki/4/#wiki_karma_farming.
17. "Article Spinning," *Wikipedia*, last modified February 16, 2025, accessed February 16, 2025, https://en.wikipedia.org/wiki/Article_spinning.
18. Eileen Cartter, "The Pope Francis Puffer Photo Was Real in Our Hearts," *GQ*, archived February 10, 2025, https://web.archive.org/web/20250210110802/https://www.gq.com/story/pope-puffer-jacket-midjourney-ai-meme.
19. "Deepfake," *Wikipedia*, last modified February 16, 2025, accessed February 16, 2025, https://en.wikipedia.org/wiki/Deepfake.
20. *Urban Dictionary*. "Myspace Whores." *Urban Dictionary*, accessed August 1, 2024. https://web.archive.org/web/20240801144047/https://www.urbandictionary.com/define.php?term=myspace+whores.
21. "Karma Farming," *Encyclopaedia of Reddit*, last modified February 16, 2025, accessed

February 16, 2025, https://www.reddit.com/r/EncyclopaediaOfReddit/wiki/4/#wiki_karma_farming.

22. "Sock Puppet Account," *Wikipedia*, last modified February 16, 2025, accessed February 16, 2025, https://en.wikipedia.org/wiki/Sock_puppet_account."

23. Wikipedia. "Poke - List of Facebook Features." Last modified date unavailable. Accessed February 18, 2025. https://en.wikipedia.org/wiki/List_of_Facebook_features#Poke.

24. "Predation," *Wikipedia*, last modified February 16, 2025, accessed February 16, 2025, https://en.wikipedia.org/wiki/Predation.

25. Kullin, Hans. "Instagram's Increasing Problem with Spam," *Media Culpa*, November 7, 2012, archived September 13, 2024, https://web.archive.org/web/20240913010244/https://www.kullin.net/2012/11/instagram-spam/.

26. "Instagram Platform Update," *Instagram Developers*, March 12, 2017, archived February 16, 2025, https://web.archive.org/web/20170312194745/https://developers.instagram.com/post/133424514006/instagram-platform-update.

27. "Psychological Warfare," *Wikipedia*, last modified February 16, 2025, accessed February 16, 2025, https://en.wikipedia.org/wiki/Psychological_warfare.

28. Yoree Koh and Betsy Morris, "Kids Love These YouTube Channels. Who Creates Them Is a Mystery," *Wall Street Journal*, April 11, 2019, 5:30 AM ET, archived May 9, 2024, https://web.archive.org/web/20240509171329/https://www.wsj.com/articles/kids-love-these-youtube-channels-who-creates-them-is-a-mystery-11554975000.

29. Chris Buetti, "How I Eat for Free in NYC Using Python, Automation, Artificial Intelligence, and Instagram," *Medium*, archived February 24, 2019, https://web.archive.org/web/20240829062747/https://medium.com/@chrisbuetti/how-i-eat-for-free-in-nyc-using-python-automation-artificial-intelligence-and-instagram-a5ed8a1e2a10.

30. "Bread and Circuses," *Wikipedia*, last modified February 16, 2025, accessed February 16, 2025, https://en.wikipedia.org/wiki/Bread_and_circuses."

31. "What Is This Site's Policy on Content Generated by Generative Artificial Intelligence Tools?," *Stack Overflow*, archived February 8, 2025, https://web.archive.org/web/20250208223241/https://stackoverflow.com/help/gen-ai-policy.

32. Confessore, Nicholas, Gabriel J. X. Dance, Mark Hansen, and Richard Harris. "The Follower Factory." *New York Times*, January 27, 2018. Accessed February 15, 2025. https://web.archive.org/web/20250112143607/https://www.nytimes.com/interactive/2018/01/27/technology/social-media-bots.html.

33. Maheshwari, Sapna. "How Bots Are Inflating Instagram Egos." *The New York Times*, June 6, 2017. Accessed February 15, 2025. https://web.archive.org/web/20250217042425/https://www.nytimes.com/2017/06/06/business/media/instagram-bots.html.

34. "Multiple Accounts," *Wikipedia*, last modified July 10, 2023, accessed February 16, 2025, https://en.wikipedia.org/wiki/Multiple_accounts.

35. Jason Koebler, "Reddit's Favorite Scientist Just Got Banned for Cheating the Site," *Vice*, July 31, 2014, archived February 8, 2025, https://web.archive.org/web/20250208224705/https://www.vice.com/en/article/reddits-favorite-scientist-just-got-banned-for-cheating-the-site/.

36. "Internet Manipulation," *Wikipedia*, last modified February 16, 2025, accessed February 16, 2025, https://en.wikipedia.org/wiki/Internet_manipulation.

37. Backlinko Team, "Instagram Statistics: Key Demographic and User Numbers," *Backlinko*, last updated January 30, 2025, accessed February 16, 2025, https://backlinko.com/instagram-users.

38. IlluminatiPirate, "Dead Internet Theory: Most of the Internet is Fake," *Agora Road's Macintosh Cafe*, January 5, 2021, https://forum.agoraroad.com/index.php?threads/dead-internet-theory-most-of-the-internet-is-fake.3011/.
39. "Russian Interference in the 2016 United States Elections," *Wikipedia*, last modified February 16, 2025, https://en.wikipedia.org/wiki/Russian_interference_in_the_2016_United_States_elections.
40. "Explainable Artificial Intelligence," *Wikipedia*, last modified February 16, 2025, https://en.wikipedia.org/wiki/Explainable_artificial_intelligence.

21. Unfollowed

1. "White-label Product," *Wikipedia*, last modified February 16, 2025, https://en.wikipedia.org/wiki/White-label_product.
2. Annie Lowrey, "The Latest Instagram Trend Is Called 'Gatsbying.' Here's What It Is," *HuffPost*, June 27, 2018, archived February 8, 2025, https://web.archive.org/web/20250208163152/https://www.huffpost.com/entry/gatsbying-instagram-social-media_n_5b5766c3e4b0fd5c73c97a23.
3. Fitzgerald, F. Scott. *The Great Gatsby*. Charles Scribner's Sons, 1925.
4. "Thirst Trap," *Wikipedia*, last modified February 16, 2025, https://en.wikipedia.org/wiki/Thirst_trap.
5. Fitzgerald, F. Scott. *The Great Gatsby*. Charles Scribner's Sons, 1925.
6. "FDA Warns Against Use of Selective Androgen Receptor Modulators (SARMs) Among Teens and Young Adults," *U.S. Food and Drug Administration*, December 18, 2020, archived February 8, 2025, https://web.archive.org/web/20250208165422/https://www.fda.gov/consumers/consumer-updates/fda-warns-use-selective-androgen-receptor-modulators-sarms-among-teens-young-adults.

Printed in Great Britain
by Amazon

60406933R00248